AFTER LAVINIA

AFTER LAVINIA

A LITERARY
HISTORY OF
PREMODERN
MARRIAGE
DIPLOMACY

JOHN WATKINS

CORNELL UNIVERSITY PRESS

Ithaca and London

First published 2017 by Cornell University Press

Printed in the United States of America

Library of Congress Cataloging-in-Publication Data

Names: Watkins, John, 1960– author.
Title: After Lavinia : a literary history of premodern
    marriage diplomacy / John Watkins.
Description: Ithaca ; London : Cornell University Press,
    2017. | Includes bibliographical references and index.
Identifiers: LCCN 2016047310 (print) | LCCN 2016049375
    (ebook) | ISBN 9781501707575 (cloth : alk. paper) |
    ISBN 9781501708510 (epub/mobi) | ISBN
    9781501708527 (pdf)
Subjects: LCSH: Marriage—Political aspects—Europe—
    History. | Arranged marriage—Europe—History. |
    Europe—Social life and customs—History. |
    Diplomacy—History.
Classification: LCC HQ611 .W38 2017 (print) | LCC
    HQ611 (ebook) | DDC 306.81094—dc23
LC record available at https://lccn.loc.gov/2016047310

Cornell University Press strives to use environmentally
responsible suppliers and materials to the fullest extent
possible in the publishing of its books. Such materials
include vegetable-based, low-VOC inks and acid-free
papers that are recycled, totally chlorine-free, or partly
composed of nonwood fibers. For further information,
visit our website at www.cornellpress.cornell.edu.

For Leigh Harbin

❧ Contents

❦ ACKNOWLEDGMENTS

This book has grown out of numerous conversations with scholars across the humanities and social sciences. The last decade or so has transformed diplomatic history into a richly speculative transdisciplinary investigation. Throughout that period I have been inspired, taught, admonished, and encouraged by my friends and colleagues in the vanguard of this enterprise, including Douglas Biow, Joanna Craigwood, Paul Dover, Timothy Hampton, Jan Hennings, Mark Netzloff, Jane O. Newman, Toby Osborne, Diego Pirillo, Jason Powell, William Rossiter, Linda Shenk, and Tracey Sowerby. They rank among the most astute readers and listeners any scholar could desire. I have also profited from my long association with historians and literary critics working on European monarchy, and especially on queenship, such as Charles Beem, Ilona Bell, Anna Bertolet, Denis Crouzet, Susan Doran, Helen Hackett, Thomas Herron, Carole Levin, Glenn Richardson, and Donald Stump. They will recognize immediately how much this book owes to their collective reflections on the marriage negotiations of Elizabeth I. I am also grateful to several other scholars of premodern history and literature for their friendship and kind support, including Colin Burrow, Eric Carlson, Patrick Cheney, Curtis Perry, Charles Ross, Susan Shapiro, Debora Shuger, James Simpson, and William Kennedy.

I have learned much at the numerous academic conferences and research networks that have given an institutional form to the new diplomatic history. Several years ago, Carole Levin and Robert Buckholz invited me to give the keynote address at a queenship conference hosted by the University of Nebraska. That keynote, which the organizers published soon afterwards, turned out to be the first of my several attempts to make sense of the 1559 Peace of Cateau-Cambrésis, and more generally of the cultural and literary aspects of interdynastic marriage. I returned to the many questions raised by Cateau-Cambrésis in yet another keynote, this time for a diplomacy conference at Liverpool Hope University organized by Jason Powell and William Rossiter. Soon afterwards, I joined about fifteen other diplomacy scholars for a landmark workshop organized by Isabella Lazzarini, Stéphane Péquignot, and John Watts at the Centro de Ciencias de Benasque Pedro Pasquale in Benasque, Spain. My work continued to develop at the workshops and conferences hosted by the British Arts and Humanities Research Council Textual Ambassadors Network, a group convened by Tracey Sowerby and Joanna Craigwood at the universities of Oxford and Cambridge. Finally, Jason Dittmer and Fiona McConnell gave me an opportunity to deepen my project's underpinnings in international relations theory by inviting me to speak at their AHRC Network on the Cultures of Diplomacy.

This project has benefited greatly from the criticism I have received as a speaker at the International Medieval Studies Conference at the Medieval Institute of the University of Western Michigan, the Renaissance Society of America, the Mediterranean Studies Association, the Elizabeth I Society, and a conference on the history of France organized by Thomas Herron at Eastern Carolina University. Several institutions invited me to share my work as a guest lecturer, including the Newberry Library's Center for Renaissance Studies; Stanford University's Center for European Studies; the University of California at Los Angeles; Queens University in Kingston, Ontario; the Institute of International Studies at the University of California at Berkeley; the University of Nebraska at Lincoln; Yale University's Center for Historical Inquiry and the Social Sciences; the Institute for Advanced Studies at the University of Bristol; and the Centre for Medieval and Renaissance Studies at Oxford. I am especially grateful to my hosts: Philippe Buc, Barbara Fuchs, Bernard Gowers, Roland Greene, Timothy Hampton, Edward Holberton, Carole Levin, Ayesha Ramachandran, Charles Ross, and Asha Varadharajan.

The University of Minnesota has been an ideal place to work on a project that crosses so many boundaries of time, place, and discipline. I have received advice and encouragement from my friends and colleagues in the departments of history, English, French and Italian, and religious studies and in the Center for Medieval Studies, Center for Early Modern History, and Center for the Study of the Premodern World: Bernard Bachrach, Daniel Brewer, Mary Franklin-Brown, Siobhan Craig, Lianna Farber, Shirley Garner, Nita Krevens, Rebecca Krug, Patricia Lorcin, Michael Lower, Nabil Matar, Ellen Messer-Davidow, Oliver Nicholson, Kay Reyerson, Andrew Scheil, Katherine Scheil, and Daniel Schroeter. Early in the project, Marguerite Ragnow, curator of the University of Minnesota's James Ford Bell Library, opened up new worlds of inquiry by encouraging me to think more about the early Middle Ages. Nobody writing on premodern marriage could hope for a better, more knowledgeable colleague than Ruth Karras.

Several scholars have read and commented on my research proposals, draft chapters, and finished manuscript: Michael Lower, Nicholas Paige,

Curtis Perry, Jason Powell, David Quint, William Rossiter, and the reviewers at Cornell University Press. Andrew Scheil, Mary Franklin-Brown, and Daniel Brewer provided invaluable help with my translations, respectively, from medieval Latin, Old and Middle French, and classical French. This is a stronger book because of their patient criticism. Remaining errors are my own. All translations are mine unless otherwise noted.

Generous fellowships and grants from the American Philosophical Society, the American Council of Learned Societies, and the John Simon Guggenheim Foundation have supported my research. I have also benefited from the Distinguished McKnight University Professor endowment at the University of Minnesota.

I completed the final version of this book during my tenure as a Senior Research Visitor at Keble College, Oxford. My host Tracey Sowerby, along with the generous and hospitable Warden and Fellows of the College, made this one of the happiest periods of my life. Ian Archer and Michael Hawcroft deserve special thanks for their generous research advice.

These awards allowed me to carry out my research in some of the world's greatest libraries. I could not have completed this project without the patience and assistance of librarians at the Bodleian, the Queen's College Library, the Keble College Library, the Codrington Library at All Souls College, the Bibliothèque Nationale de France, the Newberry Library, the Folger Shakespeare Library, and the University of Minnesota Libraries.

A portion of chapter 4 appeared as an essay in *Authority and Diplomacy from Dante to Shakespeare*, edited by Jason Powell and William T. Rossiter (Ashgate, 2013). A portion of chapter 5 appeared as an essay in *Shakespeare and the Middle Ages*, edited by Curtis Perry and John Watkins (Oxford, 2009). The Taylor and Francis Group and Oxford University Press granted me permission to publish revised versions of this material.

I would like to thank the British Museum for permission to reproduce the image on the jacket.

Working with Cornell University Press has been a joy. This book owes much of its shape to my conversations with Peter Potter, who led me past so many of the dangers inherent in writing a book that begins with Virgil and ends with the Enlightenment. His successor at Cornell, Mahinder Kingra, guided the project from its acceptance to its final appearance. My production editor Karen Hwa was a model of patience. Amanda Heller was the ideal copyeditor for a project that posed significant linguistic and editorial challenges.

As the project neared completion, Caitlin McHugh and Jesse Izzo proved to be reliable and imaginative research assistants. Morag Scheinwald provided invaluable technical assistance.

This book treats only a small segment of the ever-changing institution of marriage. Andrew Elfenbein and I stepped into that larger history in 2008 when we stood before a Toronto judge and pledged our love for each other in words echoing the Book of Common Prayer. Like many other marriages that have taken place in recent years, this one was decades overdue. Andy has sustained me with love, encouragement, intellectual companionship, and criticism for over thirty years. He will always be my best, most patient, and most highly valued reader. When I began this project, our son Dima could point out most of the countries I discuss on the map. He now argues with me about politics and international relations theory. The child I have always loved has grown into a man who shares my passion for languages and a complex, interconnected world. The good humor and abiding friendship of Eric Pressel, Morag Scheinwald, and Leigh Harbin lightened the burdens of research and writing, often on a daily basis. My cat Charlotte never failed to join me in the late afternoon for tea and a half hour of music.

❧ AFTER LAVINIA

Introduction
The Voice of Lavinia

In the fourteenth century BCE, Kadashman-Enlil I of Babylon berated Amenhotep III for not sending him an Egyptian princess as a token of their alliance. From the Babylonian perspective, the Egyptian custom that prevented a pharaoh from marrying his daughters to anyone outside their own family seemed strange. But Kadashman-Enlil still sent Amenhotep a Babylonian princess and asked for a hefty bride price in lieu of an Egyptian bride.[1] In the third century BCE, the Han emperors of China stabilized their northern border by intermarrying with the powerful Xiongnu confederation. *Heqin*, or "peace through kinship," became a familiar feature of subsequent relations between China and its neighbors. Writers honored *heqin* brides for their patriotic willingness to marry barbarians.[2] The *mais*, the rulers of the Kanem-Bornu Empire around Lake Chad, formed alliances by marrying their daughters to elite men of surrounding states.[3] On the other side of the globe, the Incas cultivated a caste of select women, the *aqllakuna*, who performed special duties in the imperial court and in religious centers. The Incan king bestowed many of them on provincial rulers as rewards for their loyalty to the central regime.[4] These transprovincial marriages fostered a common imperial culture that lessened the hold of older, potentially subversive territorial identities. In Mesoamerica, Mexica rulers like Huitzilihuitl of Tenochtitlán used similar marriage alliances to build the vast Aztec Empire.[5] Hawaiian polygamy, which allowed both men and women to have multiple spouses, created an opportunity for multiple marriages between rival dynasties to resolve conflicts.[6]

Despite significant cultural and political differences between European and non-European societies, these Asian, African, and American marriages look strangely familiar to historians of medieval and early modern European foreign policy. The chronicles, annals, "barbarian" histories, dispatches, *relazioni*, plays, commemorative poems, paintings, tomb sculptures, and early novels on which scholars base their accounts of the premodern state document countless marriages uniting European dynasties. From Theodoric the Ostrogoth to Leopold I of Belgium and his niece Queen Victoria, marriages wove the European ruling caste into a vast extended family.

By the early Carolingian period (ca. 800–924), European marriage diplomacy had acquired a systematic character that persisted, with variation, for centuries. Charlemagne and his descendants used their children's marriages to form alliances with neighboring rulers or regional leaders within their own domains. Louis the Pious, for example, married Ermengarde of Hesbaye and, upon her death, Judith of Bavaria. His eldest son, Lothair I, married Ermengarde of Tours. Lothair's half brother Charles the Bald married Ermentrude of Orléans and, upon her death, Richilde of Provence. Charles's children also married the sons and daughters of provincial nobility. Rothild, for example, married Roger, Count of Maine.

But as Charles the Bald and many later royal fathers discovered, the systematic nature of marriage diplomacy did not guarantee the diplomatic or personal success of individual marriages. Some marriages were doomed before the bride and groom reached the altar. As part of a peace settlement with Erispoë of Brittany, for example, Charles planned to marry his son and future heir Louis the Stammerer to Erispoë's daughter. But the deal fell through with Erispoë's murder a year later.[7] Charles planned next to marry Louis to the daughter of the Count Palatine of Paris. But Louis himself complicated that scheme by secretly marrying Ansgarde of Burgundy against his father's will. Charles had the marriage annulled and promptly married Louis to Adelaide of Paris, as he had originally planned. The annulment hardly solved the problem, however, since the children from both of these marriages held rival succession claims.[8]

Louis the Stammerer's sister Judith of Flanders also thwarted their father, Charles the Bald's, dynastic ambitions. As a teenager, she dutifully married two Wessex kings in quick succession, first Æthelwulf and, upon his death, Æthelbald. These marriages created a trans-Channel alliance that served both England and Francia in their struggles against the Vikings.[9] But the alliance broke down when Æthelbald also died. Judith returned to France, where Charles sent her to a monastery for safekeeping until he found an appropriate third husband. About a year later, however, she absconded with Baldwin of Flanders. When Charles sought an annulment this time, the pope denied it. Despite the initial drama, all parties were eventually reconciled, and Baldwin ended up becoming one of Charles's staunchest allies.[10]

Judith's story attests to an important aspect of marriage diplomacy: its inseparability from the history of literature. Most of what we know about it comes from the *Annales Bertiniani*, one of the few extant sources documenting ninth-century political history. As in any written document, generic conventions, narrative expedients and imperatives, and its author's aesthetic tastes and ideological biases skew its representation. In this case, the *Annales* introduce Judith primarily as the focus of a quarrel between two powerful men, her father and her third husband. They tell us so little about Judith's feelings and motivations that some scholars have wondered whether she eloped with Baldwin or was abducted by him.[11]

The narrative interest of Judith's third marriage sets it apart from numerous other marriages that the chronicles simply record as having taken place. But the fact that we know a lot more about some marriages than others has influenced the history of marriage diplomacy in crucial ways. Scholars have spent much time discussing why one noteworthy match came about, or why a king decided to marry his son to the daughter of one dynasty rather than another. But they rarely comment on the practice of marriage diplomacy per se, which they treat as a perennial feature of political experience. The seeming ubiquity of marriage diplomacy has given it a de facto explanatory value in treatments of negotiations. When the king of one country decided to make peace with the king of another, scholars write as if the two naturally settled their differences in a marriage treaty. The few who have analyzed the pattern have generally decried it as patriarchal trafficking in women's bodies, an analysis that reinforces rather than questions its transhistoricity.

But when we compare interdynastic marriages—or, more precisely, extant writings about them—across time, differences become apparent. Some of these differences are source effects. The fact that there was simply more production and preservation of records in the sixteenth century than in the tenth, for example, means we know more about marriages of state in the later period. It does not mean that early modern negotiations were more complex than medieval ones. But other differences arise from demonstrable shifts in the practice and cultural significance of marriage in general and of diplomatic marriage in particular. By the thirteenth century, for example, artworks celebrated foreign brides as types of the Virgin Mary mediating between their families of marriage and origin. That enduring association derived from devotional practices that arose in the eleventh and twelfth centuries, the so-called cult of the Virgin. New theological perspectives on the Incarnation, on Christ as the offspring of a quasi-marital alliance between God the Father and errant humanity, reinforced Marian associations.

Despite the impression that marriage diplomacy was a premodern constant, changing social and political circumstances altered its practice and meaning over time. No single volume could recount its history in a comprehensive way. Scholars have devoted numerous books to prominent marriages, such as those between Henry VIII and his six wives and between Louis XIV and Maria Teresa.[12] Even failed negotiations, like James I's doomed pursuit of a match between his son Charles and the Spanish Infanta Maria Anna, have inspired books and articles.[13] If historians can retell and analyze the story of individual marriages from many perspectives, the history of marriage diplomacy writ large, in western Europe alone, invites even more methodological variety. David D'Avray, for example, has published two volumes on the developing laws of marriage as a flashpoint between monarchs and ecclesiastics over degrees of consanguinity, dispensations, and annulments.[14] One might concentrate as well on shifting patterns of negotiation; legal differences in treaties; the economics of bride price and dowry; or the ceremonial details of betrothals, nuptial rites, beddings, proxy consummations, and consort anointings and coronations. One could construct a compelling cultural history around any of these topics. A full account of European marriage diplomacy—something that can exist only in fantasy—would call on the expertise of musicologists, art historians, literary scholars, political and social historians, specialists in gender and ethnicity, economists, political theorists, and international lawyers.

While this volume draws on scholarship from numerous fields, its primary focus is the place of marriage in the formation, maintenance, and disintegration of a premodern European diplomatic society. On an abstract level, the argument develops in dialogue with critical international society theory, the so-called English school of international relations theory, with its emphasis on the contemporary international system as a society of states sharing certain values, norms, and common interests rather than as an anarchy driven solely by power struggles.[15] It would be anachronistic to speak of "an international society of states" in the premodern world, when there were neither "states" nor "nations" as we know them today. But the kingdoms, principalities, city-states, ecclesiastical jurisdictions, trans-Channel imperiums, and Holy Roman empires that made up western Europe during the Middle Ages and early modern period did not relate to one another solely as an anarchy either. For much of this period, they shared a common religion, a *Hochsprache*, and a body of canon law that structured diplomatic understanding and exchange. So even if we cannot speak of an "international society" in premodernity, we can at least speak of a diplomatic society whose regime proliferated throughout the post-Roman period, especially during the waves of Christian conversion. Interdynastic marriage was not only an aspect of that society but also a principal avenue for its expansion.

But marriage also provided occasions for interrogating, challenging, and contesting that expansion. In adapting the English school's concept of "international society" to an analysis of premodern political culture, I also address some of the problems that recent scholars have identified in the concept's earliest formulations.[16] The founding figures of the English school, especially Hedley Bull, nostalgized the Middle Ages as a period of diplomatic consensus that was difficult, if not impossible, to achieve in a more complex, culturally divergent world.[17] This characterization of premodernity is troubling on several levels. It implies that the sooner non-European nations begin to act like the Christian and post-Christian West, the more readily they will cooperate to create a stable world order. It also overlooks how other parts of the world have existed in diplomatic systems with their own shared cultures, practices, values, and interests. The empires and kingdoms of East Asia, for example, developed their own set of diplomatic norms and conventions. Just as Latin became a *Hochsprache* for western Europe, classical Chinese became one for China, Japan, Ryukyu, and the kingdoms of the Korean peninsula.[18] Classical Arabic functioned in a similar way throughout the Islamic world. Nor was European diplomatic society immured from the rest of the world. As I show, its distinctive traditions developed through contact, confrontation, and cooperation with non-Christian societies. During its early medieval expansion, it was arguably more receptive than it later became to diplomatic encounters and even marriages between Christians and non-Christians. The loss of that earlier openness is part of the previously untold history of marriage diplomacy. It offers a timely reminder that the solidification of one diplomatic society often makes relations more difficult with those outside its borders.

While wrestling on an abstract level with the nostalgias and idealizations of English school international relations theory, this volume primarily resists, on a more practical and historiographical level, the idealizations with which premodernity itself reflected on marriage and its role in solidifying a society of sovereign principalities. Marriages of state often elicited some of premodern Europe's most eloquent descriptions of itself as a cohesive, ordered society in which war—at least among Christians—was an anomaly disturbing a peaceable status quo. The 1515 Treaty of Paris, for example, established a Hapsburg-Valois truce on the basis of a marriage between the newly crowned Francis I's four-year-old sister-in-law Renée of France and the future Charles I of Spain. But the preamble placed the truce in a broader moral and political context by hailing it as a benefit to all Christendom: "for the welfare and increase of the entire Christian commonwealth and the exaltation of the holy Catholic faith [au bien et augmentacion de toute la chose publique chrestienne et exactacion de la saincte foy catholicque]." "La chose publique chrestienne" translates literally the Latin phrase *res publica christiana* which had appeared in writings about diplomacy since the Hundred Years War. It expresses the ideal of a Christian continent peacefully united in a common Catholic faith, often in opposition to a threatening Muslim enemy. The 1515 treaty, like many others, privileges interdynastic marriage as the surest way to overcome irreligious and unnatural divisions that beset Christendom and weaken its ability to defend itself against the infidel.[19]

Despite such idealist claims, however, few things underscore the dynamic, often even volatile character of premodern diplomatic society more than interdynastic marriages. The marriage underwriting the 1515 Treaty of Paris, for example, never happened. Francis and Charles soon resumed their war, and Renée eventually married the future Ercole II d'Este, the Duke of Ferarra. That marriage alliance proved equally unstable. Ercole turned against the French after becoming duke and denounced his wife as a heretic.[20] In some cases, even relatively successful marriage alliances planted the seeds for future wars. Unexpected deaths and infertility in the male line strained relations between polities almost as much as the ambitions and rivalries of princes. Almost by definition, marriages tied foreign affairs to the quirks of biology. Perhaps the most famous case of a treaty undermined by early deaths, the 1303 Anglo-French treaty that married Philip IV's daughter Isabelle to the future Edward II, paved the way for the Hundred Years War, since it gave their son Edward III a credible claim to the French throne. Throughout history, marriage diplomacy often proved to be a source of conflict as much as stability.

The heyday of marriage diplomacy was virtually coterminous with the notion of a *res publica christiana*. When the latter began to wane after the Reformation, foreign marriages became an increasing source of contention. The difficulty of marrying across confessional lines exposed larger questions about peacemaking and alliance formation in an era when half of Europe repudiated oaths sworn on relics and threats of ecclesiastical penalties that had underwritten agreements in prior centuries. But perhaps even more critical than the Reformation was the gradual shift from a foreign policy invested in dynastic interests to one grounded in the interests of individual states. An expanding political nation had commercial and religious ambitions that sometimes ran counter to those of the Crown, and those ambitions did not necessarily favor the vision of international relations on which marriage diplomacy depended. Especially after the Reformation, newly arrived merchants and urban professionals began to resent dynastic alliances with foreign powers. From their perspective, the foreign brides once hailed as peacemakers patterned on the Virgin Mary appeared instead to be patrons of heresy and treason.

Cultural attitudes and ideologies—all the mythmaking that once ennobled foreign brides as mediators between their families of origin and marriage—do not change in a neat one-to-one relationship with shifting material circumstances. Ideas often lag behind, and sometimes anticipate or even create new empirical possibilities. Some queens consort wielded considerable diplomatic influence well after the emergence and proliferation of bureaucratized ministries of state. But as Europeans crossed into modernity, the merchants, professionals, and wealthy gentry whose interests often conflicted with those of the monarchy focused their wrath on meddling foreign consorts. The tragedy of Marie Antoinette was an extreme case, but other women suffered opprobrium long after the collapse of the *ancien régime*. The Empress Elisabeth of Austria, for example, played an important role in the 1867 creation of the dual monarchy of Austria-Hungary. But a vicious pamphlet campaign underscored the fact that such diplomatic enterprise had become the exception rather than the rule by asserting that a meddling consort was "merely a foreigner in the state, and a very dangerous foreigner too."[21]

My investigation of the place of marriage diplomacy in questions of monarchical and national sovereignty draws on interdisciplinary methodologies that have long characterized academic studies of queenship and, more recently, European diplomatic culture. Since the rhetorical abilities that make one a successful diplomat might also make one a distinguished poet, diplomacy lends itself especially well to cross-disciplinary, and especially literary, investigation. Many of premodern Europe's greatest writers spent a portion of their lives in diplomatic service. Writing sonnets, elegies, verse letters, and civic orations demonstrated one's credentials as a future envoy or ambassador. By the end of the period covered in this book, for example, César Vichard de Saint-Réal set out on his diplomatic career quite self-consciously by writing histories. Like other writer-diplomats, he hoped to convince future employers that he had the intelligence, wisdom, political expertise, prudence, clarity of expression, abilities to persuade, and tact that contemporary commentators deemed essential to a successful diplomatic career.

It would be a mistake, however, to reduce the complex relationship between writing and diplomacy in premodern Europe to credentialization. Like Roman Christianity, a shared literary heritage was yet another component of medieval and early modern international society. It, too, provided common vocabularies, attitudes, and ethical norms that promoted understanding among diplomats negotiating terms of alliance and settlement. Even after the Reformation had broken the religious consensus, humanist literary practices preserved memories of a shared Roman origin behind the contemporary system of kingdom and principality. Virtually every Renaissance dynasty claimed a Roman, if not a Trojan, origin.[22] Even the first codifiers of modern international law, often Protestant and hostile to all vestiges of scholasticism, drew heavily on Roman poets, historians, and jurists in sorting out the terms of just war and settlement. Early modern theorists like Jean Hotman and Alberico Gentili developed their arguments by using examples from Livy, Cicero, Suetonius, Tacitus, and Virgil. The *Aeneid*'s story of a translated empire provided an authorizing myth underlying these jurists' efforts to describe contemporary international relations as an extended imitation of Roman precedents.[23] As the friendships between jurists like Gentili and writers like Sidney suggest, literature and international law developed in a complex, mutually reinforcing dialogue.

Timothy Hampton's *Fictions of Embassy: Literature and Diplomacy in Early Modern Europe* has shown how effectively a concerted reading of the literary and diplomatic archives can illuminate aspects of European culture that have eluded more conventionally disciplined investigations.[24] Whereas Hampton addresses ambassadorial authority and the credentializations that allowed diplomats to represent their respective states and princes, this book focuses on actual, fictional, and possibly fictional marriages that were bound up in incalculable ways with literary production. Numerous European writers served on embassies related to specific interdynastic marriages, including Geoffrey Chaucer, Pierre de Ronsard, Diego de Hurtado de Mendoza, Garcilasco de la Vega, Thomas Wyatt, Philip Sidney, John Donne, and César Vichard de Saint-Réal. The weddings themselves occasioned orations, masques, and volumes of commemorative verse. The 1559 marriage between Philip II of Spain and Elisabeth de Valois alone inspired about two dozen volumes of mostly pastoral poetry by such writers as Ronsard, Rémy Belleau, and Joachim du Bellay. Not all the writing associated with interdynastic marriages was complimentary. In England, a proposed match between Elizabeth I and François Hercule, Duke of Alençon, inspired John Stubbs to write a scurrilous pamphlet denouncing not just this particular marriage but foreign marriage in general. An even greater outcry accompanied the negotiations between the future Charles I and Maria Anna of Spain, satirized by Thomas Middleton in his thinly veiled allegorical drama *A Game at Chess* (1624).[25]

The literature occasioned by such negotiations can tell us much about how premodern Europeans thought of marriage as a diplomatic practice. But interdynastic marriage loomed so large in the medieval and early modern political imagination that writers addressed it in works that had nothing to do with any particular match. Imagining monarchy, nobility, cycles of war and peace, and relations between states inevitably entailed imagining marriage. The classic Renaissance comedy ends in a marriage, and many are marriages of state. Almost every dynastic epic includes passages tracing the patron's descent from a mythic marriage between two illustrious houses. A few of these weddings happened in the historical past, but the majority are imagined.

For the purposes of this book, these fictional works are at least as valuable as ones associated with real marriages. Precisely because they are not clouded by immediate topical associations, they sometimes reveal more clearly the ideological assumptions underlying actual practice. The farther back we go in time, moreover, the more difficult it becomes to distinguish between the literary, the mythic, and the "authentically" historical. My opening chapters, for example, deal with periods in the European past for which there are few historical sources. Almost everything we know about sixth-century French politics comes from three works: Gregory of Tours's *Historia francorum*, the *Chronicle* attributed to Fredegar, and the Neustrian *Liber historiae francorum*. None of these works conforms to modern canons of historiographic accuracy and objectivity, and all contain legendary and mythic material. In the absence of corroborating evidence, we often cannot tell if a given bride existed, much less if an account of the politics surrounding a purported marriage is accurate. While such evidentiary circumstances make it difficult to talk about "what happened" in sixth-century France, these sources still tell us much about the cultural significance of interdynastic marriage: the brides deemed appropriate for men of the ruling caste, the imagined social functions of these marriages, and their assumed utility in establishing order among Roman successor states.

Like numerous works commemorating and condemning interdynastic marriage, this book begins with Virgil. For artists, scholars, and statesmen steeped in Roman literature, Aeneas's marriage to Lavinia was the paradigmatic interdynastic marriage. After a bitter war, the Trojan and Latin peoples come together in a peaceful settlement confirmed by the union between the Trojan leader and the daughter of the Latin king. Their prior national identities subsumed, both peoples emerge from their troubles to begin their common life as Romans destined to command the world.

Later writers such as Tasso and Spenser incorporated this optimistic *Aeneid* in their tributes to their respective dynasties.[26] Other writers, however, read the marriage and the poem itself in less celebratory terms. Virgil's poem is notoriously ambiguous. As scholars have often noted, misgivings about the destructiveness of human desire and the corrupt underside of imperial politics shadow its apparent compliment to Augustus as Aeneas's descendant.[27] They also infect its representations of interdynastic marriage. One of the poem's most influential episodes, Aeneas's affair with the passion-driven Carthaginian queen Dido, indicts relations with foreign women in the wake of Augustus's defeat of Antony and Cleopatra. Since Lavinia had already been promised to the Rutulian prince Turnus, her betrothal to Aeneas paradoxically triggers the war their marriage later resolves. In the poem's extended imitation of Homer, Lavinia's role recalls not only that of Penelope, the faithful wife, but also that of Helen, the cause of an international cataclysm. This unsettling intertextual juxtaposition foreshadows structural weaknesses in later marriage settlements, including their tendency to sow the seeds of future wars. Lavinia's silence throughout the epic raises questions about the proper role of foreign brides that will recur throughout the history of diplomatic marriage. Did the marriage system take into account their desires and feelings? How were they supposed to manage conflicting loyalties to fathers and husbands? What would happen if they broke Lavinia's silence?

Recollections of Virgilian marriage organize my transhistorical account of European peacemaking. Given the impossibilities of writing a comprehensive history, my analysis concentrates on texts foregrounding the development and later disintegration of a discourse of marriage as the preeminent means to restore and maintain the peace of Christendom. The three chapters in part one focus on the literary traces of the rise and consolidation of this myth up to its initial flowering during the Crusades. The three chapters in part two examine factors that precipitated its disintegration: the sixteenth-century reformations, new technologies of print and the large public theaters for promoting diplomatic literacy, expansion of the political nation that challenged dynastic hegemony, and the growth of bureaucratized ministries of state.

From the moment of its mythic Virgilian origin, the history of European marriage diplomacy was inseparable from the history of literary genre. This book thus unfolds chronologically by foregrounding moments when these parallel histories intersected to reinforce, expand, exalt, and ultimately undercut the value of marriage as an instrument of peacemaking and alliance formation. From its opening account of epical ambiguities, it turns to the chronicle histories of the Latin Middle Ages, French romances with their darker attitudes toward marriage's sacramental inviolability, and the humanist revival of pastoral as a tribute to the great dynastic unions between the Hapsburgs and Valois. It ends with the challenge to marriage diplomacy posed by Shakespeare, Corneille, and Racine. The rise and fall of genres mark, and sometimes even hasten, the passage from one diplomatic order to the next, with the great drama of the Renaissance adumbrating the emergence of a *raison d'état* that disentangled the erotic lives of princes from the destiny of nations.

My first chapter traces the initial stage of this generic history in a late antique turn from imperial epic to ethnic history. For the chroniclers and historians of the Germanic kingdoms that rose to power after the fall of the western Roman Empire, interdynastic marriage provided ethnic legitimation. The Ostrogothic ethnic historian Jordanes, for example, recounts his people's immigration from Scandinavia to the Mediterranean as an increasing assimilation to Roman culture. Just as the *Aeneid* celebrated the union between the relatively primitive Latins and the more urbane Trojans, the *Getica* traces that between the barbarian Goths and the Byzantines, crowned at last by the marriage between Matasuntha and Germanus, a cousin of Justinian.

As the tradition of ethnic historical writing matured, darker recollections of the *Aeneid* resurfaced. By the time Paul the Deacon, the greatest writer of the eighth-century Carolingian Renaissance, wrote his *History of the Lombards*, Pope Stephen III was castigating Charlemagne for marrying foreign women. This more negative view of intermarriage compromises Paul's belief in it as a means to establish a peaceful shared future between former belligerents. His story of Rosamund, the Gepid princess who murdered her husband, Alboin, when he tried to make her drink a toast from her father's skull, foregrounds passions that resist diplomatic closure.

My second chapter investigates interdynastic marriage during the northern European conversions to Christianity. Gregory of Tours's account of the Burgundian princess Clothilde's conversion of her Frankish husband, Clovis, established a model that later writers adopted in recounting the ecclesiastical histories of places from England to Poland. Although some historians have treated these stories as a more or less accurate account of the past, they are better understood as adaptations of the Virgilian topos of intermarriage as cultural exchange, one that preserved the prestige accorded classical texts and precedents while liberating them from their polytheistic foundations. For Gregory and Bede, these accounts of Christians marrying and converting pagans provide an image of their own revisionary relationship to classical literature, their conversion of Virgil and other Roman writers into models for Christian historiography.

These conversion stories document the expansion of a Latin-based, pre-modern diplomatic society. The Roman successor states had some diplomatic relations with one another before the conversions, or their cross-confessional marriages would never have happened. Their incorporation into Christendom, however, strengthened these relations by providing them a common *Hochsprache* to facilitate subsequent negotiation; a new body of shared values and interests; and, perhaps most important, a pan-European network of bishops, abbots, and other clerics well suited to serve as diplomats. Christian princesses rarely traveled to their new homes alone. Gregory and Bede both emphasize the role played by bishops in particular not only in promoting Christianity but also in establishing communications with the rest of Europe. Eventually this expanding cadre of ecclesiastic diplomats diminished the role of the women themselves as mediators between their families of origin and marriage. Particularly in Bede, women recapitulate Lavinia's silence in their role as disappearing facilitators of relations between and among their fathers, husbands, and bishops.

The book's first half concludes with a chapter on the flourishing of marriage diplomacy during the eleventh and twelfth centuries. Several historical developments—the Peace of God movement with its emphasis on new ways of regulating violence, the cult of the Virgin, and the preaching of the Crusades—placed more emphasis than ever before on women as peacemakers. Lavinia emerged *rediviva* as a type of the Virgin Mary. At the same time, the chronicles recounting the Viking expansion into Normandy and thence into England exposed uneasy compromises between the Virgilian, and now Christian, myth of foreign queens as agents of cultural assimilation and alternative views of them as tragic victims of ethnic rivalry. Dudo of Saint-Quentin's *De moribus et actis primorum Normanniæ ducum*, one of the period's most influential ethnic histories, honors a Lavinia-like princess who probably never existed to offset Scandinavian recollections of tragic peace-weavers incapable of reconciling the differences between their families of origin and marriage.

The Norman incursions into southern Europe complicated the idealization of interdynastic marriage even further by bringing Normans and other northerners into contact with Arabic literary discourses. The so-called courtly love tradition that emerged from this encounter destabilized the received Virgilian conquest narrative by retelling it from the perspectives of interdynastic brides. Writers of vernacular romances like the *Roman d'Enéas* invited their readers to imagine their heroines not as saintly mediators but as women whose private desires might counter their fathers' dynastic ambitions. The love that brought different polities, cultures, and ethnicities together in the romances was more volatile than the *caritas* of Christian churchmen, and less likely to underwrite lasting settlements. Figures like Isolde, Guinevere, and Chrétien de Troyes's Fenice, for example, raised the specter of adulterous liaisons rather than the Virgilian vision of a common progeny extending into the distant future. In the romances, interdynastic marriage leads to secret longings, jealousy, deceit, erotic despair, broken promises, and sometimes war rather than epic greatness.

As I argue in my chapters on the Middle Ages, misgivings dampened the confidence that rulers placed in interdynastic marriages even as the practice was weaving the European aristocracy into a giant network of familial relations. By the sixteenth century, the practice had become so routine that it was burdened with a sense of belatedness and predictability. One French jurist quipped "that as a comedy usually ends in a marriage, so is it with the most serious wars."[28] Statesmen continued to negotiate marriage alliances and settlements throughout the early modern period. But expectations that such marriages might establish lasting peace between belligerent parties began to wane, especially with recollections of prominent marriages that had failed to resolve either the Hundred Years War between the Plantagenets and the Valois or the Great Italian Wars between the Valois and the Hapsburgs.

My fourth chapter traces the earliest stages of this decline with respect to the sixteenth century's most important marriage treaty, the 1559 Peace of Cateau-Cambrésis, which ended over a half century of war between France and Spain. That war and its eventual resolution looked like a replay of the later phases of the Hundred Years War. Once again, negotiators availed themselves of a marital alliance between the principal belligerents—in this case Spain and France—to end the war. Proponents of the treaty used the new medium of print to interpret Philip II's marriage to Elizabeth de Valois according to the centuries-old discourse of Virgilian peacemaking. The texts themselves drew especially on the quasi-millenarian rhetoric of Virgil's First and Fourth *Eclogues*, with their celebrations of universal peace after a period of universal war.

But changing political conditions made such claims ring hollow. Powerful nobility had made implementing marriage settlements difficult enough in the Middle Ages. By the sixteenth century, monarchs were beginning to make them untenable. The expansion of monarchical authority in Tudor England and post-conquest Spain meant that a ruler like Philip II was less likely than ever to extend significant political authority to a foreign wife. In England, yet another force arose to complicate the older model: an increasingly obstreperous House of Commons. Henry VIII had expanded the size and authority of that body during the Reformation to serve the king's will. But that body soon had a will of its own and a membership ready to voice nationalist interests that ran counter to the monarch's dynastic ones. Whereas French poets had supported a Franco-Spanish marriage in 1559, English poets and propagandists championed the most ardent Protestants in Parliament in their opposition to a Franco-English match in 1579. They too evoked Virgil, but this time the Virgil who castigated a foreigner like Dido as an impediment to the Roman imperial project. Poets like Spenser and tract writers like John Stubbs viewed the prospect of a Catholic consort not as a step toward peace but as a betrayal of England's destiny to foster the Reformation throughout Europe and around the globe.

My next chapter focuses on Shakespeare's plays because they voiced a negative view of interdynastic marriage as subservience to a foreign power that later dominated European politics. Shakespeare came of age after the failure of Elizabeth's bid to marry the French Duke of Alençon. When Shakespeare began his career in the 1590s, Elizabeth's virginity reinforced, and in turn was reinforced by, England's position as an embattled Protestant nation waging war against Catholic Spain and nervously eyeing political developments in Catholic France. In *King John* and *Henry V*, Shakespeare retold the medieval history of England as an indictment of the humiliations of the interdynastic past and the baleful influence of foreign queens consort. *King John* casts Eleanor of Aquitaine as a manipulator who orchestrates treaties that deprive a rightful heir of his claim to the English throne and put dynastic interest above the welfare of the English people. A few years later, Shakespeare developed *Henry V* as an interrogation of just war theory in its conventional tripartite division: justice in waging, conducting, and ending war. Scholars have long noted how Henry and his English advisers twist canons of international justice to defend a legally dubious invasion of France and atrocities on the field of battle. But they have neglected how the weirdly comic turn of its final scenes presents the Treaty of Troyes as a violation of the third aspect of just war theory: justice in ending a war.

Less than a century after Shakespeare undercut the traditional justifications for interdynastic marriage by exposing its threats to an anachronistically imagined medieval English nation, neoclassical dramatists in France undercut them further by recalling disastrous marriages from classical antiquity. Whereas the English critique of diplomatic ideals stemmed from the protonationalist, insistently Protestant gentry and mercantile interests represented in the House of Commons, the French critique came from the Crown itself. Louis XIII's chief minister, Cardinal Richelieu, dismissed marriage treaties as ineffectual. Louis XIV wrote in Richelieu's spirit when he advised his son to keep women out of serious political discussion. Behind such views lay the revolutionary sense that war rather than peace was the normative condition of European life. From the perspective of Louis XIV and his advisers, the dream of Europe as a *res publica christiana* had become as much an anachronism as the pieties of queenly mediation that accompanied it.

Louis XIV's vision of state created a crisis in the French theater, since it demeaned the queen and other royal and aristocratic women who ranked among its principal patrons. As I argue in my penultimate chapter, Corneille's early *Horace* cast the country's turn away from older diplomatic ideals as a tragic necessity. Based on Livy's account of a failed alliance between the Oratii and Curiatii, the play dramatizes the suffering and degradation of aristocratic women in a state that has abandoned peacemaking for perpetual war. Later in his career, Corneille and his rival Racine were invited to return to the theme by Henriette of England, a daughter of England's Charles I who had wed Louis XIV's brother Philippe in a traditional but also politically belated marriage alliance. Both playwrights adapted the story of the Jewish princess Berenice, whom the emperor Titus loved but renounced because of a law forbidding the emperor to marry a foreign queen. Imagining a state that had abandoned marriage diplomacy allowed both playwrights to comment obliquely on the changing role of women in French politics. Corneille's *Tite et Bérénice* continues to mourn the passing of an older international order that accorded women a place of unique dignity and respect. In contrast, Racine's *Bérénice* looked to the future by creating an alternative sphere for women's expressive and persuasive power. The diva derived her power and illusory authority from distant recollections of the role once played by great queens in the French state. In an especially powerful intertextual gesture, Racine links Bérénice not to Lavinia, the woman whose marriage to Aeneas united Troy and Latium, East and West, Europe and Asia, but to Dido, the woman deserted by a hero who abandoned love for the glories of a future *imperium*.

My story ends with the French late seventeenth century. By then, the hope for European peace had lost its foundations in a shared sacramentology and confidence in women's intercessions. When discrete national historiographies celebrating nation-states rather than dynasties appeared, their writers cast the women whose marriages bound Europe in a single family as tragic victims of their fathers' ambitions and husbands' infidelities. Perhaps even more often, they condemned them as traitors. Isabelle of France, Margaret of Anjou, Catherine de' Medici, and Henrietta Maria rank among the most castigated women of the European past. Their perpetual denigration throughout the nineteenth and twentieth centuries contributed to the construction of the *ancien régime* as the corrupt order from which the revolutions of 1688 and 1789 liberated the enlightened peoples of France and England.

After Lavinia ends on a tragic note, with the exclusion of women from official diplomatic roles as a consequence of Europe's fragmentation into a system of discrete nation-states. Ever since the 1990s, historians of diplomacy and scholars of international relations and international relations theory have acknowledged a persistent need to incorporate greater attention to gender into their research.[29] There is something ironic about that need, given the role Europeans once assigned women as natural peacemakers binding their fathers, brothers, husbands, and sons into a single *res publica christiana*. I hope that by bringing the histories of marriage, gender, diplomacy, and state formation into a closer dialogue, I may complicate the received triumphalist narratives of the origin of modern diplomacy in either the Italian Renaissance or the Westphalian negotiations of the mid-seventeenth century. The following chapters document the flourishing of a diplomatic society centuries before either of those watershed moments, one in which women enjoyed, in theory if not always in practice, an exalted role in the relations between states. To the extent that the Treaty of Westphalia marked the rise of a new diplomatic order, it also marked the end of an earlier one that was every bit as robust. Like all historical transitions, the rise of the discrete nation-state and the ascendancy of *raison d'état* over dynastic interest came with a human cost. Women continued to have important roles behind the scenes. But in the official ideologies of the new European state, Lavinia once more fell silent.

❧ PART ONE

Origins

❧ Chapter 1

After Rome

Interdynastic Marriage during the First Christian Centuries

On October 24, 1441, Francesco Sforza's wedding to Bianca Maria Visconti staved off a succession crisis. Bianca was the illegitimate daughter of Filippo Visconti, the last Visconti duke of Milan. Filippo had betrothed her to Sforza when she was six years old, in order to ensure the celebrated mercenary's loyalty. But the scheme did not work particularly well, since Sforza ended up fighting for the Venetians against Visconti. Nevertheless, the two men were eventually reconciled, and the marriage took place.

During the festivities, the Lombard poet Ludovico Carbone honored the couple with an oration praising Bianca in Virgilian terms as a second Lavinia:

I ask you, esteemed gentlemen, what would have been the state of Italy? How utterly wretched the condition of everything? What a disturbance when the Milanese prince Filippo Maria passed away without any male heir and only the divine Bianca, like another Lavinia, preserving the Visconti house and all its lands, had not the great prince Francesco Sforza, afterwards strongest in the memory of men, been found worthy, who received that government by right of marriage?

[Quaero a vobis, viri praesentissimi, quisnam futurus erat Italiae status? Quam miserrima rerum conditio? Quanta perturbatio cum Mediolani princeps Philippus Maria sine ulla virili prole diem suum obiisset

et sola Diva Bianca, tanquam altera Lavinia, Vicecomitum domum et
tantas sedes servaret, nisi magnanimus et post hominum memoriam
fortissimus imperator Franciscus Sfortia dignus esset inventus qui id
gubernaculum iure coniungii exciperet?]¹

The Virgilian allusion transforms the potentially embarrassing fact of Bianca's marriage to her father's sometime enemy into a reenactment of the marriage that laid the foundation for the Roman Empire. Just as the Trojan Aeneas first waged war against the Latin King Turnus but later married his daughter Lavinia, Francesco's past enmity against Filippo ends in a marriage establishing a new dynasty. In each case, marriage legitimizes the suitor's arriviste claims to his father-in-law's lands. Even as the Roman Empire rose on Latin and Trojan bloodlines, Visconti and Sforza blood will flow in the veins of Bianca and Francesco's heirs. Allusions to Aeneas's marriage to Lavinia recur throughout Renaissance poems, orations, paintings, and tapestries honoring particular marriages. Francesco Bertini quoted Virgil's description of Lavinia's blush when praising Ippolita Sforza's beauty on the day she married the Duke of Calabria, "as if someone stained Indian ivory with crimson murex, or myriad white lilies mixed with roses blushed."² Aeneas and Lavinia's wedding was a common subject on *cassoni*, the chests containing the trousseau a bride brought with her to her husband's house.³ When Cambridge University students compiled a volume of verses honoring the Princess Elizabeth's marriage to Frederick V, Elector Palatine, in 1613, they filled it with references to the bride as another Lavinia and the groom as a second Aeneas.⁴ Many of the period's great vernacular epics incorporate the Virgilian couple as models for foundational marriages for the dynasties they honor.⁵ In *Orlando Furioso*, Ariosto casts Ruggiero and the warrior woman Bradamante as the mythical founders of the Estense dynasty of Ferrara. Spenser followed suit in *The Faerie Queene* by casting Arthegall and Britomart as progenitors of the Tudors. The fact that Virgil's narrative ends before the promised marriage takes place did not stop them. The Renaissance assumption that the narrative ought to have concluded with the marriage was so strong that the Italian poet Maphaeo Vegio wrote a "Thirteenth Book of the *Aeneid*" depicting the ceremony.⁶ Numerous humanist editions of Virgil included Vegio's text, giving it a kind of posthumous Virgilian authority.⁷

These recurrent allusions to Virgil derive from a centuries-old desire to endow the political present with the aura of Roman greatness. As I argue in this chapter, the first texts to imagine later marriages as a repetition of Aeneas's marriage to Lavinia date from antiquity. Writing in the sixth century, the Goth Jordanes prioritized a marriage between his people and the

Byzantines as the final proof of their incorporation into the Roman world. For the Romano-Gallic Gregory of Tours and the Anglo-Saxon Bede, Virgil's story of an amalgamation between Trojan and Latin cultures provided a model for the Christianization of the barbarian kingdoms that succeeded the Roman Empire in the West.[8]

From the perspective that numerous medieval and early modern writers adopted, the *Aeneid* upheld marriage between rival ruling families as a way not only of resolving differences and putting an end to hostilities but even of blending alien races into a single, coherent people drawing on the finest attributes of each. A crucial passage for later encomiasts was Juno and Jupiter's negotiation of the terms of the Latins' final surrender in book 12. Within the poem's Olympian fiction, the war between the Trojans and Latins, like the greater war between the Trojans and the Greeks it mirrors, derives from a conflict among the gods that must be resolved first. Juno, the champion of the Latins as she was before of the Greeks, must accept the will of Jupiter and the Fates ordaining Rome as a second Troy. When she realizes at last that Aeneas will prevail and the Trojans triumph over the native Latins, she makes one final request:

> So be it, when with happy marriage rites
> they make peace, and join through laws and treaties,
> that you neither command them to become Trojans, nor be called
>   Trojans,
> nor change their speech or old attire.
> Let Latium remain, let there be Alban kings for centuries,
> Let the Roman offspring be powerful through Italian virtue.
> Troy fell: Let it remain fallen along with its name.

> [cum iam conubiis pacem felicibus (esto)
> component, cum iam leges et foedera iungent,
> ne vetus indigenas nomen mutare Latinos
> neu Troas fieri iubeas Teucrosque vocari
> aut vocem mutare viros aut vertere vestem.
> sit Latium, sint Albani per saecula reges,
> sit Romana potens Itala virtute propago:
> occidit, occideritque sinas cum nomine Troia.] (12.821–828)

In Juno's vision, the Trojans' destined triumph does not efface their past defeat. Nor does it annul the Latins' own virtues.

Jupiter accepts her recommendation in great part, although he notes that certain Trojan rites and customs will persist. In the final diplomatic synthesis, neither culture is utterly effaced. While Latin-speaking, the new Roman people arising from the Latins and Trojans derives its character from both civilizations. This compromise finds its perfect emblem and embodiment in the marriage between the Trojan hero and his Latin wife. In coming together as husband and wife, Aeneas and Lavinia unite their countrymen in a common purpose and destiny.

More is involved here than mythic idealism. Throughout dynastic history, such royal marriages sometimes preceded other marriages between the two groups farther down the social scale. Livy, for instance, notes that numerous marriages united the Romans and Albans before the Romans finally annexed the latter. Interdynastic marriages also occasioned cultural exchanges, albeit rarely on the scale of transformation that Virgil imagines. But later marriages certainly precipitated changes in religion, commercial networks, artistic and literary styles, and manners.

Read in this way, the *Aeneid* provided support for a later ideology of marriage as a proper basis for peacemaking, cultural and economic transformation, and nation building. But this interpretation would strike modern commentators as misleadingly optimistic. As Craig Kallendorf has shown, moreover, some readers throughout the centuries have responded to the *Aeneid* as a profoundly pessimistic work that resists ideological certainties.[9] Instead of glorifying the Augustan regime for bringing peace to the Mediterranean, their *Aeneid*s underscore the fragility of that peace in a cosmos threatening a continual reversion into chaos. From their perspective, chthonic drives, lusts for vengeance, and conquest rather than reason structure the Virgilian universe. In that world, perpetual war rather than a pacified *imperium sine fine* looms as the true end of history. Diplomacy achieves at most temporary alliances doomed to violation, and the brides who underwrite them are destined for misery.

Virgil's story lends much to support these darker interpretations. Despite its future as a vehicle of diplomatic compliment, it had an unsettling ending: not with the projected marriage of Aeneas and Lavinia but with Aeneas's brutal slaying of his enemy Turnus, still pleading for his life. Early codifiers of international law like Alberico Gentili talked less about Jupiter and Juno's compromise than about this violation of what they saw as a basic moral principle: suppliants ought to be spared. The fact that Gentili excuses Aeneas on the grounds that Turnus could not be trusted to refrain from future violence only reinforces the sense that the *Aeneid* portrays a profoundly disordered world where fears, doubts, and second-guessing accompany every negotiation.

Nothing measures the poem's pessimism more effectively than Aeneas's relations with other human beings, especially women. For a poem that builds toward a union of peoples resting on his marriage to Lavinia, it repeatedly suggests the fragility of human ties. Aeneas leaves behind a company of corpses: his first wife, Creusa; his lover Dido; his friend Pallas; and his noble enemy Turnus. The Dido narrative in particular complicates the poem's later role in marriage encomia, since, at least from Dido's perspective, she and Aeneas entered into a marriage agreement that he betrayed. Within the poem, their love affair serves as the antitype of his projected marriage to Lavinia, a parody of the interdynastic marriage it ultimately endorses. Dido and Aeneas do not share a future, but they do share a past in their origin as exiles from the Levant seeking new kingdoms in the western Mediterranean. On an Olympian level, a truce between Juno and Venus heralds their union as much as that between Juno and Jupiter finally sanctions Aeneas's with Lavinia. Here too the marriage entails a fusion of cultures, although voices within the poem condemn Aeneas for adopting Carthaginian fashions. But unlike the later alliance with the Latins, the one between the Trojans and the Carthaginians fails, with Dido's funeral pyre foreshadowing the later Punic Wars between Rome and Carthage.

Even the peace associated with Aeneas's marriage to Lavinia is troubling. Insofar as Virgil structures his poem as a Romanization of the *Odyssey*, the war in Latium recapitulates Odysseus's struggle with the suitors and casts Lavinia as a second Penelope waiting to reward the hero with her embrace. But insofar as the second half of the *Aeneid* also imitates the *Iliad*, the Latin war repeats the Trojan War, a clash of civilizations triggered by a Trojan's determination to take a foreign bride away from her husband. In this intertextual frame, Aeneas appears as a second Paris and Lavinia a second Helen, a woman already betrothed to Turnus. Lavinia's role in the drama of war and peace is contradictory. She is at once the war's primary cause and a partner in the marriage settlement that concludes it. Writers using the *Aeneid* as a model for praising later marriages needed to tread carefully, since Virgil's poem suggested that heterosexual love was just as likely to cause a war as settle one.

The poem's ambiguities complicate its apparent attitude toward any foreign marriage, whether diplomatic or not. The opposition between Lavinia and Dido, Latium and Carthage, as legitimate and illegitimate alliances might seem to have nothing to do with the acceptability of intermarriage per se. Dido is arguably less foreign to Aeneas than the western, Latin Lavinia. After all, both Dido and Aeneas are city-building urbanites from the ancient, more civilized eastern Mediterranean. To the exiled Trojans, the Latins might seem more primitive than the Carthaginians in their tribal social organization, much as Dido finds herself isolated among the barbarian princes of North Africa. But the poem finally dismisses such cultural similarities between Dido and

Aeneas as less significant than ancient genealogies. Aeneas's deeper mythic and cultural affinities are with Lavinia, since he is descended from the Trojan founder Dardanus, who came originally from Italy.[10] This revelation not only justifies his conquest of Latium as a kind of Odyssean homecoming but also makes him seem a more suitable, ultimately less foreign suitor for Lavinia than Turnus, whose Argive ancestry diminishes his status as someone born on Italian soil. The Latins are really not that foreign at all.

As often happens in the *Aeneid*, things that first seem distant turn out to be familiar: Aeneas is simultaneously the foreign son-in-law predicted by one oracle and a fellow Italian. The reverse happens as well, as when the once familiar Turnus becomes increasingly Hellenized the more he steps into his role as a second Achilles. Dido, too, becomes more foreign by book 4, when she acquires her own Hellenized identity as a second Medea hurling curses at the departing Trojans. By the end of book 4, the reader and Aeneas alike have learned the significance of his misreading of the murals portraying the fall of Troy in Dido's temple to Juno. Instead of lamenting the Trojans' defeat, they celebrate it as Juno's triumph.

The more Virgil depicts Aeneas's and Lavinia's alternative lovers as the true foreigners, more aligned with the hated Greeks than either the Trojans or the native Italians, the more he complicates the *Aeneid*'s legacy as a celebration of interdynastic marriage. The poem endorses exogamy only within carefully circumscribed limits. The cultures that Jupiter and Juno agree to unite through marriage are less disparate than they first appear. In the Latins, the Trojans discover their own primitive, Italic origins; in the Trojans, the Latins see their own glorious, urbanized Roman future. The differences are less those between two civilizations than between early and later phases of a single society. While the Trojans bring a new sophistication to the Latins, the Latins restore to the Trojans their original austere Italian virtues, which were threatened by the effeminizing and exotic lures of Dido's Carthage.

The paradoxes that structure the *Aeneid*'s qualified endorsement of interdynastic marriage derive from and reinforce the conflicted attitudes and practices typical of the *renovatio*, Augustus's project to revive what he imagined to be the political and moral character of the republic. Several new laws attempted to bolster the size and integrity of the family by punishing celibates for not marrying, rewarding legitimate couples for having multiple children, brutally punishing adultery, and limiting marriage across lines of social rank.[11] In general, the laws exalted but also restricted marriage to individuals within the Roman patriciate. Under long-standing Roman law, moreover, *connubium* was a right enjoyed by Roman citizens permitting them to marry other Romans.[12] Relations between a Roman and a non-Roman were not considered *connubium*, or marriage as such. The more the empire expanded, and the more contacts that existed between Romans and non-Romans, the more these laws seemed to limit the choice of possible spouses. In *De beneficiis*, for example, Seneca notes that if a father promised his daughter to a man and then learned that the man was a foreigner, he had every right to break off the engagement.[13] Although such marriages did take place with the assumption and sometimes the decree that the non-Roman partner had been granted Roman citizenship, the laws officially discouraged intermarriage.

There was another problem. The emperor held the courtesy titles of *princeps senatus et princeps civitatis*, the first in the Senate and first among citizens. He was not a king, and the office was never, at least in Roman legal theory, hereditary. Drawing on vocabularies of the old republican constitution, the fiction was that the emperor was a highly trusted and respected citizen elevated to dictatorial authority to preserve the legal and social establishment. Regardless of how autocratic he might be in practice, legal theory distinguished him from both Near Eastern despots and the kings who ruled Rome before the republic. The emperor owed his succession to multiple factors. In some of the earliest cases, he was related by blood or adoption to previous emperors who may have named him as an heir. But he was also subject to army proclamation and/or Senate confirmation. Nothing as systematic as high medieval primogeniture regulated the succession, which depended as much on personal power, charisma, and influence as anything else. In short, the dynasties were barely dynasties in later understandings of the term.

In order to bolster imperial claims, often shaky at best, early emperors typically married women from within their own extended family or from other important Roman families, including daughters of ranking generals. A few, like Caligula, married women of lower rank because of erotic obsession. They generally did not marry foreign women, and certainly not women from foreign dynasties, which might suggest that they were overstepping their status as first among citizens and aspiring to dynastic monarchy. Roman propaganda frowned on men who married foreign queens. A revered figure like Julius Caesar might have an affair with a queen like Cleopatra, but if, like Mark Antony, he actually married her, posterity saw that act as part of his more general treason against the Roman Senate and people.

The dichotomy that Virgil draws between Dido and Lavinia supports the Augustan marriage project on numerous levels. As scholars have long recognized, book 4 of the *Aeneid* casts Dido as a type of Cleopatra, a North African queen who deflects a Roman hero from his duties to the *patria*. But the episode unfolds eventually as a correction of historical experience. Like Mark Antony, Aeneas falls for the queen of an exotic and opulent civilization but, through the gods' intervention, resumes his quest for Italy. Dido is left alone to kill herself in an anticipation of Cleopatra's suicide.

Cleopatra appears in her own person on the shield that Vulcan crafts for Aeneas in book 8, an ekphrastic representation of future Roman history that repeatedly disparages erotic unions between Romans and non-Romans. The Virgilian narrator, for example, notes that the Sabine women were "seized against custom [raptas sine more]" (8.635). In recounting the wars between Rome and the Etruscan Porsena, he honors Cloelia, a Roman hostage, for escaping from her captors. He conveniently cuts both stories off before their conclusions in Livy, where the Sabine women learn to love their Roman husbands and the Romans return Cloelia to Porsena to fulfill the terms of their original agreement. He thus removes any hint that Roman custom permitted either intermarriage or exchanges of female hostages with enemy powers. The representation of Actium at the shield's center condemns Antony and Cleopatra's marriage as a trespass against the *patria*. While Octavian stands proudly on his ship and commands a mono-racial fleet of Italians, Antony and Cleopatra lead a motley assembly of Egyptians, Arabs, Bactrians, Sebaeans, Indians, and other races displaying "barbarian wealth and various arms [ope barbarica variisque . . . armis]" (8.685). Perverse mingling reappears in the contrast between the noble, anthropomorphic Roman gods and the monstrous, zoomorphic gods of the Egyptians, complete with "barking Anubis" ("omnigenumque deum monstra et latrator Anubis / contra Neptunum et Venerem contraque Minervam" [8.698–99]). The passage brushes Antony and Cleopatra's marriage with a hint of bestiality, as if nothing could be more grotesque than a marriage between a Roman and a woman from one of the barbarian, dog-worshipping eastern races.

For writers who turned to Virgil in weighing the cultural and political significance of later dynastic marriages, the *Aeneid* provided both an endorsement and a repudiation of marrying people from different countries and cultures. As European history unfolded, both messages merged with other discourses in shaping and reshaping attitudes toward marriage diplomacy. Book 4's admonitions, for example, sometimes reinforced another strand of opposition to foreign marriage that derived from the Hebrew Bible. Exodus 34 condemned not just intermarriage but all negotiations and settlements with non-Israelites:

15. Avoid any alliance with the inhabitants of the land, or, when they go wantonly after their gods and sacrifice to them, you, any one of you, may be invited to partake of their sacrifices,

16. and marry your sons to their daughters, and when their daughters go wantonly after their gods, they may lead your sons astray too.[14]

Deuteronomy 7 repeats the admonition almost verbatim. After the Israelites return from the Babylonian captivity, Ezra the priest learns that Jewish men, including even priests and Levites, had intermarried with the Canaanites, Hittites, Perizzites, Jebusites, Ammonites, Moabites, Egyptians, and Amorites. When the people see Ezra weeping, rending his garments in despair over this news and casting himself down before the Temple, they repent their evil ways. In a prayer of national repentance, Ezra repeats the dual Mosaic prohibition against treaties and intermarriage with the surrounding nations. The Book of Ezra concludes with a list of the Israelites who had defiled themselves by taking foreign wives and an account of how they all pledged before God to put the women aside. Like Aeneas, each one abandons his foreign woman to fulfill a divinely authorized national destiny.

Constructions of racial alterity are notoriously slippery, with shifting political, social, and economic circumstances altering the boundaries of the pool of acceptable marriage partners. Ancient texts like the *Aeneid* and the Bible provided later writers with a variety of discourses to use in voicing their attitudes toward particular marriages or toward foreign marriage in general. For every Dido there was a Lavinia, and for every Jezebel a Ruth, the Moabite ancestor of David and, according to the New Testament, of Jesus.

The rest of this chapter examines two writers who pondered the imperial significance of interdynastic marriage along antithetical Virgilian lines in responding to later efforts to restore the western Roman Empire. Jordanes finished *De origine actibusque Getarum*, or the *Getica* (ca. 550), just when the eastern emperor Justinian was fighting to reconquer Italy and the western Mediterranean. A work resounding with Virgilian allusion, the *Getica* traces the gradual assimilation of the Gothic peoples to Roman law and custom, a process that culminates with the marriage of the Gothic princess Matasuntha to Justinian's cousin Germanus. For Jordanes's neo-Virgilian perspective, the marriage has the same mythical valences as Aeneas's marriage to Lavinia. Just as Aeneas's marriage merged the primitive Latins with the more civilized Trojans, the marriage between Matasuntha and Germanus merges the once barbarian Goths and the sophisticated, highly urbanized eastern empire.

Writing shortly before Charlemagne's 800 coronation as the head of a revived western empire, the Lombard Paul the Deacon commemorated the history of his people in the *Historia langobardorum*, yet another work with strong Virgilian resonances, which was directly influenced by Jordanes. Unlike Jordanes, however, Paul the Deacon darkens Virgil's myth of cultural and racial fusion through marriage. His ambivalences register crucial shifts in Carolingian marriage diplomacy after Charlemagne began the territorial expansions that eventually created an empire. No people experienced that transformation earlier or more brutally than the Lombards, whose relations with their Frankish neighbors had often been turbulent. At first, the last Lombard king, Desiderius, related to the Frankish king Charlemagne as a peer ruler and established an alliance with him that seems to have included the offer of his own daughter's hand in marriage. But Charlemagne eventually broke the alliance, repudiated Desiderius's daughter, conquered the Lombards, and confined Desiderius himself in a monastery. Paul's *Historia* cuts off before these events. Nevertheless, in its retelling of prior Lombard history, it suggests that marriage alliances are just as likely to end in tragedy and subjugation as in an increase in national glory.

Both the *Getica* and the *Historia langobardorum* are known today primarily among specialists in late antiquity and the early Middle Ages. But they are rich, even haunting works that deserve a wider audience. Early modern Europeans knew, edited, and even occasionally imitated and adapted these texts. As I go on to argue, their alternative appropriations of Virgil raise questions about the ethics and efficaciousness of marriage diplomacy that recurred for centuries. But in turning to these texts, scholars of the later Middle Ages and especially early modernity need to keep several points in mind. Throughout the early Middle Ages, European politics unfolded as a series of military and diplomatic exchanges between, among, and within an aggregate of loose polities that succeeded the Roman Empire. The eastern half of the empire, Byzantium, was still intact, with an emperor ruling from Constantinople. It did not fall until 1453, at the height of the Italian Renaissance. The West gradually gave birth to a series of Germanic kingdoms: the Franks in what is now much of France, western Germany, and the Low Countries; the Visigoths in southern France and Spain; the Vandals in Mediterranean Africa; and the Anglo-Saxons in England. As usual, Italy was a particularly tricky site, where Byzantine, old Roman, Vandal, Gothic, and later Lombard and Frankish forces fought for domination. The last western emperor, Romulus Augustulus, yielded to Odoacer, the first "barbarian king of Italy," in 476. Theodoric murdered Odoacer and established an Ostrogothic kingdom of Italy in 493 that was ruled from Ravenna. That kingdom in turn fell to Byzantine forces in 553. But the struggle for Italy so drained the Byzantines' resources that they could not maintain their conquest. Fifteen years later, Alboin established a Lombard kingdom of Italy that lasted for almost two centuries, from 569 until 774, when Charlemagne deposed the last Lombard and declared himself king of the Lombards, and, effectively, king of Italy.

There has never been a transhistorical definition of marriage that could be applied to every human culture at every moment of its existence. Societies differ widely over questions of partner eligibility, appropriate number and gender of spouses, the relationship of the institution to property transmission, its religious aspects, and procedures of licensing and legitimation. In the Latin West, Gratian codified the first canon law of marriage in the twelfth century, hundreds of years after Jordanes and Paul the Deacon wrote their ethnic histories. It is not always clear what kinds of relationships they, or any of their contemporaries, considered marriages and what kinds they did not. Another late antique writer I consider in the next chapter, Gregory of Tours, for example, praises some women as wives (*uxores*) and condemns others as concubines (*concubinae*). But we cannot assume that Gregory's contemporaries would have agreed with his distinctions. He may simply be disparaging women he disliked as concubines, even though their clients and allies might have honored them instead as wives. Frankish polygyny compounds the problem, since Frankish men sometimes had multiple *uxores* and multiple *concubinae*.[15]

Anyone who comes to these texts and the cultures that produced them confronts fundamental problems of historicity. Theorists have made us rightly skeptical of any truth claims about the past. But those working on early modernity can generally weigh one account of the past against multiple corroborating, qualifying, or contradictory accounts of the same things. Scholars of late antiquity are rarely that lucky. The reconstruction of entire centuries of European political history often rests on one or two sources that resist modern canons of accuracy. We sometimes cannot separate what is legendary or purely invented by a given writer from what constitutes a more or less accurate picture of what happened. In some cases, we simply cannot know if a given *uxor* or *concubina* ever really existed. Even if there is some germ of truth in these accounts, generic and folkloric convention, loyalties and prejudices of patronage, and imitation of specific literary models overdetermine the women's representation.

The blur of fact, possible fact, probable fiction, and sheer fantasy that characterizes the ethnic histories, chronicles, and saints' lives on which we must rest our knowledge of post-Roman Europe, and especially the lives of post-Roman queens, can trip up even the most careful scholar. Pauline Stafford, for example, prefaced her seminal book on early medieval queens by admitting how little we can ever really know for sure about women in this period, given the paucity of sources, particularly before the ninth century, when the apogee of Carolingian power led to the production and better preservation of family and property records, as well as the patronage of more writers chronicling royal lives.[16] But Stafford often makes generalizations about "early medieval queens," implying that many Merovingian and Lombard queens enjoyed the same powers and lived under the same constraints as later Carolingian ones. We simply cannot assume that. For every Brunhild or Fredegond, the great Merovingian consorts who wield so much authority in Gregory of Tours's *Historia francorum*, there are numerous other women we know only by their names. There were undoubtedly many more about whom we do not even know that much. It is not at all clear, for example, that all were foreign brides, like the Visigothic princess Brunhild, married in order to seal an alliance with their families of origin. Some were local girls of low social standing, some daughters of prominent local families, and probably an appalling number were spoils of battle or other women simply forced into concubinage or marriage. At the end of this chapter I discuss one such woman, the Lombard queen Rosamund, and her revenge against her captor.

In what follows, I resort repeatedly to a literary methodology, best suited to analyzing the social and cultural work of fictions, in assessing the significance of two particularly important earlier sources for the history of European attitudes toward marriage diplomacy. Even if they invented every one of their interdynastic brides, their stories still idealize marriage as a significant force in orchestrating relations between and among the kingdoms that succeeded the Roman Empire. In the Virgilian myth they all inherited, marriage had brought that empire into existence out of its mixed Trojan and Latin components. In the new myth they were inventing, marriage provided a way of rebuilding the economic, social, and cultural infrastructures that existed before the collapse of the western imperium. Italia, Gallia, Hispania, Britannia, Dalmatia, and the other old provinces were no longer part of a single political system. But as the men and women who now ruled these regions as separate kingdoms intermarried, they laid the foundations for a new European civilization on the ruins of Rome. For those who chronicled their story, the driving question was whether the unifying promise of marriage diplomacy could offset the centrifugal forces of ethnicity, localism, and individual greed.

Marriage and the Reintegration of Empire: Jordanes's *Getica*

One of the earliest and most controversial ethnic histories of late antiquity, Jordanes's account *Of the Origin and Deeds of the Goths* (*De origine actibusque getarum*), or *Getica*, established marriage as a principal narrative device for organizing reflections on the cultural, military, and political relations among the Roman successor states. The work was enormously influential in the early Middle Ages and was rediscovered in 1442 by the Italian diplomat and humanist Enea Silvio Piccolomini, the future Pope Pius II, a few years before he negotiated an important marriage between the Hapsburg emperor Frederick III and Eleanor of Portugal. The Venetian playwright Carlo Goldoni launched his career with *Amalasunta*, a tragedy based on Jordanes's account of the most famous Gothic queen and her struggles with her son. Much of the *Getica* is mythic, particularly the sections recounting the Goths' alleged Scandinavian origins and early immigrations. But scholars still value it as one of the chief sources of information about an ethnic group that sometimes supported and sometimes menaced Rome, established a short-lived Ostrogothic kingdom in Italy, and founded a Visigothic kingdom in Spain that lasted until the Umayyad conquest of 711–12.

The *Getica* is not simply a history of the Goths, their origin, early immigrations, and eventual organization into kingdoms. It is also a history of their continual contact with the older, more cultivated societies of the Mediterranean. Above all, it is a history of Gothic-Roman relations and of the Goths' eventual absorption within the Roman political order. Foreshadowings of that final assimilation give that narrative telos the force of destiny, as if the Goths were driven by fate itself to leave their original home in Scandinavia and find a new home and a new imperial identity on the Mediterranean shores.[17] Since that identity is one of subjugation, the work has had a conflicted reception history. To this day, scholars debate whether Jordanes meant to celebrate Gothic accomplishments or to signal Gothic inadequacies that cried out for ultimate absorption within the Roman order.[18]

Roman literature offered Jordanes two antithetical models for his history of the relations between the Romans and his own barbarian race, the Goths: Virgil's *Aeneid* and Tacitus's *Germania*. These works foreground the contrast between the primitive simplicity represented by one group of people and the urban sophistication of another at two critical moments in Roman history, the mythic origin of its empire and its projected fall. Virgil's earlier and more optimistic narrative imagined an *imperium sine fine* founded on the Trojans' intermarriage with the arguably less sophisticated Ausonians. In the same passage where the Ausonian king Latinus first proposes a marriage between Aeneas and his daughter Lavinia, he identifies his people as descendants of Saturn who remain in a Golden Age without the need for laws or external compulsion. Tacitus's Germans share many of the nobler attributes of Virgil's Ausonians. But for Tacitus, writing about eighty years after Virgil, Germanic continence, frugality, fidelity to commitments, and monarchy held in check by public consensus epitomized what Rome had lost by becoming an empire. His Germans scorn marriage across ethnic lines and preserve a racial purity that Tacitus admires. Instead of looking forward to a possible merger of Roman and non-Roman bloodlines, he hints that the Germans might overwhelm the empire if they ever abandoned their own intertribal conflicts.[19]

As a Goth writing after a barbarian army defeated the last western Roman emperor, Jordanes might have followed Tacitus's pessimistic view of the Roman imperium, particularly in contrast to the moral and military virtues of his fellow Germans. At several points he stresses the Romans' need for Gothic *foederati*, or allies, to fight their wars: "Nam sine ipsis dudum contra quasvis gentes Romanus exercitus difficile decertatus est" (Now for a long time, it had been difficult for the Romans to fight against any peoples whatsoever without them).[20] The Romans themselves often alienated their Gothic allies by infidelity to treaties and, more generally, through the penchant for soft, luxurious living that Tacitus decried.

But for Jordanes, even periods of open warfare between the Goths and the Romans turn out to be interruptions in an overarching story of mutual admiration and alliance. As much as the Romans depend on the Goths for military support, the Goths need the Romans to teach them civilization. Writing from a republican perspective, Tacitus equated imperial culture with decadence. Jordanes, in contrast, openly admires Roman sophistication and the Roman ability to unite vast territories through a deft combination of conquest, diplomacy, and commerce. This admiration, which he attributes to many generations of his Gothic predecessors, allows him to reject the Tacitean model of an empire falling prey to barbarism for the more optimistic Virgilian one of ethnic assimilation on the basis of interdynastic marriage.

Jordanes sets the stage for this exchange of Gothic military power for Roman refinement in his opening mythic account of the Gothic migrations from the far northern island of Scandza, "a land not only inhospitable to people but truly cruel to beasts [non solum inhospitalis hominibus, verum etiam belvis terra crudelis est]" (3). In Virgil, the more civilized Trojans are the immigrants rather than the more primitive Ausonians, but in Jordanes, for whom the racial burden is not the preservation of civilization but its acquisition, the barbarians are the wanderers. Over several generations the Goths trek southward, encounter the Mediterranean civilizations of Greece and Rome, and eventually find homes in Italy and Spain. This southward trajectory constitutes a migration not only into civilization but also into a common European history. Jordanes splices his people into famous moments of the Greco-Roman mythic past to give them their own exalted legacy: a Gothic king named Telefus supposedly married Priam's sister, fought with Ajax, fell from his horse while pursuing Ulysses, was wounded in the thigh by Achilles, and still managed to drive the Greeks from his land. His son fell in love with Cassandra and enlisted in the Trojan War to win her parents' favor but died shortly after his arrival (9). Other Goths clash with Darius and Xerxes and form an alliance with Philip of Macedon (10). Even the Amazons appear as Gothic women gone wild. According to Jordanes, they took up arms in the course of defending themselves against a neighboring tribe when their husbands were off fighting elsewhere (7–8). Jordanes also notes several apparent references to the Goths in Roman literature, such as Virgil's description of Aeneas offering a sacrifice to Mars, who rules the Getic fields: "Gradivumque patrem, Geticis qui praesidet arvis" (3.35).

For Jordanes, the more the Goths associate with Greco-Roman history, the more they reveal a moral and intellectual affinity with it. In Jordanes's eyes, the Goths merit an eventual incorporation into Mediterranean society precisely because they are more like the Greeks than other barbarians. Like the Trojan conquest of Latium in Virgil, this is the telos of Jordanes's epic narrative. A marriage marks its achievement, but as in the *Aeneid*, it is long deferred and troubled by many false starts and simulacra of the final political synthesis. While the Romans often depended on the Goths as allies, they also frequently betrayed them. In Jordanes's account, retaliatory wars between the two peoples alternate with truces that, however fragile, carry the promise of an ultimate reconciliation. One such truce followed the cataclysmic battle of Adrianople in 378, in which an army of Visigoths routed the emperor Valens and his army. Valens's successor, Theodosius I, finally made peace with the Goths and invited their king Athanaric to Constantinople. Jordanes's memorable description of the visit signals the Goths' appreciation of and predilection for the refinements of urban Mediterranean society:

> [Athanaric], having freely consented to everything, entered the royal city and marveled at it. "Behold," he said, "I see what I have often heard without belief, namely the fame of such a city." And turning his eyes here and there, he now admired the city's site and the convoys of ships. He now gazed on the shining walls and the people of various races flowing like a wave from diverse parts into a single fountain. Thus too he looked upon the soldiers in their ranks. He said, "Without a doubt, the emperor is an earthly god."

> [Qui omnino libenter adquiescens regiam urbem ingressus est, miransque, "En," inquit, "cerno, quod saepe incredulus audiebam; famam vidilicet tantae urbis"; et huc illuc oculus volens, nunc sitem urbis commeatumque navium, nunc moenia clara prospectans miratur, populosque diversarum gentium quasi fonte in uno e diversis partibus

scaturriente unda, sic quoque milite ordinato aspiciens, "Deus," inquit, "sine dubio tereneus est imperator."] (28)

Jordanes's focus on Athanaric's wonder suggests that the Goths may eventually assimilate to the Byzantine social and political order. Athanaric may be a barbarian, in the sense of someone who is not ethnically Greek or Roman, but he is no savage looking at the city with envy, resentment, or incomprehension. Far from wanting to conquer it, he recognizes that its centrality to world commerce—its status as a place where "the people of various races flowing like a wave from diverse parts into a single fountain"—ultimately derives from the emperor's supreme authority: "Without a doubt, the emperor is an earthly god."

Unfortunately, Constantinople is a paradise that the Goths can glimpse from afar but not fully enter, at least as completely integrated subjects of the godlike emperor. The conspicuous absence of an interdynastic marriage linking the Goths to the imperial family underscores the tentativeness of the peace. After Athanaric and Theodosius die, war resumes under their successors. Throughout this period, the Goths and the Romans alike enter disastrous alliances with other barbarian peoples which prove that destiny will not be fulfilled until they have finally allied with each other. The Visigothic king Theodoric I (reigned 419–451), for example, marries his daughter to the Vandal prince Huneric. The marriage is happy enough at first, but Huneric's inherent cruelty and jealousy lead to tragedy. Suspecting that his Gothic bride has tried to poison him, Huneric cuts off her nose and ears and sends her back to her father, who promptly avenges her. The mutilation not only expresses Huneric's rage but also preempts the possibility that Theodoric might use her again to forge another interdynastic marriage unfavorable to the Vandals. The narrative reinforces one of Jordanes's favorite themes: his insistence that the Goths are actually far more civilized, more Roman in character, than other non-Roman peoples. The real barbarians are people like the Vandals, who go around mutilating princesses. The story also serves as a demonic parody of the right kind of marital alliance that the Goths ought to have been seeking: one with the Romans rather than the Vandals.

Jordanes locates a significant moment of Gothic-Roman cooperation in the reign of Theodoric the Great (454–526), the Ostrogothic king who conquered Italy and ruled it as a successor state on an explicitly Roman model. Steeped in classical learning and the cultural values of *romanitas*, Theodoric won the favor of successive emperors and gained the offices of *magister militum* and consul. After a series of complicated diplomatic negotiations whose details are not fully known, the Byzantine emperor Zeno (425–491) encouraged him to move his people from the Balkans to Italy and to wrest control of the peninsula from Odoacer, its first barbarian king. From 493 to 526, Theodoric ruled Italy as a Byzantine viceroy. But in practice, he enjoyed tremendous independence and effectively established himself as the sovereign of the Latin West.

Scholars have long noted how Theodoric heightened his power and prestige through acts of conspicuous Byzantine imitation. With his 493 murder of Odoacer, Theodoric became the de facto heir to what had been the western Roman Empire and had to hold multiple factions and interests—old Roman, Gothic, and Byzantine—in balance. He did this primarily by preserving as much of the old Roman legal and social system as possible. But Jordanes has nothing to say about these internal matters and focuses almost exclusively on Theodoric's diplomatic marriages:

> Theodoric, as we noted, in the third year of his entrance into Italy cast aside his private clothes and, upon the advice of the emperor Zeno, put off the costume of his people. Now as ruler of [both] the Goths and the Romans, he took on the great royal mantle and sent a delegation to Lodoin, the king of the Franks, to seek his daughter Audefleda in marriage.

> [Theodoricus . . . tertioque, ut diximus, anno ingressus sui in Italiam Zenonisque imperiatoris consulto privatam habitum suaeque gentis vestitum deponens, insigne regio amictu, quasi iam Gothorum Romanorumque regnator, adsumit, missaque legatione ad Lodoin Francorum regem, filiam eius Aodefledam sibi in matrimonium petit.] (57)

Jordanes then notes how Theodoric quickly married one daughter to Alaric, king of the Visigoths, and another to Sigismund, king of the Burgundians. Within a single paragraph, Jordanes traces how deftly Theodoric established alliances with most of the western empire's successor states through interdynastic marriages. He later married a third daughter to a descendant of the powerful Amali dynasty living in Visigothic Spain. Theodoric finally married his sister Amalafrida to Thrasamundus, the king of the North African Vandals, and her daughter Amelaberga to Hermanafrid, king of the Thuringians (58). By this point Theodoric had established close ties between his own Amal dynasty and the ruling families of every major barbarian state that succeeded the old empire.

Jordanes's syntax suggests that this extraordinary series of marriages was Theodoric's primary response to the Byzantine emperor Zeno's insistence on Romanization. Zeno first asks Theodoric, the Ostrogothic king, to take off his native garb and assume a Roman mantle of kingship. One sentence later, Theodoric starts marrying off his relatives. Jordanes's characteristically rapid narration glosses over the lack of logical transition between the two sentences, and on a deeper level, the possibility of discord between the two leaders' projects. The Byzantine emperor wanted to stabilize the frontiers between Italy and the Vandal and Frankish states that threatened it. To an extent, Theodoric's marriages helped to accomplish this. But Theodoric practiced marriage diplomacy on a patently imperial scale. Jordanes depicts him less as a king of Italy than as someone whose vision, authority, and influence reached from one end of the Mediterranean to another. Just when the Byzantine emperor was trying to tighten his control over the West by setting up Theodoric as a viceroy, Theodoric used diplomatic marriage to supplant the emperor as the source of primary diplomatic initiative throughout the old Roman world.

A history of the Goths that concluded with Theodoric stepping into a fully imperial role would have been the perfect historiographical complement to the ambitious artistic and architectural projects that Theodoric undertook at his capital of Ravenna. But this is not where things end in Jordanes, who carries his narrative through the subsequent Gothic wars, Justinian's reimposition of direct Byzantine rule over Italy, and the absorption of Theodoric's Amal dynasty into the Byzantine nobility. This later material casts a retrospective shadow over Jordanes's narration of Theodoric's reign. As much as Theodoric proved that a Goth was capable of effective leadership in diplomatic and military matters alike, his Romanization was incomplete.

Within the context of a chronicle that uses the topos of interdynastic marriage to signal a non-Roman people's access to *romanitas*, the catalogue of marriages that Theodoric arranged for his family contains one glaring absence. He married his relatives to Franks, Burgundians, Visigoths, and Vandals, but not to Romans. Their marriages never gave them access to imperial bloodlines. The implications of this failure within Jordanes's narrative are enormous. As much as Theodoric might fashion his reign on imperial models, as much as he might cast aside his native garb and dress in a royal mantle, he still remained a Goth.

Within Jordanes's emphatically assimilationist vision, the Goths would achieve their full potential as citizens within a revitalized Roman world only when they ceased to exist as a separate people. In the years after Theodoric's death, relations between the Gothic kings and the Byzantine emperors decayed and another cycle of war erupted in which the Goths were effectively crushed. At the climax of Jordanes's narrative, the Gothic king Vitiges and his wife, Matasuntha, Theodoric's own granddaughter, surrender to the great Byzantine commander Belisarius. From Jordanes's perspective, the surrender is more ennobling than humiliating. Belisarius grants Vitiges the title of patrician and takes him to Constantinople, where he becomes "bound by ties of affection" to the emperor Justinian. When Vitiges dies, the emperor marries Matasuntha to his own nephew Germanus, a member of the elite Roman Anicii family. The *Getica* concludes with the birth of their son Germanus Junior, "in whom the race of the Anicii, joined with the Amali stock, yet promises hope, the Lord willing, to both peoples [in quo conjuncta Aniciorum gens cum Amala stirpe spem adhuc, utriusque generis domino praestate, promittit]" (60). As Walter Goffart has noted, this long-deferred marriage between the Amali and a Roman noble family betokens the Goths' decisive incorporation into the Roman world.[21]

The costs of this assimilation, however, are enormous. Germanus's relation to Justinian carries no direct claim to the imperial crown. Jordanes conspicuously downplays Germanus's imperial connections and emphasizes instead his association with the Romano-Byzantine Anicii senatorial family. The Amal dynasty, which came so close, particularly in the reign of Theodoric, to setting up a fully independent kingdom that might have substituted Gothic cultural ideals for Roman ones, effectively disappears from history with its absorption in the Byzantine nobility.

In the end, Jordanes is true to his Virgilian origins and his commitment to a Roman *imperium sine fine*. As in the *Aeneid*, a greater empire rises from the fusion of two peoples, one bringing a sophisticated urban heritage and the other the virtues of a pre-urban simplicity. But once again, the price of a stake in that imperial future is the de facto disappearance from history of the very race that the text presumably exists to commemorate. The epic ends on an elegiac note that dampens the joys attendant on its culminating dynastic marriages. Turnus's defeat looms larger than Aeneas's marriage to Lavinia, which does not even take place in Virgil's poem. By Jupiter's decree, Trojan blood will run in Roman veins, but the Romans will be known by language and by custom as Latins, and the name "Trojan" will be confined to the past. To that extent, Juno prevails over Venus. By Justinian's conquest, Ostrogothic blood will run in Roman veins as well, but like the Trojan history with which it coincides, Ostrogothic history ends at the moment of its final absorption into the Roman order. Unlike Lavinia's marriage to Turnus, Matasuntha's to Germanus takes place within Jordanes's narrative. But its understatement is telling. Theodoric the Great's ambition to marry his family into every Roman successor state ends in this marriage between his widowed granddaughter and the relative of an emperor bent on reestablishing Roman imperial authority throughout the Mediterranean.

Drinking from Your Father's Skull: *Historia langobardorum*

Over two hundred years stand between Jordanes and the other writer I want to discuss, the Lombard historian Paul the Deacon. Those were monumental years in Mediterranean history. Despite Jordanes's closing confidence in a perpetual Roman order, Byzantine domination of Italy lasted only fifteen years. Justinian's successor, Justin II, was a singularly ineffective ruler who went insane. According to his contemporary John of Ephesus, Justin liked to be drawn through his palace on a cart while taking bites out of his servants. While this petty cannibalism was unfolding in Constantinople, another barbarian people, the Lombards, conquered much of the Italian peninsula and established an independent kingdom. About two centuries later, the Lombards yielded to the Franks under their great leader Charlemagne in 774. Charlemagne conquered the Lombards and half of Italy relatively early in his career, a full quarter century before Pope Leo III crowned him emperor of the Romans on Christmas Day, 800.

At some point during that twenty-six-year period, the Lombard writer Paul the Deacon, a leading figure of the so-called Carolingian Renaissance, wrote an extended history of his people. The *Historia langobardorum* ends with the death of King Liutprand in 744, three decades before the Lombards' national catastrophe at the hands of Charlemagne. It remains our principal source of information about the Lombards, although, like Jordanes's *Getica*, it challenges the modern reader with its mixture of plausible and outrageously implausible material. Paul stands apart from other early historians in the detail with which he imagined the inner lives of two women, the Gepid princess Rosamund and the Bavarian princess Theudelinda, who entered Lombard history through radically different types of interdynastic marriage. In creating the two women, Paul conflated probable fact with folklore, legend, and conspicuous literary imitation. Their two narratives not only stand out from the more chronicle-like core of the *Historia* but also inspired a whole canon of later plays, operas, and even Pre-Raphaelite paintings that brought aspects of Paul's conflicted views of interdynastic marriage to early modern and nineteenth-century audiences. The English poet George Turberville included a poem about Rosamund in his 1587 collection of *Tragicall Tales* from Italian sources. The playwright William Davenant began his career with a play about Rosamund in 1628, the same year that the Duke of Buckingham's assassination allowed Charles I's French consort, Henrietta Maria, to wield greater influence at court. The Swedish chemist-playwright Ulrich Hjarne wrote another Rosamund play a few decades later, about the time the former queen Christina, now openly Catholic and cross-dressing, was mulling over the possibility of returning to Sweden to the alarm of its Protestant establishment. Whereas Theudelinda provided a Lavinia-like model of the good foreign bride who ennobled her adopted country, Rosamund provided later writers with a Dido-like type of a queen—either consort or regnant—whose foreign ways might subvert a society otherwise destined for greatness.

Just as the Virgilian contrast between Lavinia and Dido expressed complex attitudes toward Cleopatra, Octavia, and the Augustan *renovatio*, Paul's contrast between Rosamund and Theudelinda voiced ambivalence toward the Carolingian conquest of Lombardy and the traumatic marriage diplomacy that seems to have accompanied it. Paul's own loyalties could not have been more conflicted, since he ended up profiting from both Lombard and Carolingian patronage. Until the conquest, he enjoyed close ties with ranking Lombard nobility and with the Lombard royal family. But after the Lombard catastrophe, he moved to Francia and worked for the Carolingians. The *Historia langobardorum* is a particularly slippery text whose exact dating continues to elude scholars, in part because, unlike with other works dedicated to specific Lombard or to specific Carolingian patrons, its political affinities and even its place of composition are unclear. Paul may have started it in Francia, or perhaps a few years later, after he retired to the great monastery of Monte Cassino in the southern Lombard duchy of Benevento.[22]

In order to appreciate Paul's political virtuosity most fully, we need to grasp the complexity of Lombard and Carolingian marriage diplomacy in the years immediately preceding the conquest of Lombardy. The archival record—based primarily on the *Annales francorum*, some surviving papal correspondence, an epitaph honoring Ansa, the last Lombard queen, and some remarks in Einhard's early biography of Charlemagne—leaves some crucial questions unanswered. Nevertheless, it suggests in broad outlines the concerted effort by two late eighth-century kings, Desiderius of the Lombards and Charlemagne of the Franks, to promote their interests through marriage diplomacy. Desiderius had four daughters. While Anselperga became the abbess of Salvatore Brescia, her sister Adelperga strengthened her father's relations with the duchy of Benevento by marrying Duke Arechis II. Two other sisters married potentially hostile foreign rulers, Duke Tassilo III of Bavaria and Charlemagne. The case of the latter is the most mysterious. Her name may have been Gerperga, but even that is uncertain.[23]

There is also some evidence that at least two royal women, Desiderius's queen, Ansa, and Charlemagne's mother, Bertrada, may have played a role in the negotiations. In an epitaph for Ansa, Paul the Deacon honored her for orchestrating three marriages uniting the Lombards with the lands bathed

by the Ofanto, the Rhine, and the Danube, in other words, Benevento, Francia, and Bavaria: "Binding the severed ones whom the swift Ofanto flows
around, / Joining in love of peace those whom the Rhine and Hister sur-
round [Discissos nectens rapidus quos Aufidus ambit / Pacis amore ligans
cingunt quos Rhenus et Hister]."[24] In arranging the Frankish marriage, Ansa
may have found a kindred spirit in Bertrada, whom the *Annales francorum*
depict going to Italy in 770. According to the *Annales mosellani*, Bertrada met
with Desiderius and brought his daughter back for Charlemagne.[25]

Since the papacy had long depended on Frankish military and diplomatic
support against the Lombards to maintain the balance of power on the Italian peninsula, the alliance between Charlemagne and Desiderius unsettled
Pope Stephen III. Stephen did not trust the Lombards and, like his predecessors, hoped to find an ally against them in the Frankish king. In the summer
of 770, Stephen wrote Charlemagne and his brother a letter urging them to
abandon any plans for a Lombard marriage. Stephen attacked the negotiations both on the political grounds of the Lombards' long-standing contempt
for the church and, more generally, on an ideological opposition to intermarriage. The letter unfolds as a heady mixture of praise for the Carolingians,
invective against the Lombards, scriptural allusion, ecclesiastical menace,
and blatant misogyny. It opens with injunctions to remain steadfast against
the devil's "perfidious flatteries [pestiferis . . . blandimentis]," which, acting
upon "the weak nature of woman [per infirmam mulieris naturam]," had
cost Adam paradise itself and allowed "the destruction of cruel death to
steal into the human race [dirae mortis humano generi inrepsit excidium]."[26]
According to Stephen, Holy Scripture instructs us with numerous examples
of men lured away from God's commandments through an "unjust coupling
with an alien race [sicut divinae scripturae historia instruimur, per aliene
nationis iniustam copulam a mandatis Dei deviare]" (561). Stephen reminds
the brothers that they are already married to women of their own nation,
who could not be cast aside without committing a grave sin. Remarriage
with a Lombard woman would compound that fault: "The splendid and
noble offspring of your royal authority might be polluted—may it not be
so!—by the perfidious and most fetid race of the Lombards, who are not at
all counted among the [ordinary] races, but from whom the race of lepers is
certain to have sprung! [splendiflua ac nobilissima regalis vestrae potentiae
proles perfidae, quod absit, ac foetentissimae Langobardorum genti polluca-
tur, quae in numero gentium nequaquam conputatur, de cuius natione et
leprosorum genus oriri certum est!]" (561). According to Stephen, none of
the brothers' progenitors had ever married a foreigner. In their endogamy,
they remained true to Scripture, which repeatedly teaches that "nobody who

has taken a wife from a foreign race has remained unharmed [Itaque nullus, exterrae gentis assumta coniuge, innoxius perseveravit]" (561).

Charlemagne ignored the pope and went through with the wedding. In this case, it was not the man who suffered from the "unjust coupling with an alien race" but Desiderius's daughter. Although the details here are sketchy, neither the marriage nor the Frankish-Lombard alliance lasted very long. The death of Charlemagne's brother, and Charlemagne's subsequent seizure of his lands, seems to have kindled territorial ambition. Charlemagne repudiated his Lombard wife, invaded her country, imprisoned her royal parents in a monastery, and declared himself king of the Lombards.

As Pauline Stafford has noted, Charlemagne's ill-fated Lombard marriage was his only one to the daughter of a foreign king. Although he and his successors continued to foster political alliances through marriage, they married into the nobility of annexed territories rather than into the royal families of independent realms.[27] By 817, Louis the Pious's *Ordinatio imperii* insisted that his sons marry women from within the three Carolingian kingdoms rather than foreign women.[28] The contrast with the Byzantine practice related by Jordanes is striking: the Carolingians showed no interested in the daughters or widows of defeated royalty. They allied themselves instead with the local nobles, who were often at odds with their former rulers and betrayed them into Carolingian hands. Not everyone approved of this marriage revolution. Charlemagne's first biographer, Einhard, notes that Charlemagne's mother, Bertrada, strongly opposed her son's repudiation of his Lombard bride, and this was the only time she did not support his actions. But in her loyalty to her daughter-in-law, Bertrada exposed her allegiance to an obsolete diplomatic vision. Charlemagne's shift in marriage policy from marrying princesses to marrying the daughters of dukes and counts eventually reinforced an emerging practice and ideology of empire.[29] As king of the Franks, Charlemagne ruled over the Franks. But as an emperor, he would soon rule over Franks, Lombards, Bavarians, Alemanni, and the various Slavic peoples whose indigenous rulers he defeated.

Almost paradoxically, a king might marry the daughter of another king with whom he wanted to stabilize a relationship between peer dynasties, but an emperor had either to marry down or marry into another imperial family. Charlemagne entered twice into negotiations with the Byzantines, first in the 780s with an eye to marrying his daughter Rotrude to Constantine VI. After a formal betrothal, Constantine's mother, the empress Irene, sent a monk to teach Rotrude Greek and to prepare her for her future duties in Constantinople. But the alliance collapsed before the marriage was finalized. Many years later, after Irene had blinded and deposed her son, she and

Charlemagne discussed the possibility of marrying each other and uniting the Roman empires, East and West. But this too came to nothing. The possibility of further legitimizing the revived western empire through a Byzantine marriage remained an elusive dream until Otto II married Theophanu, the niece of Emperor John I Tzimiskes, almost two hundred years later. Even then, Germanic history seemed to repeat itself, since the Ottonians, like the Gothic Amals before them, had hoped for an actual Byzantine princess rather than a more distant member of the imperial family.

Ultimately unable to secure a Byzantine marriage, Charlemagne contented himself with marriages to women who were noble but not royal, in the sense of being a scion of a dynasty with autonomous territorial claims. He was very interested in allying himself through marriage with the dukes, counts, and other aristocrats, both Frankish and non-Frankish, who supported his imperial efforts as a way of consolidating his power in newly acquired territory. He replaced his Lombard bride almost immediately with Hildegarde, the daughter of Gerold, Count of Vinzgau. His later wives Fastrada and Liutgard were the daughters, respectively, of east Frankish and Alemannian counts. While Charlemagne's own daughters—whose love affairs shocked Einhard—never married, his successors undertook a systematic policy of aristocratic marriage alliances: rarely was a Carolingian son or daughter wasted. Sons were married to the daughters of powerful magnates, and daughters were either married to aristocratic sons or appointed abbesses of leading abbeys. This system laid the foundations for a pan-European nobility that persists to the present.

Paul wrote his *Historia langobardorum* in the confusing first stages of this transition to a more imperialistic practice of marriage diplomacy, when Charlemagne was just turning from marrying neighboring royalty to decisively conquering them and marrying instead his internal political supporters. Charlemagne's change in marriage precipitated a major change in Paul's relationship to patronage and political authority. The same Benedictine monk who had commemorated Queen Ansa with an epitaph and dedicated his important *Historia Romana* to her daughter Adelperga now found himself writing a history of the bishops of Metz, the *Historia episcopis mettensibus*, for Angilram, a pro-Carolingian bishop. The work has a decisively pro-Carolingian bias. He later dedicated an epitome of Sextus Pompeius Festus's *De significatu verborum* to Charlemagne himself, the emperor who had crushed Paul's own Lombard people and deposed the Lombard royalty he had once served.

The nature of early medieval literary production makes it impossible to cast Paul as a crass opportunist, a collaborator, or someone who tragically embraced historical necessity. He says nothing about his own experience of the Lombard conquest or ever reflects on it. The *Historia langobardorum* conveniently ends before those events, so we never get even a scholarly, historiographical perspective on them.[30] Nevertheless, the fact that some of the work's least scholarly, most historiographically problematic passages treat Lombard interdynastic marriage suggests that Paul responded in powerful, albeit not fully decipherable ways to the tragedy of the Lombard monarchy and particularly the tragedy of King Desiderius's daughter, the woman repudiated by Charlemagne. Filled with bed-tricks, kings and queens running around in disguises, long invented speeches, displays of extravagant emotion, and improbable voyages to distant locales, these episodes may strike the historian as some of the most supplemental, patently unreliable sections of Paul's narrative. But as Goffart once remarked, "The dominant preoccupation of a history is often best revealed by its most fictional pages."[31] In Paul's case, marriage fantasies voice multiple responses to the more abstract question of the suitability of marriage diplomacy as a way of negotiating relations between potentially hostile powers. Some of these embedded romances suggest the benefits that the Lombards gained through interdynastic marriages with other states, the kind of marriage that Charlemagne originally contracted with the Lombards. But these exist in an uneasy tension with other stories suggesting the fundamental instability of such unions and substantiating Pope Stephen's warning that "nobody who has taken a wife from a foreign race has remained unharmed."

The story that most supported Pope Stephen's position, and which also had the greatest post-Carolingian influence, was that of the marriage of the great Lombard king Alboin (ca. 569–572) to Rosamund of the Gepids. Early sources depicted Alboin as an ethnic hero who first led his people into Italy and modern-day Lombardy.[32] Two sixth-century continuations of Jerome's *Chronicon*, or *Temporum Liber*, one by Marius of Avenches and the other by John of Biclaro, note that Alboin's wife conspired with some of Alboin's enemies at court to kill him. Gregory of Tours notes that the woman who murdered him was a second wife, his first having been a daughter of the Frankish king Chlothar. Finally, various seventh-century sources identify Alboin's murderous wife as the daughter of a defeated Gepid king. One gives her the name Rosamund.

Paul's story elaborated greatly on the sketchy accounts he inherited, which may themselves have invented or misrepresented some of the details, including the assertion that she was a Gepid or that her name was Rosamund. Like other writers of his time, Paul was less interested in providing an account that would be accurate by standards that were yet to be invented than in telling a morally compelling story. His version portrays everything that can go wrong in a marriage between the king of one people and a princess of another, and in his version, Rosamund ends up bearing most of the responsibility for the disaster.

Paul's version, by far the most detailed and influential, heightens Rosamund's culpability, enhances the story's general horror, and associates it with a conspicuously primitive stage of the Lombards' religious and cultural development. Writing in the late eighth century, Paul creates a lasting impression of the sixth as something akin to the modern stereotype of the Dark Ages. In general, Paul reveres Alboin as a national founder, one whose military acumen and intermarriage with the Franks establish him as a prototype of Charlemagne. But as Paul notes, a disastrous second marriage ended Alboin's illustrious career prematurely. Cunimund, a new Gepid king, broke an alliance with the Lombards and resumed their long-standing feud. Alboin crushed the Gepids, killed Cunimund, and had his skull fashioned into a drinking cup that he wore on his belt. He also captured Cunimund's daughter Rosamund and forced her into a marriage.

Three years after relocating the Lombards to Italy, Alboin committed the only act for which Paul explicitly censures him. He had one drink too many:

> When the merry [king] sat at a feast in Verona longer than was seemly, he ordered that wine from the cup which he had made from the head of the queen's [Rosamund's] father, King Cunimund, be given to her. And he gleefully invited her to drink with her father. . . . Thus when Rosamund realized what was going on, she conceived a great sorrow in her heart that she could not prevail in quenching. Soon she burned to avenge her father's funeral by her husband's death.

> [Cum in convivio ultra quam oportuerat apud Veronam laetus resederet, [cum] poculo quod de capite Cunimundi regis sui soceri fecerat reginae ad bibendum vinum dari praecepit atque eam ut cum patre suo laetanter biberet invitavit. . . . Igitur Rosemunda ubi rem animadvertit, altum concipiens in corde dolorem, quem conpescere non valens, mox in mariti necem patris funus vindicatura exarsit.] (2.28)[33]

Rosamund conspired with Alboin's foster brother Helmichis to murder him. Upon Helmichis's advice, she lured a "most powerful man [vir fortissimus]" named Peredeo into the scheme by pretending to be his mistress, sleeping with him, and then revealing herself as the queen: "'It's not at all what you think,' she said, 'but I am Rosamund. And you have certainly done such a thing, Peredeo, that either you will kill Alboin or he will kill you with his sword' ['Nequaquam ut putas, sed ego Rosemunda sum' inquit. 'Certe nunc talem rem, Peredeo, perpetratam habes, ut aut tu Alboin interficies, aut ipse te suo gladio extinguet']" (2.28). While Alboin is taking his afternoon nap, Rosamund hides his armor and ties his sword to the head of the bed. When the murderer attacks him, Alboin is unable to draw his sword and dies trying to defend himself with a footstool. Paul comments on the indignity: "A consummately warlike man, of the greatest boldness, powerless against the enemy, finished off like one drained of power, died by the plots of a single woman [Vir bellicosissimus et summae audaciae nihil contra hostem praevalens, quasi unus de inertibus interfectus est, uniusque mulierculae consilio periit]" (2.28). Alboin's death spells disaster for the Lombard monarchy and, more generally, for the people of Italy.

After Alboin's murder, Rosamund and Helmichis run away to Ravenna with Alboin's daughter and "all the treasure of the Lombards [omnem Langobardorum thesaurum]" (2.29). Right after their arrival in Ravenna, however, the Byzantine prefect Longinus seems to have taken a fancy to Rosamund. "Prompt to every villainy [ad omnem nequitiam facilis]," she plots with Longinus to murder Helmichis and marry him instead (2.29). When Helmichis realizes that she has poisoned him with a drink while he was taking his bath, he forces her to drink the final drops. As Paul concludes, "Thus by the judgment of omnipotent God, these most unjust killers perished in a single moment [Sicque Dei omnipotentis iudicio interfectores iniquissimi uno momento perierunt]" (2.29).

Paul is the only source for two details in the story that seem more suited to a romance or folktale than to a chronicle from the Carolingian Renaissance: the bedtrick with the strongman Peredeo and the skull-cup with which Alboin seals his doom. The addition of Peredeo to the basic storyline is puzzling. We already have two capable assassins: Rosamund and her lover Helmichis. These two carry off the murder perfectly well in other accounts. By bringing Peredeo into the story, however, Paul simultaneously magnified Alboin's heroism and heightened Rosamund's depravity. Identifying Peredeo, "qui erat vir fortissimus," as someone renowned for his strength, he suggests that Alboin himself was so powerful that no ordinary man could have overcome him. The paradigmatic biblical fable of a foreign woman who destroys a hero, the story of Samson and Delilah, figures as a subtext in the grotesquerie of the murder itself, when Alboin is overcome less by strength than by trickery. Like the blinding of Samson, the image of the once invincible Alboin trying to untie his sword and fighting instead with a footstool carries a powerful image of castration, of a king unmanned by a barbarian princess.

Paul makes the Samson subtext even more explicit in a coda describing Peredeo's fall. Peredeo follows Rosamund and Helmichis to Ravenna and eventually ends up in Constantinople, where he kills a huge lion in a public spectacle. The emperor immediately has him blinded because of the danger that his strength poses to the city. But Peredeo eventually sneaks two small knives into the palace and kills two of the emperor's top advisers. Paul then compares this act to Samson's destruction of the Philistines: "Thus not at all unlike that mightiest Samson, he had avenged his wrongs [Sic Samsonis illius fortissimi ex aliqua parte non absimilis, suas iniuras ultus est]" (2.30).

Paul thus casts Rosamund as a double Delilah with respect to her husband, Alboin, and to her coerced accomplice Peredeo. But she is not the only barbarian here. As the story's reception history reminds us, the skull-cup looms over the narrative in ways that subvert Paul's tributes to Alboin as a Lombard hero whose only fault was a little overdrinking. In a very literal way, the skull-cup outlives all the protagonists: Paul claims to have seen it with his own eyes, when it was two hundred years old: "Lest this seem impossible to anyone, I speak the truth in Christ. I myself have seen King Ratchis holding that cup in his hand to show his guests on a certain feast day [Hoc ne cui videatur impossibile, veritatem in Christo loquor; ego hoc poculum vidi in quodam die festo Ratchis principem ut illud convivis suis ostentaret manu tenentem]" (2.28). Paul avers his story's authenticity because the whole business of making your enemy's skull into a goblet and wearing it on your belt sounds so bizarre to his late seventh-century audience. The Christian oath with which he swears to the cup's existence subtly increases the story's probability by reminding his audience of the historical distance that separates them from Alboin and Rosamund's world. Paul and his readers are Christians; Alboin and Rosamund were not. They belonged to a pre-Catholic, perhaps even polytheistic past that may adumbrate the Carolingian world and provide it with instructive *exempla*, but there are crucial differences between them and Paul's contemporaries, who enjoy the benefits of Christianity, greater civility, and literacy.

By implying such differences instead of explicitly stating them, however, Paul leaves open the question of what kind of comment his story makes on the Carolingian present. Is Alboin a prototype of Charlemagne, the first Carolingian king of Lombardy? Does the Lombards' conquest of the Gepids comment on the Franks' conquest of the Lombards? If so, what is the place of marriage in that conquest and in other instances of Carolingian expansion? If Alboin is a type of Charlemagne, however imperfect, how does the story of his involvement with Rosamund comment on Charlemagne's ill-fated marriage to the Lombard daughter of the king he eventually deposed and drove into a monastery?

By leaving these questions unanswered, Paul wrote a story that might accommodate a range of Carolingian and Lombard-Beneventan attitudes. One could read the story as a confirmation of Pope Stephen's advice about the dangers of foreign marriage, advice that Charlemagne originally ignored but ultimately followed, at least to the extent of not marrying daughters of autonomous rulers. But the story's conspicuous derivation from a pre-Christian past does not necessarily discredit all marriages between foreign royalty. Rosamund was a bride by conquest, a spoil of war rather than the focus of a peaceable diplomatic exchange. Alboin's previous marriage to Clovis's granddaughter, the fruit of such a negotiation, presumably went much better. Within Paul's narrative, in fact, Alboin's acquisition of Rosamund seems like a movement backwards into a more barbarous, pre-diplomatic past. But for some readers, and quite possibly for Paul's quondam patron, the Duchess of Benevento, who was the sister of Charlemagne's repudiated wife, such distinctions between past barbarism and contemporary diplomacy may have seemed beside the point. One can imagine her reading the story of Alboin's murder as a projected revenge fantasy, one in which the victimized wife, the daughter of an undone king, takes matters into her own hands and kills her father's conqueror.

To some extent, the subsequent story of King Authari's short but happy marriage to Theudelinda, a Bavarian princess, redeems the possibility of interdynastic marriage as a successful way to establish alliances. Like Rosamund's marriage, Theudelinda's marks a shift in genre from the flat summaries that characterize most of the *Historia langobardorum* to romance and folktale. When an alliance between the Franks and the Byzantines threatened the Lombards with decimation, they restored their monarchy and proclaimed Authari (540–590) king. He spent most of his six-year reign at war against the Franks. In the course of this conflict, he negotiated an alliance with King Garibald of the Bavarians, despite the latter's nominal allegiance to the Franks. According to Paul, Authari was so excited about his marriage to Garibald's daughter Theudelinda, which was to seal the alliance, that he could not wait to meet her. He disguised himself as an "ambassador" (*legatus*) and went to her father's court. After telling Garibald that he had been commissioned by Authari to report about the bride's appearance, he is introduced to her. She was, of course, strikingly beautiful. The disguised Authari then asks to take a cup of wine from her hand, "as she will do for us hereafter [sicut nobis postea factura est]" (3.30), in a classic gesture of hospitality familiar to readers of *Beowulf*. When he returns the cup, he touches her hand when nobody is looking, which her nurse later correctly interprets as a sign that the *legatus* is actually the Lombard king himself. Theudelinda is just as impressed with his looks: "And in fact Authari was then in the flush of youth, of fitting stature, with a shock of fair hair, and handsome enough in appearance [Erat autem tunc Authari iuvenali aetate floridus, statura decens, candido crine perfusus et satis decorus aspectu]" (3.30). He eventually reveals himself by a great display of strength, and the two are joyfully married in Verona on the Ides of May.

Within Paul's narrative, the story stands in conspicuous contrast to the horrors endured and later perpetrated by Rosamund. The secret dalliance with the cup in the presence of Theudelinda's father revises the earlier episode in which Rosamund was forced to drink from her father's skull. In retrospect, that horrible incident appears as an inversion of traditional hospitality, one in which the king serves the queen in an expression of sheer domination rather than friendship. Here civility and hospitality are restored. This is a negotiated marriage, not a marriage by conquest. The father is present as the groom's living ally. If the Rosamund story was the stuff of Gothic fiction, this episode reads like a comic opera. Paul is one of the very few earlier writers on diplomacy and international relations to say anything at all about the bride's and groom's personal feelings. The way he tells it, this is a private love story as well as a critical moment in the history of the Lombards' struggle against the Franks and Byzantines.

If Rosamund was a second Delilah, a foreign bride whose malice threatened both a hero and his race, Paul emphasizes Theudelinda's easy assimilation to Lombard society. When she built a palace for herself in Monza, for example, she commissioned a painting commemorating the achievements of the Lombards, a pictorial anticipation of Paul's own *Historia*. According to Paul, Theudelinda became so popular among the Lombards that they allowed her to keep her queenly dignities after Authari's death and to select and eventually marry his successor, Agilulf.

Even though she triumphed in her role as an adopted Lombard, however, Theudelinda's cosmopolitan identity as someone who had lived in more than one place, spoke more than one language, and had experienced more than one culture made her a powerful advocate for peace. In perhaps the earliest European attribution of diplomatic agency to a queen consort, Paul honors her not only for advancing Lombard interests, but also for settling a major territorial dispute involving the Lombards, the Byzantines, and the papacy. He appends a letter from Pope Gregory the Great thanking her "that she applied herself, earnestly and generously, as she is accustomed to do, to peacemaking [ad faciendum pacem studiosius et benigne se, sicut solet, inpenderit]" (4.9) The pope assures her that God will greatly reward her for staving off carnage: "For do not believe, my most excellent daughter, that you will receive a meager prize, for the blood that would have been shed from both sides [Non enim, excellentissima filia, de sanguine, qui ab utraque parte fundendus fuerat, parvam te credas adquisisse mercedem]" (4.9). Paul's emphasis on Theudelinda's intercessory authority, as well as on her ability to transcend partisan interests and work for the greater good of Christendom, is not the only aspect of this episode that looks ahead to later diplomatic discourses. In a second letter to her husband Agilulf that anticipates the eleventh-century Peace of God movement, the pope makes it clear just whose blood Theudelinda's peacemaking has spared: "For if [peace] had not been made, what would have come about, except the blood of the unfortunate peasants—whose labor avails both sides—would have been spilled with sin and danger to both parties? [nam si . . . facta non fuisset, quid agi habuit, nisi ut cum peccato et periculo partium miserorum rusticorum sanguis, quorum labor utrisque proficit, funderetur?]" (4.9) By the end of the episode, Paul has embedded Theudelinda's diplomacy in what would later become the full-blown medieval discourse of a *Pax Christiana* protecting the rights of nonbelligerents and underwritten by the intercessions of foreign queens.

With the wisdom of eleventh- and twelfth-century hindsight, Theudelinda's peacemaking looks like an unambiguously positive achievement. But as Goffart has pointed out, Paul may have written with an eye to his old patrons, the Lombard Beneventans. Among Charlemagne's most hardened enemies, the Beneventans had competed with the Byzantines over the domination of southern Italy and would have resented any rapprochement with them either in the present or in the distant Lombard past. Paul is generally so wary of the Byzantines throughout his narrative that his characterization of Theudelinda may be tinged with irony. Paul notes, moreover, that she never quite succeeds in bringing the Arian Lombards around fully to Catholic Christianity.[34] She is finally not a Clothilde, who converts the Franks in Gregory of Tours, or the various Anglo-Saxon queens who convert the Anglo-Saxons. Even Theudelinda's diplomatic outreach raises some unsettling questions: Does she spare the shedding of peasant blood only to expose the Lombards to Byzantine wiles? Finally, whatever she and Agilulf achieved in raising the Lombards' prestige and pacifying their relations with their most powerful neighbors, their accomplishments prove short-lived. As Paul's *Historia* continues, her descendants turn out to be ineffectual rulers who may have been pious but made wrong decisions that weakened the Lombards' military and diplomatic standing within Europe.

To the extent that this context tempers Paul's ostensible praise of Theudelinda, it weakens the apparent dichotomy between a bad interdynastic marriage grounded in conquest and abduction and a good one grounded in negotiation and consent. On balance, neither story espouses interdynastic marriage as a reliable means either to achieve national greatness or to maintain stable relations with one's neighbors. At the moment of the *Historia*'s composition, this heavily qualified, ambiguous historiography of marriage served the interests of multiple readerships, both Lombard-Beneventan and Carolingian. The collapse of the alliance between Desiderius and Charlemagne made all parties skeptical of how effective any alliance might be that was grounded in marriage. The Rosamund story appealed in obvious ways to Paul's old patrons, the Beneventans. It could even be read as a thinly veiled commentary on their recent tragedy. But the Theudelinda story complicates that transient expression of Lombard-Beneventan sympathy in ways that endorse the alliance of church and empire that was becoming, at least in theory if not fully in practice, a characteristic of the Carolingian state. With a relatively weak elective monarchy that was never more than semi-hereditary, a legacy of fractious ducal subterfuge, and a mixture of paganism and Arianism that seemed particularly resistant to Catholicism despite the proximity of Rome, the Lombard kingdom that Theudelinda honored in her murals was not sustainable. The Catholic Paul mourned the passing of an ethnic Lombard kingship. But he also embraced the hope of a universal political authority working in harmony with the universal Church.

Jordanes and Paul inherited the same Virgilian myth of marriage as the basis of political harmony and intercultural accommodation. As a Latin-writing, ethnically Ostrogothic Constantinopolitan, Jordanes embodied the Romanization of the Gothic people that constitutes the *Getica*'s central theme. A convert to Latin Christianity, he welcomed the Goths' incorporation into the empire, which the marriage between Germanus and Theodoric's granddaughter Matasuntha completes in his version of the *Aeneid*. There is little darkness in Jordanes's recollections of the *Aeneid*, and he all but forgets that Virgil ended his poem not with the promised marriage between Lavinia and Aeneas but instead with the slaughter of Turnus. Recognizing the inevitability of empire, but more ambivalent about myths of ethnic incorporation, Paul the Deacon draws on the darker Virgilian resonances that have come to dominate readings of the *Aeneid* in our own pessimistic age, when realist doubts continually undercut our cosmopolitan hope for better understandings between nations. As a revision of the contrast between Dido and Lavinia, the opposition between Rosamund and Theudelinda that structures the *Historia langobardorum* teases us into a renewed confidence in the efficacy of marriage diplomacy. But as we have seen, that effect is only temporary and is overshadowed by the rise of Charlemagne's empire and a renewed insistence on internal rather than foreign marriage.

CHAPTER 2

Interdynastic Marriage, Religious Conversion, and the Expansion of Diplomatic Society

The last chapter focused on the role of marriage in ethnogenesis, the creation from groups of human beings of a single people with common interests, cultural practices, institutions, and a common, often mythic history. Virgil's story of Aeneas's marriage to Lavinia is paradigmatic: the surviving leader of the Trojans marries the daughter of the Latin king, and their respective peoples become one. At least officially, Jupiter's decree achieves a compromise between conquest and cultural subjugation. The Trojans conquer the Latins, but then surrender their culture to the people they conquered by adopting the Latin language and modes of dress. As we have seen, that resolution was unstable enough for historians indebted to Virgil's example to recast it with varying degrees of conviction in narrating their own stories of ethnic assimilation, of Goths becoming Romans and Lombards becoming Carolingians.

This chapter turns from the Mediterranean heartlands of the old Roman Empire, with its twin capitals in Rome and Constantinople, to marriage diplomacy in Roman successor states beyond the Alps, the kingdoms of the Merovingian Franks and the Anglo-Saxons. Before the rise of the Carolingians in eighth-century Francia and of the Wessex dynasty in ninth-century England, these ranked among the most fractious political geographies in Europe. On both sides of the Channel, kingdoms and subkingdoms competed against one another, sometimes consolidated under powerful and charismatic kings, and then fragmented back into their component states. Partible inheritance exacerbated the situation in Francia, where divisions of a father's kingdom among his sons encouraged fratricidal wars.

The rulers of these small, unstable kingdoms did not think of themselves or of their closest neighbors in imperial terms. From their perspective, the eastern emperor, the acknowledged possessor of Roman authority, ruled in distant Constantinople. Unlike the Ostrogoths, they did not pursue marriage as a route of honorable incorporation into the Roman system. They remained independent, at least until Charlemagne crafted his simulacrum of Roman authority at the end of the eighth century. Frankish and Anglo-Saxon royalty married each other as rulers of autonomous kingdoms on more or less equal terms. Although the sources for these marriages are often less complete and reliable than those for the final years of the Ostrogothic and Lombard kingdoms, they suggest that Merovingian and Anglo-Saxon kings married into neighboring dynasties to secure alliances, to gain land and wealth, and to heighten prestige. In conspicuous contrast to Aeneas and Lavinia, they did not marry to achieve political and cultural fusion.

This distinction, however, did not render the Virgilian example irrelevant. Although the Merovingian Franks and Anglo-Saxons did not imagine themselves as part of a present or future Roman system, they knew that the lands they governed had a Roman past. Especially in France, many rhythms of Roman life never disappeared.[1] Roman cities contracted but remained part of the landscape, and an old Gallo-Roman elite preserved certain administrative structures. Writers like Gregory of Tours remained native speakers of Latin. Above all, the Church kept the memory of Rome alive through its Latinity and its diocesan organization. Early medieval Christianity was deeply Roman.

The Roman past also shaped the diplomatic present as Merovingian and Anglo-Saxon kings communicated with one another, their neighbors, and more distant parties such as the eastern emperors.[2] As former provinces of the western empire, the successor states had once been part of the same imperial system. Even after the central government that once united them collapsed, they still lived in a close relationship with one another, sometimes as enemies, but at least as often as allies and trading partners. Whenever they interacted, they turned to Roman precedents for guidance. The letters that their kings exchanged followed the same formulae that Roman provincial governors had used in writing to one another and the imperial court. Their envoys followed similar instructions, wrote and spoke at least in versions of the same Latin, and even traveled along many of the same roads.

The Roman legal, administrative, and cultural heritage that facilitated communications between and among the successor kingdoms gave rise to an early version of what modern political theorists call "international society." In one of the most influential descriptions of the concept, Hedley Bull and Adam Watson defined international society as "a group of states (or, more generally, a group of independent political communities) which not merely form a system, in the sense that the behaviour of each is a necessary factor in the calculations of the others, but also have established by dialogue and consent common rules and institutions for the conduct of their relations, and recognize their common interest in maintaining these arrangements."[3] In Bull and Watson's analysis, modern states exist simultaneously in an anarchical system and in an international society. As components of an anarchical system, they are not subject to any overarching sovereign power but must therefore be vigilant in protecting their interests against encroachments from other members of the system. To that extent, "the behaviour of each is a necessary factor in the calculation of the others." But they are also part of a society, a group of states that abide by understood rules, such as the principle that foreign envoys should not be molested or that treaties ought to be observed by the signatories. Bull even argues elsewhere that when modern states go to war, they fight according to certain rules, such as the imperative to limit civilian causalities.[4]

The Roman successor kingdoms related to one another in ways that Bull ascribes to modern states, although their limited bureaucratic development makes me reluctant to call them states. For the same reason, I prefer to think of them as members of a "diplomatic society" rather than an "international society," with its anachronistic implications. Their commission and reception of envoys, formal written communications, and other shared Roman legal conventions signal that they constituted something more complex and conducive to dialogue and consensus than a mere collection of states wary of one another's encroachments. Above all, the fact that their rulers sometimes married into one another's families to strengthen their relations suggests their societal underpinnings.

I have introduced critical international society theory not only because it helps us recognize the societal nature of relations between and among the Roman successor states, but also because greater attention to these relations can address some of the most frequently noted shortcomings of this body of theory, especially its inattention to gender and its inadequacies in dealing with radical cultural difference. As many scholars have noted, Bull and other English school theorists of international relations "developed their ideas thinking primarily about western, traditionally Christian states."[5] They also conceived of state affairs as a male undertaking.[6] One simply cannot talk about Merovingian or Anglo-Saxon diplomacy, or government in general, without talking about gender. During the periods that we know best, those covered by Gregory of Tours and Bede, interdynastic marriage was a key part of interstate relations. Gregory wrote his *Historiae*, later and more familiarly known as the *Historia francorum*, under the patronage of the Austrasian queen Brunhild, who served as regent for her son and grandson. A Visigoth by birth, she became the most powerful woman in Francia through her diplomatic marriage to Sigebert I. She seems to have played some role in negotiating the marriage of her niece Bertha to Æthelberht of Kent. Bede takes up the story from that point and gives Bertha a major role in the conversion of the Anglo-Saxon kingdoms to Christianity.

Gregory and Bede also expose the process through which European diplomatic practices and institutions became so bound up with Christianity that it limited the ability of Europeans to negotiate with non-Christian states. They ostensibly depict a diplomatic society that grew stronger as generations of interdynastic marriages between Christian princesses and formerly non-Christian kings diminished the ideological and cultural boundaries that separated neighboring kingdoms. This is not to say that they necessarily became more peaceful. But it does mean that they developed common discourses for diplomatic conversations and settlements among Christian Europeans. Perhaps most important, the conversions established a network of bishops and other clerics who became the primary agents in diplomatic exchange. But this development introduced a potential problem that becomes especially visible as we turn from Gregory to Bede: Once Europe became more Christian and clerics became primary agents of negotiation, how did that affect the gendering of domestic society? Did the royal women who married always have a role in later diplomatic developments? Or did they become disappearing mediators in the expansion of clericalized diplomatic society? Bede in particular offers us insight not only into the gendering of diplomatic experience but also into the broader historical and historiographic contexts that make gender so elusive in diplomatic studies.

Gregory of Tours: Foreign Queens and the Christianization of Kings

One of the most historiographically influential works of the early Middle Ages, Gregory of Tours's *Historiae* captured a critical moment in the post-Roman dynastic system: the emergence of a Christianized diplomatic society that offset the empire's fragmentation into competing ethnic monarchies. Interdynastic marriage was not merely a linchpin of that society but one that reconciled, at least on occasion, the tension between these centripetal and centrifugal forces. Within individual kingdoms, wedding a foreign princess enriched the king through both the immediate wedding gifts he received from her family and the subsequent advantages he gained from the alliance. A king with powerful allies, for example, was more inclined to win territories and plunder through warfare.[7] The queens who converted their husbands to Christianity enhanced their status in less calculable ways with new claims to sanctity that distinguished them from their rivals. But if interdynastic marriage heightened the prestige and strength of individual monarchs, it also made those gains increasingly dependent on their cooperative relationships with other monarchs and with a church claiming universal authority. Christian brides came with bishops, who, like the brides, were both loyal servants of their kings and international agents reinvigorating the old imperial networks.

Like Paul the Deacon's *Historia langobardorum*, Gregory's *Historiae* confronts its reader with a bewildering mixture of plausible, implausible, and patently legendary claims. His marriage and conversion narratives are so indebted to writers from Virgil to Eusebius that their value lies more in their expression of ideals than in any factual reportage. He was also patently biased in his account of the major divisions within Frankish society. At the time he was writing, partible inheritance had divided the Frankish land into opposing kingdoms. A forty-year struggle ensued between two powerful regents, Brunhild of Austrasia and Fredegond of Neustria, which ended only when Fredegond's son Chlothar II captured Brunhild and had her torn apart by wild horses. Gregory was an Austrasian partisan who benefited directly from Brunhild's patronage.[8] To a considerable extent, he cultivates his new ideology of marriage as a way of exalting Brunhild, the daughter of a Visogothic king, at the expense of Fredegond, a Frankish servant girl before her marriage to Chilperic I.

Gregory's conspicuous literariness, his imitations of prior writers, and his political biases do not invalidate his prominence in the history of interdynastic marriage. Quite the contrary, they are an important component of that history. Gregory gave a lasting form to a set of values and beliefs about gender, monarchical dignity, and post-Roman diplomatic society that eventually became widely accepted throughout western Europe. But we should not assume that they were widely accepted in his day. If we bracket Gregory's opinions, his insistence that some modes of conjugal relationship are contemptible and others honorable, his text confronts us with many different kinds of royal marriages and expressions of monarchical desire.[9] Some kings married members of neighboring royal families in unions charged with diplomatic significance. But others married commoners, even women—like

Fredegond—from the lowest social ranks. King Guntram married a slave. Balthild, the powerful queen of Clovis II, began her career as an East Anglian slave captured by Danish raiders and sold to the Neustrian mayor of the palace. Gregory often calls such women *concubina*, but we have no reason to trust his designations. Many of his contemporaries honored them as wives.[10] Other kings, much like Paul the Deacon's Alboin, captured noble and even royal wives in battle. Others married royal refugees who brought their husbands neither wealth nor powerful connections. Many of the kings had several wives, some in succession and living together in polygynous households.

Throughout the *Historiae*, Gregory orders these possible configurations into a moral hierarchy, with marriages between Trinitarian Christians and non-Trinitarian or even non-Christian royalty that lead to national conversions at the top. One story after the next honors men and women who marry and convert an Arian or polytheistic spouse. But concerns with rank give nuance to his dominant narrative focus on religion. Although Gregory embraces marriage across religious lines as an opportunity for proselytization, he has nothing good to say about marriages across rank or caste. The one time he depicts a king's marriage to a poor girl positively, she turns out to be disenfranchised royalty.

The touchstone for all marriages in the *Historiae* is an example of this last case, Clovis I's marriage to Clothilde. Clothilde was the exiled daughter of a Burgundian king murdered by his own brother. According to Gregory, Frankish ambassadors met her on an embassy and noted that she was "elegant and wise and born of royalty [elegantem atque sapientem et . . . de regio esset genere]" (2.28).[11] When they reported this to Clovis, he sent them back to get her. Her murderous uncle was so intimidated by Clovis's growing power that he could not object to their eventual marriage.

As the king who united the Franks into a nation, Clovis holds a critical place in Gregory's story as a military hero of the first order. But under Clothilde's influence, he acquires a new and even higher dignity as the Franks' first Christian king. His conversion and the subsequent conversions of his subjects transform them into a Christian people prepared to evangelize Europe. Recent scholarship has challenged the historical accuracy of Gregory's account.[12] It is not clear from any source what Clovis believed before he became a Christian. Gregory suggests that he worshiped the old Roman pantheon, but he may have worshiped the German gods, or been an Arian Christian like his Visogothic neighbors. The text is evasive enough to admit the possibility that Clovis, again like other neo-Christian rulers, simply added Jesus to his existing gods. Nor were Clovis's motives exclusively or necessarily spiritual. By identifying himself with the Roman Church, he gained multiple political advantages. He ingratiated himself not only with the Latin Christian Gallo-Romans within his own territories but also with those living in areas ruled by the Arian Visigoths. As a Trinitarian, Clovis could justify his encroachments on Gothic territories as an attempt to advance the true faith and to relieve his co-religionists suffering under Arian tyranny.

These alternative interpretations of Clovis's conversion expose the literary and propagandistic brilliance of the story that Gregory tells and help us to see it as part of his larger idealization of interdynastic marriage as a channel for Christianizing Europe. In Gregory's narrative, Clothilde's aura of saintliness is so strong that it influences Clovis even before he sees her. He decides to marry her the moment his envoys inform him that she is elegant, wise, and born of royalty. These qualities look like markers of rank and good breeding. But as the narrative unfolds, they become inseparable from moral characteristics that set Clothilde above her peers and moved her husband to conversion. Gregory notes, for example, that Clovis was so delighted with her that he married her even though he already had a son by one of his "concubines." From his perspective, embracing Clothilde as a wife rather than yet another concubine marks the first stage in Clovis's repudiation of paganism: devotion to one woman goes hand in hand with devotion to one true God.

Clothilde's efforts to convert her husband manifest a *sapientia* whose primary end is evangelization. Clothilde bases her rhetorical strategy on the intimate knowledge of Clovis's character that she enjoys in her capacity as his wife. Because she is a woman secure in his affection and her own rank, she can speak to him with a candor to which nobody else seems entitled. Instead of talking to Clovis about the finer points of theology, she directly questions the utility of his gods: "The gods whom you worship are nothing, who can't help either themselves or anybody else. . . . What have Mars and Mercury ever been able to do? [Nihil sunt dii quos colitis, qui neque sibi neque aliis potuerunt subvenire. . . . Quid Mars Mercuriusque potuere?]" (2.29). Clovis is stubborn, but Clothilde persists. She has their first son baptized to make him a Christian and to impress Clovis: "She commanded that the church be decorated with draperies and curtains, that he . . . might more easily be called to belief by the ceremony [adornare ecclesiam velis praecipit atque curtinis, quo facilius . . . hoc misterio provocaretur ad credendum]" (2.29). Although the baby's death poses a setback, Clothilde remains undaunted in her prayers "that [Clovis] might recognize the true God and pay no mind to idols [ut Deum verum cognusceret et idola neglegerit]" (2.30).

Clothilde's absence when Clovis's conversion takes place paradoxically underscores her influence. As scholars have long recognized, Gregory associates the moment with Constantine's conversion.[13] Like his Roman model,

Clovis becomes a Christian after Christ grants him a victory in battle. In Eusebius's *Vita Constantini*, however, Constantine's own realization of the futility of pagan worship, as well as pious recollections of his Christian father, laid the groundwork for his conversion.[14] In Gregory, by contrast, credit falls not to a father or to the sovereign's insight but to the foreign bride. Clovis's prayer to God promising conversion in exchange for victory underscores that Clovis's conversion and that of his people depended on Clothilde:

> Jesus Christ, whom Clothilde proclaims to be the son of the living God, who is said to give help to laborers and to confer victory on those hoping in you . . . if you will grant me victory over these enemies . . . I will believe in you and be baptized in your name.

> [Iesu Christi, quem Chrotchildis praedicat esse filium Dei vivi, qui dare auxilium laborantibus victuriamque in te sperantibus tribuere diceris . . . si mihi victuriam super hos hostes indulseris . . . , credam tibi et in nomine tuo baptizer]. (2.30)

Clothilde mediates everything that Clovis knows about Christ. He approaches Christ in the first place because Clothilde proclaims him "to be the Son of the living God." After Clovis wins the battle, the first thing he does is tell her that he won by calling on the name of Christ ("per invocationem nominis Christi" [2.30]). Only then does she arrange for Bishop Remigius to provide him with more formal instruction. Throughout the episode, she has been his initiator, spiritual model, and primary instructor in Christianity.

Clothilde's foreign birth and gender are both necessary elements in this story.[15] Had she been a Frank, she would not have been a Christian; if she were not a beloved wife, she could not have spoken to Clovis so persuasively. Clothilde's legacy was a lasting association between interdynastic marriage and the dignity, spiritual welfare, and integrity of the monarchy. But her legacy also included something that tempered monarchical ambition: the realm's integration into what remained of the Christian western empire, with its allegiances to Rome. Saint Remigius was the first of countless Frankish bishops who served the Church while serving their king. They soon became the king's primary envoys on diplomatic missions, including those entrusted with the arrangement of future interdynastic marriages. Later bishops accompanied or assisted other Frankish princesses in other kingdoms, Christian and non-Christian alike, as the cycle of conversions and subsequent integration and reintegration into Catholic Europe continued. Just as Clothilde converted Clovis with the help of Remigius, her great-granddaughter Bertha would convert Æthelberht of Kent with the help of Saint Augustine of

Canterbury; their daughter Æthelburh would marry and convert Edwin of Northumbria with the help of Bishop Paulinus.

Gregory himself was a Christian bishop, a partisan of Queen Brunhild, who converted from Visogothic Arianism to Trinitarianism upon her marriage to Sigebert I. He was aware of his own place in the northern and western expansion of an originally Mediterranean, Latin Christian civilization. As the primary chronicler of that process, he adapted Roman and Greco-Roman writers like Virgil and Eusebius as freely as his brother bishops adapted Roman diplomatic protocols. When Clothilde harangues Clovis about worshiping incestuous gods, for example, Gregory cites a line from the *Aeneid* in which Juno identifies herself as "both the sister and consort of Jove [*Iovisque / et soror et coniunx*]" (*Aen.* 1.46–47; *Historiae* 2.29). This is not a mere passing allusion. Gregory had thought long and hard about the passages in which Juno clashes with Jupiter for ignoring her prerogatives as his sister and wife in his fondness for the Trojans. Just as the divine couple finally reconcile their differences in a wedding settlement that Latinizes the Trojans, so Gregory reconciles his devotion to Christianity and to *romanitas* by incorporating both in a new literary culture transforming Europe into a single diplomatic society. Jupiter and Juno reemerge as Clovis and Clothilde, and the Virgilian drive to empire becomes a commitment to that society's Christian expansion.

With Clothilde and Clovis, Gregory establishes an early benchmark for assessing other queens and other regimes. Good queens follow Clothilde's example in patronizing the Church, enhancing the dignity of their husband's throne, and drawing the continent into a common diplomatic culture grounded in Latin Christianity. Even if they are poor, they are of high rank. Bad queens are women of lower social rank. Gregory reserves his greatest scorn for those Merovingians who degrade their patrimony by marrying commoners.[16] Such women often appear as greedy, impious, meddlesome, and even murderous. Marrying them instead of foreign nobility, moreover, thwarts the diplomatic progress of Europe and the ecclesiastical progress of the Church. They will not serve as ecclesiastical patrons or work to harmonize the interests of neighboring kingdoms.

The contrast between admirable royal wives and loathsome women of low degree first emerges in Gregory's treatments of four of Clovis's grandsons: Sigebert, Charibert, Guntram, and Chilperic. These four brothers divided the Merovingian lands according to the long-standing Frankish principle of partible inheritance. They were a fractious lot, and in their wars, plots, and counterplots, it is often hard to tell where virtue lies. Gregory's long, digressive accounts of their reigns make difficult reading for the nonspecialist. But these sections of the *Historiae* played a key role in the history of marriage diplomacy by privileging marriage to royal women as a kingly obligation. Throughout many of Gregory's narrative and genealogical tangles one thing remains clear: while two of the brothers, Charibert and Chilperic, degraded themselves by marrying below their rank, the other two, Sigebert and Guntram, upheld, albeit not always consistently, the principle of marriage to women of noble birth.

Gregory casts the first of the errant brothers, Charibert I, as a lecher whose marriages brought disgrace to the Merovingian monarchy. After putting away his wife, Ingeborg, the mother of the first Frankish queen of Kent, Charibert married several poor women in succession. After marrying two sisters, Merofled and Marcovefa, "daughters of a certain pauper [pauperis cuisdam filias]," he was excommunicated. It may have been for bigamy or even incest. But Gregory never tells us. He was far more disturbed by the fact that Charibert's wives were poor than by the canonical grounds for the excommunication.[17] When Merovingian polygamy appears here and elsewhere, Gregory hardly raises an eyebrow, unless one of the women is poor. Caste miscegenation looms throughout the *Historiae* as a greater offense than fornication, bigamy, or marriage to two sisters.

Gregory's narrative grows darker yet when Charibert fails to learn his lesson. After the sisters, he marries yet another pauper, Theudechild, the daughter of a local shepherd (4.26). Gregory portrays Theudechild as a foolish and vulgar opportunist. After Charibert died, she offered herself and her late husband's treasure to his brother Guntram, a generally wise, virtuous, and generous king. But instead of marrying her, Guntram confiscated the treasure and confined her in a nunnery on the grounds that it was "more just that these treasures should remain in his control than with her who unworthily visited [his] brother's bed [Rectius est enim, ut hi thesauri penes me habeantur, quam post hanc, quae indigne germani mei torum adivit]" (4.26).[18]

A third royal brother, Sigebert I, shares Guntram's contempt for "unworthy" matches. According to Gregory, Sigebert was so disgusted by his other brothers' marriages that he was determined to marry a royal woman, even it if meant marrying an Arian:

And when King Sigebert saw his brothers taking to themselves unworthy wives and even, in their own worthlessness, marrying their own servants, he sent a delegation to Spain and, with many gifts, asked for Brunhild, the daughter of King Athanagild. For she was a maiden elegant in her acts, comely in appearance, honest and proper in her manners, prudent in counsel, and alluring of speech. Her father did not say no, and sent her to the aforesaid king with great treasures.

[Porro Sigyberthus rex cum videret, quod fratres eius indignas sibimet uxores acciperent et per vilitatem suam etiam ancillas in matrimonio sociarent, legationem in Hispaniam mittit et cum multis muneribus Brunichildem, Athanagilde regis filiam, petiit. Erat enim puella elegans opere, venusta aspectu, honesta moribus atque decora, prudens consilio et blanda colloquio. Quam pater eius non denegans, cum magnis thesauris antedicto rege transmisit.] (4.27)

The bride and groom share comparable wealth and status; the gifts with which Sigebert loads his messengers effectively return in Athanagild's offer of a large dowry. The description of the Visigothic Brunhild echoes and expands upon that of the equally elegant, wise, and royally born Clothilde. She equals her grandmother-in-law in every grace suitable to queenship and surpasses her in fortune, with a father who still retains his throne.

Brunhild's Arianism is the only liability that might prevent her from stepping into the role of a second Clothilde. But Gregory transforms that potential embarrassment into another conversion story that seals a transgenerational association between interdynastic marriage and the expansion of Trinitarian Christendom:

And since [Brunhild] had been subject to Arian law, she converted through the preaching of the priests and the persuasions of that same king. She professed the blessed Trinity in unity, believed, and was anointed. A Catholic, she abides in Christ's name.

[Et quia Arrianae legi subiecta erat, per praedicationem sacerdotum atque ipsius regis commonitionem conversa, beatam in unitate confessa Trinitatem credidit atque chrismata est. Quae in nomine Christi catholica perseverat.] (4.27).

By this point in Gregory's narrative, Brunhild's conversion amplifies themes already present in his previous accounts. Her apparent alacrity in embracing Trinitarian Christianity, for example, contrasts with Clovis's stubbornness about renouncing his Roman gods. Royal women seem to embrace Trinitarian belief quicker than men, hold to it in the face of brutal efforts to make them renounce it, and do everything to advance it, from building churches and endowing monasteries to evangelizing those still in the grip of false belief and patronizing the expanding cadre of bishops.

At first, Sigebert's marriage to Brunhild inspired at least one of his brothers to higher marital standards. After promising to put away his lowborn "concubine" Fredegond, Chilperic married Brunhild's sister, the princess Galswintha. Once again, an exchange of generous gifts underscored the fact that this was a match between equally illustrious parties. Like Brunhild, Galswintha soon converted to Trinitarian Christianity with every expectation of becoming a royal patroness of the Church. But Chilperic's commitment to interdynastic marriage between people of equal social rank was short-lived. He soon recalled Fredegond, resumed their affair, eventually murdered Galswintha, and married Fredegond in her stead. This flagrant backsliding triggered the struggle between the noble Brunhild and the baseborn Fredegond, who becomes the *Historiae*'s chief villain. Her numerous crimes serve as a continual reminder of the dangers of giving women of low rank monarchical authority, powers, and resources.

In insisting that kings ought to marry the daughters of kings and in honoring princesses who converted their husbands, Gregory advocated an expansion of diplomatic society. Kings who married servants missed the chance to weave themselves into the interests of other ruling families and to create a common progeny. Catholicization too provided a basis for common interests, alliances, and oppositions. It supplied Europe with highly trained clerics sharing vocabularies, procedures, sanctions, and juridical orientations. As envoys, they were prepared to represent their kings as well as their church. Their ambivalent loyalties, which sparked some of the most heated juridical conflicts of the Middle Ages, made them useful as diplomats. They could cultivate at least the appearance of rising above parochial interests and seeing both sides of a quarrel between Christian rulers of goodwill.

An undercurrent of skepticism necessarily dampens the idealism of that last sentence. Like modern critical international society theorists, Gregory is less concerned with peace per se than with the expansion of a civil order, one, in his mind, inseparable from the authority of the Roman Church. Hedley Bull famously insisted that war was itself an instrument for the reinforcement of international society, as when countries ally against a power that violates their fundamental assumptions about state sovereignty and nonintervention.[19] One would be hard-pressed to demonstrate that the conversions Gregory recounts created a peaceable society. Clovis's sons were all baptized and raised as Latin Trinitarian Christians. That fact did not stop them from going to war and trying to kill one another. Clothilde herself, the woman who brought Christianity to the Franks, incited a war of vengeance against her cousin Sigismund of Burgundy. The first major European effort to limit war lay five hundred years in the future, with the eleventh-century Peace of God movement. But the men who conceived and promulgated that first articulation of post-Roman international law were Christian bishops, and they proposed it as binding only for Christian believers. To that extent, they drew on the work of Clothilde and her king-converting descendants.

Bede's Nuptial History of the English Peoples

One of our most important sources for understanding how diplomatic society expanded in the period, Bede's *Historia ecclesiastica*, suggests that clerics may have supplanted royal women as actors in this process after the great conversions. Because Bede, like the other writers I have examined, incorporates legendary materials and shapes his story according to received literary conventions, we approach his text with similar reservations about its historical accuracy.[20] The more we have learned about the Anglo-Saxon past from archaeological evidence, the more reasons we have to doubt Bede's account. But at the least, the *Historia ecclesiastica* suggests the beliefs and values one prominent eighth-century cleric held with respect to Christian diplomatic society, to the relative importance of familial and clerical networks, and to the place of women in the society's expansion.

As Walter Goffart has noted, Bede continued the historiographic tradition pioneered by Gregory of Tours.[21] The fact that his account of the English conversions parallels the Frankish and Visigothic ones recounted in Gregory provides us with more evidence for assessing diplomatic changes during and after the great conversions. In revising Gregory's *Historiae*, Bede depicts an increasingly exclusive diplomatic society. His Christian kings still enter marriage negotiations with non-Christians, but in contrast to Gregory's kings, Bede's begin to insist that the non-Christian party convert before the marriage can take place. Even though interdynastic marriage remains the primary channel for conversion and the religious homogenization of European society, moreover, Bede's brides are passive. Bishops figure prominently in Gregory's *Historiae* as envoys and provide religious instruction *after* wives convert their husbands or husbands convert their wives. But in Bede, bishops, rather than foreign queens, lay out the case for conversion and persuade the groom to become a Christian. Like Lavinia in the *Aeneid*, brides stand in reverential silence.

Earlier historians sometimes assumed that this difference between Gregory and Bede reflected actual differences between royal women in Frankish and Anglo-Saxon society. More recent scholars have been cautious about such generalizations and have noted that Bede's representations tell us more about him than about his society.[22] In a particularly nuanced account, Stacy Klein argues that Bede writes less from misogyny than from a determination to replace a pre-Christian concern with wealth, prestige, and valuable alliances—the usual fruits of an interdynastic marriage—with transcendent Christian values. The bishops who accompany brides urge non-Christian kings to turn from earthly gain toward the greater good of heaven.[23]

As compelling as Klein's analysis is, it risks getting caught up in the bishops' transcendentalism. As a monk interested in the spread of Christianity, Bede reduces complex and wide-ranging diplomatic encounters to conversion dialogues between bishops and pagan auditors. Yet these conversion stories still retain the basic form of a negotiation between a ruler and a foreign envoy who simultaneously represents a foreign king, a foreign church, and the Kingdom of Heaven. The bishop asks the king to exchange one set of things—his indigenous religion and the temple infrastructures that supported it—for something else: a young wife, a new cultic infrastructure, and the promise of salvation. The bishop himself stands as a de facto part of the offer. As in any negotiation, the king must weigh the external advantages of the deal against such internal disadvantages as alienating a powerful, once loyal priesthood. But if the king accepts the deal, he will soon have a new cadre of educated, Latin-speaking ministers to serve him and his new God in further expanding the new diplomatic society. He and his new wife will produce royal offspring to marry in later marriages under similar terms and with similar advantages.

Like Virgil's Romans and Trojans, each male party to this negotiation—the king, the bishop, the Christian king who either commissioned or at least supported his travels, and ultimately the Roman Church—gains something. It is not so clear what Bede's brides gain from it, or if their lives would not have been better had they married a continental Christian prince. While some of Gregory's brides ended up in bad marriages, others, like Clothilde and Brunhild, acquired new moral and rhetorical authority, as well as wealth and political power. Bede's *Historia ecclesiastica* includes some politically influential women, such as the Abbess Hild, who presides over the climactic Synod of Whitby. But they are celibate nuns rather than brides in a narrative that privileges clerical networks over familial ones.

These contrasts between Gregory and Bede first appear in the latter's account of the earliest English conversion, that of Æthelberht of Kent under the influence of his Frankish wife, Bertha. As a foreign princess who, at least in some sense, introduces her husband and his subjects to Christ, Bertha recapitulates her great-grandmother's role as the patroness of a national conversion. At precisely that point of potential resemblance, however, Bede departs from his source in ways that both diminish Bertha's agency and limit the freedom with which Merovingian predecessors had married across religious lines.[24] Bede focuses on the monks whom Pope Gregory sent to convert the English after he saw some handsome Northumbrian boys in the Roman slave market. When the monks arrive in Canterbury and start preaching about the eternal kingdom awaiting Æthelberht, however, they discover that Æthelberht has already learned something about Christianity from his Frankish wife:

> Having heard these things, [Æthelberht] ordered them to remain in that island and to be given anything they might need, until he knew what to do with them. For the fame of the Christian religion had already reached him, since he had a Christian wife of the royal Frankish race, called Bertha. He received her on this condition from her relatives, that she might have an inviolable right to practice the rites of her own faith and religion with a bishop, name Liuthard, whom they gave to her as an assistant in the faith.

> [Qui haec audiens manere illos in ea . . . insula, et eis necessaria ministrari, donec videret, quid eis faceret, iussit. Nam et antea fama ad eum Christianae religionis pervenerat, utpote qui et uxorem habebat Christianam de gente Francorum regia, vocabulo Bercta, quam ea condicione a parentibus acceperat, ut ritum fidei ac religionis suae cum episcopo, quem ei adiutorem fidei dederant nomine Liudhardo, inviolatum servare licentiam haberet.] (1.25)[25]

As the range of scholarly interpretations of this passage suggests, we do not know exactly when Æthelberht converted or who converted him. He allows the monks to stay and make converts, although he does not commit himself personally to abandoning "those things, which [he has] observed for so long, together with all the English people [relictis eis, quae tanto tempore cum omni Anglorum gente servavi]" (1.25). Since Gregory later addresses Æthelberht as a Christian king, he presumably became one at some point.

Some scholars have suggested that the historical Bertha had already converted her husband before the monks arrived.[26] The fact that Gregory's monks worship in a nearby church dedicated to Saint Martin, the patron of the Franks, may indicate that she was already sponsoring an aggressive campaign of building and proselytizing on the Frankish model. But nothing in Bede confirms that. Quite the contrary, he frames the story in ways that prevent her from acquiring the authority of Gregory of Tours's Christian heroines. He mentions her only in passing, to provide a context for Æthelberht's hospitality toward the monks. In medieval Latin, *parens* can mean either "parent" or "relative," which leaves open the question whether Bede knew that Bertha's father was long dead and that her brothers had arranged her marriage. In either case, his Bertha experiences neither Clothilde's initial abjection nor her authority as the woman who ushers her husband into the Church. Bede presents her as the cherished daughter of parents or other relatives concerned about her spiritual welfare. They shield her against apostasy and ensure the integrity of her faith by negotiating her freedom to observe the rites of her religion and by sending a bishop with her as a spiritual guardian. Did this conspicuously infantilized Bertha provide Æthelberht with his first instruction in the Christian religion? Or was it done by the bishop who came as her "assistant"? Bede leaves such questions unanswered. Bertha drops out of the picture in a story that focuses on the Gregorian mission, with which she has had nothing to do, at least in Bede's account.

Bede's passing remark about Bertha's *parentes* introduces a further contrast with Gregory: the idea that Christian kings were wary about marrying their daughters to pagans. In Gregory, royalty marry across confessional lines with abandon, and sometimes with tragic consequences. But neither Gregory nor anyone in his text condemns the practice. In Bede, each new Christian generation distances itself more emphatically from religious intermarriage. Bede repeats these scenes of negotiation often enough in recounting the advancement of English Christianity that they establish a principle of literary revision within his own text: each time the scene gets replayed, the Christian party becomes even more stringent in the conditions that he or she places on the non-Christians. As more kingdoms embrace the faith, the less they are prepared to tolerate its coexistence with indigenous polytheism. In the case of Bertha, her Frankish parents simply insisted that she be free to practice her faith and to maintain a Christian bishop in her retinue. A generation later, Æthelberht's son Eadbald—who himself married a Frankish princess—was more emphatic about protecting Christian interests when he negotiated his sister Æthelberga's marriage to King Edwin of Northumberland (ca. 586–632/33). Bede's account of that marriage includes a lengthy discussion of the stipulations and of Edwin's assurance that he would not only abide by them but also be open to conversion.

In Bede's third account of a kingdom's conversion, the bride's father insists that the pagan groom convert to Christianity even before the wedding takes place. Because of conflicting territorial interests, Oswiu of Northumberland was in an almost constant state of war with the Mercian king Penda. But despite this feud, or possibly even to resolve it, Oswiu's son Alhfrith married Penda's daughter Cyneburh, and Oswiu's daughter Alflæd married Penda's son Peada. As a peacekeeping strategy, the double marriages proved useless. But according to Bede, the marriages succeeded in Christianizing the Mercians:

> At this time, the Middle-Angles, that is, the Angles who lived in the Midlands, received the faith and the sacraments of truth under Prince

Peada, the son of King Penda, who was a most fine youth, most wor-thy of the name and person of a king. He was raised by his father to the government of that people. He came to King Oswiu of the Nor-thumbrians, asking that his daughter Alflæd might be given to him in marriage. But he could not get what he was seeking by any means other than receiving the faith of Christ and baptism, along with the people whom he commanded. But when he had heard the preaching of the truth, and promise of the heavenly kingdom, and the hope of the resurrection and of future immortality, he gladly confessed that he wanted to become a Christian, even if he did not receive the virgin. He was mostly persuaded to receive the faith by a son of King Oswiu named Alhfrith, who was his friend and brother-in-law, since he had married his sister Cyneburgh, the daughter of King Penda.

[His temporibus Middilangli, id est Mediterranei Angli, sub principe Peada filio Pendan regis fidem et sacramenta veritatis perceperunt. Qui cum esset iuvenis optimus, ac regis nomine ac persona dignissimus, praelatus est a patre regno gentis illius, venitque ad regem Nordan-hymbrorum Oswiu, postulans filiam/ eius Alchfledam sibi coniugem dari. Neque aliter quod petebat inpetrare potuit, nisi fidem Christi ac baptisma, cum gente cui praeerat acciperet. At ille, audita praedica-tione veritatis et promissione regni caelestis speque resurrectionis ac futurae inmortalitatis, libenter se Christianum fieri velle confessus est, etiamsi virginem non acciperet, persuasus maxime ad percipien-dam fidem a filio regis Oswiu, nomine Alchfrido, qui erat cognatus et amicus eius, habens sororem ipsius coniugem, vocabulo Cyniburgam, filiam Pendan regis.] (3.21)

Instead of insisting that his daughter be allowed to practice her faith in a pagan court, Oswiu demands that Peada convert and bring his subjects with him to the font. The alacrity with which Peada accepts attests not to his love for Alflæd but to the persuasive force of Christianity throughout England. The fact that Peada has already learned about the religion from his friend and brother-in-law Alhfrith adds a preemptive note to the story. Peada was already so close to conversion that he did not even need the opportunity of his own marriage to a Christian to bring it about. As he says after hearing the Gospel, he would be happy to convert even if he did not win the bride.

We can only wonder what Alflæd thought of Peada's remarks, especially in light of the role she possibly played in his later assassination. But in terms of Bede's revisionary stance toward Gregory, the passage comes close to writing the queen out of the story of interdynastic marriage. In a sense, the Gregorian theme of the queen who brings her husband to Christ is pre-empted by Peada's friendship with Oswiu's son. That friendship may not have sealed the Mercian conversion, but it initiated and sustained it in ways that diminish Peada's marriage to Alflæd.

Although Gregory of Tours and Bede both advocated interdynastic marriage as a vehicle for the Christianization of Europe, they inhabited contrasting ecclesiastical worlds. Clerical marriage was a regular feature of diocesan life in sixth-century Francia, and Gregory frequently refers to the wives of priests and of his brother bishops. As a metropolitan bishop of one of the most important Frankish sees, Gregory was directly involved with political life. He knew powerful queens firsthand. He helped Ingeborg write her will, turned down a bribe from Fredegond, and staunchly supported Brunhild in her quarrel with her sister-in-law. Whereas metropolitan bishops had played a decisive role in the conversion of the Franks, the Anglo-Saxons owed their Christianity to monks, Irish and Roman alike. These monks, like Bede himself, had taken vows of celibacy. Bede entered the monastery at Wearmouth at the age of seven and spent the rest of his life there and at nearby Jarrow among his books. His knowledge of politics, albeit extensive, is mediated through his readings and his conversations with other men, mostly ecclesiastics.

In both Gregory's *Historiae* and Bede's *Historia ecclesiastica*, interdynastic marriage arises from and occasions conversations among major political and ecclesiastical figures. For both writers, one of the most significant effects of these conversations is the expansion of a Christianized diplomatic society uniting the former provinces of the Roman world. For the metropolitan bishop Gregory, directly involved with a world dominated by powerful queens, the most important conversations in this process are those between the Christian queen and the pagan king whom she converts. In adapting Gregory as a principal model for his ecclesiastical history of England, Bede assimilated these to the condition he knew best as a monk living among other monastics: they become conversations among men. Conversion happens in discussions not between Christian queens and pagan kings but between pagan kings and the queens' fathers, bishops, and brothers. Interdynastic marriage remains the occasion of the Christianization of Europe. But the queens who are married in these arrangements are no longer the exhorting catalysts of this momentous process. For Bede, they are merely part of the occasion.

The Christian diplomatic society that Bede portrayed was paradoxically both wider and narrower than Gregory's. It expanded beyond Francia to the most distant Anglo-Saxon kingdoms. But with a long-established corps of bishops, abbots, and other clerics to carry out further expansion and conversion, it set firmer limits on those entitled to participate in diplomatic conversations. In the process, Bede reduced interdynastic brides to disappearing mediators. Their marriages occasion the expansion of the Christian community, but only because they bring along the clerics who do the actual work of conversion. At the same time, their bishops and fathers eventually limit their choice of marriage partners to those men willing to convert to Christianity. By the end of Bede's narrative, this process has precluded the kind of marriage that originally brought Christianity to the Franks and the Visigoths, in which a Christian princess persuaded her husband to convert through her words and moral example. It would be a mistake to read into Bede the reservations about marriage, and open hostility to clerical marriage, that later became normative in Catholic society. But he privileges clerical over familial networks as the basis of relations between the Anglo-Saxon kingdoms in ways that return us to the question of Lavinia's silence: What did all these women think and feel who found themselves married to foreign kings? In the next chapter, we will see how a tradition of vernacular romance arose to answer that question.

❦ CHAPTER 3

From Chronicle to Romance

Interdynastic Marriage in the High Middle Ages

Throughout the first Christian millennium, writers from Jordanes to Bede and Paul the Deacon credited interdynastic marriages with enriching and exalting individual monarchs, reintegrating the old Roman world by building alliances between and among its successor states, and expanding Christendom. But these writers rarely mention marriages between former enemies as a path to peace. Many of the marriages they recount took place between parties who were already allies.[1] Others took place between groups like the Franks and the Visigoths, who alternated between periods of open war and periods of peace. Frankish-Gothic intermarriages happened regularly, but during times of relative stability. As far as we know, such intermarriages were never part of peace negotiations.

As late as the ninth and tenth centuries, marriage still played a role in expanding the Christian frontier. Fearing domination by the Holy Roman Empire, for example, King Mieszko I of Poland formed a counter-alliance with Duke Boleslaw I of Bohemia. In 965 Mieszko married Boleslaw's daughter Dobrawa on the precondition that he convert to Christianity. Dobrawa acquired a place in Polish national mythology analogous to Clothilde's in the French, but she was no peacemaker. To the contrary, the marriage was part of a defense alliance.[2]

On the other side of Europe, however, marriage diplomacy reacquired its mythic Virgilian association with peacemaking. In 911, at least according to the account written over a hundred years later by Dudo of Saint-Quentin, Rollo the Viking had devastated all Francia and menaced Paris itself: "For in truth, driven and possessed by bitter furies, Rollo began to lay waste and obliterate the whole land and to burn it with fire [Rollo vero ita exagitatus, furiis acerrimis bacchatus, coepit totam terram vastare et delere, atque incendia concremare]."[3] King Charles III finally pacified Rollo and saved his own realm by offering him Normandy and the hand of his daughter Gisela in "conjugal friendship [connubiali amicitiae]" (col. 248D). Rollo—following what had now become standard practice—converted to Christianity and became a great patron and protector of the Church. But Dudo also emphasizes how Rollo—now christened Robert—maintained his fiefdom in justice and peace:

> He married Gisela, the king's daughter, for whom he had reconciled himself with the Franks and made peace. He maintained security for all people wanting to live on his land. He divided his land into portions among his followers. . . . He reestablished rights and sacred, lasting laws with princely consent. He revealed ordinances to the people. And he made them live peaceably together. . . . Thus men rejoiced in continual peace and lasting rest, secure under Robert's sway; they were abundant in all good things, not fearing the army of any hostile party.

> [Gislam filiam regis uxorem sibi duxit, pro qua se Francis conciliando pacificavit. Securitatem omnibus gentibus in sua terra manere cupientibus fecit. Illam terram suis fidelibus funiculo divisit . . . iura et leges sempiternas voluntate principum sancitas et decretas plebi indixit; atque pacifica conversatione morari simul coegit . . . Continua igitur pace, diuturnaque requie laetabantur homines sub Rotberti ditione securi morantes; locupletesque erant omnibus bonis, non timentes exercitum ullius hostilitatis.] (cols. 652C, 654A)

Pax and its inflections recur throughout this part of the chronicle. At least for a time, the peace that Rollo establishes with Charles for Gisela's sake radiates to the entire region. Dudo's description of a just king dividing his lands among his followers, governing them according to well-established laws, and keeping them secure from all enemies contrasts with the king's previous violence in ransacking the countryside. The marriage treaty transforms violence into a fantasy of regeneration, a restitution of violated pastoral innocence. In a work resonant with Virgilian echoes, Dudo honors Rollo as his Aeneas, the invader who marries a native princess whom he wins in battle and establishes a new dynasty with a hybridized culture.[4] Just as the Trojans gave up their language and adopted the Latin of their new home, Rollo's Vikings become the francophone Normans.

This chapter examines this new emphasis on peacemaking in marriage diplomacy and its competition with other, generally negative attitudes toward marriage diplomacy. The first section observes how theological and devotional developments in the eleventh and twelfth centuries attributed a new sanctity to marriages between former belligerents by honoring brides as types of the Virgin Mary. The next returns to Dudo's chronicle, a work written at the earliest stages of the Christianization of Lavinia's legacy. It reveals a conflict between this new discourse and an older Germanic skepticism toward interdynastic marriages as ineffectual. In *De moribus et actis primorum Normanniæ ducum*, triumphant Christian brides never fully exorcise memories of tragic Germanic peace-weavers. The chapter's final section examines another Christian encounter with non-Christian representations of marriage and desire, the courtly love tradition, with its roots in Arabic and Ovidian accounts of erotic despair. A renewed emphasis on the bride's feelings and desires allowed the ancient Virgilian conflict between private desire and public responsibility to resurface.[5] Jilted lovers and adulterous queens undercut the period's official idealization of foreign brides as peacemakers and provided themes to which opponents both of individual marriages and of marriage diplomacy *in toto* would return centuries later.

In Mary's Office: Marriage and the Peace of God

After Charlemagne died in 814, authority and military clout within the Frankish empire devolved to numerous warring kingdoms, duchies, and principalities. The ninth and tenth centuries also witnessed renewed troubles on the borders of Christendom, with Vikings invading from the north, Magyars from the east, and Arabs from the south.[6] At the dawn of the eleventh century, when Dudo wrote his history of the Normans, the Church began to preach peace, at least among Christians, as an abstract ideal and took concrete steps to promote it. Beginning in the south of France and later throughout much of the Latin West, bishops promoted the Peace of God and Truce of God movements.[7] While the Peace protected the interests of such nonbelligerents as peasants and clerics, as well as of churches and other ecclesiastical properties, the Truce banned fighting during such sacred seasons as Christmas and Eastertide.

The Crusades brought this discourse of peace to its fullest expression.[8] Popes and bishops pleaded with feuding Europeans to put aside their quarrels and make common cause against the Muslim enemy. Although no definitive text of Urban's words survives, several accounts suggest that he stressed the need for Christian Europeans to make peace among themselves. According to Fulcher of Chartres, Urban presented the Crusade as the primary mission awaiting his audience after they first put aside their differences:

> Now that you, O sons of God, have consecrated yourselves to God to maintain peace among yourselves more vigorously and to uphold the laws of the Church faithfully, there is work to do, for you must turn the strength of your sincerity, now that you are aroused by divine correction, to another affair that concerns you and God. Hastening to the way, you must help your brothers living in the Orient, who need your aid.[9]

Urban's emphasis on peace is even more pronounced in the version recorded by Robert the Monk:

> This land which you inhabit, shut in on all sides by the seas and surrounded by the mountain peaks, is too narrow for your large population; nor does it abound in wealth; and it furnishes scarcely food enough for its cultivators. Hence it is that you murder one another, that you wage war, and that frequently you perish by mutual wounds. Let therefore hatred depart from among you, let your quarrels end, let wars cease, and let all dissensions and controversies slumber. Enter upon the road to the Holy Sepulchre; wrest that land from the wicked race.[10]

Almost like a modern social historian attributing the crusading impulse to the problem of finding land for younger sons, Robert associates it with a demographic imbalance, the land's inability to support an expanding population.[11] Until the people turn to the Holy Land, they will continue to fight over inadequate resources. Not only must a general European peace precede the Crusade, but also the Crusade will preserve that peace by focusing martial energies on common enemies of Christendom. Subsequent popes, statesmen, and diplomats echoed Urban's words in urging Europeans to stop fighting one another as a precondition of success in the East.[12] Sometimes it is difficult to judge the depth of a given speaker's commitment to a Crusade: Was he primarily interested in waging war on Muslims or using the Crusade as a pretext for making peace among Christians?

By the twelfth century, writers narrated the central events and mysteries of Christianity through this emergent discourse of peacemaking. They spoke of the Incarnation as an event that opened up new experiences of peace by reconciling the Father to errant humanity. Saint Anselm had made this a key theme in his seminal treatise *Cur Deus Homo* (ca. 1095–1098), but

Saint Bernard of Clairvaux gave it a popular devotional significance in his sermons for Advent and Christmas (ca. 1128–1140).[13] From Bernard's perspective, peace was central to the mystery of God's coming into the world: "But it is delightful to consider the way of His manifest coming, since His ways are beautiful ways, and all His paths are peaceable [Libet autem manifesti adventus viam considerare: quoniam viae eius, viae pulchrae; et omnes semitae eius pacificae]."[14] According to Bernard, God chose to be born of Mary not only because she was a virgin—the primary issue in Anselm—but also because she was "humble and peaceable [humilem et quietum]" (col. 104D). Contemplating how the Incarnation offers humanity the hope of salvation, Bernard identifies peace as heaven's greatest gift for the redeemed:

> And indeed peace is even now on earth to men of goodwill. But what is that peace in comparison to the fullness and superiority of [heavenly peace]? . . . [Y]ou are not yet capable of that, and for that reason, I offer you a homeland of peace, and leave you in the meantime a way of peace.
>
> [Et quidem pax nunc est etiam in terra hominibus bonae voluntatis: sed quid est pax ista ad illius plenitudinem et supereminentiam? . . . necdum capaces estis: propterea do vobis patriam pacis, et relinquo interim viam pacis.] (col. 104A)

The word *pax* or its synonyms and derivatives occurs twenty-three times in a single sermon which concludes by asserting that "the Son is Peace, our peace [Filius pax est, pax nostra]" (col. 105A). For Anselm, the Incarnation is primarily about satisfying the debt of sin and recovering humanity's claim to the rational contemplation of God; in Bernard, it is about a peace that transcends rational contemplation.

Bernard and his contemporaries often centered their thoughts about incarnational peacemaking on the Canticles, or Song of Solomon, which they read as a general allegory about Christ and the Church but also as a more intimate personal allegory about Christ's relationship to Mary.[15] More than any other biblical text, the Canticles encouraged Christians to see a link between marriage and peacemaking, perhaps because, with its secluded gardens and sexual intimacy, the book differs so strikingly from the many biblical stories of wars, rebellions, conquests, and conflicts. Numerous commentaries and sermons treated the work as a tribute to the peace that flowed from the union between the Heavenly Bridegroom and His mother, the Heavenly Bride. Bernard begins his First Sermon (ca. 1135) on it by noting that Solomon's name derives from the Hebrew word for "peace": "Observe first of all that the name of Peacemaking, which is Solomon, is suited to the opening of the book, which begins with the sign of peace, which is a kiss [Observa in primis Pacifici nomen, quod est Salomen, convenire principio libri, qui incipit a signo pacis, id est ab osculo]."[16] In Sermon 23, on the bridegroom's palace, Bernard honors the bedroom where he will bring his bride as "here truly it is calm. A peaceful God pacifies all things, and to look on peace is to be at rest [Hic vere quiescitur. Tranquillus Deus tranquillat omnia; et quietum aspicere quiescere est]" (col. 893 B); "that is the only place where peace comes about [solus factus est in pace locus iste]" (col. 893C). The bride is herself a preeminent peacemaker who "rather has strived to be a peacemaker with those who have hated peace" [Magis autem cum his qui oderunt pacem, studuit esse pacifica]" (Sermon 25, col. 899C).

The Premonstratensian Abbot Philip of Harveng's commentary on the Canticles gave these associations between the heavenly marriage and incarnational peacemaking their fullest expression. His *Commentaria in Cantica Canticorum* (mid-twelfth century) explains the Incarnation through a parable about a peace settlement sealed by a marriage between former belligerents. A great king had obtained a vast kingdom. But the people of one region were rebellious and defied his laws. Although they deserved to be imprisoned, the king decided instead to send his son to live with them and to marry one of their virgins. He knew that if his son married one of their women, he would be bound to them not only as a friend but also as a brother: "Indeed he saw that as a benefit of this marriage, anger, strife, and hatred would be turned far away, while joy, justice, agreeable society, peace and love would be called back [Videbat quippe quod nuptiarum beneficio, ira, rixa, odium, simultas longius avocantur: gaudium, aequitas, grata societas, pax, dilectio revocantur]."[17] Rebellion ended in joyful reconciliation.

For Bernard and Philip, marriage diplomacy provided a means of understanding the Incarnation, and their emphasis on incarnational peacemaking provided ideological support for such marriages. The Incarnation became for them the ultimate peace settlement, and the celestial union between Christ and his Heavenly Bride the paradigmatic interdynastic marriage. The resulting fusion of human and divine natures in the person of Christ, son of God and son of Mary, overcame the enmity between God and fallen humanity.

Similarly, a marriage contracted between a mortal ruler and the daughter of his enemy paved the way—at least theoretically—for peace on earth. Every settlement supposedly offered a glimpse of the peace that churchmen like Alcuin longed to sow among Christians, and in turn provided an image, however imperfect, of the great peace achieved by the Incarnation. The Virgin Mary joined Lavinia as a prototype of the royal bride mediating between her families of origin and marriage. This combination of Christian and classical legacies enhanced the prestige of marriages between former belligerents, which began to occur, at least according to extant records, with greater frequency around the year 1000.[18]

By the beginning of the thirteenth century, interdynastic marriage had acquired an association with peacemaking that it would retain for centuries and had become a regular feature of European diplomacy. Richard I of England even seems to have considered settling the Crusades through a match between his sister Joan and Saladin's brother. It failed, presumably because of the difference in religion, so it becomes an example of how the same Christian beliefs that integrated Europe limited diplomatic relations with the non-Christian world.[19] But within Christian Europe, marriage diplomacy flourished. It reached its apogee in the fifteenth and early sixteenth centuries, when families like the Valois dukes of Burgundy, the Hapsburgs, and the Trastámaras used it to build regional and, in the case of the Hapsburgs, global empires. It helped to resolve—at least temporarily—intractable intra-European conflicts, including the Franco-English struggle over Gascony, the perennial war between England and Scotland, the Hundred Years War, and the Hapsburg-Valois wars of the late fifteenth and early sixteenth centuries.

By the later Middle Ages, hailing foreign queens as types of the Virgin Mary had become a commonplace. As John Carmi Parsons has noted, the English queen's coronation *ordo* instructed her to pattern her reign on the models of Esther and the Virgin Mary, both powerful figures of intercession.[20] Paintings and sculptures, like the bas-relief tympanum depicting the Coronation of the Virgin over the Porte Rouge on the north flank of Notre-Dame de Paris, gave the association visual expression.

The figures of Louis IX and his queen, Marguerite of Provence, kneel on either side of the Heavenly Bridegroom and his Bride. As the angel places a crown on Mary's head which closely resembles those worn by Louis and Marguerite, the scene underscores the mystical connection between earthly and celestial. As much as Louis, anointed at Reims with the sacred oil believed to have descended from heaven, derives his authority from Christ, Marguerite derives hers from Mary.[21] Just as Mary reigns as the supreme mediator in heaven, Marguerite served as the supreme intercessor in France.

Across the Channel in England, Henry III ordered an image depicting a Jesse Tree—an illustration of Jesus's human ancestry that foregrounded Mary in her role as mother—to be installed in the bedchamber of Marguerite's sister, his bride, Eleanor of Provence. He then placed an image of Eleanor herself kneeling before a Madonna and Child in her palace at Clarendon.[22] Such

FIGURE 1.   Tympanum, Porte Rouge, Notre-Dame Cathedral, Paris. Courtesy Wikimedia Commons.

symbolism had a long afterlife. In Anglo-French affairs alone, artistic tributes to foreign queens as types of the Virgin Mary committed to intercession and peacemaking persisted until the Reformation. When Henry VI's bride, Margaret of Anjou, made her 1445 formal entrance into London, pageants along the way linked her coronation to the Virgin Mary's crowning in heaven and praised her for establishing peace between war-torn France and England.[23] Pageants celebrating Mary Tudor, queen of France, the sister of Henry VIII and bride of Louis XII, stressed the same points.[24]

In practice, complex and variable political circumstances determined whether individual queens could fulfill these coronation injunctions to pattern themselves on the Virgin Queen of Heaven. Scholars have long challenged Marion Fancinger's claim, based on the evidence of royal charters, that the later Capetian queens lost their public status and operated solely through personal influence on their husbands.[25] Some queens were indeed excluded from politics. But others—including Blanche of Castile, Marguerite of Provence, Eleanor of Provence, Margaret of Anjou, Isabeau of Bavaria, and Mary Tudor, queen of France—were major political agents, as both consorts and regents. Eleanor and Marguerite of Provence, for example, were the daughters of Count Berenguer IV, whose two other daughters married the Angevin king of Sicily and the king of the Romans (the elective king of Germany). Although Eleanor's enemies, and later nationalist historians, often condemned her for bringing in a horde of alien relatives, these connections gave England a more central role in European affairs. She and Marguerite actively promoted the 1259 Treaty of Paris, which ended a hundred-year conflict between France and England over Normandy, Anjou, and Maine. These same family connections also encouraged Louis IX to support Henry III in his recurrent disputes with his English barons.[26]

In recent decades, scholars have traced the careers of numerous queens who tried to fulfill their image as types of the Virgin Mary reconciling rival dynasties. Some succeeded more than others. The fact that prominent aristocrats often opposed them and the alliances they embodied reminds us that, regardless of how much theologians, chroniclers, and artists trumpeted the res publica christiana, it competed with local interests, ambitions, and resentments. Honor might lead powerful factions within a signatory realm to repudiate their king's desire for peace with a former enemy. Kings entered into treaties, including marriage treaties, with varying levels of commitment. Under any of these circumstances, the foreign queen—the enemy's daughter, sister, or other close relative—might become the focus of hostilities.

Virgilian Subtexts in the Norman Chronicle Tradition

Practical circumstances were not all that resisted idealizing foreign brides as types of Mary. The expansion of Christian diplomatic society throughout northern and southern Europe brought writers into contact with radically different ways of thinking about interdynastic marriages. Arguably the most famous of these was the discourse of peace-weaving, a mainstay of Germanic saga, chronicle, and poetry. The evidence for peace-weaving is primarily literary, and in most cases even legendary. There are no reliable contemporary descriptions of how pre-Christian Germans, Scandinavians, or Anglo-Saxons arranged such marriages. Instead we have narratives of events written centuries after the marriages allegedly took place, typically by Christian authors reconstructing the lives of pre-Christian ancestors whom they regard with a mixture of admiration, pity, and occasional disgust. These writers offer us at best a glimpse of how earlier Europeans may have attempted to contain violence between rival groups by intermarriages between ruling families. But their sense that violence was an inevitable fact of pre-Christian society, if not of human existence itself, led them to present such diplomatic efforts as doomed to failure. Regardless of how effectively peace-weaving may have functioned in a distant and undocumentable past, literary peacemaking ends in failure. As Ruth Karras has remarked, no text records peace-weaving that achieved a lasting peace between belligerents.[27]

The moral valence of peace-weaving in Germanic narratives shifts, but the basic narrative structure tends to be the same. Two parties are at war. Eventually they negotiate a truce sealed by the marriage of a "peace-weaver" (Anglo-Saxon *freoðuwebbe*), a woman selected from one group to marry a man selected from the other. In theory, social taboos against killing relatives will contain any future violence, since the two groups will be united by blood with the birth of the couple's offspring. But the peace never holds. Something reminds one party of the losses suffered at the hand of their new ally, and the quarrel resumes. The sense of betrayed trust often makes the renewed feud even bloodier than before.

Not all writers approached the collapse of the truce from the same perspective. If they felt that a peace had been contracted with a base or unworthy party, for example, they may have welcomed renewed hostilities. The twelfth-century Danish historian Saxo Grammaticus scorned Valdemar II's diplomatic overtures to the German Empire.[28] His contempt for all things German was behind his version of the legendary hero Ingeld's adventures. Saxo cast Ingeld as the son of a Dane murdered by Saxons. Instead of avenging his father's death, Ingeld marries a Saxon peace-weaver and allies himself with his father's slayers, whom Saxo condemns in extravagant terms as a debased race:

> From that bilge no small nourishments of debauchery have flowed into our country's throats. For hence run the lavish tables, more fashionable kitchens, the sordid offices of cooks; hence flows the filth of various sausages.

> [Ex cuius sentina in patriae nostrae fauces haud parva luxuriae nutrimenta fluxerunt. Inde enim splendidiores mensae, lautiores culinae, sordida coquorum ministeria variaeque farciminum sordes manavere.][29]

From Saxo's perspective, war is the only acceptable response to sausage-eating Saxons, not because they are aggressors, but because their taste for fine foods and luxuries threatens a proud Danish people hardened to battle. Peace-weaving itself is the ultimate decadence, a retreat from the honorable vengeance demanded by the heroic code that will mire Denmark in further decadence. Saxo sides with the old Danish hero Starkad, who shames Ingeld into divorcing his Saxon wife and avenging his father's death with Saxon blood.

Ingeld's feud reappears in *Beowulf*, but this time in a tragic rather than a heroic key. The Danish king Hroðgar has betrothed his daughter Freawaru to Ingeld—a Heaðobard in this version—to resolve a feud. Beowulf predicts that the marriage will end in a resumption of the quarrel: "Very rarely, after a people's fall, / does the slayer-spear rest a little while, / even though the bride is suitable [Oft seldan hwær / æfter leodhhryre lytle hwile / bongar bugeð, þeah seo bryd duge!]" (2029–31).[30] Assuming that the compulsion to avenge a murdered kinsman can never be slaked, Beowulf envisions the collapse of the Danes' diplomacy even before the marriage takes place. In a detailed passage, almost certainly drawing on the same legendary materials as Saxo, he imagines an old Heaðobard warrior seeing Freawaru's Danish retainers sporting weapons taken from his fallen comrades. He chastises his peers for leaving their kinsmen's deaths unavenged, and the quarrel resumes. A deep-seated "slaughter-rage" (wælniðas) then wells up in Ingeld as his more superficial "love for his woman" (wiflufan) grows cold (2064).

In the Gesta danorum, Saxo endorsed the call for vengeance that rekindled the feud by assigning it to Starkad, a legendary hero. The Beowulf poet, in contrast, undermines its moral authority by attributing it to an unnamed, embittered warrior. Here the truce's failure adds to a pathos that pervades the poem in its acknowledgments of humanity's inability to ward off death, violence, and mutability. The poet heightens this tragic focus in the name he gives to the peace-weaver. Unlike the unnamed Saxon woman scorned by Saxo, Freawaru is the daughter of Beowulf's friend and ally Hrothgar, and she embodies a fragile gentility that the poet honors even as he recognizes its vulnerability. The fact that Freawaru's name means "peace-guard" underscores the poignancy of her role as a woman destined for the impossible task of warding off the violence that eventually destroys the Danish kingdom. Allusions elsewhere link her to Hildeburgh, a Danish woman married to her father's enemy in yet another vain attempt to achieve peace. Like Hildeburgh, who lived to see her brother, husband, and son die in battle, Freawaru too will find herself torn between her families of origin and marriage.

Divergent, sometimes even antithetical discourses of gender thus reinforced the retrospective critique of pre-Christian marriage diplomacy. Writers either condemned foreign wives as temptresses seducing men from honorable vengeance or pitied them as victims. Peace-weaving placed too much of the responsibility for a successful alliance on women and their children, both figured as too weak to maintain it against men's hunger for vengeance. Whether writers portrayed peace as desirable or inherently ignoble, they agreed that pre-Christian peoples could not sustain it.

This construction of the futility of pagan peace-weaving contrasted with the hopes surrounding the alliances that Europeans wanted to achieve with Christian matrimony. At least in theory, Christian brides were types not of Freawaru, Hildeburgh, or the unnamed slattern in Saxo but of the Virgin

Mary. As sowers of peace among Christians, they worked not in tragic isolation but—again in theory—in harmony with the Church Universal and the whole *res publica christiana*. From the twelfth century on, theologians and canonists emphasized the permanent, sacramental nature of marriage. Bishop Ivo of Chartres, for example, stressed the indissolubility of a validly contracted marriage. If both the man and the woman consented to be married, their union was binding. Johannes Faventius saw the union's stability as essential to its sacramental nature. Unlike other sexual unions, marriage could not be dissolved. Other canonists concurred.[31]

The principle that a legally contracted marriage could not be dissolved influenced adjudications in ecclesiastical courts. With divorce per se deemed impossible, those who wanted a legal separation had to prove that their marriage had never been legal in the first place. From now on, high-profile annulment cases would figure prominently in interdynastic marriage negotiations. The difficulty of obtaining a separation provided a kind of *post hoc* proof that Christian marriage was indeed a better basis for diplomacy than non-Christian marriage. When Philip I of France fell in love with Bertrade de Montfort and tried to put away his wife, Bertha of Holland, for instance, Hugh of Die, the archbishop of Lyon, excommunicated him. Urban II later placed him under a ban of papal excommunication.[32] Innocent III followed suit by excommunicating Philip II and placing France itself under interdict when Philip put away Ingeborg of Denmark and married Agnes of Merania. After considerable struggle, Philip finally submitted to ecclesiastical authority and resumed his marriage with Ingeborg.[33] Despite the fact that some princes resisted or even ignored bans of excommunication, church courts made sure that the freedom with which Ingeld divorced his Saxon wife in the *Gesta Danorum* existed no longer.

Few works are more self-conscious about the Christian repudiation of Germanic marriage practices than Dudo's *De moribus et actis*. In it, when Bishop Franco approaches Rollo with Charles III's proposal for a settlement, he stresses that everything depends on Rollo's willingness to become a Christian. He greets Rollo, hails him as a great warrior, and then, without batting an eye, informs him that he is nothing but food for worms, dust and ashes: "Nonne es esca vermium, cinisque et pulvis?" But if Rollo were to convert, Franco assures him that he would enjoy great riches in this life, peace in the world to come, Normandy in perpetuity, and Gisela's hand in a lasting, Christian marriage (col. 648B12).

As Dudo's history unfolds, other Franco-Norman marriages reinforce this sense of a dynasty fully integrated into Christian diplomatic society. But as Norman historians have always realized, this rising European profile is only part of Dudo's story.[34] Alongside this neo-Virgilian saga of foreign invaders becoming better guardians of Frankish religion and civilization than the Franks themselves, Dudo introduces a counter-narrative of persistent marital irregularity. As it turns out, the first several Norman dukes *marry* Frankish women. But they *beget their heirs* on Norman women whose marital and ethnic status embarrasses Dudo's ostensibly Virgilian project. Although Rollo marries Gisela to great acclaim, that marriage produces no offspring. Dudo says almost nothing about the mother of Rollo's son William Longsword, other than that her name was Poppa. In a slightly later continuation of Dudo's chronicle, William of Jumièges notes that Rollo simply "bedded" her ("Popam . . . sibi copulavit").[35] Although their son's marriage to Luitgarde of Vermandois proved just as barren, William produced an heir through a relationship with a woman whom Dudo calls a wife but William of Jumièges dismisses as a mere Breton captive. Throughout the chronicle, William distinguishes between "Christian marriages" (*Christiano more*), like Rollo's to Gisela, and "Danish marriages" (*more danico*), like William Longsword's with his captive. Scholars continue to debate what the terms meant, but the implication is clear enough: the Scandinavians, from William of Jumièges's perspective, practiced concubinage that fell short of full Christian marriage.[36]

From the perspective of both Christian chroniclers, relations "after the Danish manner" may have produced heirs but were immoral and politically insignificant. They did nothing to expand or further integrate Christian diplomatic society. But that does not mean they lacked diplomatic significance. Although Dudo writes as if the Normans cohered as a single people under Rollo's leadership, the "Danish" marriages that trouble his narrative suggest another possibility. Norman society was almost certainly less unified than Dudo acknowledges. The early dukes had their hands full. In addition to developing their ties to various kings, dukes, and counts, they also had to manage rival Norman clans. The "Danish" marriages that Dudo retrospectively dismisses may be the traces of efforts to appease intra-Norman conflicts. In short, they may have resulted from the internal Scandinavian peace-weaving that other Christian writers condemned as ineffective.[37]

This counter-narrative of internal rivalry seems to underlie Duke Richard I's decision to remarry after the death of his well-connected Frankish wife, Emma of Paris. At first, Richard goes through a series of concubines (*ex concubinis*) and sires a number of children (col. 748C). But he then falls in love with a woman, Gunnor, whom Dudo identifies as a member of a high-ranking Norman family. Gunnor is beautiful, talented, and politically prudent. Nevertheless, instead of marrying her, Richard joins her in a "contract of forbidden coupling" (*prohibitae copulationis foedere* [col. 748C]).

Once again, a Norman duke slips into what Dudo condemns as an unsanctioned endogamous relationship. The irregular nature of the relationship also bothers the Norman nobles, who approach him just as their predecessors approached Rollo two generations before. This time, however, they ask not for *conubium* but for full-fledged Christian marriage: "We ask that she be joined to you with the indissoluble prerogative of a marital treaty [Hanc tibi inextricabili maritalis foederis priuilegio petimus connecti]" (col. 749A).

Eleanor Searle has noted that Richard's marriage to Gunnor looks like traditional peace-weaving.[38] A later continuation of Dudo's chronicle by Robert of Torigni identifies Gunnor as a woman from the Pays de Caux in western Normandy. Since Rollo's descendants settled in the eastern part of the duchy, Searle proposes that Richard married Gunnor to unite the eastern and western factions and to defuse a possible threat to his rule. In Dudo's text, the word *inextricabili* counters the issue that Christian writers foregrounded in their representations of Scandinavian peace-weaving: its impermanence and its decisive inability to resolve underlying conflicts. The Normans who ask Richard to marry Gunnor under Christian forms are worried about what will happen to them if he dies without an heir and leaves them to the mercy of "foreigners" (*exterae gentes* [col. 659C]). But what they really want is for this to be a Christian marriage, one that will result in "inextricable ties" lasting beyond Richard's death. It cannot be another instance of a peace-weaving that never stabilized relations between competing clans in earlier Scandinavian history.

Richard's subjects get their way. Seeing the errors of his wanton ways, Richard agrees: "Therefore the most holy Duke Richard, enthusiastically favoring their counsel, betrothed her according to the matrimonial law, in the presence of bishops, clergy, satraps, and laity [Huic igitur consilio libenter dux sanctissimus richardus favens; ascitis episcopis cum clero satrapisque cum populo; eam lege maritali desponsavit]" (col. 749A–B). Numerous offspring follow, and the Norman succession is assured. Like so much else in the chronicle, the passage commemorates the Normans' inscription in a Christian diplomatic society where bridal exchanges are sealed by sacred laws of matrimony. Later readers would know that subsequent Norman dukes persisted in irregular marital practices. Most famously, Richard's great-grandson William the Conqueror, known less flatteringly as William the Bastard, was presumably the son of one Herleva, the daughter of Fulbert the Tanner of Falaise. But within Dudo's narrative, Richard I's concession to his retainers' request that he marry Gunnor under Christian auspices marks a fitting end to the story of Norman assimilation to Christianity.

Like other histories and chronicles indebted to the Virgilian story of inter-dynastic marriage, Dudo's rests as much on fiction as on anything modern historians might accept as fact.[39] He was so committed to his story of assim-ilation through marriage that he minimizes one potentially embarrassing fact after another, above all the extent to which the Norman dukes he hon-ors were descended from successive concubines and other women of lower birth. At least one of the high-profile interdynastic marriages he privileges, that between Rollo and Gisela, may be a fabrication.[40] No prior source attests to Gisela's existence, or to any such marriage. We do not know whether Dudo drew on an intervening source that no longer survives, or whether he was so determined to find a Lavinia for his Viking Aeneas that he sim-ply made one up. In any event, his chronicle attests that much of what we might think of as a history of marriage diplomacy is a history of a diplomatic *ideology*, the beliefs, ideals, and aspirations that guided Christian and newly Christian powers in relations with one another but did not always conform with diplomatic practice.

Subsequent Norman writing confirmed the power of Dudo's fiction-making and canonized his account of interdynastic marriage as the basis of ethnogenesis and lasting alliances. In the process, it abandoned all traces of the Germanic peace-weaving tradition. Within a few generations, the descendants of Rollo and his invaders had managed to set up other Nor-man realms from Sicily to Britain. Wherever they went, chroniclers adapted Virgil's story of a foreign invader who reconciles himself to his new sub-jects by marrying a woman from their indigenous royal family. Marriage plays an important role, for example, in William of Apulia's *Gesta roberti wis-cardi*, a hexameter epic recounting the Norman occupation of southern Italy. Following Dudo, William appeals to Virgilian conventions to trans-form a story of conquest into one of a people's possession of a destined homeland. Like Rollo and his Vikings, the sons of Tancred of Hauteville, who conquered much of southern Italy in the early eleventh century, were fierce warriors, "a people more fond of war than peace treaties [Bella magis populi, quam foedera pacis amantes]."[41] William depicts them at first as greedy mercenaries whose alliances are unreliable and who are even treach-erous to one another. But by joining local leaders in a common fight against southern Italy's Byzantine overlords, they gain legitimacy as the region's liberators. The Hautevillian hero Robert Guiscard confirms that alliance and legitimizes a Norman succession by marrying Sichelgaita, the daughter of Guaimar IV of Salerno.

Modeling his account of the marriage on Aeneas's to Lavinia, Wil-liam stresses the native aristocracy's reluctance to embrace the newcomer.

Sichelgaita's brother objects to the marriage "because the Gauls seemed to him a wild and barbaric race, cruel and lacking a human heart [Galli / Esse videbantur gens effera, barbara, dira, / Mentis inhumanae]" (Book 2). Just as characters in romance versions of the *Aeneid* question the fates of Aeneas's first wife, Creusa, and his lover Dido, Sichelgaita's brother mistrusts Robert's repudiation of his first wife on grounds of consanguinity. But eventually the family consents not only to Sichelgaita's marriage to Robert but also to one between her younger sister and Robert's nephew. The marriage diplomacy transforms Robert's relationship with the people he has effectively conquered:

> Joined in a marriage of such nobility,
> The noble name of Robert began to increase,
> And a people who had formerly been compelled to serve
> Now paid him the obedience due to ancestral right,
> For the Lombard people knew Italy was
> Subject to the great-grandfathers and grandfathers of his spouse.

> [Coniugio ducto tam magnae nobilitatis,
> Augeri coepit Roberti nobile nomen,
> Et gens, quae quondam servire coacta solebat,
> Obsequio solvit iam debita iuris aviti.
> Nam proavis et avis subiectam coniugis huius
> Noverat Italiam gens Longobarda fuisse.] (Liber 2)

Marriage turns the conqueror into a de facto heir of the Salernian dynasty. The illustriousness and Italic legitimacy of Sichelgaita's ancestry reconcile the people to the fact that the son of a relatively obscure Norman nobleman will eventually rule them. Sichelgaita's grandfathers and great-grandfathers have effectively become Robert's in the popular imagination.

After the 1066 Conquest of England, British chroniclers, too, adopted the Virgilian story. Henry I became the Anglo-Norman Aeneas par excellence. William of Malmesbury hailed him as one whose accomplishments were so great that Cicero would scarcely attempt to describe them in prose, and in verse, "not even a rival of the Mantuan Bard."[42] Within a year of his accession, Henry stepped fully into the role of the Virgilian hero by marrying Edith of Scotland, who eventually became known as Matilda, a name that linked her to Henry's mother, Matilda of Flanders. Although Edith/Matilda was the daughter of the Scottish king Malcolm III, her mother was Margaret of Wessex, a scion of the Wessex dynasty that ruled England from 871 to 1016, and again from 1042 to 1066. Yet another worthy Norman had found his Lavinia.

Stressing the affection between the couple, chroniclers like William of Malmesbury and Orderic Vitalis endowed them with all the heterosexual passion they found so lacking at the court of Henry's bachelor brother William Rufus. William of Malmesbury presents it as a love match. Although Edith/ Matilda's marriage portion was small, Henry was determined to possess the woman "whom he so ardently desired" (428). By "being grand-niece of king Edward, by his brother Edmund," Matilda brings Henry something much more valuable than property: a Wessex heritage that legitimizes him and his descendants in the eyes of their English subjects (428). When William later praises her piety, learning, patronage of the arts, and even excessive generosity, he attributes her virtues to her descent from "an ancient and illustrious race of kings" (452).

From Dudo to William of Malmesbury, from William of Apulia to Wace, Norman chroniclers used interdynastic marriage to transform the descendants of Viking conquerors into master diplomats. They showed how the people whose arrival on the borders of Carolingian civilization in the ninth and tenth centuries seemed to harbinger its collapse became its heirs and perpetuators. By the time Robert Guiscard married Sichelgaita or Henry I wed his widowed daughter to Geoffrey of Anjou, descriptions of such marriage alliances drew on an ever-thickening web of intertextual associations. Gregory of Tours's seminal account of Clothilde's marriage to Clovis underlies Dudo's account of Rollo's marriage to the daughter of Charles III. As a revision of the original Merovingian story, Dudo's hints that the Normans might soon outstrip the Franks as paradigmatic champions of Christianity. Rollo's marriage in turn shapes the later chroniclers' accounts of other marriages that domesticated Norman conquerors to their new subjects. But the tables turn in the later stories: it is no longer the father of the bride who initiates the marriage but the Norman hero who seeks her out and takes the lead in creating new diplomatic relations. Robert Guiscard and Henry I emerge as the true heirs of Aeneas, the hero whose marriage bridges times and places to create a common European diplomatic culture.

Romance Countertexts

The *Aeneid* that chroniclers from Dudo to William of Malmesbury adapted as the basis for their diplomatic narratives was optimistic and celebratory. Its Aeneas was a hero destined to create a new home for his people in a distant land. Although he had to subjugate its native Latin inhabitants in war, his marriage to the daughter of their king restored order and allowed Trojans and Latins to come together as one people. As late as the twelfth century, something of that empire survived in the language and in the administrative and judicial infrastructures of the Roman Church, which continued to champion marriages between rival families as a way of sowing peace among Christians.

But this triumphal *Aeneid* was only one among several interpretations available to medieval writers, and it was arguably less popular than darker interpretations of Aeneas's rise to power. While chroniclers wrote in Latin for learned audiences, vernacular writers drew on an anti-imperial reading of the poem, dating back to Ovid, that condemned Aeneas as an unfaithful subject and lover.[43] In the *Heroides*, Ovid featured a letter written by Dido to Aeneas condemning him for abandoning her and denouncing his talk about the gods and a future homeland in Italy as lies. Two late antique writers, known to posterity as Dares, the author of *De excidio trojae historia* (ca. 600), and Dictys, the author of *Ephemeris belli trojani* (ca. 200–400), claimed to have been eyewitnesses to the Trojan War. They argued that Aeneas was a treacherous counselor who betrayed his city to the Greeks. These versions were extremely popular throughout the Middle Ages and inspired such works as Benoît de Sainte-Maure's *Roman de Troie*, Guido delle Colonne's *Historia destructionis Troiae*, and Chaucer's *Troilus and Criseyde*.

These counter-characterizations of Aeneas as a villain, one who betrayed his lover and his nation, countered his mythic authority as a bridegroom whose marriage to Lavinia brought peace to troubled Italy. The Aeneas that derived from Dares and Dictys was the antitype, almost a demonic parody of a good diplomat. As a corrupt counselor, he poisoned his king with misleading counsel and colluded with the enemy to the detriment of his own people. In these narratives, peace is bad. The truce that Aeneas and his sidekick Antenor advocate lets the Greeks catch the city off guard. In several versions of this story, Aeneas urges the Trojans to bring the fatal horse into the city as a sign of their trust. On the night the city falls, he even leads Pyrrhus to murder Priam. This Aeneas embodied suspicion about divided loyalties and secret treachery that had always shadowed the diplomatic career: Can anyone ever fully trust individuals who must simultaneously represent their own state and be open to dialogue with its enemies?

As competing versions of the *Aeneid* proliferated throughout Christian diplomatic society, they inscribed both its highest ideals—sowing peace among Christians—and the suspicions and fears that undercut them. These contradictions in Virgil's reception history made his epic the perfect vehicle for expressing a range of equally contradictory attitudes toward interdynastic marriage, honored by some writers as an image of the Incarnation and, for the first time, condemned by others as a violation of human feelings in the interest of family ambition. The same canonical reforms that heightened its promises of stability and permanence, moreover, also heightened its volatility by placing new emphasis on consent as a necessary, even definitive, component of a valid marriage.[44] While some canonists insisted that marriage required the consent of the couple's families as well as of the bride and groom, the majority insisted that the feelings of the latter were decisive.[45]

In rendering his opinion, Gratian drew on a case from the late eleventh century, when Sanchez I Ramirez of Navarre appealed to Urban II because his niece was refusing to marry a man to whom he had promised her.[46] While marriage seems to have been part of Sanchez's attempts to strengthen relations with the southern French nobility, we do not know the details or even the name of the niece. But one thing is clear: the papal appeal backfired because Urban II sided with the bride. Decreeing that those who are joined in body ought also to be joined in mind, Urban argued that marriage without consent opened a window to abandonment, fornication, and even adultery. Partners who were not happy in their conjugal life might start looking elsewhere.

Although canonists built a body of legal theory on Urban's decision, I have found no recorded instances of its application. Richard I's sister Joan may have spoiled a deal between her brother and Saladin by refusing to marry the latter's brother on religious grounds, but that story rests on only one source. We have no idea how often formal consent—which was almost always forthcoming in cases of high-profile diplomacy—masked hidden histories of silent suffering, thwarted love affairs, broken hearts, intrafamilial quarrels, psychological coercion, threats, and worse.

Even in the most high-profile annulment of the period, in which the woman's feelings had enormous diplomatic consequences, the legal case centered on consanguinity rather than consent. On March 21, 1152, four French archbishops annulled Eleanor of Aquitaine's marriage to Louis VII of France.[47] Contracted in an effort to stabilize relations between the French Crown and nominal, but fiercely independent, aristocratic subjects in the south, the marriage was troubled from the start. By the time Eleanor accompanied Louis on the Second Crusade, they had separated and returned home on separate ships. When they appealed to Eugene III for an annulment, he acted on the principle of indissolubility and refused to grant it. But things deteriorated further, and Eugene consented to an annulment on the basis that they were related within the canonically forbidden fourth degree of consanguinity through their common descent from Robert II. The case rested entirely on genealogical matters that had nothing to do with their feelings for each other.

Eight weeks later, Eleanor married Henry II of England, Louis's titular subject in his simultaneous role as Duke of Normandy and hereditary heir to several other French territories. The marriage drastically shifted the balance of power in western Europe and made Henry II—Louis's de facto enemy—the head of the largest European imperium since Charlemagne.[48] In terms of the history of marriage diplomacy, Eleanor's marriages demonstrate three important facts about the High Middle Ages. First, marriages between rival dynasties could have vast territorial, economic, and military consequences. If played well, marriage diplomacy could bring families unparalleled power and prestige. But if played badly, it could cost them. Louis's position in internal French affairs and in the larger European calculus of power eroded after 1152. Second, feelings could, at least on occasion, have practical consequences. Eleanor and Louis sought an annulment because they disliked each other. Some scholars have argued that feelings mattered just as much in her subsequent decision to marry Henry II: they married because they were in love. Third, even though feelings mattered in Eleanor's case, it was a grand and scandalous exception to a more general—unspoken and even officially denied—rule that most people married and remained married for political reasons, regardless of their feelings. Few women, even daughters of powerful kings and aristocrats, had the inheritances, resources, and other advantages that brought Eleanor's feelings to the center of European state affairs. Even in her case, the separation rested on a genealogical loophole rather than an appeal to the official but probably ineffective legal principle of consent.

This final contradiction between legal theory and legal practice—between the principle that a woman's consent mattered and the fact that we have no cases of men or women claiming to have been coerced into marriage—resonated throughout the medieval European literary system with its competing claims to Virgilian authority.[49] Lavinia, the paradigmatic interdynastic bride, is a conspicuously and troublingly silent character in a poem that swirls with disruptive and destructive passions. Aeneas's marriage to her ruins one character after the next. In his renewed commitment to a Latin future with a Latin bride, Aeneas abandons Dido and drives her to suicide. When Latinus accepts him as his future son-in-law, the agreement outrages his wife, Amata, who counted on their daughter marrying Turnus. Turnus, the formerly betrothed but now jilted suitor, becomes one of literature's most terrifying embodiments of passion, more a demonic force than a human being. Lavinia's marriage to Aeneas itself is a perfect diplomatic paradox: it settles a brutal and dehumanizing war that it triggered in the first place by unleashing Fury throughout the land. Each of her victims expresses his or her misery in memorable imprecations and lamentations. Through it all, Lavinia is silent.

With almost no exception, the ethnic histories and chronicles that documented marriage diplomacy throughout the twelfth century were complicit in that silence. Except for Rosamund of the Gepids, no bride challenged their testimonies to an expanding Christian diplomatic society built on the administrative foundations of the Roman past. As we have seen throughout this book, we often do not even know the names of the women whose marriages forged alliances, secured truces, and enhanced dynastic wealth. Bede stripped his brides of the persuasive force with which Gregory endowed Clothilde, and, in the process, left doubts about their contributions to British Christianity. Later chronicles documenting the expansion of Norman society into Sicily and Britain generally adopted Bede's model. William of Malmesbury, for example, praises Edith / Matilda for her piety and other virtues but spends little time trying to imagine her feelings or her words.

Yet the chronicles were not the whole story.[50] Drawing on both the counter-Augustan, counter-Virgilian discourse of Ovid and Arabic love poetry introduced into northern Europe from Spain and Sicily via Provence, courtly romance gave brides the language that the chronicles did not.[51] Its vernacularity alone underscored its potential resistance to the Latinate, neo-Virgilian ideal of a Christian diplomatic society sealed by silent brides. It also gave it an edge in terms of potential influence: more people could understand it and its criticism of a diplomatic system that privileged the peace of Europe and goodwill between Christians over individual happiness. The role of marriage in diplomatic society would continue to expand. But as I argue in later chapters, writers who heralded and subsequently celebrated the collapse of the dynastic order would draw heavily on topoi about overbearing fathers, unhappy brides, and adulterous queens that date from the twelfth century.

In the Anglo-French Angevin imperium, one work in particular led the way in criticizing marriage as a means to resolve interdynastic conflict. Written three years after Henry II's marriage to Eleanor of Aquitaine, Wace's *Brut* identified its central hero, King Arthur, and by implication the later Anglo-Norman kings, as Aeneas's heir. The *Brut* is a classic *translatio imperii* narrative appropriating Virgil's story of Aeneas's journey from Troy to Rome as the basis for Wace's own story of Aeneas's great-grandson Brutus's journey from Rome to Britain. Like several later works that adapted Virgilian materials, the *Brut* presents itself as a Norman *Aeneid* and exalts its author as a Norman Virgil. Its focus on immigration and the relocation of empire becomes a metaphor for the translation of cultural authority to which the work itself contributes. Wace had also honored Henry II with his account of Rollo and the first Norman dukes, the *Roman de Rou*. With the *Brut*, he honored him as a second Arthur and as yet another Aeneas extending Norman power from Britain to the Pyrenees.

Like Aeneas, Henry owed his imperium to a combination of interdynastic marriage and conquest, two themes that run throughout Wace's vernacular chronicle. Unlike Latin chronicles, however, Wace's adaptation of Virgil is ambivalent toward imperial authority and to the marriage diplomacy that extended it into newly conquered territories. Whereas other twelfth-century writers imagined interdynastic marriages underwritten by sacramental authority and *caritas*, Wace stressed their vulnerability to lingering resentments, irreconcilable cultural and racial differences, and, above all, sexual passions that resist canonical restraint. The *Brut* opens, for example, with a short synopsis of Troy's fall and Aeneas's arrival in Italy. The moment Aeneas lands, the rich but feeble Latinus—"who held all that realm in peace" [Ki tut cel regne en pais teneit]" (38)—offers him his daughter, a generous portion of coastal land, and a commitment to making him his heir.[52] For the Latin chronicles, that was the end of the story. Wace, however, dampens the chronicle's recollection of Aeneas's marriage as a model peace settlement by noting both Amata's objections and Turnus's outrage over seeing a woman promised to him handed to another. As in Virgil, their passions resist rational settlement and erupt in warfare.

Although Wace initially depicted Latinus *giving* ("dunout" [55]) Lavinia, the war recasts Aeneas as a conqueror *taking* her as part of the spoils:

> After Aeneas had taken Lavinia
> and had conquered all the land,
> he lived and reigned four years
> and named a castle
> he completed after her,
> it was called "Lavinium."
>
> [Puis k'Eneas Lavine out prise
> E la terre tute conquise,
> Vesqui il quatre anz e regna
> E a un chastel k'il ferma
> De Lavine posa le nun,
> Si l'apela Lavinium.] (67–72)

The rhyme on "prise" and "conquise" degrades Lavinia—as silent here as in Virgil—to a battle prize. That degradation continues in the references to

Lavinium as a "chastel," or fortress, rather than the town mentioned in the *Aeneid*. The Normans were famous castle builders, and their castles had one primary purpose: dominating their conquered territories. Like building the castle he names after her, Aeneas's "taking" Lavinia is just one more proof of the Trojans' victory.

Although this particular marriage-conquest succeeds, Wace diminishes the prestige it had acquired in early medieval literary history by linking it to Paris's prior abduction of Helen, the sexual violation that precipitated the Trojan War. Wace first mentions Paris and Aeneas in the same sentence:

> As books tell it,
> when the Greeks had conquered Troy
> and razed the whole land
> in vengeance on Paris
> who had ravished Helen from Greece,
> Aeneas the Commander had some trouble
> escaping from the great slaughter.

> [Si cum li livres le devise,
> Quant Greu ourent Troie conquise
> E eissillié tut le païs
> Pur la venjance de Paris
> Ki de Grece out ravi Eleine,
> Dux Eneas a quelque peinne
> De la grant ocise eschapa.] (9–15)

Aeneas escapes "la grant ocise," but the verse taints him with recollections of the Trojan crime punished by his city's destruction. These associations hint that his marriage to Lavinia reenacts Paris's abduction of Helen, with Turnus doubling as the outraged Menelaus. In a literary system replete with works like Benoît de Sainte-Maure's *Roman de Troie*, in which Hecuba condemns the traitor Aeneas as "Satanus," his similarity to Paris may have been especially obvious and damning.[53]

Although Wace mentions several later marriage negotiations and settlements, most of them fail. Either the parties never agree on terms, or if they do, the settlement does not last. When Brutus first sets out from Rome, for example, he tries to free thousands of Trojan slaves from the Greek king Pandrastus. After capturing Pandrastus in a fierce war, Brutus and his war council have to decide what to do with him. Finally, they agree that Brutus should marry the king's daughter Innogen and receive tribute. Like Lavinia, the equally silent Innogen appears less as a mediator between former enemies than as spoils taken by the victors. The latter reject the idea of settling down with the Greeks and insist instead on sailing on to Britain:

> Then we will go and seek a home
> in foreign places,
> for if we remain with him,
> if we have experienced evil, we will have worse.
> We will never have peace with the Greeks,
> for they will never forget
> their relatives, their uncles, their fathers,
> their cousins, their nephews, their brothers,
> nor their other close friends,
> Who have died at our hands.

> [Puis irrum quere mansions
> Par alienes regions
> Kar si nus od lui remanons,
> Si mal eümes, pis avroms;
> Jamais as Greus nen avrom pais,
> Kar il n'ublieruent jamais
>   Lur parenz, lur uncles, lur peres,
> Lurs cosins, lur nevuzs, lur freres
> Ni lurs altres amis precains
> Que nus avum morz a noz mains.] (525–34)

The passage sounds so much like similar ones in Saxo Grammaticus and *Beowulf* that one wonders if it is an intertextual recollection of unsuccessful Germanic peace-weaving, the predicament that Norman chronicles had evaded since Dudo. Brutus's marriage to Innogen could never halt the residual hostilities. As in early Germanic writings, the vanquished parties would always desire revenge for their murdered kinsmen. Once an interdynastic marriage takes place, peace can last only as long as the enemies live fifteen hundred miles apart.

On a fundamental level, Wace believed that some cultures were too incongruous to become part of a single diplomatic society and settle their differences through marriage. The Britons, for example, are presumably right to refuse intermarriage with the Picts (5192–5198). Other nations in the poem share what Françoise H. M. Le Saux has identified as an underlying fear of miscegenation.[54] King Ebrauc sends thirty British maidens to Italy to marry men of Trojan descent whom the women of Lombardy have rejected on racial grounds. Conan, the legendary founder of Brittany, imports British women to prevent his men from marrying Gauls. Wace castigates the British leader Vortigern not only for marrying a Saxon himself but also for allowing his subjects to do the same. Arviragus's marriage to the Roman Genissa works well enough because they share a common Trojan ancestry. From Wace's perspective, Roman-Briton marriages succeed because they unite two halves of the same diasporic race. When King Cole of Camulodunum marries his daughter Helena to the emperor Constantius to foster peace between the two peoples, the strategy paves the way for mutual respect. Their son Constantine the Great "loves the Britons for his mother / And those of Rome for his father [Les Bretuns ama pur sa mere / E cels de Rome pur sun pere]" (5687–88). Helena's uncle also marries a Roman. Instead of drawing different cultures into a single people, these marriages restore a lost ancestral unity.

But even if the parties to an interdynastic marriage are sufficiently similar, there are still no guarantees. Throughout the poem, Wace focuses on the aspect of interdynastic marriage that Latin chroniclers ignored: sexual passion. Urban II first broached the dangers that a couple's feelings for each other might raise when he ruled against Sanchez I Ramirez. As the pope cautioned Ramirez, settlements are worthless if they drive brides and grooms to abandonment, fornication, and adultery. Wace, too, treats adultery as the underside of marriage diplomacy. From its opening allusions to Paris's theft of Helen, the *Brut* foregrounds the violation of betrothals and solemnized marriages in which the bride's and groom's feelings for each other fall short of the *caritas* that ought to have drawn their families into a Christian commonwealth. When the British king Brennius falls in love with a Norwegian princess already promised to the king of Denmark and steals her, for example, Denmark launches a disastrous invasion of Britain. Within Wace's Virgilian master narrative, such marriages reenact Aeneas's to Lavinia as an example not of successful peacemaking but of the disasters that occur when two men pursue the same woman.

The Aeneas-Lavinia-Turnus triangle recurs most tragically in the relationship of Arthur, Guinevere, and Mordred. Although Wace, like Geoffrey of Monmouth, is sketchy about the origins of Arthur's marriage, it seems to have been a political alliance with Guinevere's guardian, Cador of Cornwall. But in this new narrative world, where personal feelings overwhelm diplomatic resolution, Guinevere's charms and their effect on Arthur are what matter:

> When Arthur had settled his lands
> and established justice throughout them,
> and all his realm restored
> to its ancient dignity,

he took Guinevere and made her his queen,
a pleasant and noble lass,
she was beautiful and courteous and gentle, . . .
She was greatly polished,
and of noble conduct,
of generous and excellent speech,
Arthur loved her greatly and held her dear.

[Quant Artur out sa terre assise
E par tuit out bone justise,
E tuit sun regne out restore
En l'ancïene digneté,
Genuevre prist, sin fist reïne,
Une cuinte e noble meschine;
Bele esteit e curteise e gent . . .
Mult fu de grant afaitement
E de noble cuntienement,
Mult fu large e buene parliere,
Artur l'ama mult e tint chiere.] (9641–48, 9653–56)

On the surface, Arthur's marriage seems the next prudent step after he has restored order and dignity to his realm. Guinevere is well born, another member of the Roman diaspora, and gracious. But some aspects of Wace's encomium hint that trouble might follow. Once again, a hero "takes" a woman and "makes" her his queen, and the narrator does not refer to her feelings. Unlike her precursor Lavinia, however, Guinevere is not silent: "Mult fu large e buene parliere." She is also "cuinte," a loaded word in Old French that can denote anything from elegance to cunning. The fact that her beauty and grace have such a powerful impact on Arthur leaves open the possibility that they will have a similar effect on other men.

In the only prior treatment of the story, Geoffrey of Monmouth revealed Mordred's determination to steal his uncle Arthur's throne before he mentioned Mordred's theft of Arthur's wife. In Wace, by contrast, passion precedes and overdetermines politics.[55] When Arthur departs for his continental wars and entrusts his realm to his wife and nephew, Wace notes that Mordred already loves Guinevere shamefully and dishonorably: "Feme sun uncle par putage / Amat Mordret si fist huntage" (11185–86). By foregrounding Mordred's secret desires first, Wace makes them seem like the primary motive for the betrayal that follows. For reasons that are never specified, Guinevere returns his love. Wace's silence with respect to Guinevere's motives leaves us to wonder whether the fault lay with Mordred's powers as a seducer, Guinevere's frailty or even her inherent cunning, or Arthur's inadequacies.

If Wace is silent about Guinevere's feelings going into the affair, he reveals her remorse when Arthur returns and the realm collapses around her:

> She sojourned at York,
> pensive and sad,
> recalling to herself the villainies
> with which she had dishonored herself for Mordred . . .
> she was most sad, most pensive;
> she fled to Caerleon,
> and entered a nunnery.

> [A Everwic iert a sujor,
> En pensé fud e en tristur;
> Membra lui de li vilainie
> Que pur Modred s'esteit hunie, . . .
> Mult fud triste, mult fud pensive;
> A Karliun s'en est fuïe,
> La entra en un abeïe.] (13205–8, 13214–16)

Wace underscores the poignancy of Guinevere's fall by echoing the cadences with which he once praised her. The woman "Mult fu de grant afaitement . . . Mult fu large e buene parliere" now mourns her villainies: "Mult fud triste, mult fud pensive." As she shuts herself away from a realm in chaos, the insistent interiority of this passage sets it apart from most of Wace's writing. While it underscores the isolation that is an important part of Guinevere's punishment, it also exposes the inner life that, from Wace's viewpoint, makes marriage diplomacy so risky. Despite the best intentions of the canonists, marriage is too bound up with unpredictable and unmanageable forces to yield a reliable basis for policy.

With the appearance of Wace's *Brut*, questions of nuptial consent and, more generally, questions of diplomatic credibility began to dominate the vernacular literary system. When Henry II, Louis VII, and their heirs relied on marriage alliances for their foreign policies, vernacular writers turned out works that questioned the reliability of such alliances. Rulers worried less about these questions than the comparative advantages and disadvantages of particular matches. As we have already seen, Eleanor of Aquitaine marched out of one royal marriage into another with little concern for the theoretical permanence of marriage. She left it to the canonists to argue that her marriage to Louis had never happened. In the same spirit, rulers throughout western Europe betrothed their daughters to one prince only to back out and betroth them to someone else as political conditions shifted. In 1159, for example, Henry II agreed that his two-year-old son, the future Richard I, would marry a daughter of Ramon IV Berenguer, the Count of Barcelona. That match never materialized, and by the 1160s, Henry was planning to marry him instead to Alys, Countess of the Vexin, a younger daughter of Louis VII. That did not happen either. Richard finally married Berengaria of Navarre, the daughter of Sancho VI, whom he had met at a tournament. Richard I's history of near-miss marriages was typical, and the pattern of promising young royals to one party and then another persisted through early modernity.

If rulers and their representatives seldom asked whether such practices undermined the credibility of a diplomatic culture based on marriage, poets did. Dominated by the presence of adulterous queens like Guinevere and Isolde, romance refined and sometimes even attempted to answer the paired questions of what constituted consent and what assured the credibility of a settlement. Almost certainly in intertextual response to Wace's exploration of these questions, the first French romance, the anonymous *Roman d'Enéas*, reformulated them in a rewriting of the *Aeneid* that gave a voice to the long-silenced Lavinia.[56] The *Roman* downplayed Virgil's supernatural machinery and heightened the love interest. Most important for its place in the history of twelfth-century diplomatic consciousness, it added several thousand lines in which Aeneas and Lavinia fall in love with each other, so that true consent underwrites their marriage settlement. Hero and heroine meet, fall in love, worry about the mutuality of their affections, finally voice their feelings, live happily ever after, and create an empire that stands as a model for all future polities, including the conspicuously imperial and multicultural realm governed by Henry and Eleanor.

Despite this final happy and consensual ending, however, the *Enéas* author himself poses some unsettling questions. He overgoes Wace not by reasserting imagined Virgilian certainties but by giving the doubts with which Wace, Benoît de Sainte-Maure, and other Norman writers undercut them a more nuanced articulation. His Aeneas is not a traitor, his Lavinia is not a mere pawn to be "taken" and bartered, and his denouement unfolds, albeit anachronistically, according to the most rigorous standard of canonical consent. Yet the *Enéas* poet retains just enough of Virgil's Olympian machinery to make us wonder if the diplomatic success of Aeneas's interdynastic marriage with Lavinia warranted the security of later marriages patterned on it. Is the lasting settlement between the Romans and the Trojans a solution to the problem of diplomatic credibility that later monarchs can adopt? Or does its success depend on *fatum*, an irrational, incalculable element of divine caprice that human beings have a limited capacity to discern or influence?

As it stands, the *Roman d'Enéas* is one of medieval literature's most searching inquiries into the problem of diplomatic trust. As the poet retells Virgil's story, he questions what underwrites the agreements that hold powers together in a common diplomatic society. The poem opens, like Wace's *Brut*, with references to the Trojan War imagined as the consequence of a violation of trust:

> When Menelaus had Troy besieged,
> He never turned back until he had taken it,
> Laid the country waste and the whole realm,
> In order to avenge his wife.

> [Quant Menelax ot Troie asise,
> Onc n'en tourna tresqu'il l'ot prise,
> Guasta la terre et tot le regne
> Por la venjance de sa femme.] (1–4)[57]

As an apt *contrapasso*, the treachery of the Trojan horse provides Menelaus with the perfect means to avenge Paris's treachery in abducting his wife. The poet reduces the tragedy of Troy's fall to one inversion of sound diplomatic practice after the next. A foreign prince abducts a sovereign's wife. An arguably just war results to recover stolen property. But in fighting it, the Greeks become even more deceptive than the Trojans. Sinon, the Greek who reports falsely reassuring information about the Greeks and their mysterious horse, parodies a proper envoy conveying truthful, reliable information about his sovereign's intentions. The horse itself parodies the gifts that rulers exchanged in diplomatic encounters. Later in the *Enéas*, as well as in both classical and other medieval texts, horses appear in the inventories of items exchanged. But in the Trojan War, a conflict that begins and ends in broken trust, the horse turns out to be a secret, ultimate weapon. In the carnage that follows, the slaughter of women and children signals once more a violation of the ideals of the Peace of God. In stealing Helen, Paris throws the diplomatic order into chaos, and his crime tragically returns against Troy, her ruling family, and her people.

As a refugee from Troy, Enéas—who lacks the epithet *pius* that offers some reassurance about his Virgilian counterpart—labors under suspicions that he embodies his country's legacy of deception and violated trust. Whenever Enéas arrives at a foreign court, such as Didone's or Latinus's, people initially or eventually doubt his motives, his claims about himself and his mission, and his promises. When he tells Didone that he must leave, for example, she accuses him of treason and bad faith:

> So much evil has my kind service met,
> The lovely visit, the kind hospitality
> That I offered you in Carthage! . . .
> You were plotting an evil deed
> And an extraordinary treason . . .
> The Trojan keeps bad faith.

> [Tant mar ai fait le bel servise,
> le bel sejor, le bel ostage
> que ge vos ai fait en Cartage. . . .
> molt pensastes grant felonie
> et merveillose traïson . . .
> Malvaise fei ont Troïan!] (1688–90, 1692–93, 1700)

As Didone sees it, Aeneas comes to Carthage as another Sinon, a faux refugee happy to receive her hospitality while plotting against her. His nationality alone should have warned her about his deceptive nature: "Malvaise fei ont Troïan!"

Enéas's treatment of Didone reinforces the stigma he carries as a Trojan whose word cannot be trusted. The moment Latinus's queen learns that her husband has promised their daughter Lavine to Enéas, she reminds him of past Trojan perfidy, beginning with Paris's theft of Helen and ending with Enéas's betrayal of Didone. Whereas Latinus insists that marrying into the Trojan's famous lineage will make the Latin lineage renowned, she argues that the Trojan lineage is nothing but a legacy of crime:

> Don't even think it
> For the Trojan has no faith
> Nor does he hold to any law . . .
> I will never trust their lineage.

> [Nel te penser!
> que Troïen n'ont point de fei,
> ne il ne tienent nule lei . . .
> Ge ne crerrai ja lor ligniee.] (3288–90, 3298)

When the queen later learns that her daughter has fallen in love with Enéas, she repeats the charges of Trojan infidelity and lawlessness, but with greater emphasis on the Trojan's amorous unreliability: "No woman has gotten anything good from him [Onkes femme n'ot bien de lui]" (8581). In addition to the usual catalogue of crimes, the queen tells Lavine that Enéas is a sodomite: "He doesn't want to hunt the doe, / Much more he loves the flesh of the buck [il ne vuelt pas bische chacier, / molt par aime char de maslon]" (8570–71). From the queen's perspective, sodomy is perhaps the Trojans' greatest infidelity, a betrayal of nature itself. Their not-so-secret preference for Ganymedes over women makes them singularly unsuited for marriage alliances. They are incapable of loving any woman and therefore fulfilling even the most basic nuptial obligations, an accusation that the poet's extensive treatment of the Nisus and Euryalus episode reinforces.

Although the poet does not paint Enéas as the deliberate traitor who appears in Benoît de Sainte-Maure and other texts derived from Dares and Dictys, his destiny continually situates him in narratives of betrayal.[58] While this dynamic figures in Virgil, the *Enéas* poet accentuates it by deleting almost all the *Aeneid*'s divine machinery, especially the scenes in which the gods discuss and debate the future.[59] We learn about Enéas's subservience to *fatum* either through his own words or through passing narrative remarks. The characters are at an even greater epistemological disadvantage. Although the poet tells his audience that the gods ordered Enéas's departure from Carthage, for example, neither Didone nor the other characters within the poem have any reason to believe him. Didone, Turnus, and Latinus's queen all dismiss Enéas's claims about his Italian destiny as mere Trojan fabrication.

The poet's attitude toward interdynastic marriage, and indeed to diplomacy in general, seems as bleak as Wace's in the *Brut*. Every major character ends up either deliberately or inadvertently violating a prior trust. In this world where vows are retracted, pledges broken, and every diplomatic gift turns out to be a Trojan horse bringing war rather than peace, little hope exists for lasting agreements. The rapidity with which Latinus reneges on his promises to Turnus and offers everything instead to Enéas would defy credibility if it were not a fact of common diplomatic experience in premodern Europe. The episode's contemporary relevance, and even possible topicality, makes the narrative's significance to the history of diplomacy all the more readable. The *Roman d'Enéas*, more than Wace's *Brutus*, challenged the classical myths and sacramental theologies that exalted marriage treaties as the basis of Christian concord. From the perspective of almost everyone in the poem, diplomatic overtures were covers for ulterior designs, and all settlements were binding only until one of the signatories withdrew from them in the pursuit of more advantageous alliances.

But just when almost all the major characters join in predicting further Trojan breaches of trust, a Dido-like betrayal of Latinus, and nuptial misery for Lavine, the poem ends on a happy note. Up to this point, Ovidian perspectives from the *Heroïdes* and the *Ars amatoria* have undercut the Virgilian portrait of *pius Aeneas* working in accordance with destiny. But once the final love plot begins, Ovidian rhetoric transforms Enéas and Lavine into stereotypes of mutually devoted lovers.[60] The poet details how Lavine falls in love with Enéas when she sees him from her window, endures sleepless nights of longing, suffers the vicissitudes of hope and despair, and tries to conceal her love from everyone around her. Enéas suffers similar tortures after he falls in love with her. Finally, when Lavine orders a soldier to fire an arrow at him containing a secret missive, they know their feelings are mutual.

By falling in love with each other, Enéas and Lavine restore the possibility of lasting diplomatic relations. Because they give their hearts to each other alone, their marriage transcends political convenience. They love each other above and beyond whatever is required by Enéas's destiny and Latinus's paternal authority. Even though Latinus gives Lavine to Enéas in one sense, the lovers give themselves to each other in ways that conform to the new canonical expectations of consent—the same consent that Urban argued would prevent abandonment, fornication, and adultery. One manuscript of the poem even includes an expanded ending in which Enéas sends a ring—one with no prior history—to Lavine with a profession of his love. When she receives it, she tells his singularly trustworthy messenger that she accepts his master as her husband:

> Then Lavine said, "Now there is nothing more to do,
> I so submit myself to my lord,
> I know well that his great loyalty
> Will not let him think or do
> Anything cruel to me."

> [Or ni a plus dit lors Lavine,
> a mon segnor tante mencline
> bien sai que sa graut layauté
> ne li laisseroit cruauté
> penser ne faire contre moi.][61]

Lavine's consent breaks the spell of the Trojan past. Against predictions to the contrary, she knows that she will suffer no cruelty at Enéas's hands. In marked contrast to Virgil's silent heroine, she gives herself to her beloved with a free and open heart. As the poem concludes, their faithful, unwavering love for each other underwrites long-deferred peace and concord throughout the realm: "And they lived in goodly peace the rest of their days, without the fret and trouble of war [et vesquirent en bonne pais / tant com de lor jors i ot mais / sanz anui sanz destor de guerre]."⁶²

Although the author does include notes that counter the seeming perfection of this final marriage, the love of Aeneas and Lavinia did, however, serve as a model for later French and Anglo-Norman literature. As the genre developed, it dismantled the *Enéas's* concluding reconciliation between private desire, formal consent, and diplomatic expedience. As Patricia Ingham has noted with respect to the Arthurian romances: "Women are powerful in these texts, and their desires are important. They constitute repetitive obstacles to communitarian wholeness."⁶³ One romance after another recounts the story of rulers wanting to marry their children, typically a daughter, into a foreign dynasty against their wishes. Often such marriages threaten to separate young people who truly love each other, and, as if in direct response to Urban's pronouncements, they often end in adultery. Tristan and Iseult are one example among many. Although most Arthurian texts do not focus on Guinevere and Arthur's marriage, Guinevere's infidelity generally conforms to the pattern. Peggy McCracken has attributed this preoccupation with adultery to anxieties about dynastic succession.⁶⁴ But the possibility of a queen's adultery posed a parallel threat to relations between her dynasties of origin and marriage. If it were ever to happen, it would be a diplomatic catastrophe.

One of the earliest Arthurian romances, Chrétien de Troyes's *Cligès*, transforms the usual story of flight from a loveless interdynastic marriage into the fantasy of a new diplomatic order in which young love establishes its own lines of diplomatic alliance. As a two-generation story of interlocking British, German, and Greek marriages, *Cligès* intervened in the discourse of western-Byzantine relations at a period of especially heightened intensity. The Crusades began with the emperor Alexios I Komnenos's request for western aid to ward off the Seljuq Turks. But once the Crusaders arrived in the East, their relations with the Byzantines were often fraught. One diplomatic disaster followed the other. The Franks, for example, blamed the alleged treachery of Emperor Manuel I Komnenos for the disastrous Second Crusade (1145–1149), the campaign that most immediately preceded Chrétien's writing in the mid-1170s. Sharon Kinoshita has argued that in *Cligès*, the Greek heroes recuperate that bitter memory in the interests of King Arthur, an imaginary western leader, through their cunning use of disguise on the battlefield.⁶⁵ According to Kinoshita, the poem's depiction of Byzantine princes who travel to Arthur's court so that they might be schooled in chivalry reverses a westward-moving *translatio imperii* and *translatio studii* that dated back to Virgil and treated western Europe as a derived, belated culture. In Chrétien's fantasy, by contrast, the West has clear moral and military advantages over the East.

I want to build on Kinoshita's insights by focusing on the romance's projection of an imaginary diplomatic society, founded on a new kind of marriage, that promises to overcome the mutual doubts and suspicions that prevented a more effective alliance between the West and Byzantium. *Cligès* traces the abandonment of an older, tyrannical marriage regime associated with the Virgilian past in favor of a more emotionally generous diplomatic culture associated with Britain. The stakes in the game of state are high. Marriage diplomacy between western rulers and the Byzantines had always been difficult. As we have seen, northern rulers had been seeking an alliance with Byzantines since at least the reign of Charlemagne. The hope of such an alliance was usually elusive, since the Byzantines preferred to marry their fellow Greeks and often selected the imperial consort by means of an internal bride show. The Holy Roman Emperor Otto II's 972 marriage to Theophanu, the niece of John I Tzimiskes, was a rare exception.[66] Islamic and Norman expansion on the borders of the Byzantine Empire gradually eroded the preference for endogamous imperial matches. In 1140, for example, John II Komnenos sought an alliance with Conrad III, king of the Germans, as a counter to the Mediterranean ambitions of Roger II of Sicily. Conrad eventually married his sister-in-law Bertha of Sulzabach to John's son Manuel I. Manuel himself married several Byzantine princesses to western rulers and his son Alexios to one of Louis VII's daughters, Agnès of France. After Bertha's death, he married another "Frank," Maria of Antioch.[67]

But Manuel's attempts to stabilize eastern-western relations never dispelled the mutual distrust between Byzantium and the West. In *Cligès*, Chrétien implicitly links the failure to establish a stronger alliance to a problem in contemporary practice, the possibility that a woman's formal consent may mask hidden contempt for her chosen partner and love for someone else. In Chrétien's corrective fantasy, what finally unites the Arthurian, Holy Roman, and Byzantine empires is not high-level negotiation but lovers' determination.[68] Like the *Roman d'Enéas*, *Cligès* overturns Lavinia's silent willingness to marry Aeneas by introducing several female characters—Guinevere, Soredamors, Fenice, and Fenice's governess—whose words, perceptions, and sheer determination removed impediments to young love. In the first part of the romance, for example, Guinevere is the primary negotiator. When Alexander, the heir to the Greek imperial throne, arrives at Camelot in the hope of being knighted by Arthur, he falls in love with Arthur's niece Soredamors, who had previously committed the grave mistake of closing her heart to love. Soon Love avenges himself on her by making her fall passionately in love with Alexander. But the two are so paralyzed by their mutual timidity that neither gives the other a clue to his or her true feelings. At last Guinevere, a seasoned lover herself, brings the two parties into negotiation. After stressing the danger of denying their desires, she encourages them to speak their hearts. Alexander confesses his feelings for Soredamors, who in turn "did not refuse this gift" and revealed "her heart's desire . . . both by her speech and by her expressions [Qui cest presant pas ne refuse. / Le voloir de son cuer ancuse / Et par parole et par sanblant]" (2331–33).[69]

Chrétien's litotes in portraying Soredamors as one who "did not refuse" Alexander's gift of love understates not only her joy but also his own transformation of diplomatic convention. In many, if not most, twelfth-century marriage negotiations, the bride and groom were the last to know what was happening. Rulers and their representatives made decisions with an eye to political and economic advantage. Queens may have joined the conversation, although their exact role is hard to document. Kings and queens alike expected their children to consent to the marriage, since canon law now required it, but not to fall in love, and certainly not in the way that love figured in Ovid and in contemporary romance. *Cligès* turns this pattern upside down. Everything starts with the lovers and their feelings for each other. Guinevere, rather than the couple's relatives, helps things along with attention to their hearts rather than the political implications of the match. Finally, Chrétien mentions only in passing that Arthur and Soredamors's brother Gawain consented to the marriage, and he does so conspicuously after the couple voice their love for each other. The diplomatic rewards for this departure from twelfth-century practice could not have been higher. The marriage achieves what European dynasts had only dreamed of since the days of Jordanes, a union between a "barbarian" northern princess and the heir apparent to the Byzantine throne. In Chrétien's fantasy, the political rewards are more certain because they have come about through love rather than political ambition.

In the second part of the poem, a generation later, Alexander and Soredamors's son Cligès struggles to marry the woman he loves while living under a more conventional diplomatic order that has little regard for young people exchanged in interdynastic marriage. In a series of plot twists that includes the mistaken belief that Alexander died at sea, Cligès's younger brother Alis takes the imperial throne. When Alexander finally returns, he agrees that Alis can continue to rule on the conditions that he never marry and that Cligès will become emperor after him. After Alexander dies, however, Alis's self-serving advisers urge him to marry Fenice, the daughter of the Holy Roman Emperor, who "was very rich and very powerful [mout riches et mout puissanz]," standard reasons for an alliance in actual twelfth-century practice (2657). In contrast to the situation many years previously in Britain, politics proceed without regard for Fenice's affections. The German emperor breaks Fenice's previous betrothal to the Duke of Saxony without the slightest hesitation to pursue a more lucrative and influential match with Byzantium. The result is war aligning the imperial Greeks and Germans against the Saxons.

The shift from the first part of the romance to the second feels like a collapse from wonderful new diplomatic order into sordid quotidian diplomatic realities. Brothers usurp their brothers' thrones, emperors violate their agreements with their relatives, and fathers break their word to one suitor and marry their daughters to a new one with minimal respect for her wishes. Family pressures and expectations compel consent, and love drops out of diplomacy.

Yet in the end, love saves the day, after significant complications. As part of the entourage commissioned to bring Fenice to her new life in Constantinople, Cligès falls in love with her. When Fenice, like Sordamors before her, "returns his present," she finds herself caught in a bind between her father's expectations and her own feelings, one that prevents her from consenting to an arranged marriage with an open heart: "But by force she must have / One who cannot please her / And therefore she is anguished and distraught [Mes par force avoir li estuet / Celui, qui pleisir ne li puet, / S'an est angoisseuse et destroite]" (2987–88). In the first part of the poem, love established its own alliances between nations. Here ambitions for powerful alliances set out to constrain love "par force." Whereas the first diplomatic regime developed in harmony with the new canonical emphasis on consent, the "force" now exerted by dynastic interests defies it.

Fenice's anguish might serve as a prelude to Urban II's direst predictions. As scholars like McCracken have noted, recurrent allusions to the story of Tristan and Iseult underscore the risk of infidelity: the triangle between Fenice, Cligès, and his uncle Alis exactly reproduces that between Iseult, Tristan, and his uncle Mark.[70] Under the traditional diplomatic regime—dominated by male rulers and driven by political fear and ambition—there would be no alternative. Fenice would either resign herself to a life with "one who cannot please her" or succumb to adultery. But as in the first part of the poem, Chrétien imagines a compelling alternative. Taking on Guinevere's role, Fenice's governess Thessala provides her with a magic potion that deceives Alis into dreaming he has made love to her when she secretly preserves her virginity for Cligès. Yet another tricky servant builds a secret retreat for Cligès and Fenice to consummate their relationship. When they are caught, King

Arthur comes to their aid with a vast army. But the war never happens: Alis dies and Cligès claims his rightful throne with the woman he loves and who loves him in return.

Cligès's denouement indulges a fantasy of what would have been the most powerful diplomatic alliance in Europe. The Angevins had certainly done well on the marriage market, and Manuel I had succeeded in marrying his children to western aristocrats and royals. But nobody had been able to unite Britain, the Holy Roman Empire, and the Byzantine Empire in such a close marital alliance. For Chrétien, the reason for that inability lay with the dynamics of consent. Even with canonists stressing nuptial consent and with queens and powerful noblewomen sometimes influencing decisions about their children's fates, powerful men remained the architects of European interdynastic marriages. The question of their children's feelings rarely entered into deliberation. If they had, Chrétien seems to imply, alliances might have been founded on a greater degree of trust, and subsequent Crusades might have met with greater success.

Cligès's final lines retreat from the new European order the poet imagined to male-dominated quotidian diplomatic practice:

> Since then, there has not been an emperor
> Who did not fear that his wife
> Would trick him,
> When he heard recounted
> How Fenice deceived Alis. . . .
> And so for this reason, she
> Is guarded as in a prison in Constantinople
> Regardless of who the empress might be
> However rich or however noble. . . .
>
> Nor [may she] have with her any male
> Who was not castrated in childhood.
>
> [Qu'ains puis n'i ot anpereor,
> N'eüst de sa fame peor,
> Qu'ele le deüst decevoir,
> Së il oï ramantevoir,
> Comant Fenice Alis deçut. . . .
> Por quoi aussi come an prison
> Est gardee an Costantinoble,
> Ja n'iert tant riche ne tant noble,
> L'anpererriz, ques qu'ele soit; . . .

Ne ja avuec li n'avra masle
Que ne soit chastrez an anfance.] (6765–69, 6772–75, 6780–81)

Instead of upholding the story of Cligès and Fenice as a blueprint for a better diplomatic future, this coda reduces it to a myth about the origins of the harem. Chrétien distances himself from the new diplomatic order he seemed to endorse, one orchestrated by ingenious women and underwritten by true affections of royal lovers. The whole fantasy of a marital alliance binding all of Europe, from Camelot to Constantinople, suddenly evaporates in emphatic orientalism: the only lasting result of Fenice's resistance to marriage "par force" is the Byzantine fear of cuckoldry.

Chrétien's retreat from his own fantasy stands as a synecdoche for the romance genre in general. Arguably more than any other writing in the Middle Ages, the romances pressed the canonist's insistence on consent to a radical conclusion: How could nobles consent to marry someone whom they did not love? The adulterous queens who people romance exposed the limits and dangers of a diplomatic order that reduced canonical consent to merely formal assent, often conceded under pressure. Less tragic works like *Cligès* inverted the political order so that diplomacy followed erotic imperative rather than dynastic ambition. Yet the genre was so contrafactual and implausible that its more radical views of gender, family authority, and diplomatic agency could be dismissed as part of the fiction. However much romances might challenge Lavinia's silence, the chronicles—with their own silent or relatively silent women—commanded the greater claim to truth. Though packed with invented speeches and even invented brides, the diplomatic culture they evoked was closer to contemporary European experience.

Consent was not the only concept at stake in the tension between Latin chronicle and vernacular romance. So was the ideal of marriage as a means of achieving peace among Christians. Dudo of Saint-Quentin hailed the marriage between the French princess Gisela and Rollo the Viking as a reenactment of Lavinia's to Aeneas, a union between two peoples that advances justice and peace throughout a troubled realm. Other chroniclers followed suit, and an idealization of women as natural intercessors developed over the course of the later Middle Ages. Despite their emphasis on women's agency, however, the romances did not emphasize peacemaking per se as a central issue. They certainly dealt with questions of trust and women's role in alliances. But women are just as likely to be the focus or, in the case of the adulterous Guinevere, the cause of wars.

The romances went only so far in their critique of medieval society. The aristocracy that patronized writers like Wace and Chrétien was still a military caste, one that benefited from opportunities for fighting and plundering.

Aristocratic women had something to gain from greater attention to their feelings. Younger women and widows might profit from a right to nuptial consent. But pacifism per se threatened the aristocracy's raison d'être. The Church had to work hard to enforce the most basic limitations on warfare covered under the Peace and Truce of God. The Church itself was inconsistent in its more pacifistic discourses, as it was in so many things. Ranking churchmen and abbesses typically came from royal and aristocratic families who had reaped the benefits of war. The ideal of a completely pacified *res publica christiana* was primarily a product of the Crusades. Even then, popes and bishops coupled their calls for peace among Christians with injunctions to kill Muslims. Their focus was more on redirecting aristocratic belligerence than on pacifying it. Even in *Cligès*, climactic alliance is probably not an end in itself. Written between the Second and Third Crusades and filled with references to kings and emperors projecting huge armies across the sea, it tacitly offers its new diplomatic vision as the basis for a renewed Crusade.

By the High Middle Ages, the ideals that would support the great marriage treaties of the fifteenth and sixteenth century were in place. At least officially, the Church urged peace among Christians first to fight the Crusades and then to ward off Muslim encroachments into the heart of Europe. Royal brides emerged as peacemakers, joining the Virgin Mary in their ministry of reconciliation. But however ardently some clerics may have embraced this discourse, other powerful forces undercut it. Through the end of the Middle Ages, the primary threat came from monarchs and aristocrats who valued their children's marriages primarily as a route to greater land, power, and influence. They resented the Church for inserting itself into their affairs through a growing body of canon law and measures like the Peace and Truce of God. The Crusades may have marked a kind of rapprochement between churchmen and aristocrats, although one that was never fully stable. Eventually, other forces would arise to thwart the dream of a *Pax Christiana* presided over by a vast network of intermarried royal and aristocratic families, including new religious divisions, the increasing clout of merchants and professionals whose wealth derived from sources other than land, new competitions between dynastic interests and emerging national interests, and new media that expanded diplomatic literacy to sectors of the population demanding greater influence on foreign policy. These new forces will be the focus of my next chapters.

❧ PART TWO

Wanings

✍ CHAPTER 4

Marriage Diplomacy, Print, and the Reformation

In theory, we should be in a better position to understand the end of European marriage diplomacy than its remote, post-Roman beginnings. An abundance of well-preserved and catalogued diplomatic correspondence dates from the late fifteenth century. We can trace a public response to major diplomatic events, including marriages of state, from the sixteenth century. But even in this better-documented period, the symptoms and trajectory of a decline prove elusive. In the twenty-first century, marrying commoners is now a regular practice among royalty in the few remaining European kingdoms. One could argue that these marriages still have some political, or more broadly cultural, significance within their respective countries. But there could be no surer sign such marriages play an insignificant role in international politics than the prevalence of marrying commoners.

Marriage still retained some diplomatic significance as late as the nineteenth century. Leopold I of Belgium, for example, famously married members of his Saxe-Coburg and Gotha family into royal houses from Great Britain to Russia. In the European West, however, foreign relations had become the concern primarily of ministers of state and not of hereditary monarchs. Leopold's marriages were arguably less about politics per se than about cultivating his family's social prestige. In the century of Metternich, Palmerston, and Bismarck, nobody looked to marriage to maintain the peace of Europe.[1] Foreign consorts certainly had an impact on culture: the great Victorian reform movements, for example, owed much to Prince Albert's patronage and his commitment to German liberal ideals. But nobody expected foreign wives to broker treaties. When women like the empress Elisabeth or the tsarina Alexandra tried to influence foreign affairs, powerful parties within the state condemned them.[2] Gone were the days when Margaret of Austria and Louise of Savoy hammered out the 1529 Treaty of Cambrai.

The rest of this book examines the political, cultural, and societal preconditions for this devaluation. This chapter focuses on changes in religion and the dissemination of diplomatic literacy to an expanding political nation whose interests diverged from those of ruling dynasts. To some extent these developments merely amplified instabilities that had been present from the beginning. Even at their apogee, interdynastic marriages often fell short of their exaltation as a means of establishing peace. As I argue in the first section, for example, diplomats and heads of state availed themselves of several marriage treaties in their efforts to end the 1337–1453 Hundred Years War. But these efforts ultimately failed, and the war ended only with France's decisive victory over England. Recollections of these diplomatic disasters haunted subsequent negotiations, including the greatest marriage treaty of the sixteenth century, the 1559 Peace of Cateau-Cambrésis, which I examine in the next section.

Cateau-Cambrésis stands as a watershed in the history of interdynastic marriage. Although it harked back to the marriage treaties of the late Middle Ages, its divergent implementations within its three signatory realms—Spain, France, and England—revealed shifts in the organization of western monarchies that diminished the traditional roles of queenly intercession. By occasioning the first major outpouring of printed poems on affairs of state, it also signaled the ascendancy of the printing press as an instrument of diplomatic significance. These 1559 poems fully supported the treaty's official self-presentation as the dawn of a new era of peace. But by the time Elizabeth I was considering marriage to the brother of the French king twenty years later, the press had become a vehicle for opposing marriage treaties that allegedly threatened increasingly important political sectors within individual kingdoms. The combination of major religious divisions with the power of the press to organize national opinion made marriages of state volatile undertakings by the century's close.

Late Medieval Diplomatic Society and Its Discontents

The history of something as complex and varied as marriage diplomacy does not always lend itself to a clear-cut narrative of residual, dominant, and emergent discourses. Nor does it develop through a series of catastrophic changes. As we saw in part one, the Christian meaning of marriage developed over the centuries, from the earliest stories of wives converting pagan husbands to a later exaltation of brides as types of the Virgin Mary reconciling their families of birth and origin. Both its political function and its cultural meaning shifted in relationship to changes in theology, canon law, and literary genre. But many things also remained constant. Regardless of what later identities might be imputed to them, for example, royal brides were first and foremost agents of dynastic continuity. They were expected to bear the next heir to the throne and, if possible, other children who could strengthen the dynasty through their own marriages or their placement in important monastic and ecclesiastic positions. The significance of these marriages could also vary with respect to geography. In northern Europe, marriage still played a role in religious conversion as late as the tenth century, long after the rest of the continent had accepted Trinitarian Christianity as the basis of diplomatic society. Even the temperaments of individual brides and grooms could affect the politics and the cultural meaning of a marriage. Some kings, for example, were less open to their wives' intercessory influences than others, regardless of the Marian tributes paid to them by poets and preachers.

During the later Middle Ages, interdynastic marriages formed and renewed some of the longest-lasting European alliances. The Auld Alliance between Scotland and France, for example, began as a defense pact between John Balliol and Philip IV against Edward I.[3] They sealed the treaty with an agreement that Philip's niece Jeanne de Valois would marry John's son Edward Balliol. Although that marriage did not take place, many other Franco-Scottish ones did that created a reliable defense against English ambitions during and after the Hundred Years War. James I married his eldest daughter, Margaret, to Charles VII's eldest son, the future Louis XI. When James died, his son James II asked for Charles to arrange marriages for him and his unmarried siblings. Charles was happy to oblige, and when French princes of the blood were not available, he married the Scottish royalty into aristocratic families with close French ties.[4] James II himself, for example, married Mary of Guelders, the niece of Charles's cousin Philip of Burgundy. With the exception of Louis XI, every French monarch renewed the general defensive terms of the alliance between 1295 and the mid-sixteenth century. The alliance played a major—some historians would argue a decisive—role in fending off a total English victory in the Hundred Years War. Some of the most prominent marriages of all took place in the alliance's final century, with James V marrying Mary of Guise and their daughter Mary, Queen of Scots, marrying the future Francis II. That final union of the French and Scottish crowns was an ultimate nightmare for Elizabeth I and her Privy Council, especially since Mary was also the heir apparent to the English throne.

The Auld Alliance entailed far more than just a military pact. Over the centuries, it became a densely intersected subset within the larger European diplomatic society sustained by trade, population exchanges, and the development of important Franco-Scottish families like the Stuarts of Aubigny, the Moneypennys, the Lyles, the Vernons, and the Greys, who owned land on both sides of the Channel. Scottish soldiers who fought with the French in the Hundred Years War settled in Touraine, Berry, and Poitou.[5] Scottish clerics and humanists studied in France and brought back a taste for French letters and French arts. Almost every major writer of the Scottish Renaissance spent time in France. George Buchanan, for example, spent much of his life in France, where he studied at the University of Paris and tutored the young Michel de Montaigne. By the time he wrote his Neo-Latin *Epithalamium* honoring Mary Stuart's wedding to the Dauphin, its ostensible grounding in French humanism complemented its hyperbolic assertion of a Franco-Scottish alliance dating back to Charlemagne:

> That same Charles
> Joined the Scots in a treaty,
> A treaty, which neither Mars with sword,
> Nor foul sedition can dissolve,
> Or the mad desire of mastery,
> Nor the passing of the ages, nor any other force,
> And beyond that, a more venerable treaty holding fast
> By its own chains. . . .
> Your wife gives you this dowry,
> A faithful people joined to yours for so many ages by an alliance treaty.

> [Carolus idem
> . . . conjunxit foedere Scotos:
> Foedere, quod neque Mars ferro, nec turbida possit
> Solvere seditio, aut dominandi insana cupido,
> Nec series aevi, nec vis ulla altera, praeter
> Sanctius et vinclis foedus propioribus arctans. . . .
> Hanc tibi dat conjux dotem, tot secula fidam
> Conjunctamque tuis Sociali foedere gentem.][6]

Mary, who embodied the Auld Alliance, had spent most of her life in France, and the Holyrood Palace to which she eventually returned resembled palaces in northern France rather than in late Plantagenet and Tudor England. The architects who built Kildrummy and Bothwell castles based them too on French design.[7] French queens like Marie of Guise patronized both French and Scottish artists. These numerous and varied ties linking the two countries made the alliance all the stronger.

Generations of intermarriage created tight bonds between other ruling families. The Hapsburgs, for example, intermarried with the sovereigns of Poland, Bavaria, and Spain.[8] Numerous marriages linked the Iberian rulers of Castile, Portugal, and Aragon. Geographically far-flung marriages, like that between France's Henry I and Anne of Kiev in 1051, were more often the stuff of romance than actual experience. Closer neighbors were more likely to share common interests and values, particularly after the 1054 schism between the eastern and western churches. They could also come to one another's defense quickly in times of invasion. Neighboring dynasties, moreover, were often the ones most in need of the pacification that intermarriage promised, since they were prone to recurring border clashes. During the sixteenth and seventeenth centuries, for example, the royal families of France and Spain intermarried almost as frequently as they went to war against each other. This was a particularly fractious relationship, since the dynasties shared two borders, one in the Pyrenees and one between northern France and the Spanish Netherlands, and had conflicting claims to the same territories in Italy. As we will see in this and subsequent chapters, attempts to stabilize Franco-Spanish relations eventually lowered the level of confidence with which rulers and statesmen turned to marriage in the hope of resolving interdynastic rivalry.

The success of treaties like those linking France and Scotland during the late Middle Ages, however, should not blind us to the many marriage treaties that failed to produce such strong alliances. There were problems with marriage diplomacy from the start. The caprices of biology—infertility, illegitimate birth, and early death—meant that the marriage that ended one war might inadvertently trigger future ones by creating multiple claimants to a throne. The most famous instance of this was the outbreak of the 1337–1453 Hundred Years War. In attempting to resolve a recurrent quarrel over Gascony, Edward I of England and Philip IV of France agreed twice, in 1299 and 1303, on a marriage between their children, Isabelle of France and the future Edward II. When the marriage took place in 1308, nobody expected any confusion over the French succession, since Isabelle had three brothers. But after the death of Philip in 1314, the three brothers died in quick succession without a viable heir. Philip's first son, Louis X, died two years later, in 1316. Louis's wife was four months pregnant, so her son—John "the Posthumous"—became king at birth. But John the Posthumous died only five days later and left the crown to his uncle, Philip IV's second son, Philip V. Philip V died five years later without an heir. His brother Charles IV, Philip IV's third son, became king. Like his brothers, Charles died young, after only a six-year reign.[9]

From 1314 to 1328, five French kings had reigned and died without leaving a biological heir. Their passing triggered the most intractable succession dispute of the Middle Ages. From an English perspective, there was a clear solution: Edward III, the English grandson of Philip IV, was next in hereditary line and ought to become king. But the French nobility did not like the idea of an Englishman becoming their king and crowned instead Philip IV's nephew Philip of Valois.[10] The ensuing Hundred Years War foregrounded a problem inherent in all interdynastic marriages: the difficulty of maintaining a balance between local and cosmopolitan interests. In theory, the subordination of local ambitions to the greater good of Christendom was always the purpose of such marriages. But in practice, nobles and even members of a monarch's own family sometimes objected to a marriage treaty in part or in its entirety. Perhaps they resisted a settlement because it required them to give up lands that they had acquired in battle. Or perhaps they wanted to keep on fighting in the hope of greater plunder or from a desire to avenge old injuries. After marriages took place, such disaffected nobles often focused discontent on foreign consorts, or on the retinues that accompanied them from their families of origin. Nothing stirred xenophobic hostilities faster than the prospect of a foreign succession resulting from a prior interdynastic marriage. Whenever such successions occurred, local aristocrats argued that they would suffer under a foreign heir insufficiently versed in local laws and customs.

Local resistance to foreign brides and their offspring was as evident in the final decades of the Hundred Years War as it was at the beginning. It undermined several attempts to resolve the conflict through traditional interdynastic marriage. For centuries, writers decried the 1420 Treaty of Troyes, for example, as a foreign attempt to subvert the French nation.[11] The treaty came to stand for everything that was allegedly wrong with marriage diplomacy, and especially with its elevation of foreign dynasts to powerful positions within a realm. It dated from one of the French king Charles VI's bouts of insanity, when his German wife, Isabeau of Bavaria, served as regent. Isabeau was an accomplished diplomat who had previously negotiated a Franco-Florentine alliance, managed the bitter rivalry between the Burgundians and the Orléanists with some success, and was invited by Jean Gerson of the University of Paris to help settle the Western Schism. But in the distorted account of her life that became canonical throughout Europe,

Isabeau was a self-serving adulteress who took advantage of her husband's illness to betray his country to the English. The treaty, one of the shortest in diplomatic history, declared that Charles and Isabeau were now the "father" and "mother" of Henry V, who was to marry their daughter and inherit the French throne upon Charles's death. The treaty merely confirmed the prior disinheritance of Charles VI's biological son, the future Charles VII, after he murdered John the Fearless of Burgundy.

The Treaty of Troyes was a bold gesture, one that might have brought peace to Europe if Henry V had not predeceased his "father" Charles VI by a few weeks in 1422 and left the French and English thrones to his nine-month-old son, Henry VI. The disinherited Dauphin eventually saw his chance, claimed to be the true heir to the throne, and capitalized on long-standing resentment of the English occupation. As scholars have often noted, the Dauphin's struggle to win his throne and drive out the English with the assistance of Joan of Arc helped to shape an emerging French national self-consciousness.[12] That proto-nationalism cankered all future interpretations of Isabeau of Bavaria, the events leading up to the Treaty of Troyes, and, more generally, the integrity of foreign consorts. Joan herself, at least according to the testimony of two witnesses at her trial, may have initiated what became a later commonplace contrast between Isabeau's betrayal of the French people and her own efforts to redeem them from occupation when she quoted an old prophecy: "Nonne alias dictum fuit quod Francia per mulierem desolaretur, et postea per virginem restaurari debebat?" (Was it not once said that France would be desolated by a woman and afterwards should be restored by a virgin?).[13] Whether or not Joan said this, the quotation exposes the contrasts on which a later nationalist myth would rest, one that demonized interdynastic marriage as a betrayal of French interests. It opposes a good woman to a bad one, a French shepherd's daughter to the daughter of a German duke, and a virgin to a royal wife whose own marriage and the marriage she arranged for her daughter brought the country to ruin.

Nationalist stirrings also colored the English response to diplomatic marriage. Although England profited from the Treaty of Troyes, its chroniclers soon decried the 1444 Treaty of Tours between Henry VI and Charles VII. To seal the peace between France and England, the treaty married Henry to a distant relative of Charles VII, Margaret of Anjou. In exchange for the impoverished and dowerless Margaret, Henry agreed to surrender the county of Maine to France.[14] The treaty did not hold for long, and the French soon brought the Hundred Years War to an end by reclaiming all the English lands in northern France. The disaster precipitated the Wars of the Roses, which pitted Henry, Margaret, and their Lancastrian partisans against

Richard, Duke of York, and his allies. Yorkist propaganda accused Margaret of betraying the English to the French, much as the Dauphin's propaganda had accused Isabeau of betraying the French a generation earlier. In 1450 Parliament imprisoned and impeached the primary architect of the treaty, William de la Pole, first Duke of Suffolk. He would have been executed, but Henry intervened and banished him. His enemies murdered him on his way to France.[15]

Suffolk's impeachment was one of the earliest instances of a representative body punishing a minister for what it perceived to be a corrupt foreign policy. It would not be the last. Especially in England, interdynastic marriages became recurrent occasions for showdowns between the Crown and Parliaments presenting themselves as the guardian of English liberties. From the once canonical medieval perspective, the value of such marriages lay in their ability to encourage kings and their ranking subjects alike to reconcile their interests with those of their former enemies. In the process, they created a common diplomatic society and fostered the development of transnational ways of thinking. But as diplomats like William de la Pole discovered, powerful sectors of their respective political nations sometimes resented that transnationalism. The more they thought of themselves as English or French, the more they saw their monarchs, born of foreign mothers and married to foreign wives, as unreliable representatives of their values.

Interdynastic Marriage and the Peace of Cateau-Cambrésis

Three intertwined developments heightened the proto-nationalist turn against marriage diplomacy: the invention of print in the mid-fifteenth century, the religious divisions of the sixteenth century, and the centralization of the monarchical state at the expense of national aristocracies. Of all these factors, the Reformation was the most cataclysmic. From the Germanic conversions of the sixth century, interdynastic marriage was bound up with the history of the Catholic Church. Catholic brides expanded the frontiers of Christendom by bringing their faith, their priests, and their bishops to their new homes. The church reforms of the eleventh and twelfth century in turn heightened the prestige of marriage diplomacy by insisting on the permanent, sacramental nature of marriage. The twelfth-century cult of the Virgin provided yet further honors for interdynastic brides as types of the Virgin Mary working to reconcile their families of birth and origin. Almost overnight, the Protestant Reformation demolished the theological and ecclesiastical superstructures that had supported marriage diplomacy for over four

centuries. It also provided new vocabularies and new argumentative strategies that could be used by opponents of marriages negotiated across the confessional divide: Protestants "of the hotter sort" famously challenged their
Protestant sovereigns' freedom to marry Catholic consorts. Staunch Catholics continued to hail brides as types of the Virgin Mary, but only when they
married fellow Catholics. In one of the great ironies of diplomatic history,
it was easier to marry your Catholic daughter to a pagan in sixth-century
France than to marry her to a Protestant in the sixteenth century.

As scholars have often noted, the printing press accelerated the pace of
both the Protestant and Catholic Reformations.[16] Presses churned out vernacular Bibles, sermons, devotional guides, and books of religious controversy that gave Christian Europeans new identities as Lutherans, Calvinists,
Anabaptists, and Counter-Reformation Catholics. The presses also gave
them something else: access to new ideas about current events, history, political geography, and foreign relations.[17] Readers of Hall, Holinshed, Cam-
den, Belleforest, Haillan, Vignier, Hotman, and Popolinière acquired new,
potentially subversive interpretations of European politics. This rapid dissemination of diplomatic literacy to the professional and merchant classes in
France and especially England eventually changed the course of diplomatic
practice. This happened most rapidly in England, where religious and commercial interests began to limit the freedom of monarchs to form alliances
that might promote their dynastic interests or even the peace of Europe. For
their subjects who were most committed to the Reformation, a group that
included some of the wealthiest and most powerful people in the realm,
peace mattered less than the preservation of the Gospel. They feared few
things more than the possibility of their sovereign's marriage to a Catholic
consort. The women once hailed as types of the Virgin Mary soon stood to
be condemned as latter-day Jezebels.

Protestantism's hostility to the traditional theological arguments for marriage diplomacy explains many of the challenges facing foreign brides north
of the Alps. But even among Catholic powers, the sixteenth century witnessed new political developments that strengthened individual states at the
expense of the old dynastic system. Catholic royalty still intermarried with
the familiar appeals to the peace of Christendom. But first, most noticeably
in Spain and later in France, royal brides saw their authority diminish as part
of a long-term process of royal centralization. In one country after another,
Renaissance monarchs appropriated powers once wielded by provincial aristocrats and sometimes by the Church and vested them instead in a bureaucracy that often included men of lower birth. This process reached its earliest
and fullest development in England, where its potentially cataclysmic impact

on royal wives became rapidly apparent during the reign of Henry VIII. But the French monarchy had been on the rise since the end of the Hundred Years War. One sign of its growing strength was Gallicanism, the unusually high degree of control exerted by the Crown over the French Church after the 1438 Pragmatic Sanction of Bourges.[18] French queens still enjoyed vast powers as regents during royal minorities. But during the lives of their husbands, they were often overshadowed by ministers, ranking aristocrats, and even royal mistresses. The Spanish monarchy too had been growing in power, wealth, and prestige ever since Ferdinand and Isabel's union of the crowns of Aragon and Castile. A hereditary queen of Castile in her own right, Isabel was one of the most powerful rulers in Europe. But subsequent queens consort often had little influence on affairs of state.

The first major marriage treaty to register the combined effects of royal centralization, the Reformation, and the printing press was the 1559 Peace of Cateau-Cambrésis between France, Spain, and England. In its general outlines, the Treaty of Cateau-Cambrésis looked like a typical late medieval settlement.[19] Everyone assumed that at least one dynastic marriage would seal it. France's Henry II was set to marry his sister, Marguerite de France, to Emmanuel Philibert, Duke of Savoy, a first cousin and partisan of Philip II. Henry also seemed ready to marry his eldest daughter, Elisabeth de Valois, to Philip's son Don Carlos. But when Philip's wife, Mary I of England, died one month after the negotiations began, plans changed. Philip was so concerned about the risks of losing the Hapsburg-Tudor alliance that he seriously considered marrying his wife's sister and successor, Elizabeth I. When Elizabeth turned him down, he married Elisabeth de Valois himself. Both marriages took place in July 1559, at the insistence of the dying Henry II.

Like numerous other medieval and Renaissance treaties, this interdynastic union purported to merge bloodlines in a commitment to international peace. Yet the treaty's implementation in all three signatory realms—Spain, France, and England—suggests anything but a determination to subject the interests of individual regimes to the common European good. Each monarch blocked aspects of the traditional practice of interdynastic marriage that might have compromised his or her authority at home. In Spain, Philip gradually turned away from the bold marriage policies that had made the Hapsburgs the most powerful dynasty in Europe. With the exception of his five-year marriage to Mary, Philip's marriages were less dynastically and territorially ambitious than those of his Hapsburg and Burgundian ancestors. His 1559 marriage to Elisabeth de Valois stabilized his claim to Italy, but because of the Salic law banning women from the French throne, it did not give the Hapsburgs any place in the French succession. In contrast to many other queens consort, and in pointed contrast to her mother, Catherine de' Medici, Elisabeth played a minor role in Spanish politics. A few sources suggest that Philip discussed politics with her, but he did not treat her as a significant consultant, and she did not pressure him to take particular courses of action. What seems to have mattered most in limiting Elisabeth's diplomatic career was Philip's reluctance to share power with anyone, even his wife.[20]

Beginning with Philip II, a principle of *intra*dynastic marriage competed with the more familiar *inter*dynastic patterns that had first brought the family to the zenith of its power. After Elisabeth died, Philip obtained a papal dispensation to marry his niece Anne of Austria, an act that provoked William of Orange's cracks about Philip's incestuous proclivities.[21] The stigma haunted the Spanish Hapsburgs for several generations. Philip II's son Philip III married a Hapsburg cousin. His grandson Philip IV first married a French princess, but after her death married yet another Hapsburg niece. In the context of other shifts in dynastic marriage taking place in western Europe, this endogamous tendency suggests a centralization of royal authority that rested uneasily beside the older medieval practice of marrying across dynastic lines.

The marriage politics of Henry II of France registered a similar turn toward consolidating the sovereign state. In France, that consolidation was badly needed. The French monarchy was arguably weaker than the Spanish one, and the French aristocracy more powerful and fractious.[22] By 1559, French nobles not only disagreed over the conduct of the war and the terms and even the desirability of a settlement but also had begun to divide along religious lines. In the final years of the Italian wars, several prominent aristocrats had converted to Protestantism. In the meantime, Duke Francis II of Guise and his brother Charles, cardinal of Lorraine, aggressively defended the Catholic Church. These divisions led to the civil wars that erupted shortly after Henry II's death.

Even before Henry embraced the two marriages at the heart of the Cateau-Cambrésis settlement, he resorted to marriage as a way of bringing these different aristocratic factions into a tighter alliance with the Crown. On April 24, 1558, his heir apparent, Francis, married Mary Stuart, the reigning queen of Scotland, but just as important, the niece of the powerful Guise brothers. On January 19, 1559, Henry married his second daughter, Claude, to Charles III, Duke of Lorraine. The marriage successfully moved the young duke, whose lands Henry had occupied since 1552, from the Hapsburg to the Valois sphere of influence. It helped to transform a possible enemy into a secure ally. On May 3, 1559, Henry counterbalanced the Mary Stuart match with one between his illegitimate daughter Diane and François de Montmorency, the son of the Guises' implacable enemy Anne, Duc de Montmorency and constable of France. By the time the Valois-Hapsburg marriages were to take place in July, Henry had established marriage alliances between his children and some of the most powerful and fractious members of the French aristocracy.

In this year-long project of marrying his children into as much of the French aristocracy as possible, Henry sought to contain faction and enhance royal authority. In retrospect, there seems to have been a kind of nuptial excess in Henry's efforts to pacify a highly militarized aristocracy through intertwining marriage alliances. Their sheer number in the last years of his reign suggests the strain of adapting an old diplomatic strategy—typically used to expand territories and to resolve interdynastic conflict—to the new ends of building and consolidating the modern state.

In England, the relationship between state building and marriage diplomacy took an even more radical turn, one that set a precedent for the eventual abandonment of marriage as peacemaking. When Elizabeth came to the throne in 1558, she found herself in a historically rare position as an unmarried queen regnant. The generally early age of royal betrothals and marriages meant that few twenty-five-year-old princesses were still unmarried. Like her sister, Mary I, Elizabeth was free to choose a husband largely because her bastardization had limited her desirability on the European marriage market when she was still young. The stigma was never quite erased, but once Elizabeth became queen, she enjoyed a power to select a husband or to remain single that few queens had ever known.[23]

Elizabeth first exercised that power in the context of Cateau-Cambrésis. The moment Mary died in November 1558, Philip II considered marrying Elizabeth to preserve the Tudor-Hapsburg alliance. When his ambassador broached the subject with Elizabeth, she hedged. At first she argued religious differences and her conviction that the pope had no power to let her marry her sister's husband. But by late February she became more emphatic. Instead of just refusing Philip, she said that she did not want to marry anyone. In a memorandum enumerating her reasons for not marrying Philip, the Spanish ambassador placed her general distaste for marriage first: "She had no desire to marry, as she had intimated from the first day." The next point then followed logically: "That she quite understood that this marriage would be advantageous to her honour and the preservation of both States, but that these ends could be attained by the maintenance of the good friendship with your Majesty, above all seeing the obligations she was under to maintain it, as she well knew."[24] Taken together, the first two points move

from an expression of personal distaste—"she had no desire to marry"—
to a boldly original insistence that good diplomatic ends might be achieved
without interdynastic marriage. This is quite a thing to say to a Hapsburg,
the family whose success in negotiating such marriages was second to none.
Philip was not happy about it, and he doubted that she had no intention of
marrying.[25]

In not marrying, Elizabeth moved toward a more abstract foreign policy
shielded against the accidents of biology and family psychodynamics: delayed
onset of menstruation, the uncertainties of pregnancy and childbirth, and
the notorious suddenness of death in early modern Europe. What brought
countries together was not the outward and physical assurance of a shared
progeny but a spirit of honest trust and agreement to work together toward
common ends. Such a policy was potentially more secure than one founded
on interdynastic marriage, but as Philip worried, it was also potentially less
secure. Elizabeth's language is richly vague with respect to what modern
diplomatic theorists would call the matter of sanction: the conditions that
guarantee an agreement's observance by both parties. Her exchange with
Philip exposes the contingency of fundamental assumptions about interstate
relations. Confidence in the old system of marital alliances was starting to
wane, but no fully developed, abstract system of international law stood to
replace it.

Elizabeth's approach to marriage proved to be the most forward-looking of
those undertaken by the three peacemaking monarchs of Cateau-Cambrésis.
In strikingly different ways, Philip II and Henry II revised interdynastic marriage to strengthen their control over hierarchical relations within their
realms. While Philip diminished the influence held by other foreign brides
over both foreign and domestic affairs, Henry attempted to gain the loyalty
and submission of powerful aristocrats by marrying them to his children.
By not marrying at all, Elizabeth escaped the foreign influence that Philip
worked to avoid. To that extent, Elizabeth came closer than either Philip
or Henry to achieving the independence that would become a hallmark of
Westphalian sovereignty. Embracing a more abstract basis for international
negotiations, however, eventually threatened to sever sovereignty itself from
the body of the hereditary monarch. While anticipating one aspect of Westphalian sovereignty, Elizabeth diminished her personal ability to achieve
the other: the ordering of hierarchical relations within her territories. In
order to understand how Elizabeth's highly original turn on the traditions
of interdynastic marriage reinvested sovereignty in the abstraction of the
nation, we need to consider the role of print in Cateau-Cambrésis and its
politico-cultural afterlife.

Print and Peacemaking

Accounts of modernization on both sides of the Channel have attributed to print an extraordinary degree of influence over one aspect of the Westphalian state, the establishment, preservation, and transformation of hierarchical relations within territorial boundaries. Historians of Britain, for example, have often treated the transition from manuscript to print as inherently democratizing: Protestantism, print, and popular sovereignty converge as markers of modernity.[26] French historians have described the development of a "republic of letters" as an important step toward the French Revolution.[27]

The contribution of print to the other aspect of the Westphalian state, its distinction from other sovereign entities, is equally significant. In abetting the rise of what Timothy Hampton has called a "literary nationhood" grounded in the vernacular, print accelerated an understanding of the world as an assembly of independent states distinguished by discrete cultures and forms of law.[28] While the role of print in Westphalian sovereignty was enormous, however, it was not inevitable. Once again, the Treaty of Cateau-Cambrésis—crafted just at the moment when older diplomatic ideals were yielding to the pressures of the Reformation, shifting commercial interests, and the acquisition of New World empires—signals the contingency of what has often been seen as a necessary link between print and the modern state system. Cateau-Cambrésis occasioned an explosion of celebratory poetry. Hailing the double marriages between Valois and Hapsburg as the beginning of a pan-European peace, these poems look back to the medieval notion of a *res publica christiana* as the basis of all diplomatic exchange. They call on the former belligerents to subsume their national identities as Frenchmen and Spaniards in a higher vocation as European Christians.

Scholars have recognized the forty or so volumes of verse commemorating Cateau-Cambrésis as France's first major outpouring of *printed* poems on affairs of state. This was arguably the first such printing event in Europe. Nothing similar happened in Spain or in England, the other parties to the negotiations. Since many of these poems are epithalamia, they pay extravagant tribute to the two couples whose marriages underwrote the Hapsburg-Valois alliance:

> The shepherdess of honor, who was led
> To the bonds of marriage by chaste Hymen
> Is that Elisabeth, of honor incomparable,
> Daughter of the doughty Shepherd, Ruler of the Gauls,
> Vowed to the Spaniard, who bathes all France and Spain in consolation.

[La Bergere d'honeur, qui a este menee
Au lien conjugal par le chaste Hymenee,
C'est ceste Elisabeth, d'incomparable honeur,
Fille du fort Berger des Gaules gouverneur,
Vouee à l'Hespagnol, dont en soulas se bagne
Universellement & la France & l'Hespagne.][29]

The beauteous day has come, when the heavenly favor abounds,
That Marguerite, sister of the greatest king in the world,
Will be joined in a knot divinely laced,
By mutual love of holy matrimony
To the Prince so valiant among all those of Europe
That Mars might single him out from among his band.

[Le beau jour est venu, ou l'heur du ciel abonde,
Que MARGUERITE seur du plus grand Roy du monde,
Sera jointe d'un neud divinement estraint,
Par l'amour mutuel du mariage saint
Au Prince autant vaillant entre ceux de l'Europe,
Que Mars pourroit choisir au milieu de sa trope.][30]

A universal transformation flows from the double Hapsburg-Valois marriages. The soldier worthy to serve in Mars's own company has now become a groom submitting to the higher power "of holy matrimony." Royal brides, Henry II's sister and eldest daughter, have brought consolation to the lands ravaged by wars between their fathers, brothers, and husbands.

The poems and commendatory addresses, written in both Latin and French, come from a remarkably diverse group of French writers: Pléiadistes like Du Bellay, Ronsard, Baïf, and Belleau; those closely attached to Ronsard and to the Pléiade circle like Guillaume des Autels, Marc-Claude de Buttet, Jean Le Gendre, and Jacques Grévin; the poet and royal historiographer François de Belleforest; and poets like the classical translator and allegorist François Habert, who did not embrace Pléiadic innovations. Several of the extant poems were written by individuals who wrote nothing else that has survived and are known to posterity only by their single contribution to what was clearly a nationwide explosion of epithalamia.[31]

The poets not only differed in literary tastes, training, and channels of patronage. They also represented the full range of religious opinion that characterized a country on the brink of civil war. Grévin, for example, was a Calvinist whose friendship with the committed Catholic Ronsard would end with the outbreak of civil war. The Savoyard poet Marc-Claude de Buttet was the son of a Genevan Calvinist mother. While he seems to have spent his life in communion with Rome, he clearly had reformed sympathies and remembered certain Protestant communities in his will. He and Grévin were both clients of Marguerite de France, who, like her aunt Marguerite de Navarre and several other Valois women, had a reputation for protecting dissenters.

Despite such differences, however, Catholics and Protestants, champions of the Valois monarchy and clients of individual nobles, Parisians and provincials, adopted a common Virgilian idiom to celebrate the possibility of a pan-European peace. As Hélène Fernandez has noted, the poetry occasioned by Cateau-Cambrésis demonstrates a thematic and stylistic uniformity which masks the conflicts that characterized French political life in the late 1550s.[32] The poems are remarkably similar in tone, attitude, argument, imagery, general effect, and underlying ideology. Many are pastoral eclogues in which shepherds rejoice that the war that ravaged their fields and disrupted their lives has ended. Although some of the poets, like Baïf, were gifted Hellenists, the dominant influence is Virgil, especially the Virgil of the First and Fourth *Eclogues*. In one poem after another, two shepherds meet, remark how war has ravaged the countryside, and rejoice in the prospect of peace.

In thinking about the *Eclogues'* impact on early modern writing, critics have focused on them primarily as Virgil's response to Octavian's arbitrary government, of his decision to reward his veterans with confiscated land. But the poets of Cateau-Cambrésis recognized something in the *Eclogues* that twenty-first-century readers often forget: Virgil's collection stands as one of western literature's most poignant expressions of the desire for peace. After a half century of war, the poets of Cateau-Cambrésis embraced Virgilian pastoral as the perfect medium for expressing their gratitude for the apparent cessation of hostilities. The *Eclogues* appealed to them because the repose they achieved in the face of ongoing division foregrounded the delicate balance of interests that attends all acts of peacemaking, on both domestic and international levels. Poets like Ronsard and Du Bellay did not see in Virgil's characteristic *otium* the mind-deadened utopia that results from suppressing dissident opinion. They embraced it instead as a testimony to virtuosic diplomacy.

The architects of Cateau-Cambrésis not only had to reconcile the conflicting demands of France, Spain, and to a lesser extent, England, but also had to forge a settlement on which different sectors within those countries' ruling classes might agree. As we have seen, this was particularly difficult for the French, since many aristocrats wanted to keep fighting. The poets of Cateau-Cambrésis depended on these same French aristocrats for patronage, and their interests were just as conflicted. For over fifty years, the proliferation of print had coincided with and reinforced France's war against the Hapsburgs. *Rhétoriquers* like Jean Lemaire de Belges, André de la Vigne, and Pierre Gringoire had trumpeted the claims of Charles VIII and Louis XII to Italy in the opening years of the Italian wars that started in 1494. During the reigns of Francis I and Henry II, an increasingly printed body of poetry exalted individual aristocrats who distinguished themselves in battle.[33] The same poets who rejoiced over the Peace of Cateau-Cambrésis had made their careers writing war poetry. Belleau, for example, served under the Duke of Guise, a hawk who did not want to lose a family claim to land in Italy. Antoine de Baïf and Du Bellay also wrote tributes to the Duke of Guise, and Ronsard composed a poem for the duke's brother, the cardinal of Lorraine.

Such poetry was insistently bellicose. In the summer of 1558, Ronsard wrote a stirring *Exhortation au Camp du Roy pour Bien Combattre le Jour de la Bataille* urging soldiers to avenge the French defeat at Saint Quentin:

> God, who now champions the French
> Will punish the Spaniard for his presumption
> And turn back on him the unfortunate fate
> That undid our army before the walls of Saint Quentin.

> [Dieu, qui tient maintenant le party de la France,
> Punira l'Espagnol de son outrecuydance,
> Et renvoyra sur luy le malheureux destin,
> Qui defit nostre armée aux murs de Sainct Quentin.][34]

In Ronsard's hierarchical vision, the common soldiers draw their valor from their aristocratic leadership, whose heroism in turn manifests the ancient virtues of their race:

> You, the greatest Lords, show yourselves diligent
> Setting yourselves and all your men well in order,
> So that the noble virtue of your race
> Might not be tarnished in this warlike honor,
> But as great Lords and the first of blood,
> In defiance of death, hold the first rank,
> And by your virtue (which cannot be brought down)
> Show your soldiers combat's way.

> [Vous, les plus grans Seigneurs, montrez vous diligens
> A renger bien en ordre & vous & tous vos gens,
> Que la noble vertu de vostre race antique
> Ne soit point demantie en cest honneur bellique,
> Mais comme grans Seigneurs & les premiers du sang,
> En defiant la mort, tenez le premier rang,

Et par vostre vertu (qu'on ne sçaurait abattre)
Montrez à vos soldas le chemin de combattre.] (A.ii.v)

A passage like this captures the heroic ethos that drove the Italian wars for half a century. The defeat of Spain is a matter of blood, honor, being and serving in the first rank, and the defiance of death. There is no national interest apart from the interests of a warlike aristocracy zealous for honor and Italian lands. The aristocrats are bound by honor to fight, and their men are bound to follow by the sheer charisma of their betters.

The speed with which the poets changed from military tributes to pastoral epithalamia measures the complexities of both internal French politics and the patronage system that underwrote artistic production in the mid-sixteenth century. In supporting the peace with Spain, they created a new role for aristocrats bred up to constant warfare and for themselves as poets by turning to Virgilian pastoral. But that solution entailed a striking change in the terms of Virgil's Renaissance canonization. The *cursus* outlined in the opening lines of the *Aeneid* as it appeared in sixteenth-century editions mapped out an artistic career that complemented the warrior ethos of the Valois courts. Like Virgil before him, the aspiring poet began his career by writing pastorals, but as he matured, he abandoned them for the martial themes of epic. The prioritization of epic reinforced an association of aristocratic honor and poetic maturity with military might.

In positing epic as the most mature and exalted form of poetic labor, Virgil also appeared to suggest that poetry's highest expression was bound up with violence. A heroic society seemed to be one in a perpetual state of war. The pseudo-Virgilian lines appended to the opening of the *Aeneid* in most Renaissance editions linked poetic progress not just to a shift in genre but to a decisive turn from peace to war:

I am the one who once measured songs on the slender reed
And having left the woods, compelled the neighboring fields
To obey the farmer, however eager,
A work welcome to farmers, and now the bristling arms of Mars
I sing, and the man . . .

[Ille ego qui quondam gracili modulatus avena
Carmina et egressus silvis vicina coegi,
Ut quamvis avido parerent arva colono,
Gratum opus agricolis, at nunc horrentia Martis—
Arma virumque cano . . .][35]

The poet surrenders the idyllic setting of pastoral in the second line, which already sounds a note of violence in its evocation of georgic labor as compulsion. The farmer eagerly, or even greedily, anticipating his harvest introduces a further note of strife that crescendos dramatically in line four with the bristling arms of Mars.

Nobody believes anymore that Virgil wrote these lines. The *Aeneid* honors its heroes' military prowess, but as readers have recognized not only in modern times but also in antiquity and during the Renaissance, it also exposes the terrible costs of war both to the individual and to society at large. Virgil offers his own metanarrative of generic development in the story of the Arcadian prince Pallas, who allies himself with Aeneas only to be killed in battle. The suffering his loss brings to his father, Evander, and more generally to the Arcadian people measures the transition from pastoral to epic in pathetic and even tragic terms. Within the *Aeneid*'s overarching narrative, war is emphatically not the end of the story. Although Virgil did not complete the poem, it projects a resolution of the Trojan-Latin conflict in the interdynastic marriage between Aeneas and Lavinia. That marriage in turn provides a mythic basis for that *Pax Augustana* that follows the victory of Actium. The *Aeneid* holds out to its readers and later imitators both a complex and an ambivalent portrayal of war and the hope for a lasting peace.

Since Virgil never described the peaceful union between the Latins and Trojans that followed Aeneas's marriage to Lavinia, we will never know what kind of poetry he may have written for a postwar society. But this was the aesthetic challenge that faced the poets of Cateau-Cambrésis. Most of them were explicitly self-conscious of their need to image a fourth stage in the Virgilian *cursus*, one that would suit the new imaginative space opened by the interdynastic marriages between the houses of Hapsburg and Valois. In general, they advocate a reconstituted, post-bellum mode of pastoral or georgic when soldiers returned from battle to resume their lives as herdsmen and farmers.

In part an imitation of Virgil's First *Eclogue*, Habert's *Eglogue pastorale* typifies the self-consciousness with which these poets imagine a post-epic world achieved by marriage diplomacy. When the shepherd Janot meets his friend Herbat—an obvious acronym for the poet himself—piping peacefully beneath the elms, he expresses his surprise:

> I am really shocked, gentle Shepherd Herbat,
> To see you happy, and frolicking
> Under these green elms, while in the shade
> Your herd and mine are looking for pasture.

[Je suis tout esbahi, (gentil pasteur Herbat)
De te voir resjouy, & prendre ton esbat
Dessoubs ces verds ormeaux, ce pendant qu'en l'ombrage
Ton troupeau & le mien cherche son pasturage.] (A.ii)

The *otium* that Herbat enjoys strikes Janot as out of character. Instead of listening to "poétiques chants" and nightingales, Herbat usually sat in silence or sang of war: "Car ta Muse plus tost se tenoit en silence, / Ou bien elle chantois de Mars la violence" (For your Muse rather kept silent, or instead sang the violence of Mars [A.ii]). But as Herbat explains, "the Celestial Pan, the King and God of Shepherds [la céleste Pan, Roy & Dieu des Bergers]," has ended the wars by bringing the former enemies together in "divine and everlasting concord [perpetualle & divine concorde]." More specifically, that great shepherd, Henry, so noble and magnificent ("Ce grand Berger, Henry, tant noble & magnifique"), has married his daughter to the Spanish shepherd, son of a powerful emperor ("Le Berger Hespagnon, fils d'un fort Empereur" [A.ii verso]). Like Tityrus in Virgil's First *Eclogue*, who hails the "young god" Octavian for endowing him with his peaceful life beneath the spreading birch tree, Herbat pays tribute to Henry II for the tranquility he now enjoys under the green elms of France.

In gratitude to his patron, Herbat recalls how the wars disrupted the shepherds' simple lives:

> The greatest shepherds were envenomed . . .
> So that in lieu of cultivating the plowman's fields,
> All their hearts were set on taking iron in hand,
> Instead of the usurped shepherd's crook,
> The sword was naked to splatter human blood . . .
> Instead of the *musette* agreeable to shepherds,
> The trumpet made a frightful cry,
> Instead of the sweet and tuneful flute,
> Falcons resounded, and odious cannons.

> [. . . les plus grands Bergers estoyent envenimez . . .
> Qu'au lieu de cultiver les champs de labourage,
> De prendre fer en main c'estoit tout leur courage
> Au de la houlete aux Pasteurs usurpee,
> Pour sang humain espandre, estoit nue l'espee . . .
> Au lieu de la musette aux Bergers acceptable,
> La trompete faisoit un cry espouventable,
> Au lieu de chalemeaux doux & melodieux,
> Resonnoyent fauconneaux, & canons odieux.] (A.ii.r)[36]

The passage not only describes the coming of war. Its conspicuous Virgilian and pseudo-Virgilian resonances also transform it into a critique of Renaissance views of the poetic career as a progression from pastoral to epic. Repeatedly echoing the lines commonly prefixed to the *Aeneid*, Habert treats the passage from the groves of pastoral through the georgic fields to the bristling arms of Mars not as a poet's triumphant Bildungsroman but as a tragedy. In this context of heightened Virgilian consciousness, the verb *envenimer* (to poison) that Habert uses to describe the shepherds' sudden desire to fight echoes Virgil's repeated descriptions of characters like Dido and Turnus who are infected with secret poisons that ultimately destroy them. Habert thus uses recollections of the *Aeneid*'s own depiction of war as madness and frenzy to disrupt the rota's conventional association of warfare with heroic maturity. War appears as a grotesque inversion of a benevolent natural order.

Now that the marriages of Cateau-Cambrésis have ended the war and restored the shepherds to their groves, however, a new pastoral order emerges, one colored by the prophecy of peace at the end of *Georgics* I:

> And surely the time will come, when within those bounds
> the farmer laboring the earth with the curved plow
> will come upon heavy javelins eaten away by the mangy rust
> or strike upon empty helmets with heavy mattocks,
> and gaze upon great bones exhumed from their sepulchers.
>
> [scilicet et tempus veniet, cum finibus illis
> agricola incurvo terram molitus aratro
> exesa inveniet scabra robigine pila,
> aut gravibus rastris galeas pulsabit inanis
> grandiaque effossis mirabitur ossa sepulchris.][37]

Virgil's georgic description of a farmer striking his plow on "heavy javelins eaten away by the mangy rust" or "empty helmets with heavy mattocks" resounds in one French poem after another. Belleau, for example, combined Virgil with Isaiah in urging the people of France to crown the heads of both Philip and Henry with laurels, so that peace might flourish:

> So that we might hope never to see war down here,
> that the standard might sprout in green branches,
> that the spider might weave its web in empty helmets,
> that the iron of bracers and of breastplates
> might be drawn into plowshares;

the cutlass, the pistol, and the mace might molder
in the scabbard hung on the wall.

[Donques affin que jamais n'esperions
Guerre ici bas, que l'estendart fleurisse
En vers rameaux, et que l'araigne ourdisse
Sa fine trame en vuides morions.
Que des brassardz, & du corps de cuirasse,
Le fer s'alonge en la pointe d'un soc,
Les coutelas, la pistolle et la masse,
Dans le foureau se moisissent au croc.]³⁸

Addressing the nobles of France, Ronsard prays for a renewal of georgic labor to mark the end of war:

That your morions might be laced forever on the hook,
and the spider, spinning with its feet, might weave its nets around them;
that the workers of honey might carry out their labors inside your
    shields,
Re-forge forever the point of your rapier,
The tip of your pike into a plowshare,
May your lances henceforth be steeped in the waves,
and your swords curved into sickles.

[Au croq vos morryons pour jamais soyent liez,
Autour desquelz l'araigne en fillant de ses piedz
Y ourdisse ses retz, & que dedans vos targes
Les ouvrieres du miel y deposent leurs charges:
Reforgez pour jamais le bout de vostre estoc,
Le bout de vostre pique en la pointe d'un soc,
Vos lances desormais en vouges soyent trempées
Et en faux desormais courbez moy vos espées.]³⁹

In relating the horrors of war, Virgil complained that war had driven the tillers away and "bent sickles into blades [curvae rigidum falces conflantur in ensem]" (1.508). In celebrating the peace of Cateau-Cambrésis, Ronsard borrows the line only to reverse it. Skillful diplomacy and two joyous marriages have brought an end to war and its devastation of the countryside. Helmets can be placed back in storage, lances thrown into the sea, and swords can be beaten back into sickles.

In creating a new Virgilian identity as pacifists, writers like Belleau, Ronsard, and Habert imply that the aristocracy must now usher in a new georgic age of peace. As part of the wedding process that Hymen leads in Roman fashion to the altar, Buttet's *Epithalame*, for example, includes a catalogue of every leading French nobleman. Beginning with the great princes of the blood, Bourbon and Condé, Buttet continues with the Duc de Lorraine, the Duc de Montpensier, the Duc de Nemours, the Duc de Montmorency, the Duc de Nevers, the Duc de Guise, and the Duc d'Aumale. He devotes a few lines to each one, often with explicit reference to their military prowess:

> There you see the Duc de Nevers, a valiant prince,
> And also Guise, the tough fighter,
> The great taker of towns, and Aumale who draws
> Behind him war, fury, and ire,
> Like a great thunderbolt bursting through the forests.

> [Là le Duc de Nevers, Prince meur & vaillant,
> On voit, & Guise aussi le rude bataillant,
> Le grand preneur de ville, & Aumale qui tire
> A la guerre après soy & la fureur & l'ire,
> Comme par les forests un grand foudre éclattant.] (B.ii verso)

The epithets and similes give the passage an unmistakably classical flavor, as if it were a catalogue of commanders from an ancient epic. But this is not a group of men about to fight a war. Despite their martial manner, they are attending a wedding. Although Buttet does not quite say it, one commander has prevailed, the Duc de Montmorency, who supported the peace negotiations against the strong objections of the Duc de Guise and his partisans:

> You see that great Constable also marching along,
> That Vulcan of the Peace, that great Montmorency,
> For whom France prepares a thousand laurels with olive,
> Honoring itself for such a wise head.

> [Ce Connestable grand on voit marcher aussi,
> Ce Vulcan de la paix, ce grant Mommorenci,
> A qui mille lauriers avec l'olive appreste
> La France, s'honorant d'une si sage teste.] (B.ii verso)

In the epic tradition on which Buttet so conspicuously draws, Vulcan furnishes the hero with the armor that allows him to prevail in battle over his enemies. But Buttet overturns that legacy by imaging Vulcan as a diplomat forging treaties. The hero now wears the olive, a tribute to his wisdom as a statesman and peacemaker, instead of laurels alone.

As a Savoyard client of the Duke of Savoy, who recovered his lands as part of the deal, Buttet was probably one of the most genuine supporters of the treaty. But he also comes closer than any of his peers to imagining how it might constrain the aristocracy's traditional military role. The noblemen he presents retain their martial bearing and all the honors they gained during the Italian wars. But in the world brought about by Montmorency's peacemaking, they are no longer active soldiers but groomsmen at a wedding honoring the very man whom once they fought. At least in the poem, the old epic energies subside in the wedding hymn of universal peace. These former soldiers are not yet the functionaries with whom Louis XIV would fill the halls of Versailles, but they have a place in the prehistory of that later development.

The poets celebrating Cateau-Cambrésis sometimes voice proleptic anxieties about the effects of a rapid demilitarization on their patrons. How long would those battle-tested soldiers be happy marching in wedding processions? Several of the poets propose a new Crusade as the perfect solution to the problem. Instead of fighting each other, French and Spanish troops could unite to liberate the Holy Land. There were many reasons for adopting this anachronistic vocabulary. Treating all Muslims as the common enemy of all Christendom, for example, glossed over the embarrassing fact that Henry II had informally allied himself with the Ottomans against Spain. More important, liberating Jerusalem recalled the High Middle Ages, when the aristocracy's military prestige was at its height. Above all, it recalled a point when diplomacy had a clear, emphatically Christian and pan-European purpose: the uniting of all Christendom as a *res publica christiana* in its struggles against the infidel. As anachronistic as the allusions to a renewed Crusade might have seemed in 1559, they nostalgized the exact period when interdynastic marriages had helped sovereigns put aside their individual interests in order to fight the infidel.

In the event, the potentially cloying amity achieved at Cateau-Cambrésis proved to be short-lived. The troubles that soon befell France make the presence of the First *Eclogue* in so many of these poems all the more poignant. Like Tityrus and Meliboeus, the country was to enjoy its pastoral joys beneath the spreading elms for only a short time. That provisionality extends to the place of these poems in the history of European print. Taken as a whole, these epithalamia mark a passing union between one of Europe's oldest diplomatic strategies, fostering peace though the interdynastic marriage of former belligerents, and the relatively new technology of print. Whatever the democratizing potential of print in the abstract, these poems reinforce the hierarchical basis of French society. While they may not have been commissioned by the king, they uphold the view that foreign policy is an absolute prerogative of the king and his closest advisers. Like Tityrus and Meliboeus, the French subject in these pastorals could not appear more passive in his grateful submission to the peace that descends from, in Habert's words, "Pan," that all-wise "god of shepherds [Dieu des Bergers]," Henry II (A.ii.v). This publication event does not, in other words, mark the emergence of anything like a public sphere in which the people who wrote, printed, circulated, and read this poetry might begin to imagine national interests detached from the dynastic interests of the king. Instead of voicing dissent or even independent interest, the poems proclaim their authors' gratitude for the king's paternalistic care of his subjects.

As later writers continued to reflect on Cateau-Cambrésis, however, their accounts of the treaty acquired an oppositional character that helped erode the dynastic basis of European diplomacy. Exactly twenty years after the Hapsburg-Valois marriages that sealed the treaty took place, recollections of Cateau-Cambrésis haunted the 1579–1581 negotiations of yet another Valois match, the notorious one proposed between the Duke of Anjou—the younger brother of France's Henry III—and Elizabeth I. Once again, the negotiations unfolded according to the traditional assumption that establishing a common royal lineage was the best way to ally realms. But this time, new technological and ideological forces combined to thwart the negotiations. In the process, some writers voiced radical interpretations both of hierarchical relations within the state and of the state's relationship to other states which would eventually transform diplomatic practice throughout western Europe.

The Anjou negotiations have figured so prominently in work on both Elizabethan history and literature by Mack P. Holt, Susan Doran, Natalie Mears, Ilona Bell, and numerous other scholars that I will not discuss them in detail here.[40] Instead, I want to think about the notorious backlash they provoked in an international perspective. That backlash constitutes an important chapter in the emergence of state-based sovereignty. It focused ostensibly on one particular marriage, but as an implicit—and sometimes explicit—refutation of the tributes to Cateau-Cambrésis, the outcry against Anjou suggested that reservations about interdynastic marriage had acquired a startling new dimension: they had gone public. In 1559, those reservations were intimated only in closed diplomatic correspondence or implied by changing arrangements within the marriages themselves, like the relative exclusion of Elisabeth de Valois from politics. By 1579, they were voiced by previously silent sectors of the English public in ways that potentially limited the freedom of sovereigns to contract the foreign marriages that had been the mainstay of dynastic diplomacy.

If the Anjou marriage had taken place, French and English writers alike might have produced a body of celebratory verse comparable to that which marked the ratification of Cateau-Cambrésis. But the marriage did not take place, and what we have instead are several works whose opposition to the match seems to suggest a more general negative sentiment. In one of the most notorious instances of a conflict between the Crown and something analogous to modern public opinion, John Stubbs lost his right hand for publishing his 1579 treatise *The discoverie of a gaping gulf whereinto England is like to be swallowed by another French mariage*. The circumstances of its publication continue to puzzle historians, who debate whether Stubbs was prompted to write the treatise by councilors opposed to the marriage or whether he voiced more widespread opinions. One thing is clear: *A Gaping Gulf* marked an unprecedented dissemination of sophisticated reflections on foreign affairs in a highly public medium. In condemning the Anjou negotiations, Stubbs developed a general argument against interdynastic marriage itself as a means of forging alliances between countries.

Drawing heavily on a historiography of the Hundred Years War popularized by chroniclers like Hall and the newly published 1577 Holinshed, Stubbs presented the long and troubled history of Anglo-French relations as a testimony to the troubles created by dynastic intermarriage. Henry I, for instance, committed a double folly in marrying his daughter Matilda to Geoffrey of Anjou and his sister Adela to Stephen of Blois. According to Stubbs, these interdynastic unions cost Matilda her kingdom and brought "civile miseries to the [English] people, who through the incertaintye of a governor, were in field and armes one agaynste another."[41] Even greater disasters came about through Henry II's marriage to Eleanor of Aquitaine, "whow through her owne wickednes and the freendes she made on the otherside, entertained many yeares an unnaturall warre betweene hir owne husbande and hys and her children" (C.4.r–v). Yet Henry was so committed to the principle of interdynastic marriage that even his tragic firsthand experience failed to prevent him from marrying his son Henry and betrothing his son Richard to two daughters of Louis VII, "which alliances proved such assurances to Henry the second as his last five or sixe yeeres were nothing but an unkinde stryfe" (C.4.v). Stubbs blames virtually every subsequent English disaster on a French marriage. Philip IV's daughter Isabelle brings down Edward II, and Richard II ends up betraying his own subjects under the influence of his second wife, yet another French Isabelle, and the "French companions, such as his wyfe brought" (C.4.v). Henry V's marriage to a French princess ultimately gained England nothing, and his son, Henry VI's, marriage to Margaret of Anjou cost him several French dominions and later his own throne.

As it turns out, the English were not the only ones who had suffered from interdynastic marriage. Stubbs attributes the miseries that gripped France since the death of Henry II to his foreign wife, the Italian heiress Catherine de' Medici. In the same way that women like Eleanor of Aquitaine and Margaret of Anjou contaminated the English monarchy, Catherine de' Medici allegedly contaminated the French one by exacerbating its hostility to the Reformation. From 1558 on, Catherine had used the marriages of her children to unite Catholic Europe in a monstrous conspiracy against the Gospel. Stubbs hails the triple alliance among France, Spain, and Savoy achieved at Cateau-Cambrésis as an early testimony to her diplomatic genius and to her ultimate ambition of eradicating Protestantism:

> For to begin with the mariage of her other daughter [Elisabeth de Valois] into Spayne, in the lyfe of her husband, what tyme a sister of hys [Marguerite de France] was maryed into Piemont, & so three greate princes linked in a threefold cord (as it were) by that alliaunce: all the world knoweth, that the capital capitulation and article of inprimis (as I may say) in that threefold mariage, was, against God and his annoynted. (unpaginated section after B.3)

In contrast to the poets of Cateau-Cambrésis, who hailed the treaty as ushering in a new Golden Age, Stubbs condemns it as a betrayal of the princes' individual sovereignty. The repeated emphasis on the threeness of "three greate princes linked in a threefold cord" makes Cateau-Cambrésis sound more like a diabolical spell, or a parody of the divine Trinity, than a treaty. Stubbs develops these suggestions of the diabolical in a grotesque image charging that Catherine herself is only "a body or tronk wherein the Pope moveth" (unpaginated section after B.3). Nor does Stubbs let his readers forget that Catherine's similar 1572 orchestration of her younger daughter Marguerite's marriage to the Protestant Henri de Navarre led directly to the massacre of Saint Bartholomew's Day. From Stubbs's perspective, marriage diplomacy was bound up with papal intrigue, diabolism, and the destruction of kingdoms.

Even more than the detested Valois, the greatest villains in Stubbs's view are the privy councilors, ambassadors, and other politicians who have encouraged the Anjou marriage. According to Stubbs, these "perswaders, as men having theyr eyes daseled wyth the golden sun," are so "over affectioned to thys match" that they have either overlooked or deliberately suppressed the objections that Stubbs raises (unpaginated section after C.4). Throughout the tract, he slights the knowledge and skills of the seasoned diplomat as irrelevant qualifications: "For what if some of these persuaders can talke a litle French: . . . think they for a little french in theyre tongues ende, to be so much set by? alas poore men, how vainely they gape at french promises, with losse of theyr Englishe possessions" (D.4.r.). The passage cuts to the heart of a diplomatic culture and practice that had embraced interdynastic marriage to forge alliances. Stubbs ridicules the mastery of foreign language and the ability to negotiate settlements on which treaties between nations typically depend. Humbler, less-educated subjects are presumably better guardians of English possessions because their monolingualism inoculates them against French seductions.

For centuries before the publication of *A Gaping Gulf*, dynastic interests had driven an English foreign policy characterized by almost constant fighting with France over territories associated with the old Angevin Empire. Fragile peace treaties, almost always sealed with an interdynastic marriage, punctuated decades of warfare. Even if such marriages failed to achieve a sustainable peace, they still strengthened the European dynastic system. Above all, they distinguished European royalty and high-ranking aristocrats from everybody else. At least since the time of Charlemagne, they created a pan-European ruling class in which heads of different states were more likely to be related to one another than to the people they ruled. This was part of the reason why English monarchs, who shared much of the governance of their realms with their Parliaments, zealously guarded the negotiations of their families' marriages as a key point of their prerogative. Interdynastic marriage was intimately connected to the mystery of royalty. Stubbs's tract threatened that mystery by suggesting that the queen ought to marry with the consent of Parliament. Urging her "not to conclude hyr mariage before she parle in parliament with hyr subiects," he casts her as a kind of parliamentary ward rather than an adult sovereign in her own right (E.1.r.). Her comfort for such a submission to Parliament will be the knowledge that her marriage "had their generall consent." The "whole land" can in turn comfort itself with the knowledge that her husband is someone by whom they are willing "in sort to be governed" (E.1.r.). In imagining the whole realm speaking in the first person, Stubbs goes beyond the question of passive consent to suggest that Parliament should actively *choose* the queen's husband: "I have chosen such a Lord as I dare put in trust with my Queene, for so much as it also is to be maried with her, and in sort to be governed by him that shal be her governor" (E.1.r.). Stubbs is quite direct in stating his reasons for this presumption: the queen's marriage will have such a direct impact on the realm that "it also is to be maried with her." On one level, the passage claims that the marriage will place the English people in a doubly subordinate position, governed by a queen who is herself governed by her husband. But on a deeper and even more subversive level, it places the queen in the most subordinate position as a bride yielded to her husband by the collective will of her people, who take on the de facto role of her guardian watching out for their common interests: "*I* have chosen such a Lord."

A Gaping Gulf anticipated Westphalia in its rejection of interdynastic marriages that compromise the sovereignty of individual states. In challenging the queen's prerogative, it even looked beyond Westphalia to something like the current state system, which since the later nineteenth century has privileged popular sovereignty as a mark of legitimate nationhood. To say that *A Gaping Gulf* anticipated these later formulations of sovereignty, of course, is not to argue that it fully articulated Westphalian doctrine. It was a product of its time and of particular polemic circumstances. Stubbs was an ardent Protestant, and nothing in his tract suggests that he was so committed to nonintervention in the abstract that he would have opposed England's fostering the Reformation in other countries. But in the face of an apparent Catholic attempt to interfere in England, he offers one of the period's strongest and most forward-looking defenses of England's independence from the rest of Europe. He also offers an incisive account of how arranged marriages between rival dynasties threatened that independence.

A Gaping Gulf was not the only revolutionary printing event triggered by the Anjou crisis. Scholars have long argued that Edmund Spenser's *Shepheardes Calender*, published in the same year and by the same printer as *A Gaping Gulf*, encoded a similarly hostile response to the negotiations. The *Calender* includes ecclesiastical satires of a distinctly Protestant character, for example, that distance Spenser from the *politiques* who were willing to tolerate Anjou's Catholicism.

While history would recall *A Gaping Gulf* as an outrageous attack on the queen's prerogative, however, generations of poets and scholars have honored *The Shepheardes Calender* as the first literary fruit of the Elizabethan Golden Age. Only in in the late twentieth century did critics like Paul McLane and David Norbrook begin stressing its oppositional character.[42] But in our growing emphasis on these oppositional aspects, critics have minimized the complexity of Spenser's response to Elizabeth, her ongoing marriage negotiations, and the shifting discourse of international relations. The poem transforms political opposition into formal ambivalence in ways that complement Elizabeth's own limited and ambivalent rejection of biologism as the grounds of peacemaking. *The Shepheardes Calender* and *A Gaping Gulf* issued from the same press, but they are not the same work. Instead of urging Elizabeth to reject Anjou, Spenser presents that rejection as a fait accompli in his tributes to her numinous, inviolable virginity. This strategy preserves the traditional hierarchies within the Elizabethan state. Spenser presents himself as an adoring subject rather than someone with the authority to advise the queen on the basis of his superior knowledge, wisdom, and piety. This tactic involved more than a clever evasion of the censors. Spenser located Elizabeth's virginity at the center of a growing myth of England's radical independence within an emerging state system.

In elevating Elizabeth's virginity to mythic status, Spenser reversed the representational patterns crafted by the poets of Cateau-Cambrésis. Throughout his earlier career, Spenser had been profoundly indebted to French poetry and even translated Du Bellay's *Antiquitez*. Throughout *The Shepheardes Calender*, he engages the same Virgilian subtexts that figured in the poetry of Cateau-Cambrésis: Tityrus and Meliboeus's colloquy in *Eclogue* I, the Golden Age prophecy of *Eclogue* IV, and the millenarian climax of *Georgics* I. But the future that he envisions is one in which England, rather than joining other nations in an era of pan-European peace sealed by an interdynastic marriage, stands apart from them in strikingly belligerent ways under the aegis of its Virgin Queen.

Whereas the poets of Cateau-Cambrésis revised the Virgilian *cursus* to admit a fourth phase of post-epic pastoral or reconstituted georgic, Spenser restores the original three-phase model in which epic stands as the national poet's crowning achievement. In a colloquy in the "October" Eclogue about the social function of poetry, an older shepherd named Piers counsels a younger one named Cuddye that it is time to abandon pastoral for the epic: "Turne thee to those, that weld the awful crowne, / To doubted Knights, whose woundlesse armour rusts, / And helmes unbruzed wexen dayly browne." The suggestion rallies Cuddye's spirits, at least for a few moments, and he confirms the source of the allusion to the opening lines of the Renaissance *Aeneid*: "Indeed the Romish *Tityrus* I heare . . . left his Oaten reede / . . . And eft did sing of warres and deadly drede." In embracing Virgil as a war poet, Piers and Cuddye repudiate the pacification of Virgil in French pastorals hailing the Peace of Cateau-Cambrésis. Piers's suggestion that it is time to rouse the knights whose "woundlesse armous rusts, / And helmes unbruzed wexen daly browne," for example, alludes to the same passage at the end of *Georgics* I that Ronsard and Belleau echoed in celebrating the achievement of a pan-European peace. In Spenser, Piers cites the topos only to invert it into a complaint against a long-standing peace. From his perspective, rusting armor and "helmes unbruzed" suggest indolence, a recession of martial vigor that needs to be stirred to action by a heroic poetry. Instead of honoring peace and imaging a post-bellum georgic society, the self-proclaimed English Virgil rouses the troops to war.[43]

Whereas the marriages of Elisabeth and Marguerite de Valois underwrote the reconstitution of pastoral and georgic in the poetry of Cateau-Cambrésis, Spenser organizes his reassertion of epic decorums around Elizabeth I's virginity. In the "October" Eclogue, he pairs her with the Earl of Leicester, a leader of the Protestant resistance against the Anjou marriage, as the proper subjects for poetry in the true, martial Virgilian tradition. The pairing rather heavy-handedly substitutes Leicester, a subject and a native Englishman, for the specter of an alien consort. As numerous scholars have noted, the allusion to Leicester could not have been more awkward. In 1579 Leicester had fallen to his lowest point ever in the queen's esteem. He had offended her both by his clandestine marriage to Laetitia Knollys and by his growing commitment to a Protestant internationalism that threatened to draw the country into war.

Like the poets of Cateau-Cambrésis, Spenser found himself in the awkward position of negotiating tensions between a monarch determined to forge an international alliance and a belligerent aristocratic faction that opposed it. Whereas the French poets tried to shift aristocratic sentiment toward the king's new alliance, Spenser endorsed the position of the Leicesterians in the hope of gaining their patronage. But he tried to reconcile the Leicesterians with their queen by exalting her virginity as the surest pledge of England's monadic independence from all foreign influences. This was a brilliant strategy, since it resonated with the language that Elizabeth herself had used in rejecting past suitors. It clearly distinguished him from Stubbs, who offended the queen by imagining her married to a suitor vetted and approved by Parliament. Spenser's Elizabeth is wonderfully independent, a royal virgin who submits to no one, either foreign suitors or matchmaking Parliaments.

Elizabeth's own drift toward an abstract basis for politics had its limits: she brooked no encroachment on her hereditary prerogatives. Spenser earned his reputation as her poet laureate by respecting those limits even while coming dangerously close to open criticism of her foreign policy. In the "Aprill" Eclogue, he implies his opposition to the Anjou match while extolling Elizabeth's hereditary authority: "For shee is *Syrinx* daughter without spotte, / Which *Pan* the shepheards God of her begot / . . . No mortall blemishe may her blotte."[44] Many of the Cateau-Cambrésis poems honor Elisabeth de Valois's descent from Henry II and Catherine de' Medici in similarly mythic terms. Spenser even calls Henry VIII "Pan," the same name that the French poets used for Henry II. In the French poems, Elisabeth de Valois inherits her virtues from her royal parents and will pass them on to her equally royal offspring. In Spenser's "Aprill," Elizabeth I similarly inherits her numinous chastity from her parents. But that is also where the similarity between Spenser and his French precursors ends. He endows Elizabeth Tudor with an aura of having been immaculately conceived, a concept that he conspicuously wrenches from its original Marian and Catholic context. As in the original theological scheme of things, Elizabeth's conception "without spotte" predicates a lifelong commitment to virginity: "No mortall blemishe may her blotte." The sovereign authority that Elizabeth inherits from her parents has become so closely linked to her personal chastity that she could not surrender the latter without diminishing the former. Like England itself, she stands sublimely, untouchably apart from her peers.

The movement from mortal to mythic and immaculate generation complements Elizabeth's own interest in the possibility of a more abstract basis for foreign relations. It joins the queen and her self-appointed laureate together in a commitment to regal authority freed from the past tradition of interdynastic marriage. Elisa-Elizabeth's exaltation among the encircling retinue of Muses, nymphs, and shepherdesses contrasts with *A Gaping Gulf's* vision of her humbly submitting herself to Parliament. It is royalist in the extreme, but also insistently isolationist. The shepherd-queen who will not even let a non-virgin into her presence prefigures by seventy years the monadic exaltation of the state as the basis of sovereignty.

The "Aprill" Eclogue marks a momentary response to one signal crisis in European marriage diplomacy. I conclude with it because its vision stands so perfectly poised between the tangled dynastic lines of the late Middle Ages and the monadic state that emerged from Westphalia. Its sheer tentativeness captures the complexity of its historical moment. At least within England, print had made possible the articulation of opinions that resisted the basic assumptions about international relations that negotiators had brought twenty years previously to Cateau-Cambrésis. These opinions did not have to be oppositional: monarchs themselves were starting to see the older diplomatic patterns as a threat to their own sovereign power within their borders. By 1581, Elizabeth effectively dropped any real interest in marrying Anjou. She fell into the role scripted by Spenser and other poets as the Virgin Queen, the "good virago" zealously guarding her nation from all foreign threats. Born of an English father and an equally English mother, she finally embraced a national identity that helped to bring a new international system into being.

CHAPTER 5

Shakespeare's Adumbrations of State-Based Diplomacy

In one important sense, the English Middle Ages ended on January 7, 1557, less than a year before negotiations began at Cateau-Cambrésis. On that day, the Duke of Guise defeated the English at Calais and reclaimed the city for the king of France.[1] Mary I famously proclaimed that the loss was her deathblow and told her subjects that if they opened up her corpse, they would find "Calais" inscribed on her heart.[2] English monarchs had claimed territory in France since the Norman Conquest, and they had claimed the French crown since 1328. Although English monarchs styled themselves kings and queens of France until 1800, the title became a romantic anachronism. Within a half century after Mary's death, English expansion shifted away from Europe to the Atlantic and Indian oceans.[3] Losing France was an important precondition for England's oceanic future, since it detached the country from the costly territorial wars that had shaped its foreign policy for centuries. Elizabeth's forty-five-year reign as a single English woman, one who rejected several foreign suitors, witnessed the first political and economic phases of this transformation. Shakespeare's theater reinforced it with a vision of England's new independence from an older European order and a profound critique of the marriage system on which it rested.

Scholars have given Shakespeare a pivotal role in their accounts of the emergence of modernity from its medieval antecedents. By identifying modernity with the consolidation of the nation-state, they often write as if English nation building took place entirely within England.[4] Doing so limits our understanding of what it means to be a nation and underestimates how nations exist as a consensus within the international community. Shakespeare himself wrote within a broadly European context. He adapted continental sources for most of his comedies and tragedies, and even in his English history plays, he often depicts medieval political life in terms of conflicts between England and France. The narrative of modernity that his plays enact ends with a clearly bounded English state, but it begins with radically different models of sovereignty that are neither nation-based, anglophone, or even insular. His history plays in particular invite us to interpret the emergence of modernity as a function less of the state's increasing internal coherence than of its changing relationship to Europe. In the process, Shakespeare associates the end of the Middle Ages with the waning of dynastic and diplomatic practices that united ruling houses despite a conspicuous disregard for the cultural and linguistic character of the territories they ruled. The plays discussed in this chapter, *King John* and *Henry V*, rank among the most diplomatically and historiographically self-conscious works of the Elizabethan period. They open up enough rifts between medieval and early modern diplomatic practice to remind us that there has not always been an England as such and that its political and cultural distinction from France is not an obvious truth but an ideologically loaded claim.

The nature of the new professional theater for which Shakespeare wrote carried his insights about history, sovereignty, diplomacy, and interdynastic marriage to a wider audience than even the most celebrated poet or pamphleteer might have reached. As many as three thousand people, many of them marginally literate, may have attended a single production.[5] Although the absence of documentable reception makes it impossible to estimate Shakespeare's original impact on popular consciousness, the plays offering some of his most negative assessments of marriage diplomacy have been especially popular during periods of heightened patriotism. *King John*, for example, was a favorite of the Victorians, who prided themselves on England's stability while much of Europe exploded in civil war and revolution. *Henry V* rose to prominence during the Second World War and in the following decade, when the country rebuilt its cultural infrastructures on an insistently nationalistic basis.[6]

Like Stubbs and Spenser before him, Shakespeare rested his patriotic tributes to England as a nation standing apart from other nations on suspicions of interdynastic marriage that generalized into a distaste for foreign alliances. The same French women whom Stubbs condemned for compromising

England's international position reappear in Shakespeare's English history plays: Eleanor of Aquitaine, who "through her owne wickednes ande the freendes she made on the otherside, entertained many yeares an unnaturall warre betweene hir owne husbande and hys and her children"; Margaret of Anjou, whose baleful influence led "to many miserable destructions of our English chevalry"; and Catherine of Valois, whose marriage to Henry V established a fragile double monarchy; its collapse triggered the Wars of the Roses.[7] Shakespeare focused on two moments of fraught Anglo-French dynastic entanglement. *King John* addresses the final years of the trans-Channel Angevin imperium, when English kings ruled larger portions of France in their joint capacities as dukes of Normandy; counts of Maine, Anjou, and Tours; and dukes of Aquitaine. Eleanor of Aquitaine, whose marriage to Henry II brought vast territories in southern France into Angevin hands, appears as a consummate Machiavel who murders her grandson in order to shore up her son King John's dubious claims to the English throne. The first and second tetralogies, by contrast, center on Anglo-French relations during the Hundred Years War, when English kings claimed not just French territory but the French crown itself by virtue of their descent from Isabelle, the ill-fated Edward II's French bride. With *Henry V*, Shakespeare uses the conspicuous artifice of the Elizabethan stage to expose marriage diplomacy as a comic, even absurdist fiction. Pressing beyond the Stubbsian concern with the alleged malice of French brides, he reflects more generally on the inadequacy of the practice to contain the mistrust, hatred, injustice, and inhumanity unleashed in war.

Losing France and Becoming England

King John, which dramatizes England's first major loss of French territory, can be read as Shakespeare's most complex commentary on his country's place in an emerging sixteenth-century European state system.[8] A major diplomatic revolution occurred in England's relationship with France during Elizabeth's reign. If Mary I was the last English monarch to hold land in France, Elizabeth I was the first to orchestrate a foreign policy without continental territorial ambitions.[9] Rather than being an enemy, France became a qualified ally against Hapsburg expansion in Europe and the Atlantic. Elizabeth achieved this cautious alliance without contracting the kind of interdynastic marriage that had served as the linchpin of European diplomacy since at least the tenth century. She certainly considered the possibility of such a marriage and, in the late 1570s, came close to marrying the Duke of Anjou. But in the end, she did not. The significance of her decision should not be underestimated. Rejecting a French marriage decisively removed England from the cycle of wars and treaties that, from a sixteenth-century perspective, compromised England's independence. Above all, it enabled the eventual emergence of a national foreign policy detached from dynastic interests and shielded against the vagaries of biology.

The cultural fallout over England's developing alliance with France and, more broadly, the shift from a dynastic to a state-based diplomacy surfaced strikingly on the English stage, where the new genre of the history play arose through revisionary recollections of the Middle Ages that commented implicitly on current events. One of the earliest plays in the genre, Shakespeare's 1 *Henry VI*, for example, is redolent of Francophobia in its burlesque treatments of Joan of Arc and of Henry's French consort, Margaret of Anjou, whose meddlings in English politics help trigger the Wars of the Roses.[10] As Linda Gregerson has noted, such plays drive home a clear propagandistic message, one fully consonant with the opposition to the Anjou match voiced by John Stubbs, Sir Philip Sidney, and Edmund Spenser.[11]

But this conspicuously Francophobic topicality marks only the surface of the plays' more important intervention in European diplomatic history. Like Stubbs's notorious *Gaping Gulf*, Spenser's poetry, and Holinshed's newly printed *Chronicles* on which they were based, the Elizabethan history plays redirected a discourse of foreign affairs once restricted to monarchs and their inner circle of advisers into a larger public arena. Traditionally, even Parliament avoided open discussion of the royal marriages that were the typical linchpins of medieval peace settlements. Elizabeth made it clear that she did not want her Parliaments discussing her marriage choices or questions about the succession. This underscores the revolutionary character of 1590s history plays as a medium that broadened the country's interest in and knowledge of affairs of state. They mark an important stage in the diffusion of diplomatic literacy beyond the court, one with major implications for seventeenth-century politics.[12]

The diplomatic vision that these plays promote depended on a tendentious interpretation of the Middle Ages that contemporary medievalists are still working to overcome. The closer writers drew to a concept of a nation-state in which sovereignty resided in the collective will of a people who shared a common culture and history, the more they read that concept back into the medieval past.[13] Elizabethan writers narrated medieval events as if words like "England" and "France" possessed uncontested transhistorical significance. Shakespeare's history plays, for example, exploited the ambiguity of these words as designators of persons—"France" meaning the *king* of France and "France" meaning the country across the Channel—to treat dynastic conflicts anachronistically as national ones. Dynastic intermarriage made it entirely possible that "France"—meaning a king of France—might have a legitimate claim to the English throne. But Shakespeare so closely associates "France" with a distinctly foreign cultural geography that the idea of a Frenchman sitting on the English throne carried suggestions of complete political, legal, and social subjugation. French kings ought to speak French and stay on their side of the Channel, and English kings not only ought to speak English but also, like Shakespeare's Henry V, should even have a hard time speaking French. But that is not how medieval dynastic politics worked.

No play exposes the contradictions between the expansionist continental agendas of medieval monarchs and Elizabeth's defensive, even isolationist one more dramatically than *King John*. Critics have often commented on the play's representational instabilities. *King John* is so contradictory in terms of plot, characterization, tone, and apparent political direction that it poses unique challenges to directors and actors. As Jean Howard and Phyllis Rackin note, "every attempt to resolve the action or make sense of it is immediately frustrated by the moral ambiguities of an episodic plot where success and failure ride on the shifting winds of chance."[14] The play seems to be moving in two different directions at once, toward a castigation of John and his associates as corrupt and toward an endorsement of them as defenders of England against foreign threats. Philip the Bastard, the illegitimate son of Richard the Lionhearted, for example, begins as a vice figure driven by self-interest but ends up as the quintessential English patriot boasting of his country's independence: "Nought shall make us rue / If England to itself do rest but true" (5.7.117–18).[15] Nothing in the plot accounts for the change. Shakespeare's portrayal of King John is just as contradictory. He appears as a child murderer with dubious claims to the throne, but he also champions England's independence and denounces the pope in soundly patriotic, albeit anachronistically Protestant, language: "no Italian priest / Shall tithe or toll in our dominions" (3.1.153–54). John is simultaneously devious and incompetent, a usurper and a patriot, a murder and a proto-Protestant.

While *King John*'s contradictions cannot be explained on the basis of its characters' psychological development, they do organize themselves around a central ideological tension between the dynastically motivated diplomacy of the Middle Ages and an early form of state-based diplomacy that would become one of the hallmarks of modernity. *King John* reminds us that the contradictions inherent in early modern state development did not manifest themselves solely internally as the conflict between rival sectors of the emergent nation. They also manifested themselves in the relationships between and among dynastic states that experienced the modernizing process of consolidation and bureaucratic centralization at different rates and in radically divergent ways.

At the heart of *King John*'s contradictions is a very odd ideological feat: it turns what might look like a national disaster—the loss of England's French territories—into a national triumph. It privileges the collapse of John's trans-Channel Angevin imperium as the beginning of England's history as a fiercely independent nation standing against the other countries of Europe. This *felix culpa* is the paradox on which most of the play's representational contradictions finally rest. The play confuses us because it presents John's dynastic catastrophe—his loss of the massive territories consolidated by the marriage of his father, Henry II, to Eleanor of Aquitaine—as the birth of a culturally, linguistically, and politically coherent England. In doing so, it also presents the *felix culpa* of John's reign as an imperfect pretext for the happy losses of Elizabeth's: the fall of Calais, her failure to marry the Duke of Anjou or any other continental suitor, and her de facto abandonment of dynastic politics.

To make sense of Shakespeare's interventions in *King John*, I turn first to the Angevin world that his play represents. Nothing could have contrasted more emphatically with the highly centralized Tudor monarchy confined to the British archipelago than the sprawling trans-Channel constellation of kingdoms, duchies, counties, and fiefdoms claimed by John, his father, Henry II, and his elder brother Richard I.[16] England's Henry II was born in what is now France. He inherited titles not only to his family's county of Anjou but also to the duchy of Normandy and to the counties of Maine and Touraine. He also achieved one of the Middle Ages' most brilliant territorial alliances by marrying Eleanor of Aquitaine, the heir to most of France's southwestern quarter. He then successfully pressed his claims to England and Ireland. Combined with shakier holds on Brittany and Toulouse, these lands gave Henry the largest landmass controlled by a western European ruler since Charlemagne.[17]

Historians still struggle to give Henry's assemblage of territories and subjects a name that does not impose on it anachronistic understandings of sovereignty, nationhood, colonization, and empire.[18] To avoid the anachronistic implications of words like "nation" or "empire" in reference to the Angevin possessions, I follow the example of the thirteenth-century chroniclers, who spoke of Henry II's "imperium."[19] Nothing united the Angevin territories into anything remotely resembling a modern nation. They lacked a common language, political administration, legal system, military organization, coinage, and even foreign policy. "King of England" was the first of Henry's titles, but only because a kingship conveyed greater heraldic glory than a dukedom.

He actually enjoyed massive wealth and power in his capacity as Duke of Normandy and Count of Anjou and Touraine. Unlike the kings in Shakespeare's two tetralogies, Henry II was a French-born and French-speaking noble identified with the *langue d'oïl* culture of northern France.

Although Henry's immediate successor, Richard I, was born in Oxford, he was arguably more Francocentric in orientation than any other English monarch. As a small child he moved to Aquitaine, where his mother, Eleanor, proclaimed him duke in 1174 and where he imbibed the Poitevin culture of troubadours in all its emphatically un-English richness. He succeeded his father as king of England in 1189 but spent only six months of his eventful ten-year reign on English soil. Much to the irritation of his subjects in England, who had to help pay his bills, Richard spent most of his reign as a Crusader in the Middle East and as a prisoner in Germany. He died from gangrene after a minor skirmish in the Limousin and was buried, like his parents, at Fontevrault Abbey in Anjou. He asked that his heart be removed and buried not in England but in the Norman capital of Rouen as a final reminder of his fundamentally French orientation.[20]

Richard's death led to a succession crisis that is the focus of Shakespeare's play. Both Richard's brother John and his nephew Arthur of Brittany—the son of Richard's deceased brother Geoffrey—claimed title to the Angevin imperium. Precisely because John had been a younger son, never expected to rule, he had spent more of his time in England—arguably, the less politically and economically significant portion of the realm—than in France. His greater familiarity with English domains helped make him the preferred choice of the English barons, while Arthur was the preferred choice of barons in France. Although the conflict was always one over seigneurial prerogatives and allegiances rather than anything like modern national identities, this territorial accident had important consequences for later historiography, including the composition of Shakespeare's play. John eventually lost everything on the French mainland, with the exception of Gascony, to the expansionist Capetian king Philip II. While Philip Augustus emerged as the most powerful king in Europe, John ended his reign fighting off an invasion of England itself by Philip's son, the future Louis VIII. John thus found himself in the humiliating role of a king of England who ruled nothing but England and its western neighbors Ireland and Wales.[21]

Had Louis conquered England, the Capetians would have ruled exactly the same imperium that John's Angevin ancestors had assembled. John himself died of dysentery during the campaign, but his leading supporters drove out the French and established John's son Henry III on the throne for an almost sixty-year reign. Although the English would continue to assert claims to Gascony and other parts of France, and actually took much of the country during the Hundred Years War, John's debacle marked the end of a truly trans-Channel imperium. When later Plantagenet kings like Edward III and Henry V recaptured territory that John lost, they were perceived primarily as English conquerors, not as French magnates with legitimate claims.

Throughout much of the period between John's 1216 death and Mary I's 1558 loss of Calais—in other words, as long as English monarchs still considered themselves entitled to lands in France—writers portrayed the Angevins favorably. Ralph Higden's assessment of Richard I was typical: the English had as much right to boast of Richard I as the Greeks to boast of Alexander, the Romans of Augustus, the Britons of Arthur, and the French of Charlemagne.[22] Holinshed praised Richard "as a notable example to all princes," and Speed honored him as "a noble prince" who "showed his love and care of the English nation as also of Justice itself."[23] While medieval writers were a little more mixed in their treatment of Henry II and John, the Reformation turned both into heroes. Extirpating the cult of Thomas à Becket allowed propagandists to recuperate his murderer, Henry II, as a kind of proto-Protestant. John Bale and John Foxe honored King John as a proto-Protestant martyr who suffered excommunication for his defiance of Innocent III over the appointment of Stephen Langton as archbishop of Canterbury.[24]

But by the final years of Elizabeth's reign—and several decades after the end of any real territorial ambitions on the continent—admiration of the Angevins and their imperium had yielded to contempt. Shakespeare's contemporary Samuel Daniel condemned Richard as an absentee landlord who "exacted, and consumed more of this Kingdome, then all his predecessors—from the Norman had done before him, and yet lesse deserved then any, having neither lived here, neither left behinde him monument of Pietie, or of any other publique worke, or ever shewed love or care to this Common-wealth, but onely to get what hee could from it."[25]

Shakespeare's *King John* occupies a similar transition point in Angevin historiography. As a Tudor writer, Shakespeare stops short of the antimonarchical republicanism that informed later negative accounts of John's career. His target is not monarchy per se, but a monarchy that privileges dynastic interests over the welfare of a new kind of political entity: English subjects imagined as members of a distinct nation. In writing *King John*, Shakespeare brought a proto-nationalist historiography to bear on a dynastic imperium that subsumed the linguistic and cultural divisions that, by the late sixteenth century, had become aligned with the nation-state. By centering the plot on the succession contest and John's subsequent loss of French territories,

Shakespeare transformed John's story into a metanarrative about the clash between medieval dynasticism and a nascent understanding of Europe as a set of autonomous competing states. In losing France, John fails as a medieval dynast. But in that failure, he opens the possibility for a new England, a fiercely independent nation proudly defying its European neighbors.

This historiographic metanarrative about England's emergence as an independent power in which politics, culture, language, and geographical space align underlies the play's notorious inconsistencies in plot and characterization. When John, Philip the Bastard, and their other allies epitomize the dynasticism that Shakespeare anachronistically associates with a betrayal of English interests, they are villains. When they champion those interests, they are heroes. More than any other Shakespearean history, *King John* is concerned less with individual characters than with England, its integrity as a political entity, and its place within an emerging European system. As the action unfolds, characters do not mature or develop in psychologically consistent ways. But England does. It outgrows the dynasticism that Shakespeare repudiates as one of the most dangerous legacies of the Middle Ages.

Whereas Foxe and Bale transformed John's story into a condemnation of the medieval Church, Shakespeare uses it to condemn medieval peacemaking. The dramatic intrigue that unfolds in acts 1 through 3 between Eleanor of Aquitaine, Constance of Brittany, and Blanche of Castile indicts interdynastic marriages that violated the boundaries, which had become significantly more aligned by the late sixteenth century with national states. The succession crisis that opens the play comes about through a kind of matrimonial excess that binds French and English, Angevin and Capetian interests together in an explosive combination. Richard I's death results in two claimants to the Angevin possessions. Eleanor of Aquitaine has one surviving son from her marriage to Henry II: John. But Arthur of Brittany, the son of John's deceased elder brother Geoffrey and Constance, also has a claim. From the play's perspective, Angevin marriage diplomacy has created an imperium that is neither culturally, legally, nor politically coherent. Writing at times as if thirteenth-century succession principles were more stable than they actually were, Shakespeare suggests that the trans-Channel titles belong by dynastic right to Arthur of Brittany. But he also suggests that Arthur is too Francocentric in orientation to serve as a proper English king.

Throughout the play, the critique of interdynastic marriages manifests itself in a pervasive distrust of women as the vehicles, and sometimes the negotiating agents, of such alliances.[26] John and Arthur appear as men excessively dominated by their respective mothers, Eleanor of Aquitaine and Constance of Brittany. As long as both women are alive, John acts primarily as the inheritor and defender of a politically unstable French territorial empire. Matters become even more confusing when he negotiates an interdynastic marriage between his niece Blanche of Castile and the Dauphin, the heir to the French throne. But after he disclaims that treaty, and after Eleanor and Constance both die, John appears in the last two acts as a legitimate defender of England itself from foreign aggression. The disappearance of all three women—Eleanor, Constance, and Blanche—complements a shift from England's initial entanglement in confusing continental alliances to its emergence as a coherent island kingdom. The play's last two acts are insistently masculinist and homosocial in their direction.[27] England establishes its independence as a sovereign power with the passing of Constance and Eleanor, and of the Angevin heirs they championed, Arthur and John. When Henry III triumphs at the end of the play, surrounded by his English lords, the realm has escaped French and female domination.

Katherine Eggert has identified the fantasy of a realm governed by a powerful, charismatic king as symptomatic of a larger cultural disillusionment with Elizabeth I in the final decade of her reign. While Eggert centers her discussion primarily on a reading of Shakespeare's *Henry V*, *King John* concentrates the history plays' general anxieties about women's rule on the specific problem of the foreign consort.[28] One of the traditional justifications for interdynastic marriages was that women would use their natural powers as mediators to cultivate peace between the former belligerents, their husbands' families and their own families of origin. Many historical queens fully embraced this role. Women like Margaret of Anjou, Isabeau of Bavaria, Catherine de' Medici, Henrietta Maria, and Marie Antoinette strove to foster benevolent relations between their countries of origin and the countries where they reigned as queens consort.[29] Yet the dubious reputations that many of these women earned by such efforts suggest the political risks inherent in the role. What one faction welcomed as queenly mediation, another might condemn as foreign meddling. The more seriously a queen consort acted as an agent of reconciliation, the more she might be suspected of working for the enemy.

Throughout *King John*, Shakespeare uses the personal predicaments in which Eleanor, Constance, and Blanche find themselves to register the perceived inadequacy of interdynastic marriage as a diplomatic practice. Eleanor, whose marriage to Henry II epitomized the Angevin territorial expansion, finds herself the mother of one claimant to the Angevin-English throne, King John, and the grandmother to the other, Arthur of Brittany. Although Shakespeare might have made her preference for an English king over a Breton duke a point of English honor, Eleanor's championship actually undermines the legitimacy of John's rule.

In the opening scene, Eleanor's behavior blurs what looks like a simple contrast between English and French claims. As long as only the male characters speak, French arrogance serves as a foil to English integrity:

> KING JOHN. Now, say, Chatillion, what would France with us?
> CHATILLION. Thus, after greeting, speaks the King of France
>   In my behavior to the majesty,
>   The borrowed majesty, of England here. (1.1.1–4)

As king of England, John acknowledges the rights of the king of France to rule within his territory. The Chatillion, or French envoy, seems about to return the courtesy, but then snubs John with the insinuation that his "borrowed majesty" is really usurpation. Just when the contrast between English dignity and French impertinence seems to anticipate *Henry V*, however, Eleanor's private conversation with John suggests that the French have the better case in their championing of Arthur:

> KING JOHN. Our strong possession and our right for us.
> ELLINOR. Your strong possession much more than your right,
>   Or else it must go wrong with you and me;
>   So much my conscience whispers in your ear,
>   Which none but heaven, and you, and I, shall hear. (1.1.39–43)

Eleanor uses the language of conscience, heaven, and right only to ironize them in supporting the king's strong but ethically problematic possession.

The more Eleanor speaks, the more she dissociates sympathy for John as an English king from respect for custom, law, and honor. Instead of fulfilling the traditional queenly role of mollifying hostilities, she exacerbates them. Like Lady Macbeth, Eleanor unsexes herself by helping John destroy Arthur. The more she parodies the role of a protective mother in championing John's illegitimate claims, the more she plays a perverse, and ultimately murderous, grandmother toward Arthur. After capturing Arthur and separating him from his mother, John assures him that his "grandame" Eleanor loves him and that he himself will cherish him as dearly as a father (3.3.3–4). Addressing Arthur tenderly as her "little kinsman," Eleanor then pulls him aside for a private "word" (3.3.18). But this apparent affection is merely a screen: Eleanor distracts Arthur so that John can plot the boy's murder with his henchman.

As villainous as Eleanor and John prove to be, Constance and Arthur are not wholly sympathetic. In terms of the proto-nationalist vision that colors Shakespeare's re-creation of the Angevin past, a king of England ought to be unambiguously English. Arthur of Brittany's status as a protégé of the Capetian king of France compromises his dynastic legitimacy. Shakespeare goes out of his way to introduce this conflict between dynastic and proto-nationalist canons of legitimacy, since the historical Arthur claimed the Angevin territories only on the French side of the Channel. By casting him as a legitimate but essentially foreign heir to the English throne, Shakespeare carries dynastic logic to what in the sixteenth century seemed a nightmarish conclusion: England's possible reduction to a French satellite.

Just as one foreign mother, Eleanor, exacerbates John's tyranny, another foreign mother, Constance, undermines Arthur's credibility by embedding him in alliances with continental powers. John is corrupt and increasingly tyrannical, but Shakespeare identifies him primarily with England in his opposition to King Philip of France. Arthur may have a better claim to the Angevin imperium, including England, but he depends completely on Philip and his imperial ally the Duke of Austria. In Constance's first lines in the play she thanks France's ally Austria for menacing not only John but England as well, imagined as a culturally and geographically independent power:

> AUSTRIA. To my home I will no more return
>   Till Angiers, and the right thou hast in France,
>   Together with that pale, that white-fac'd shore,
>   Whose foot spurns back the ocean's roaring tides
>   And coops from other lands her islanders,
>   Even till that England, hedg'd in with the main,
>   That water-walled bulwark, still secure
>   And confident from foreign purposes,
>   Even till that utmost corner of the west
>   Salute thee for her king. . . .
>
> CONSTANCE. O, take his mother's thanks, a widow's thanks. (2.1.21–30, 32)

To the extent that Constance pleads for her son's just dynastic inheritance, her gratitude is understandable. But Austria couches his offer of assistance to Arthur entirely as an attack on England. Shakespeare builds Austria's description of the country with its chalk cliffs spurning the "the ocean's roaring tides" around the same isolationist topoi that he used in John of Gaunt's speech in *Richard II*. But instead of speaking as a patriotic Englishman, Austria speaks as a foreigner intent on humbling England and its fiercely independent islanders. He is determined to crush the pride with which England "spurns back the ocean's roaring tides" and to violate its "water-walled" security. Even though Arthur has a legitimate claim to the throne, the dramatic context makes it patently clear that his kingship would reduce England to a puppet realm dominated by foreigners.

Despite all her maternal protestations, Constance of Brittany never worries that France and Austria's patronage of Arthur might ultimately deprive him of independence as an English sovereign. The alacrity with which she accepts their aid suggests either that she is naïve or that she shares their fundamental disregard for English liberties. The historical Constance had diplomatic and genealogical ties with Britain. Although her father, Conan IV, was a Breton, her mother, Margaret, was a Scottish cousin of Henry II. But instead of using such connections to give Constance an English aura, Shakespeare ignores them; she shows no loyalty to England, a country she has never seen.

Throughout the misogynistic opening acts of *King John*, the presence of foreign dowagers complicates further an already complicated succession question by blurring thirteenth-century vocabularies of dynastic right with a sixteenth-century discourse of national honor. To the extent that the play identifies Arthur as Richard the Lionhearted's heir, John is a usurper. John's mother, Eleanor of Aquitaine, never lets us forget that fact, and her murderous connivance heightens his stigma as a usurper. But even John's continental enemies refer to him as the king of England, in contrast to Philip of France, and in general he carries an aura of Englishness that Arthur, his Breton rival, lacks. Arthur's mother, Constance, is potentially sympathetic as the mother of a son who is eventually murdered. But her transports and outbursts of grief and fury—so loved by Victorian audiences—undercut her moral authority by suggesting female intemperance and irrationality. More important, she exacerbates Arthur's foreignness by encouraging his alliances with England's traditional enemies, including the man who murdered Richard the Lionhearted. The misogyny inherent in both Eleanor's and Constance's characterizations reinforces the play's running critique of medieval diplomatic convention. The tangle of gender, dynastic interest, and national loyalty ultimately indicts more than the meddling of two ambitious mothers. It suggests a fundamental inadequacy in the system of interdynastic marriages that established sovereign authority across the linguistic and cultural frontiers that, by the late sixteenth century, were important components of an emerging sense of the nation. *King John* develops the Catch-22 choice between Arthur, a legitimate but effectively French heir, and John, an English usurper, as an inevitable consequence of the fevered dynastic politics that first created the Angevin imperium.

John and Philip temporarily resolve the conflict over the succession through a formal treaty epitomizing the mélange of national and dynastic interests that Shakespeare stigmatizes as inherently unstable. The 1200 Treaty of Le Goulet developed from a plan first proposed to establish peace between Richard I and Philip II by marrying the Dauphin, the future Louis VIII, to one of Richard's Spanish nieces.[30] Richard died before the deal was completed, but Philip and John revived its essential features, including the Spanish marriage, a year later. Eleanor of Aquitaine journeyed to Spain to select one of her granddaughters for the match. After rejecting the elder, Urracha, on the grounds that her name would sound strange to northern French speakers, Eleanor settled instead on Blanche of Castile. Under the terms of the treaty, Philip acknowledged John as king of England, Duke of Normandy, and Count of Anjou and Maine and all other Angevin territories on either side of the Channel. Philip also repudiated Arthur's claim to all territories beyond his native Brittany, which he was to hold henceforth solely as a vassal of King John. John in turn gave the Dauphin the territories of Issoudon, Gracay, and portions of Berry as a dowry for Blanche. He also surrendered the Vexin, a contested portion of Normandy, directly to Philip.

Nothing about the Treaty of Le Goulet should have prevented it from establishing peace between the belligerents, except that neither Philip nor John was fully in control of his own realm. The *langue d'oc* regions to the south were especially fractious. When the Lusignan barons of Limoges rebelled against John, they appealed to Philip for assistance, which he readily gave. The war between the French and English kings resumed, and it never really ended. John scored a few major victories, but the French finally drove the English across the Channel and later invaded England itself with the ostensible aim of assisting English rebels allegedly suffering under John's tyranny.

The Treaty of Le Goulet thus marked only a short respite in the troubles between the French and English crowns that dated back to the reigns of Henry II and Richard I and that continued into the reign of John's son Henry III. But in *King John*, Shakespeare rewrites Le Goulet as a major turning point in the narrative, the beginning of the end of England's territorial confusion with France.[31] Even within Shakespeare's fiction, the treaty initially makes both political and, at least to some extent, moral sense. An unnamed citizen of Angiers first proposes it as a way to prevent John and Philip from destroying the city when its citizens refuse to acknowledge either Angevin claimant as its sovereign. Up to this point in the play, the citizen has been a sympathetic character voicing the honest quandary of the city's residents in their inability to choose between the rival claimants. Just at the point when cataclysm seems inevitable, he introduces the possibility of an interdynastic marriage as a way of staving off disaster. Shakespeare presents the citizen as the consummate diplomat who finds a way to mediate seemingly irreconcilable positions in the interest of "peace and fair-fac'd league" (2.1.417). Even the circumstance that other writers sometimes foregrounded as the central injustice of such treaties—the bride and groom's incompatibility—fails to be a problem. The Dauphin Louis and his Spanish-Angevin bride Blanche fall conveniently in love with each other at first sight.

Yet the citizen's description of a negotiated settlement as "fair-fac'd league" hints at a kind of hypocrisy that the play eventually stigmatizes as an inevitable component of any diplomatic exchange. The Bastard sums it up in his role as comic chorus: "I was never so bethump'd with words" (2.1.466). The treaty making exposes diplomacy as a kind of theater, yet another art that Shakespeare associates with the seductions and duplicity of language. As much as Shakespeare invites us to sympathize with the citizens of Angiers, their solution substitutes self-interest for a commitment to royal legitimacy. They do not care that the treaty excludes Arthur from his just inheritance; all they are interested in, albeit understandably, is their city's safety.

By exposing John's, Eleanor's, and even Philip's commitment to dynastic aspiration, the deal that Hubert brokers occasions the Bastard's paean to commodity:

> Mad world, mad kings, mad composition!
> John, to stop Arthur's title in the whole,
> Hath willingly departed with a part,
> And France, whose armor conscience buckled on,
> Whom zeal and charity brought to the field
> As God's own soldier, rounded in the ear
> With that same purpose-changer, that sly devil . . .
> Commodity, the bias of the world. (2.1.561–67, 574)

Medieval diplomatic theory upheld treaty making as a quasi-divine intervention in human affairs with the goal of establishing the Peace of Christendom. But as the Bastard notes, there is nothing divine about this particular treaty. John has simply cut his losses in a vain effort to retain some French territory. Philip, who pretended to be "God's own soldier," driven by "zeal and charity" to fight in Arthur's interest, emerges as a hypocrite. Just as much as John, he has surrendered himself to "Commodity," the insistently secular self-interest and expedience that the Bastard sees as the actual ground of diplomacy.[32]

In King John, the treaty is immoral and politically naïve. Shakespeare drastically exaggerates the amount of land that John gives away as a dowry: "Then do I give Volquessen, Touraine, Maine, / Poictiers, and Anjou" (2.1.527–28); the historical John ceded only one of these territories, the Volquessen, or

Vexin. The deal falls apart one scene later, when Philip succumbs to papal pressure to repudiate the excommunicated king of England. Even one of the few good things that the treaty accomplishes, the happy union between Blanche and Louis, takes a disastrous turn when Blanche finds herself torn between her conflicting loyalties to the belligerents: "Which is the side that I must go withal? . . . / Whoever wins, on that side shall I lose" (3.1.327, 335). She cannot be faithful to her French husband, Louis, without betraying her English uncle John, and she cannot support her uncle without violating the integrity of her marriage.

Blanche's predicament exactly mirrors that of the citizens of Angiers. Like them, she cannot stand unambiguously with either side of the quarrel. In short, the treaty fails to resolve anything.[33] Unlike Eleanor and Constance, the younger Blanche does not appear as a meddling, domineering mother. But even as misogyny yields to pathos, Shakespeare continues to develop his critique of interdynastic marriage as a basis of European statecraft. The play's few innocent characters, like Blanche and the citizens of Angiers, find themselves trapped as pawns between the rival powers. Blanche's tragedy in particular suggests that traditional diplomacy is not only corrupt, hypocritical, and ineffectual, but also destructive in its impact on the men and women whose lives are brokered by unscrupulous dynasts. The predicament in which Blanche finds herself serves as a synecdoche for the dangers inherent in the marital diplomacy that first brought about the Angevin confusion of French and English interests. The old dynastic trans-Channel imperium denied its subjects the possibility of full political and even psychological coherence by demanding loyalty to sovereigns, and sometimes even multiple sovereigns, whose aspirations did not coincide with their subjects' own welfare.

The treaty's failure signals the beginning of John's collapse and the end of the Angevin imperium. Having given up the Angevin heartlands of Maine, Anjou, and Touraine, John soon finds himself driven out of France altogether and retreating to England. His murder of Arthur is a pyrrhic victory, since the crime so alienates his English subjects that they rebel against him and encourage a French invasion to expel him from the throne.

In terms of the play's central paradox, however, the invasion also allows John at last to appear as an unambiguously English king rather than a trans-Channel dynast. Instead of compromising England's independence through treaties with Frenchmen, he and his retainers find themselves fighting to preserve England itself. The Dauphin, Lewis, is no Henry Bolingbroke. In swearing allegiance to him, Salisbury, Pembroke, and the other rebels betray not only their king but their country as well. If they placed the Dauphin on the English throne, he would eventually rule a Capetian imperium that mirrored its Angevin predecessor and reproduced its instabilities. Once more, one man would find himself in the impossible position of heading a vast collection of kingdoms, duchies, counties, and provinces on both sides of the Channel with no common linguistic, cultural, or political traditions. Once again, the only basis for such a conglomeration of polities would be the fortunes of interdynastic marriage. As Lewis himself proclaims, "I, by the honor of my marriage bed, / After young Arthur, claim this land for mine" (5.2.93–94). The only thing that might justify his de facto annexation of England to the French throne is his marriage to Blanche, a Spanish woman descended from an Angevin king. His ambitions carry the logic of inter-dynastic marriage to its conclusion: a French seizure of the English throne.

The proto-nationalist language dominating the play's final acts suppresses the fact that the men occupying the English throne since the Conquest were arguably more French than English. This convenient amnesia establishes an anachronistic distinction between the components of John's realm on oppo-site sides of the Channel. Surrendering Anjou, Maine, Touraine, and the Vexin might have been a strategic error and even a humiliation, but it left English sovereignty—imagined as something that both embraces and tran-scends the personal authority of the English monarchy—intact. The same would not be true if Lewis were to take England itself. Shakespeare imagines that as an ultimate national catastrophe, which would surpass anything yet suffered under John's incompetent and tyrannical regime.

In warding off the invasion, the Bastard and the other Angevin supporters appear less as John's partisans and more as defenders of an English nation imagined as entirely distinct from the Angevin imperium. When the Bas-tard confronts Lewis and the papal emissary Pandulph, his predictions of an English victory anticipate the full-bodied patriotism of *Henry V*:

> Shall that victorious hand be feebled here
> That in your chambers gave you chastisement?
> No! Know the gallant monarch is in arms,
> And like an eagle o'er his aerie tow'rs,
> To souse annoyance that comes near his nest. (5.2.146–50)

The Bastard uses hyperbole and sharp antitheses to augment the force of his boast: What could be more tactically futile than a French assault on English soil, since John has punished the French not just on French soil but in the private chambers of their own homes? The language is so charged that it skirts around the fact that John has shown no evidence of valor. Just when did his "victorious hand" chastise the French in their own chambers? That might have been said of the historical John after his success at the battle of

Mirabeau, but that was an unusual bright spot in a dismal military career.[34] In Shakespeare's version, Mirabeau matters primarily as the site of Arthur's capture. The boy duke's subsequent murder rests uneasily beside the Bastard's paternal image of John as an eagle protecting its nest. But such objections matter little in the face of a French invasion. What the Bastard offers is less an accurate recollection of John's reign than a celebration of him as an embodiment of England's independence as a sovereign nation.

The Bastard, in fact, has to work hard to keep John himself from spoiling the patriotic fantasy.[35] In return for the promise of a negotiated peace, for example, John surrenders his crown to Pandulph and then receives it back again as a token that he holds his "sovereign greatness and authority" from the pope (5.1.4). The Bastard repudiates this gesture and its implications of a sovereignty contingent on papal favor:

> O inglorious league!
> Shall we, upon the footing of our land,
> Send fair-play orders and make compromise,
> Insinuation, parley, and base truce
> To arms invasive? Shall a beardless boy,
> A cock'red silken wanton, brave our fields,
> And flesh his spirit in a warlike soil,
> Mocking the air with colors idly spread,
> And find no check? (5.1.65–73)

In yet another burst of familiar Elizabethan jingoism, the Bastard spurns the papal legate and the effeminate French alike for insulting a warlike English nation. As with similar passages elsewhere in Shakespeare's histories and other Elizabethan plays, the speech opts for war over peace in strikingly gendered language that discredits anything short of an ultimate military victory as a failure of English masculinity.

The Bastard's militarism finally carries the day. After a monk conveniently poisons John, England is freed from feminine and effeminate influences and can bask in the wholly masculine authority of Henry III. Henry inherits only a fraction of his father's original imperium, but nobody minds. In proclaiming that "England never did, nor never shall, / Lie at the proud foot of a conqueror" unless it somehow betrays itself, the Bastard ends the play on a cautiously triumphant note (5.7.112–13). What anxiety he might have about the future centers on England's internal welfare and not its pretensions to a continental imperium. John's French losses are his son's gain. Freed from the encumbrances of a French appanage, Henry III is a wholly English king whose relationship to the continent is military and defensive. Shakespeare never mentions his French mother, Isabelle d'Angoulême, or the fact that John's courtship of her triggered a major revolt among his French barons. Nor does he say anything about Henry's *langue d'oc* wife, Eleanor of Provence, or about the Savoyard and Lusignan relatives who dominated his court. Shakespeare writes instead as if John's reign marked an absolute separation of French and English interests that created England's national sovereignty.

King John thus transforms the political tragedy of the last Angevin king into an etiology for England's place within a European community of nation-states. From the play's perspective, England's greatness depends on its insularity. It must remain both militarily and diplomatically impregnable, "That water-walled bulwark, still secure / And confident from foreign purposes," whose fierce independence the Duke of Austria and other French partisans so bitterly resent. If this popular diplomatic vision radically rewrote the medieval history that Shakespeare encountered in Holinshed and other Tudor chronicles, it also projected an interpretation of contemporary politics that rested uneasily beside Elizabeth's foreign policy, especially for the first two-thirds of her reign. She was finally no more fully "confident from foreign purposes" than the historical Henry III. Although she gradually accepted the loss of Calais, she had opened her diplomatic career at Cateau-Cambrésis with a desperate effort to retain it. Over the next several decades, she entered into serious negotiations to establish an alliance with France based on yet another Anglo-French marriage, the exact kind of interdynastic union that, according to Shakespeare, had entangled French and English interests throughout the Middle Ages. Those marriages failed to come about, possibly more through diplomatic chance than through monarchical deliberation. But by the time *King John* was first staged and Elizabeth was in her last decade, she had accepted the role of the fiercely independent Virgin Queen and escaped the xenophobic misogyny that the play concentrates on Eleanor of Aquitaine and Constance of Brittany.

The Unjust Ending of an Unjust War: *Henry V*

The medieval ideal of Europe as a *res publica christiana* obedient to pope and emperor was never much more than a fantasy. Popes and emperors were often at war with one another; dukes, counts, princes, and municipalities chafed against their imperial overlords; the centralizing monarchs of France and England showed little patience for papal interventions in their foreign and domestic affairs. As we have seen, sacramental theology and canon law complemented the concept of the *res publica christiana* as a model for interpreting interstate relations, especially to the extent that rulers contracted alliances and made peace with one another through interdynastic marriage. But the ideals that accompanied these marriages often collapsed before bouts of renewed warfare.

The long Italian wars between the Hapsburgs and the Valois, the Reformation, and the subsequent wars of religion made the dream of a *res publica christiana* pacified by generations of interdynastic marriages less tenable than ever. By the end of the sixteenth century, European intellectuals sought alternative frameworks to describe relations between heads of state. Niccolò Machiavelli inaugurated the new era by characterizing European politics as an amoral competition driven by secular interests and applying his model equally to emperors, kings, and popes. These last appear throughout *Il Principe* and *I discorsi* less as moral authorities governing a submissive Christian republic than as temporal rulers locked in struggles against other heads of state. In this fractious environment, marriage lost its credibility as a diplomatic tool. In *Istorie fiorentine*, Machiavelli suggested that marriages triggered wars nearly as often as they brought about fragile intervals of peace. Corso Donati's marriage to the daughter of Uguccione da Faggiuola, for example, leads his enemies to take up arms against him. The Viscontis supplied Machiavelli with particularly lurid examples of the difficulties that might arise before or even after marriages contracted between powerful families. Filippo Maria Visconti acquired considerable land and money from his marriage to Beatrice di Tenda, the daughter of a cadet branch of the house of Ventimiglia and the wealthy widow of Facino Cane of Montferrat. But he promptly accused her of adultery and had her executed. When Filippo Maria sought a rapprochement with Francesco Sforza by offering him his daughter Bianca Maria, Sforza hesitated to accept: "Neither could his offer of marriage be trusted, since he had been duped many times before [ne anche al suo parentado si poteva prestare fede; sendone stato tante volte beffato]."[36] Inverting the long-held belief that marriage would create the occasion for a binding piece, Sforza notes that he will consider Visconti's *parentado* (alliance through kinship) after careful discussions with his advisers, and only after a peace has been concluded. Sforza thus separates marriage from the question of peace itself.

In their attempts to make sense of a rapidly changing international situation and a decaying religious consensus, the first generation of legal jurists—Francisco de Vitoria, Conradus Brunus, Pierino Belli, Balthazar Ayala, Francisco Suarez, and Alberico Gentili—rejected Machiavellian realism in their insistence that the *jus gentium*, the law of nations that was an aspect of natural law, governed relations between states. Gentili, a Protestant refugee who taught civil law at Oxford and had close ties to the Earl of Leicester and Sir Philip Sidney, proclaimed that "the law of nations is that which is in use among all the nations of men, which native reason has established among all human beings, and which is equally observed by all mankind."[37] Along with other Renaissance jurists, Gentili argued that every aspect of war was subject to law. He divided his magisterial 1589 treatise *De jure belli* into three books, presenting the criteria for a just decision to wage war (*jus ad bellum*), just conduct in battle (*jus in bello*), and a just resolution of the conflict (*jus post bellum*).

As scholars have often noted, however, the Renaissance just war theorists had read Machiavelli.[38] When they turned from general claims about the rules of engagement to specific historical examples, their idealism degenerated into a realist discourse similar to that of *I discorsi* or the *Istorie fiorentine*. The fact that all peoples shared a sense of what constituted just grounds for war, for example, did not prevent them from waging wars for unjust reasons. They also still killed civilians, even though the law of nations forbade it. Works like Gentili's *De jure belli* often read less like expositions of law than catalogues of international lawlessness. In their discussions of any specific precept, they note more instances of its violation than of its observance by rulers more concerned with their own interests than with justice.

This tension between juridical aspiration and realist disillusion undermined the fragile confidence that still survived in marriage diplomacy after the shock of the Reformation. In the final third of *De jure belli*—the book devoted to *jus post bello*, or justice after a war—Gentili asserts that the victor should oversee just retribution and ensure that war will not break out again in the future. Regardless of how laudable these principles might be, however, law alone fails to underwrite them in the absence of a universal sovereign. As Gentili reminds his readers, treaties are binding only so long as the signatories agree to abide by their term. Despite their best intentions, old hatreds continue to simmer, new political and material developments render former agreements obsolete, and successors renege on their predecessors' promises: "Our jurists tell us in general that every pledge is capable of being broken" (3.13).[39] In a world where rulers sealed their agreements with solemn oaths—those between Catholic powers still swore on relics—this was a grim pronouncement.

In the old sacramental theory, interdynastic marriage compensated for the fragility of oaths alone by reconciling opposing interests in a shared progeny. But, according to Gentili, agreements sealed by marriages were just as subject to failure as those underwritten by oaths alone:

> What then of relationship? Duaran wittily says that as a comedy usually ends in a marriage, so is it with the most serious wars. But what profit is there in relationship?

. . . I am speaking of Christians and of legitimate wedlock. Even those who are not Christians say that this is a firm bond of peace. "An inviolable pledge," Virgil calls it.

And yet everyone knows how much weight even Christian princes give to these ties of relationship. But what is weak cannot hold in restraint the stronger desire for power and for liberty. And it is because of those desires that treaties based on relationship are so often broken. (3.13)

Gentili begins by noting the universal assurance with which Christians and non-Christians alike have hailed marriage as a guarantee of peace. Like countless poets celebrating individual marriages, he traces that confidence back to Virgil, with his foundational fiction of Aeneas's marriage to Lavinia. But, argues Gentili, the confidence is misplaced. Even Christian marriage is too weak to counter individual rulers' lust for power and, in the case of a defeated party forced to accept a humiliating settlement, the desire for liberty from a victorious oppressor.

Even the sources Gentili enlists to prove the universality of marriage diplomacy challenge its effectiveness. He draws the Virgilian allusion, for example, from a late passage in the *Aeneid*, in which the war-weary Drances begs Latinus to end the war with the Trojans by giving Aeneas his daughter as "the sole, inviolable pledge of peace [pacis solum inviolabile pignus]" (11.363). In this particular context, however, the reference to the inviolability of the Latins' word could not be more ironic. War has broken out in the first place because Latinus had already pledged his daughter to Turnus, who happens to be standing by when Drances makes his plea. The *Aeneid* hardly offers an unambiguous endorsement of interdynastic marriage as a mode of peacemaking. Instead of fostering peace, marriage negotiations might just as well end in conflicting claims and promises subject to violation as new circumstances arise.

Gentili's allusion to François Le Douaren is just as slippery. While comparing marriage treaties to the endings of comedies acknowledges their universality, it also trivializes them by reducing sacramentality to theatrical convention. Prefaces to late medieval and High Renaissance treaties hailed marriage settlements as a manifestation of *caritas*, of God's healing presence in a fallen world. Quoting Douaren, Gentili dismisses them as mere social form, the thing one simply does after a great war: "A comedy usually ends in a marriage, so is it with the most serious wars." The theatrical simile suggests that there is something pat, unrealistic about them, as if they cannot be taken fully seriously as a means to a just and durable peace. From Gentili's perspective, such settlements are rare. The passions that lead princes to take up arms are so difficult to contain that it is absurd to think that they might be resolved by anything as frail as a marriage contract. Marriages might make good endings for comedies, but they rarely solve conflicts in the real world.

About the same time Gentili was finishing the first version of his tripartite analysis of the laws of war, Shakespeare launched his career as a writer of historical dramas and comedy. Many of Shakespeare's comedies end with marriages, and so, rather surprisingly, does one of his history plays: *Henry V*. The play's entire final act moves conspicuously, but never comfortably, into a comic mode that, like Gentili's quotation of Douaren, foregrounds disjunctions between theatrical convention and historical experience. As in Gentili, the expectation of comic closure clashes with the practical realization that wars are difficult, if not impossible, to resolve justly. Paola Pugliatti and Rosanna Camerlingo have demonstrated how *Henry V* repeatedly foregrounds the question of what constitutes just grounds for waging war (*jus ad bellum*) and just conduct in war (*jus in bello*).[40] Both scholars have attributed the play's ambiguities, its simultaneous characterization of Henry as an idealistic hero and as self-serving master of political realities, to ambiguities within the just war tradition itself. Throughout the play, the noblest ideals degenerate into strategic calculations that test the border between just and unjust conduct. Henry, for example, demands that his counselors provide a moral rationale for waging war on France. But as the audience already knows, the same clerical counselors have trumped up an excuse for the war to distract Henry from an ecclesiastical reform that threatens their carefully hoarded wealth. Similarly, Henry evokes widely acknowledged rules of *jus in bello* when he warns his soldiers not to pilfer from churches. But then he violates an equally established principle when he orders his men to kill their French prisoners. The act makes strategic sense, since his dwindling army does not have enough men to guard them while battling the French. But since the prisoners are utterly defenseless, it runs against the basic principle of all just war theory that acts of violence are acceptable only as an extension of the right to self-defense.

Although scholars have recognized Shakespeare's Gentilian engagement with *jus ad bellum* and *jus in bello*, they have not seen how the play's concluding dramatization of the Treaty of Troyes raises equally unsettling questions about the possibility of *jus post bellum*. In a play that foregrounds problems of theatrical credibility, the idea that a marriage between a dashing English king and a coy French princess might dispel the long-standing enmity between their respective nations provides one last crowning absurdity. The Treaty of Troyes is simply too good to be true. As a conclusion for the stage play, it fails to resolve the tragic ambivalences raised in preceding scenes. As a conclusion for a war that in historical fact had already lasted over a century, it fails to resolve a series of insurmountable political conflicts that constantly threaten to disrupt the final act's comic closure.

In making Henry V the heir to the French throne and investing the future succession in his descendants, the historical Treaty of Troyes was a gamble from the start. The French nobility were not united in their willingness to make peace with the English. More controversial yet was the treaty's de facto exclusion of Charles VI's eldest son, the future Charles VII, from the succession. When Henry predeceased Charles VI by a few months in 1422, he left both France and England in the hands of his nine-month-old son and a fractious regency council that gave the Dauphin ample room to organize resistance to the treaty. As Gentili observed, "What is weak cannot hold in restraint the stronger desire for power and for liberty." Henry VI's eventual loss of his father's French conquests unleashed a storm of recriminations and counter-recriminations among the English nobility that planted the seeds of civil war. In the course of that war, Henry VI followed up the loss of the French crown with the loss of the English crown itself.

In order to bring the play to an unambiguously comic conclusion, the fifth act of *Henry V* would need to suppress this tragic history, in a sense replacing the history recorded in its chronicle sources with a counterfactual fantasy. Instead, Shakespeare erects a fragile comic superstructure over an insistently tragic counter-narrative that always threatens to subvert the apparent drive to a happy ending. More than any other play in his canon, *Henry V* thematizes the gap between theatrical spectacle and lived historical experience.[41] The Chorus, for example, prefaces each act by urging the audience to imagine things that simply cannot be shown on the stage:

> O, do but think
> You stand upon the rivage and behold
> A city on th' inconstant billows dancing;
> For so appears this fleet majestical. (3.Chorus.13–16)

Inviting a sixteenth-century London audience to pretend that they are standing on the shore watching a fifteenth-century fleet sail to Harfleur, the Chorus foregrounds the gaps in time and space that separate them from the historical moment he evokes. The past can be imagined but not directly experienced or known.

As the play's self-consciousness of the gap between the spectacle and the past it purports to represent grows in act 5, it acquires a disruptive political and diplomatic significance. The Chorus and prominent characters like the Duke of Burgundy hint at a more complex story of factionalism, failed mediation, and exclusions of significant parties that, if brought onto the stage, would undermine the illusion of a binding peace created and sustained through marriage:

> Vouchsafe to those that have not read the story,
> That I may prompt them; and of such as have,
> I humbly pray them to admit th'excuse
> Of time, of numbers, and due course of things,
> Which cannot in their huge and proper life
> Be presented here. (5.Chorus.1–6)

With this disclaimer, the Chorus fast-forwards through the five years separating the 1415 victory at Agincourt from the 1420 negotiations at Troyes. He evokes in quick succession the king's embarkation from Calais, joyous arrival at Dover, and triumphant entry into London, where the people greet him as "their conqu'ring Caesar" (5.Chorus.28). The narrative pace quickens, almost at the expense of grammatical coherence:

> Now in London place him—
> As yet the lamentation of the French
> Invites the King of England's stay at home;
> The Emperor's coming in behalf of France,
> To order peace between them—and omit
> All the occurrences that ever chanc'd,
> Till Harry's back-return again to France. (5.Chorus.35–41)

The elisions and disjunctions that give this speech its epic sweep also distort the military and diplomatic character of the post-Agincourt years. Yet Shakespeare hints just enough at the elided past to establish a dissonance between it and his new epic theater. The odd reference to the French lamentation that "invites the King of England's stay at home," for example, seems to mean that the French wanted the king to give them time to bury and mourn their dead before he returned to enjoy his conquest. But the line comes off as litotes, a not so subtle reminder that Agincourt was not that decisive. Many French nobility resented the English occupation of the country and were glad to see Henry return to England. The war dragged on for five more years, albeit to the English advantage. There were also frequent diplomatic exchanges. The emperor Sigismund, for example, who suddenly appears in line 39, tried to broker a peace between England and France, but did not succeed. Although Holinshed identifies him as Henry's "coosine germane . . . the kings freend, and . . . a mediator for the peace," Shakespeare dismisses him as a French partisan.[42] As the theoretical head of the *res publica christiana*, he was the person best suited to mediate between two parties whose century-long war had strained the European economy and allowed the spread of heresy.

The Chorus's rapid summary and partial distortion of the historical narrative available in Holinshed lays the groundwork for the fifth act's definitive shift into comedy, a genre that depends on compression and exclusion of potentially unsettling facts.[43] The first scene, for example, shifts from politics to the hijinks of Fluellen, Pistol, and Gower. The French political plot returns only with the next scene, the last in the play. By this time, however, the peace is effectively a done deal. Henry greets his royal enemies as "our brother France, and . . . our sister," and they greet him as their "brother England" (5.2.2, 10, 12). Shakespeare tells us nothing about the messy French politics, all included in Holinshed, that made this happy moment possible: the murderous rift between the Armagnac and Burgundian factions, the former's opposition to any deal with the English, the French king Charles VI's bouts of madness, his queen, Isabeau of Bavaria's, controversial regency, or her ultimate rapprochement with the Burgundians and acceptance of their plan for peace with England.[44] Above all, Shakespeare downplays the fact that Isabeau's and Charles's willingness to name Henry V as their heir entailed disinheriting their own son, an Armagnac partisan implacably hostile to the English.

As in the act's opening Chorus, Shakespeare hints just enough at these complexities to undercut the apparent comedy. The Duke of Burgundy, who carries on for some forty lines about the devastation of the French countryside, presents himself as the chief advocate of a settlement:

> that I have labor'd,
> With all my wits, my pains and strong endeavors,
> To bring your most imperial Majesties
> Unto this bar and royal interview,
> Your mightiness on both parts best can witness. (5.2.24–28)

Although Shakespeare says nothing about the specifics that these "pains and strong endeavours" entailed, these lines remind us that the settlement involved more than a decisive French defeat followed by a marriage treaty. Burgundy would not have had to work so hard if there had not been reluctance on both sides to settle. The messiness of French factionalism, the Burgundians' hard-won advantage over Armagnac resistance—these hover just beyond the text's explicit historical narrative.

Now that Burgundy has brought the former belligerents together, they are set to finalize the details of the treaty. Henry insists that he has made his terms clear, and the king of France says he needs only to go over them one more time with some of Henry's counselors. Right at this most diplomatically significant moment in the play, however, Shakespeare swerves from politics to Henry's comic courtship of his French bride:

> KING HENRY V. Brother . . . Go, uncle Exeter,
>   And brother Clarence, and you, brother Gloucester,
>   Warwick, and Huntington, go with the king,
>   And take with you free power to ratify,
>   Augment, or alter, as your wisdoms best
>   Shall see advantageable for our dignity,
>   Any thing in or out of our demands,
>   And we'll consign thereto. Will you, fair sister,
>   Go with the princes, or stay here with us?
>
> QUEEN ISABEL. Our gracious brother, I will go with them.
>   Happily a woman's voice may do some good,
>   When articles too nicely urg'd be stood on.
>
> KING HENRY V. Yet leave our cousin Katherine here with us:
>   She is our capital demand, compris'd
>   Within the fore-rank of our articles. (5.2.83–97)

Raising almost as many questions as they answer, these speeches expose the counter-narrative darkening the ostensible presentation of Henry as a conqueror who forces the French to come to settle according to his terms. While the king and queen of France will both be present at the negotiations in their own person, Henry is content to send his representatives. Is his absence a sign of decisive English advantages, of a young king's naïveté, of a military hero's mistaken belief that diplomatic details are unworthy of his attention? Audiences who know the earlier *Henry VI* plays would hear in the list the names of individuals whose families were on opposite sides of the Wars of the Roses. Can we assume they were necessarily like-minded or supportive of Henry's Lancastrian policies during these negotiations? The roster raises that possibility but leaves the question open.

As a prelude to one of the most important interdynastic marriages in the late Middle Ages, Isabeau's role in this scene is brief and potentially troubling. She was herself a bride in a prior interdynastic marriage arranged by the Burgundians. At that time, Philip the Bold had brokered her marriage to France's Charles VI in order to bring the Holy Roman Empire into an anti-English alliance. Now she was working with Philip the Bold's grandson Philip the Good to advance an English settlement. In stating that "a woman's voice may do some good, / When articles too nicely urg'd be stood on," she voices one of the most familiar justifications for medieval interdynastic marriage: the belief that women were natural peacemakers. But yet again, by merely bringing her onto the scene, Shakespeare possibly admits an alternative history that dampens his story of Anglo-French reconciliation. In the century and a half that had passed since the death of the historical Isabeau, a black legend had arisen, based in part on hostile Burgundian sources, that condemned her as an adulteress, the lover of Philip the Good's father, John the Fearless. She allegedly hated her son the Dauphin and was happy to disinherit him, because he had conspired to assassinate her Burgundian lover. Holinshed condemns her championship of Burgundy over the interests of her son, her husband, and ultimately France as "womanish malice."[45] This sordid Franco-Burgundian history played to the advantage of the English claims to the throne but raises questions about the integrity of Isabeau's "woman's voice" in Shakespeare.[46] Does she want to be present at the negotiations as a natural champion of peace, or to maintain her own political interests?

On one level, none of this matters. The play concludes with the conspicuously lighthearted scene between Henry and Katherine, a kind of generic retreat into the romantic comedies of the Shakespearean past. Whatever machinations and sordid family intrigues might have transpired in the French royal family, Henry appears as a plain, honest-speaking English soldier who charms his bride even if she does not understand everything he says. The entire exchange displaces key diplomatic themes—foreign encounter, the challenges of translation and misprision, strategies of persuasion, coy evasion, the quest for acceptance and final consent—onto the comedy of courtship. The fact that Henry wants Katherine not only to accept him but to love him wards off at least one of the shadow narratives that had challenged many interdynastic marriages since the twelfth century: suspicions that the practice undervalued women's feelings. Katherine seems quite attracted to Henry, and as a glimpse into the private erotic lives of two individuals, the scene succeeds as a romantic comedy.

The pervasive tone throughout the scene almost even suppresses the darker diplomatic significance of Katherine's question "Is it possible dat I should love de ennemie of France?" (5.2.170). The whole theology of diplomatic marriage, of course, depended on the belief that women could learn to love their country's former enemy, and that their love would radiate in turn throughout their respective nations. When the king and queen of

France return, the king's words echo centuries of tributes to marriage as the perfect resolution for long-standing war:

> Take her, fair son, and from her blood raise up
> Issue to me; that the contending kingdoms
> Of France and England, whose very shores look pale
> With envy of each other's happiness,
> May cease their hatred; and this dear conjunction
> Plant neighborhood and Christian-like accord
> In their sweet bosoms, that never war advance
> His bleeding sword 'twixt England and fair France. (5.2.348–55)

The sentiment recalls the one voiced in dozens of prefaces to European marriage treaties: the union between two young people brings war to a close, establishes a common progeny, and restores the "neighborhood and Christian-like accord" of the European *res publica christiana*. But Shakespeare's poetry brings to the comparatively flat language of treaties a heightened poignancy. Katherine's "blood," from which Henry will raise up issue, has a metaphorical, even sacramental relationship to the blood shed by war when it advanced "his bleeding sword 'twixt England and fair France." That final personification of war, moreover, distances the couple even further from the hostilities of the past by metaphorically exonerating "England and fair France" of the enmities that let to bloodshed. War with its bleeding sword was the true cause of the suffering, not the collision between Valois and Lancastrian ambition.

As satisfying as this scene might be if it were simply the end of a comedy, it never fully resolves the questions raised by Henry's prior exchanges with Isabeau, her husband, Charles VI, and the Duke of Burgundy. There remain as well the troubling implications of Katherine's question: Is love really possible between former belligerents? Or, as Gentili put it, "What profit is there in relationship?" Can the marriage between one man and one woman, even if they love each other, dispel the hostilities that drew their countries into war? Can it make their peoples forget the lives that were lost during the conflict? Or will vindictive passions fester on both sides?

The Chorus gives a brutally short answer to these questions in the play's final lines:

> Thus far, with rough and all-unable pen,
> Our bending author hath pursued the story,
> In little room confining mighty men,
> Mangling by starts the full course of their glory.
> Small time; but in that small most greatly lived

This star of England. Fortune made his sword;
By which the world's best garden be achieved,
And of it left his son imperial lord.
Henry the Sixt, in infant bands crown'd King
Of France and England, did this king succeed;
Whose state so many had the managing,
That they lost France, and made his England bleed:
Which oft our stage hath shown. (5.Chorus.1–13)

The passage violates the happy ending by foregrounding the countertexts broached but quickly evaded throughout the play. One last time, the Chorus measures the gap between historical experience and theatrical representation. With the fifth line, however, that theme acquires a new, unexpectedly tragic valence: "Small time, but in that small most greatly lived / This star of England." The brevity of theatrical time, what Shakespeare elsewhere calls the "two hours' traffic of our stage," no longer simply contrasts with the "full course" of complex historical events. With the second "small" it becomes a metaphor for the brevity of Henry V's life. The fact that "Fortune made his sword" reinforces this transition with its play of double sense. Henry was fortunate in his victories, but Fortune was a notoriously capricious goddess, one whose ravages had been lamented in a large canon of *de casibus* tragedies that haunted the entire *Henriad*.

As happened often during the history of interdynastic marriage, biological accident—in this case an early and unexpected death—defeats whatever dreams of peace a marriage treaty may have inspired. Many of the men to whom Henry had entrusted the negotiation of the Treaty of Troyes, for example, return now as the fractious regency council whose "managing / . . . lost France and made his England bleed." That reference to bleeding England echoes the imagery just used by the king of France in looking forward to the glorious issue that Henry would raise up from Katherine's French blood. That happy future will never take place. With the marriage treaty long broken and forgotten, Henry and Katherine's son will lose France to the once bastardized and disinherited Dauphin. As the eerie rhyme on "succeed" and "bleed" reminds us, the Treaty of Troyes finally yields a succession of blood only too familiar to those who recall the first tetralogy, "which oft our stage hath shown," and its parade of murdered princes.

Along with other writers of the period, Shakespeare valued peace over the nearly perpetual war that had characterized Anglo-French relations in the late Middle Ages. But along with the earliest writers on what would later be called international law, he realized that there were multiple ways to achieve peace, and that some were more just than others. In *Henry V* he reframed the question of *jus post bellum* as a problem of theatrical representation, of the credibility of a conspicuously contrived happy ending. Throughout most of his career Shakespeare ignored the neoclassical decorums that forbade the mixing of genres and assigned noble characters to tragedies and lower-rank characters to comedies. Yet most of his histories, even if they have comic interludes, end on a tragic note with the deaths of kings or noble rebels like Hotspur. *Henry V* is an exception, or at least would be without the ominous final Chorus. The young king marries his princess with hopes of a secure Anglo-French succession, a happy revival of the trans-Channel imperium whose loss Shakespeare had previously chronicled in *King John*. The ending, however, is radically unstable. Shakespeare no sooner broaches the promise of living happily ever after than he refutes it with the devastating return to war. Happy endings finally have no place in history. Achieving them requires too many deletions and oversimplifications, too may distortions of the historical record.

Arguably more than any other writer in English literary history, Shakespeare helped to dismantle a marriage ideology that dated back to the High Middle Ages. He gave that ideology moving expression in the speeches he attributes to Charles VI and Isabeau of Bavaria. But the action in which he embeds their hope for peace questions whether interdynastic marriages were ever a just or even reliable means to resolve hostilities between states. At best, his interdynastic brides were tragically ineffective. At their worst, they could subvert the integrity of proudly independent nations.

Shakespeare crafted these dramatizations of interdynastic marriage at a moment when numerous forces were beginning to undermine credibility in the European West. The confessional divisions attendant on the Reformation were only part of a larger story. In England, political power was passing from the descendants of Norman aristocrats—many related to the Crown by blood—to wealthy gentry, urban professionals, and merchants. Represented by a drastically expanded House of Commons, they had their own opinions about foreign relations. Among the staunchest Protestants in the nation, they were more concerned with religion and commercial opportunity than dynastic prestige and disdained treaties that might limit their trading freedoms or compromise their religion. Shakespeare offered them a revisionary history that confirmed their sense of England as a country standing proudly apart from other European powers.

✦ CHAPTER 6

Divas and Diplomacy in Seventeenth-Century France

A reorientation of peacemaking took place in seventeenth-century Europe. From about the First Crusade, those who negotiated, drafted, signed, and ratified European treaties assumed that war was an anomaly. At least in the dominant theory, best articulated by churchmen like Bernard du Rosier, a fifteenth-century archbishop of Toulouse, Christians were meant to live in peace.[1] If they went to war, something was wrong and had to be fixed. This discourse provided the rhetorical framework for treaties during the Hundred Years Wars and the Italian wars between Valois France and Hapsburg Spain in the first half of the sixteenth century. Treaties culminated in sacramental expressions of forgiveness and brotherly reconciliation.[2] But by the middle of the seventeenth century, statesmen like Richelieu spoke of war as inevitable. Numerous factors contributed to this reorientation, including changes in the scale and technology of warfare, new demographic challenges, the rise of state bureaucracies, and the growing realization that the post-Reformation divisions of Christendom were not going away.

Instead of focusing on the political and socioeconomic factors that made the acceptance of war a perpetual fact of European life, this final chapter focuses on how it affected one of the mainstays of European peacemaking: interdynastic marriage. The new normal reduced, and in some cases eliminated, the role of royal women, especially consorts, in state affairs.

Since these women patronized the arts, the theater and the salon emerged as battlegrounds for the clash between antithetical diplomatic opinions that became especially visible in commentary about women in negotiations and settlements. Rarely do the histories of gender, cultural production, and statecraft converge in such readable ways as in the plays of Corneille and Racine. The neoclassical theater cast women not as peacemakers but as impassioned commentators on their abjection before a belligerent destiny. The heroine's eloquence, and the actress's power over her audience, grow in inverse relation to the eclipse of women's traditional, albeit often only mythic, influence as peacemakers and intercessors on the future of Europe.

The intertwined histories of marriage diplomacy and cultural production did not unfold as a linear progression from dynastic, even personal interests to reasons of state. Throughout the French seventeenth century, diplomatic correspondence and literary works voiced conflicting and often incoherent understandings of sovereignty, the traditional role of women in relations between polities, a growing internal state bureaucracy, and an emerging international system that operated by its own competitive and defensive logic, often without regard to dynastic *gloire*. French drama in particular registered the personal and cultural impact of marriage diplomacy's declining prestige. Its dialogic character made it the perfect medium for capturing the moral and emotional costs of rapidly shifting diplomatic values. Plays like Corneille's *Horace* and *Tite et Bérénice*, as well as Racine's *Andromaque* and *Bérénice*, offer their own genealogies of the modern state system's emergence from its medieval and Renaissance antecedents. With their greater attention to the gendered nature of that transition, they challenge more familiar presentations of reasons of state as an enlightened alternative to the darkness of the dynastic past.

Horace and the Devaluation of Queenly Intercession

The history of diplomacy entails everything from the most idealizing pronouncements to the most jaded, cynical practices. Both ends of the continuum matter. This is why international relations have provoked some of today's richest and most productive political theory. Articulations of ideals matter, even if disregarded. They can still establish the terms and limits of negotiations, and there is often no way to predict whether and how long negotiating parties will live up to them. I raise this caveat because my story begins with some of the most idealistic articulations in diplomatic history, the language of medieval and early modern marriage treaties after prolonged periods of war. These treaties opened and closed with ringing affirmations of peace as the state of Europe:

> This supreme God, who holds the hearts of kings in his hand, and to whom alone is reserved the precious gift of Peace, had the goodness, through his infinite mercy, to inspire the two Kings, and to guide and conduct them in such a manner, that, without any other intervention or purpose except the sentiments of compassion that they have had for the sufferings of their good subjects, and from a paternal desire for their welfare and relief, and for the repose of all Christendom, they have succeeded in ending such great and enduring calamities, in forgetting and extinguishing the causes and the seeds of their divisions, and in establishing to the glory of God and to the exaltation of our Holy Catholic Faith, a good, honest, whole, and lasting peace and brotherhood between them and their successors.

> [Ce Dieu supreme, qui tient en sa main les cœurs des Roys, et qui s'est particulierement reservé à luy seul le precieux don de la Paix, a eu la bonté, par sa misericorde infinie, d'inspirer dans un même temps les deux Roys, et les guider et conduire de telle maniere, que sans aucune autre intervention, ni motif, que les seuls sentimens de compassion qu'ils ont eu des souffrances de leurs bons Sujets, et d'un desir paternel de leur bien et soulagement, et du repos de toute la Chrétienté, ils ont trouvé le moyen de mettre fin à de si grandes et longues calamitez, d'oublier et d'éteindre les causes et les semences de leurs divisions, et d'établir à la gloire de Dieu, et à l'exaltation de nostre Sainte Foy Catholique, une bonne, sincere, entiere et durable Paix et Fraternité entre eux, et leurs Successeurs.][3]

This quotation comes from the preface to the 1659 Treaty of the Pyrenees, which ended a war between France and Spain that began as part of the Thirty Years War but lasted long after the 1648 Treaties of Westphalia had ended the conflict elsewhere in Europe. Peacemaking here unfolds in a deocentric Catholic universe. It begins in the mind of God, through the action of his mercy on his divine goodness. It then passes into the world through the agency of kings committed to the welfare of their subjects and to the propagation of the faith. The negotiations carried out by their appointed deputies restore harmony not only between the belligerents but also between the kings, their respective realms, and God. The treaty emphatically denies the importance of any considerations other than the most pious: "que sans aucune autre intervention, ny motif." Exhaustion of supplies, pressing concerns on the domestic front, pressure to treat from third parties, and all the other factors that typically lead parties to the negotiating table do not enter into the picture. The peace is about the will of God, manifested through mediating the benevolence of their majesties the Most Christian and Most Catholic Kings.

The sacred language of the preface returns at the end of such treaties, when they introduce the marriages that will unite the rival dynasties. They invariably present marriage as a solution to what modern international relations scholars call the problem of "sanction": Just what guarantees that signatory powers will abide by the settlement? According to those who drafted the Treaty of Cateau-Cambrésis and numerous other late medieval and Renaissance treaties, the answer lay in marriage as an indissoluble sacrament:

> And for a greater confirmation of this peace, and to render the friendship, union, and confederation firmer and more unshakeable, the aforementioned deputies by virtue of their said powers . . . have settled and accorded marriage . . . between the aforesaid Catholic King and the aforesaid Lady Elisabeth, in form and following the laws and ordinances of Our Mother the Holy Church.

> [Et pour plus grande confirmation de cette Paix, et rendre l'amitié, union et confederation plus ferme et indissoluble, les Deputez avant dits, en vertu de leurs-dits pouvoirs . . . ont traité et accordé Mariage . . . entre ledit Seigneur Roy Catolique et ladite Dame Elizabet, en la forme et ensuivant les Constitutions et Ordonnances de Nôtre Mere Sainte Eglise.][4]

In the case of Cateau-Cambrésis, a marriage between the Spanish king and a French princess promised to achieve a "firm and unshakeable" peace because it created a set of common interests and gestured toward transcendence. With this sacramental union, peacemaking circled back to its divine origin. It attempted to establish a bond between the two countries as inviolable and unalterable as Christian marriage, itself a type of the immutable life of God.

Such passages remind us that canon law provided a foundation for diplomatic thought throughout the Middle Ages and well into the early modern period.[5] Amplifying basic legal and theological premises, artists and writers exalted the bride as a type of the Virgin Mary, herself an interdynastic bride mediating between God and a fallen humanity. Not every treaty, nor every marriage, was a success, but on many occasions, the ideal translated into valuable practice. From at least the twelfth century on, the sacralization of interdynastic marriage authorized numerous royal women to mediate in the political realm between their husbands and their families of origin.[6]

Sacramental language was still included in the treaties that married Louis XIII of France to Anne of Austria, the daughter of Spain's Philip III, in 1615 and, a generation later, Louis XIV to Maria Teresa, the daughter of Philip IV. The latter marriage took place in 1660, just over one hundred years after Cateau-Cambrésis promised perpetual peace between the realms of France and Spain. The treaty was an echo chamber of pious phrases from Cateau-Cambrésis and intervening Franco-Spanish agreements:

> And in order that this peace and union, confederation and good rapport might be, as is desired, even more firm, durable and indissoluble, the two said principal ministers, the Cardinal Duke [Mazarin] and the Marquis Count Duke [Luis Méndez de Haro y Guzmán], by virtue of the special power that they have received from the two Lords Kings to this end, have agreed to and decreed in their name upon the marriage of the Most Christian King with the Most Serene Infanta, Lady Maria Teresa, eldest daughter of the Catholic King.

> [Et afin que cette Paix et Union, Confederation et bonne correspondance soit, comme on le desire, d'autant plus ferme, durable et indissoluble; lesdits deux principaux Ministres, Cardinal Duc, et Marquis Comte Duc, en vertu du Pouvoir special qu'ils ont eu à cet effet des deux Seigneurs Roys, ont accordé et arresté en leur nom, le Mariage du Roy Tres-Chrestien, avec la Serenissime Infante, Dame Marie Terese, fille aisnée du Roy Catholique.][7]

Once again, the designated representatives of the French and Spanish kings agreed to a marriage in the hopes of establishing a firm and durable peace. While the formulaic rhetoric grounded the new treaty in the authority of the past and suggested a long-standing affinity between the two powers, it also, most troublingly, exposed the fact that previous treaties had not worked. France and Spain were pledging perpetual peace because they were always on the verge, or in the midst, of war.

This was hardly the first time perpetually contested frontiers resulted in bouts of war punctuated by declarations of peace. What had shifted, however, was the underlying theoretical orientation. Particularly after the rise of Richelieu in the 1620s, French statesmen began to repudiate the ideological framework that had upheld diplomatic marriage as an instrument of state policy since the High Middle Ages. In the process, they created an alternative view of diplomacy not as a means to lasting peace but as an inevitable component of the state as an increasingly bureaucratized culture.[8] From this perspective, the long succession of Franco-Spanish treaties was a sign not of failure but of the perpetual negotiation that created the bureaucratized state and continually redefined its place in European commerce and politics.

The *Testament Politique* that Richelieu wrote as an advice manual for the young Louis XIV articulates this alternative understanding of diplomacy and of interdynastic marriage. In a chapter on the benefits of negotiation, Richelieu writes that

> endless negotiation, openly or secretly, in all places—even if no present benefit is received from it and any future benefit is uncertain—is something absolutely necessary for the good of states.

> [négocier sans cesse, ouvertement ou secrètement, en tous lieux, encore mesme qu'on n'en reçoive pas un fruit présent et que celuy qu'on en peut attendre à l'avenir ne soit pas apparent, est chose tout à fait nécessaire pour le bien des Estats.][9]

In practice, the exchange of resident ambassadors, first in Italy and later throughout western Europe, had made continual negotiations common for over a century.[10] But no prior diplomatic treatise had ever extolled it as a perennial feature of the state. With rapid cadences and quick asides, Richelieu presses beyond his ostensible concern with negotiation "sans cesse" as a means to practical advantage and upholds it as a dynamic vital to the state's existence. His prose captures a fervor for deal making that had become a hallmark of the professional diplomat, without whom such continual diplomatic activity would have been impossible. His tone contrasts sharply with the solemnity of the treaty prefaces and their adumbrations of perpetual peace as the proper end of all negotiations, an end that Richelieu repudiates.

In rejecting peace as the proper and expected condition of European life, Richelieu also repudiates the hope that it might be achieved through interdynastic marriage. Although he does not state that such marriages should not take place, he stresses their limitations:

> Even though the alliances that are often contracted by various marriages between crowns do not always produce the benefit that one might desire from them, still they must not be neglected, for they are often one of the most important issues of negotiation.

> [Encore que les alliances, qui se contractent souvent par divers mariages entre les couronnes, ne produisent pas toujours le fruit qu'on en peut désirer, si est-ce qu'il ne les faut pas négliger et que c'est souvent une des plus importantes matières des négociations.][11]

As Richelieu pursues his argument through the twists and turns of his syntax, he notes that interdynastic marriages, though frequent, do not always yield the "fruit" parties might expect from them. Since their promised "fruit," at least officially, was almost always a durable alliance and perpetual peace, his word choice could not be more dismissive of the older, sacramental diplomacy. By the end of the passage, he inverts the traditional value of marriage as the cornerstone of alliance formation. In the older diplomatic model, negotiations were important because they ended in settlements, including the great marriage treaties that had realigned the map of Europe numerous times in the past. For Richelieu, marriage is important because it encourages extensive negotiation. Whatever practical advantages royal marriages might achieve—such as rendering bloodlines even more illustrious ("d'autant plus Illustre")—is secondary to their role in sustaining the endless negotiation on which the bureaucratic state system depends.

Richelieu suavely notes that these alliances typically fall short of their promised perpetuity:

> One can always derive this advantage: for a time, they hold states in a respectful relation with one another. . . . Moreover, alliances sometimes serve to extend relationships and leagues between states, and although they do not always produce this good effect, the utility that the House of Austria received from them shows well enough that they should not be neglected.

> [Toujours on tire cet avantage, qu'elles retiennent pour un temps les Estats en quelque considération de respect les uns envers les autres. . . . Au reste, les alliances servent quelquesfois à esteindre les ligues et les liaisons entre les Estats et, bien qu'elles ne produisent pas toujours ce bon effet, l'utilité qu'en recçoit la maison d'Autriche fait bien voir qu'elles ne sont pas à négliger.][12]

At best, marriage treaties hold "for a time [pour un temps]," or at least they do "sometimes [quelquefois]." There are certainly no guarantees. Stripping away any hope that marriage might resolve the rivalries between dynasties, Richelieu undercuts the Hapsburgs' success in building a world empire on their marriages with the Burgundians and the Trastámaras. Even if their example shows that marriages "should not be neglected," Richelieu reminds us that they do not always yield an impressive result. The Hapsburgs' good fortune was an exception rather than a rule.

The failure of most marriage alliances results in future wars, further negotiations, and yet more treaties, all orchestrated by men like Richelieu and the bureaucrats who had come to dominate the French state. And in Richelieu's vision, the negotiators were always men. Rejecting the older, sacramental diplomacy, he also rejected the intercessory power that it invested in royal women. According to Richelieu, women were temperamentally unsuited to offices of trust:

> Thus it comes that women—by nature lazy and little capable of secrecy—are so little suited to government that if one further considers that they are highly subject to their passions, and, as a result, scarcely capable of reason and justice, this principle alone excludes them from all public administration.

> [De là vient que les femmes paresseuses et peu secrettes de leur nature sont si peu propres au gouvernement, que si l'on considère encore qu'elles son fort sujettes à leurs passions et, par conséquent, peu susceptibles de raison et de justice, ce seul principe les exclude de toute adminstration publique.][13]

Marriage diplomacy of the past assumed that women's capacity for love and compassion made them perfect intercessors. This new diplomacy dismissed those virtues as emotionalism jeopardizing a statecraft of perpetual warfare and a culture of secrecy that permitted negotiations only through official, bureaucratized channels.

Theory dovetailed with practice. When war broke out again between France and Spain in 1635, Anne of Austria tried to mediate between Louis XIII and her brother Philip IV. Richelieu accused her of treasonable correspondence with Spain, confiscated her letters, and searched the monastery where she went on retreats for further evidence. Far from honoring her as a valuable mediator, Richelieu treated her as a suspect.[14] Many foreign queens had suffered calumny and suspicion. But this time the attack came from the king's government rather than from an opposition faction, as if it were simply wrong for a queen to perform her traditional role as intercessor.

The same year the war erupted and Anne became the focus of official suspicions, Richelieu founded the Académie française to maintain the integrity of the French language and to determine the linguistic and literary value of new works. In one of its first actions, the Académie condemned Pierre Corneille's 1637 Le Cid, a popular tragicomedy about the Reconquista hero Rodrigo Díaz de Vivar. While the Académie focused its critique on the play's violation of the classical unities, it also complained that honoring a Spanish hero was inappropriate when France was at war with Spain. The querelle du Cid became one of the most contentious literary debates of the century.

While scholars continue to argue about the role that Richelieu played in the affair, one thing is certain.[15] After a hiatus of three years, Corneille returned to the theater with *Horace*, a tragedy he eventually dedicated to Richelieu. Scholars also continue to debate the significance of the dedication and the question of whether or not it signals a chastened deference to the Acadé-mie.[16] *Horace* certainly adheres more closely to the unities than *Le Cid*. But in light of Richelieu's struggles with Anne of Austria, its focus on interdynastic marriage and female intercession could not have been more daring. Nor does it necessarily endorse Richelieu's belief that women should stay out of politics.

Scholars have sometimes argued that Corneille's play comments on Anne's relationship with Richelieu.[17] But the characteristic delicacy and ambiguity of *théâtre classique* make the play too slippery to support any single topical reading. Instead, the play derives its pathos from a profound understanding of Anne's plight as symptomatic of a more general, overarching shift in European politics, one that challenged the traditional understanding of all diplomatic encounters as steps toward peace. Based on Livy's account of the war between the Romans and the Albans, the play transfigured the intersection of loyalties that lay at the ideological heart of marriage diplomacy into a tragic conflict of interests.

As the play opens, war has resumed between Rome and Alba Longa, despite so many years of intermarriage that almost every Roman family has Alban relatives:

> And while our happy destinies lasted, Hymen's bonds have so many times united peoples so closely related that there are few Romans whom the opposite side does not interest in the death of a son-in-law or brother-in-law.

> [Et les noeuds de l'hymen, durant nos bons destins,
> Ont tant de fois uni des peoples si voisins,
> Qu'il est peu de Romains que le parti contraire
> N'intéresse en la mort d'un gendre ou d'un beau-frère.] (5.2.1493–96)[18]

Intermarriage has made the Roman-Alban war more like a civil than a foreign conflict. The Albans may be technically foreign, but they are also sons-in-law and brothers-in-law of the Roman warriors. In such a case, any victory would be tinged with remorse.

Intermarriage may have staved off conflict between the two city-states for a time. But the tragedy of such marriages is that they intensify the suffering of both sides once war resumes. As the play unfolds, the women characters in particular measure the pain of being in a situation that will end inevitably in family tragedy. Either their husbands will kill their brothers or their brothers will kill their husbands. As Sabine, the Alban woman married to the Roman hero Horace, laments:

> You are enemies in this famed combat, you of Alba, you of Rome, and myself of both. What? Are you saving me to see a victory where, for the high trappings of a solemn glory, I will see the laurels of a husband or a brother steaming still with a blood I will have so cherished? Will I then be able to guide my soul between you two? Satisfy the duties both of sister and of wife? Embrace the victor while weeping over the vanquished?

> [Vous êtes ennemis en ce combat fameux,
> Vous d'Albe, vous de Rome, et moi de toutes deux.
> Quoi? me réservez-vous à voir une victoire
> Où, pour haut appareil d'une pompeuse gloire,
> Je verrai les lauriers d'un frère ou d'un mari
> Fumer encor d'un sang que j'aurai tant chéri?
> Pourrai-je entre vous deux régler alors mon âme,
> Satisfaire aux devoirs et de sœur et de femme,
> Embrasser le vainqueur en pleurant le vaincu?] (2.6.645–53)

Such speeches adapt Petrarchan antinomies to suggest the divisions in the soul caused not by unrequited love but by irreconcilable personal commitments: How can one exult in triumph over the body of a husband or brother? One cannot honor the victor without betraying the vanquished, or fulfill the duties of the wife without leaving unperformed the duties of the sister. Characteristically in this play that foregrounds the failure of diplomacy to contain imperial violence and ambition, insisting on a truce only deepens the protagonist's anguish. Just when battle is about to begin, the Alban dictator makes an impassioned speech stressing the fratricidal character of a war between two cities linked by the closest personal bonds and suggests that they resolve their differences through personal combat between champions selected from each side. In theory, the compromise exemplifies the best diplomatic principles, since it contains the violence in as tight a circle as possible. Most women will be spared the misery of seeing one's husband murder one's brothers. Unfortunately, the cities select as their champions the intermarried heroes, the Curiatii and the Horatii brothers. Given the play's neoclassical concentration on them, the compromise hardly seems to be a successful diplomatic outcome. It appears instead as a meaningless deferral of the inevitable tragedy, one that teases the wives and sisters with false hope.

As the Horatii and Curiatii prepare to fight, Corneille evokes moments from the earliest history of interdynastic marriage to underscore its futility under an emerging Roman order that prioritizes conquest over negotiation. The name of Horace's Alban wife, Sabine, for example, recalls one of the first episode's in Livy's account of Roman history: the rape of the Sabine women. Within this context, the allusion encompasses the double role women play in Livy, first as objects of Roman conquest but then as powerful intercessors who forge a peace between their Sabine fathers and their Roman husbands. Livy's story provided an extended meditation on marriage as an expression of the mutual hospitality that ought to reign between neighboring peoples:

> Then upon advice from the elders, Romulus sent envoys among the neighboring peoples, to petition an alliance and marriage with the new people. . . . Nowhere was the delegation kindly received. So together they spurned them at the same time they feared such a great population growing in their midst, for both themselves and their posterity.

> [Tum ex consilio patrum Romulus legatos circa vicinas gentes misit, qui societatem conubiumque novo populo peterent. . . . Nusquam benigne legatio audita est; adeo simul spernebant, simul tantam in medio crescentem molem sibi ac posteris suis metuebant.] (1.9)[19]

When the Sabines refuse the Romans' civil request to marry their daughters, they effectively condemn the new city to die off in a single generation. Since their denial threatens Rome's existence, the Romans have the right to abduct the women as an act of self-defense. Although the women are initially terrified, Romulus and his men show them such great kindness and hospitality that they become loving and dutiful wives. By the time the Sabines come to wage war on Rome, the Sabine daughters stand before their armies "with loosened hair and torn garments" and plead that fathers-in-law and sons-in-law not stoop to mutual slaughter ("crinibus passis scissaque veste" [1.13]). Their words prove effective and offer an early testimony to the power of intermarriage to reconcile the bitterest enemies.

In Livy, the Sabine women acquire their new authority as peacemakers almost overnight. In Corneille, the Roman ethos of conquest reverses the Livian progression from abjection to diplomatic authority, so that Sabine and her sister-in-law Camille find themselves reduced to an original abjection as victims of the Roman drive to empire. Before the action begins, Sabine has married Horace as a token of Roman-Alban friendship. The openness and mutuality that her marriage expresses between the two peoples are diametrically opposed to the violence of the Sabine women's abduction. But whatever role she and her sister-in-law might have enjoyed as intercessors between Alban and Roman interests disappears after the war resumes. As the brothers prepare to fight, Old Horace, the Roman paterfamilias, locks them inside the family home precisely so that they cannot fulfill their traditional intercessory role. Lamenting her confinement, Sabine imagines how she and Camille might have otherwise averted the pending tragedy:

> And do you not know that they have made a prison of this house for Camille and me? . . . They are afraid of us and of our tears. Without this, we would be in the midst of their arms and by the despairs of a chaste amity would have drawn some pity from the two camps.

> [Et ne savez-vous point que de cette maison
> Pour Camille et pour moi l'on fait une prison?
> . . . on a peur de nos larmes;
> Sans cela nous serions au milieu de leurs armes,
> Et, par les désespoirs d'une chaste amitié,
> Nous aurions des deux camps tiré quelque pitié.] (3.2.773–78)

The spectacle that Old Horace and his fellow Romans hope to avoid is one that recurred throughout later European history, as royal women acted according to their idealized roles as advocates of peace and reconciliation. The intercessory work honored for centuries in a diplomatic theory steeped in Christian idealizations has no place in the Roman order supported by the Horiatii. War has become for them a perpetual fact of life, not an aberration that must be healed through diplomatic grace. They value the men of other cities not as potential brothers, friends, or peers but as combatants who can test the integrity of their Roman manhood. In the process, they transvalue the ties of marriage and affection that link the Roman and Alban states. For the Horiatii, such ties become proof of an even greater commitment to Rome, something precious that they can sacrifice to show that nothing matters to them but the imperial future.

In its balanced presentation of the claims of two competing diplomatic visions, *Horace* conforms to the Hegelian notion of tragedy as an impasse between incompatible ethical claims.[20] Corneille signals that opposition linguistically through recurrent rhymes on the words "romain," "humain," and their variants. Old Horace, for example, imagines that Roman honor depends on a combat that exceeds the limits of common humanity: "Et de l'événement d'un combat plus humain / Dépendrait maintenant l'honneur du nom romain" (3.5.977–78). But when other characters adapt the same rhyme, the superhuman degenerates into the "non-human" or "inhumane." For this reason, Sabine resists assimilation to her husband, Horace's, race:

> But finally I renounce Roman virtue, if I must be inhuman to possess it. And I can't see in myself the wife of a conqueror without seeing there the wretched sister of the vanquished.

> [Mais enfin, je renonce à la vertu romaine,
> Si pour le posséder je dois être inhumaine,
> Et ne puis voir en moi la femme du vainqueur,
> Sans y voir des vaincus la déplorable soeur.] (4.7.1367–70)

From the perspective of Sabine, her brother Curiace, and even the Roman daughter Camille, the Romans are not more but rather less than human. The play resounds with the charge that they are "inhumane," "brutal," and "barbaric" in their disregard of fundamental human affections that characters such as Camille suggest ought to transcend the more abstract love of country (4.5.1278, 1294).

That inhumanity culminates in the most controversial moment in the play: Horace's sudden execution of his sister Camille for her refusal to celebrate his victory over Curiace, her Alban lover and fiancé. When Camille confronts him, she flaunts her grief for Curiace and denigrates all the Roman values Horace embodies:

> Rome, the sole object of my indignation! Rome, to whom your arm has just sacrificed my lover! Rome, who saw you born and whom your heart adores! Rome, whom finally I hate because she honors you!

> [Rome, l'unique objet de mon ressentiment!
> Rome, à qui vient ton bras d'immoler mon amant!
> Rome, qui t'a vu naître, et que ton cœur adore!
> Rome enfin que je hais parce qu'elle t'honore!] (4.6.1301–4)

From Camille's alternative, arguably more universal perspective, Rome has become a rogue state trampling not just other countries but the common humanity that binds them together in the hope for peace and coexistence. In the fantasy that drives her brother to kill her, she imagines all the nations of the world—"cent peuples unis des bouts de l'univers"—amassing to destroy the city (4.6.1309). This is more than her brother can stand in his single-minded devotion to the *patria*. He drives her from the stage at sword point and, in conformity with neoclassical decorum, kills her offstage.

Camille's murder marks a final abandonment of the old diplomatic order in which polities turned to the bond between husbands and wives to transcend their rivalries and to unite in their common humanity. From Horace's perspective, such an ideal constitutes treason. For him, Rome is prior to all other claims, those of love and common humanity alike. Throughout the play, he and other champions of the Roman state prove deeply suspicious of women, sexuality, friendship, love, and everything else that figured in the diplomatic culture that once united them as a common aristocratic family with the Albans. From their perspective, Rome can conquer and expand, but it can never submit or compromise itself again in its relations with a foreign power.

Horace is a notoriously ambiguous play that has had a long and tortured reception history, typically focused on characters and their actions. From the moment it premiered, audiences have found Camille's death shocking and debated the extent to which it compromises Horace's heroism.[21] John Lyons has moved the conversation usefully beyond questions of which character is most sympathetic or defensible to see the play as foregrounding a moment in the evolution of the Roman state which stigmatized that state's own past as archaic. Emphasizing the conflict between public and private imperatives, Lyons accounts for an aspect of the play that has troubled critics as well as Corneille himself: its division into two sections. In the first, Horace kills the Curiatii brothers, establishes unrivaled Roman domination, and is proclaimed a hero. In the second, Horace kills his sister, is proclaimed a criminal, and escapes execution only because the Roman king declares that his past heroism sets him above the law he has defied. Instead of seeing the division as an aesthetic fault, Lyons sees it as expressing two sides of the same movement from the Roman past to the Roman future. In each case, the emerging republic privileges public over private rights and values. The first section of the play discredits the private bonds linking the Roman and Alban families in order to expand and clarify the boundaries of Rome. The second discredits an older legal principle that allowed males to execute their own family members. Even though Camille committed a grave offense against Rome, the state itself rather than her own family ought to have meted out justice.[22]

While Lyons discusses the relationship between the two halves of the play in terms of new historiographic possibilities, I see it as a double response to new diplomatic ones. Premiered eight years before the Peace of Westphalia, *Horace* dramatizes the two aspects of the classical Westphalian state: its ordering of hierarchical relations within its boundaries and its monadic isolation from other polities. Even though the king pardons Horace for killing his sister, his judgment arrogates authority that families once had over their own errant members to the state itself. At the same time, Horace's prior victory over the Curiatii dismantles the relationships that once upheld Rome and Alba as states that were simultaneously separate but so closely integrated that neither one could act fully on its own initiative.

Even though the Romans triumph over the Albans, however, I am reluctant to see the play as an unambiguous endorsement of that order, even despite its dedication to the same Richelieu who intercepted Anne of Austria's correspondence with her Spanish brother. Other voices in the play are simply too compelling to be ignored or consigned to a past that has lost its power to affect the present. Corneille presents the collapse of the older diplomatic culture from so many competing aesthetic, moral, and historiographic perspectives that it is impossible to identify the author himself with any single attitude. As the first major writer to engage a moment of radical transformation in French diplomatic practice, one that would have major consequences for the role of women in international affairs, Corneille achieves a fragile equipoise between the sacramentology of the past and the masculinist legal regimes of the future. The same coexistence of mutually exclusive visions of the relationship between polities that transformed the Treaty of the Pyrenees into the *casus belli* of the next war gave birth in *Horace* to a new kind of heroine. As French drama matured over the next decade, it derived ever greater aesthetic power from the powerlessness of women to avert catastrophe.

Diplomatic Innovation and the Treaty of the Pyrenees

Life improved for Anne of Austria with Richelieu's death in late 1642 and the death of Louis XIII, the husband she despised, a few months later. Almost immediately, the Parlement de Paris overturned Louis XIII's will, which had limited Anne's authority as regent for her son, the four-year-old Louis XIV.[23] With her historical status restored, Anne's regency harked back to the older diplomatic order, when women regents like Blanche of Castile and Catherine de' Medici—respectively Spanish and Italian by birth—wielded significant power. It also refuted the counterexample of Marie de' Medici, who had found her authority challenged on all fronts before Richelieu and her own son Louis XIII drove her into exile. Rather surprisingly, Anne got along well with Jules Mazarin, Richelieu's protégé and successor. The two may even have become lovers, with Mazarin taking a kind of paternal interest in the young king. As their relationship deepened, Anne entrusted him with the real work of running the country and managing its foreign policy.

Despite the closeness of his relationship with Anne, however, Mazarin persisted in Richelieu's anti-Spanish policies. The war dragged on for another decade and a half. But by the late 1650s, Spain was sufficiently weakened for Mazarin to expect a settlement favorable to France. In addition, a now almost traditional Franco-Spanish match would solve an awkward problem on the domestic front. Louis XIV had fallen in love with Anna Maria Mancini, one of Mazarin's Italian nieces, and the situation was causing all parties considerable embarrassment. Anne and Mazarin sent Mancini back to Italy and forced through the 1659 Treaty of the Pyrenees, a landmark event in diplomatic history. As Mazarin expected, the treaty was a French triumph. France acquired Roussillon, a portion of the Cerdanya Valley, and several other territories in both the Pyrenees and the Spanish Netherlands. At the same time, it solved the problem—at least officially—of Louis XIV's love life by marrying him off to the Infanta, his first cousin Maria Teresa.[24]

Traditional diplomatic history remembers the Treaty of the Pyrenees for creating a "fossilized," or "cold," border, one that has persisted to the present without a major territorial contest.[25] From that perspective, the treaty was a success. But for the historian of marriage diplomacy, the treaty's legacy is more complicated. It not only failed to ward off future Franco-Spanish wars but also sowed the legal seeds for the 1667–68 War of Devolution, the only war in European history fought explicitly over a woman's dowry. The treaty's volatility derived from its incorporation of many of the same conflicted attitudes toward women, their role in international politics, and the sacramental promise of perpetual peace that *Horace* had brought to the French stage a generation earlier. Once the settlement began to unravel, the ensuing propaganda war revealed a major contradiction in France's ostensible drift away from the sacramental diplomacy of the past. Although the French state had much to gain from the devaluation of queens as peacemakers, the French monarchy had something to lose. Kingly and queenly authority had developed throughout the Middle Ages in a close symbiosis. Could one now diminish a queen's powers without damaging kingship itself?

With its pledges of perpetual peace grounded in the sacramentology of marriage, the Treaty of the Pyrenees looked much like a traditional marriage treaty. As we have already seen, the drafters borrowed much of its language from prior Franco-Spanish agreements, particularly the great 1559 Treaty of Cateau-Cambrésis. But there was a major point of controversy during the negotiations that ended with the insertion of a compromise article that not only lacked historical precedent but also embodied Richelieu's revolutionary sense of the transience of all treaties and alliances. Drawing on the precedents of previous marriage treaties, the Spanish wanted Maria Teresa to renounce any claims she might have to a paternal inheritance. They were especially worried that the French would use the marriage as an excuse for annexing the Spanish Netherlands. The French, by contrast, wanted her to retain her hereditary rights. Mazarin's protégé Hugues de Lionne broke through the impasse by claiming a novel compromise: Maria Teresa would renounce her inheritance in exchange for a dowry payment of 500,000 ecus, an extraordinary amount of money. The Spanish agreed, both parties signed the treaty, and the marriage took place.[26]

The renunciation clause was unusual, although it did have precedents. More innovative, however, and more in keeping with Richelieu's critique of traditional marriage alliances, was the demand for an outrageously high dowry. In fact, Lionne and the other French negotiators demanded it because they knew that the Spanish would probably never pay it. The Thirty Years War, the 1635–1659 war with France, and an ongoing war with Portugal had exhausted a Spanish treasury still suffering the inflationary effects of the sixteenth-century American gold and silver rush. Delivering on the promise of 500,000 ecus was impossible. Instead of promoting a durable and permanent peace, the French established a *casus belli* for another round of almost certain war. They had acquired a wife for their king, and they had won some time to lay the diplomatic and military foundations for what they hoped would be future victories. John B. Wolf has argued that the war plans began immediately, and that the French joined the Dutch war against England in 1666 merely to mask their military preparations against Spain.[27]

The War of Devolution came with the 1665 death of Philip IV.[28] The Spanish were in arrears on the dowry payments, so Louis XIV immediately claimed the Spanish Netherlands in the interest of his wife. The French also claimed that Burgundian law protected Maria Teresa's inheritance from her younger brother Carlos II, since he was the son of Philip IV's second wife. To make sure that nobody in Europe missed the point, the French made their case in a widely disseminated pamphlet, Antoine Bilain's *Traité des droits de la reine très chrétienne* (1667), which was published in multiple languages. The Spanish quickly shot back by noting, correctly, that other Spanish women, including Louis's own mother, had surrendered their inheritance claims upon marrying Frenchmen.[29]

Throughout this escalating pamphlet war, different principles of international relations moved in open contradiction. On the surface, the French seemed to pit dynastic right against a Spanish insistence on contract and precedent. Their primary claim was that the succession was an inalienable right that could not be negotiated away. Yet at the same time, for numerous pragmatic and strategic reasons, they did not extend their claim to the Spanish crown itself. By focusing instead on local Burgundian laws and customs,

they tried to justify an international action on the basis of the law of one particular region. Finally, they also repeatedly noted that the Spanish had broken
the 1659 treaty by failing to make the appropriate payments. In searching
everywhere for anything that might support their case, they ended up arguing for universal hereditary rights at the same time they were also arguing
about contract violation and local precedent.

Like the Treaty of the Pyrenees, the French case for war was rhetorically,
theoretically, and practically inconsistent. The logical rifts and fractures all
pointed to a central tension in Louis's identity as an aggressively centralizing
monarch who wanted to enhance the glory of hereditary kingship without
respecting the diplomatic theory that had once supported it. The diplomacy
that produced the treaty and led effectively to the later war was innovative
in the extreme. In 1659 the French agreed to Maria Teresa's renunciation of
her inheritance in exchange for a hefty dowry. In 1665 they castigated the
Spanish for failing to pay the full amount. But they also attacked the Spanish
for bargaining away her rights in the first place. The French certainly had
alternative motives for wanting war that had nothing to do with the marriage, including the need to regularize the French borders in ways that made
them less subject to attack. But there were also more offensive motives, such
as the king's determination to advance his *gloire* and develop an ambitious
and influential military bureaucracy eager for a theater to demonstrate its
abilities. The French state had expanded in ways that made war a likely, and
even necessary, condition for its existence. Promises of perpetual peace were
ringing more hollow than ever.

Richelieu's diplomatic principles had made a lasting impression on the
French court and had become a basis for its later foreign policy. In his *Mémoires*,
composed as a *Fürstenspiegel* for his son and heir apparent, Louis recalled
the circumstances that led to the War of Devolution and expounded more
generally on his thoughts about war, alliance formation, and peace. Even
more than Richelieu, Louis maintained that marriage treaties just bought
time before the next war. He discounted their most exalted expressions of
amity, their gestures toward a kind of sacramental permanence, as "specious
clauses . . . meaning far less than they sound."[30] They may suspend and even
mask hostilities, but only for a time. To invert Clausewitz, policy becomes
the continuation of war by other means. Despite moralizing moments when
he echoes Richelieu on the need for princes to keep their word, Louis's advice
to his son owes nothing to the late medieval notion of Europe as a *res publica
christiana* linked by interdynastic marriages. His France stands in a competitive isolation from its neighbors. In fact, what Louis most mistrusts—and this
sentiment grew over the course of his career—is alliances.

He was especially suspicious of marriage diplomacy. With the exception of the Dauphin, who married the daughter of the Bavarian elector, he married his children to French nobility. In his *Mémoires*, he cautioned his son against taking women into his counsel:

> But the second consideration, which is the most delicate and the most difficult to keep and practice, is that in abandoning our heart, we must remain the absolute master of our thoughts, that we might separate the tenderness of the lover from the resolutions of the sovereign, that the beauty that gives us pleasure might never have the liberty to speak to us of our affairs nor of the people who serve us, and that these two things be absolutely separate.

> [Mais la seconde considération, qui est la plus délicate et la plus difficile à conserver et à pratiquer, c'est qu'en abandonnant notre cœur, il faut demeurer maître absolu de notre esprit; que nous séparions les tendresses d'amant d'avec les résolutions de souverain; que la beauté qui fait nos plaisirs n'ait jamais la liberté de nous parler de nos affaires, ni des gens qui nous y servent, et que ce soient deux choses absolument séparées.][31]

At least until his final years, when Louis almost certainly entered into a secret marriage with Madame de Maintenon and discussed state business with her, he shared Richelieu's sense that women could not be trusted with sensitive information and that their counsel was worthless. Although he spent many hours of the day in the company of Maria Teresa and various mistresses, he generally held to his principle. As Joan DeJean has noted, this bias effectively drove women's political agency into the opposition.[32] Women played an important role in the Fronde and in other expressions of resistance against Louis's ever greater appropriations of power. But Maria Teresa had no opportunities to exercise the traditional queenly role of intercession between her families of origin and marriage.

Maria Teresa's exclusion from such offices was apparent from the moment she arrived in France. Abby E. Zanger has noted that the broadsides and spectacles celebrating the marriage downplayed suggestions of a mutual alliance and stressed instead Spanish subordination.[33] The story of Jason and Medea, for example, figured both in celebratory fireworks displays and in the *Conquête de la Toison d'Or*, which Corneille wrote for the occasion. On the surface, such cultural productions complimented the Order of the Golden Fleece, Spain's highest order of knighthood. The order had originated in Burgundy and come to Spain through the many marriages linking the Burgundian Valois, Hapsburg, and Trastámara dynasties. But as Zanger notes, these works ultimately demoted Maria Teresa, and Spain itself, to a golden fleece captured by the French. A secondary association of Maria Teresa with the sinister Medea presented her as a potential threat to Louis's reign who needed to be domesticated within the French monarchical order.[34]

Whereas Zanger treats such entertainments as symptomatic of Louis's absolutist control over the French state, I want to stress their diachronic force as a repudiation of the centuries-old tradition of honoring the queen as a mediator and peacemaker. The poets and dramatists who arranged the spectacles did not invent them out of thin air. They patterned them on the basis of prior entertainments, but in the process of revising their models, they drastically transformed their ideological significance. I want to focus on one especially telling example, the pastoral eclogue written for the occasion by the young Jean Racine. He based his poem conspicuously on the many pastorals that greeted the 1559 Peace of Cateau-Cambrésis exactly one hundred years before. As in the poems by Ronsard, Du Bellay, Habert, Belleau, and others, a devastated countryside welcomes the long-awaited peace in heavily Virgilian language:

And after the harsh tempests, it is a pleasure to see that the powerless north winds no longer rumble above our heads, that everyone loves the repose after the great travails, that the pleasure is sweet that follows so many evils, that the spring has some charms after a long winter.

[O qu'aprés de rudes tempestes,
Il est agreable de voir
Que les Aquilons sans pouvoir
Ne grondent plus dessus nos testes:
Qu'on aime le repos aprés de grands travaux!
Que le plaisir est doux qui suit beaucoup de maux!
Qu'aprés un long Hiver le Prin-temps a de charmes!][35]

Springtime and pastoral itself return with the cessation of war. In this particular poem, the pastoral speaker is the Nymph of the Seine, who addresses her ode to the new bride. The moment Maria Teresa appears along her banks, the voice of Love ("Amour") breaks from the heavens to assure her that her sufferings, as well those of all Europe, are at an end. In the familiar language descending from *Georgics* I, Racine proclaims that the "sheathed swords will no more see the day, or else will be seen as trophies consecrated to Love by the hands of Peace [Les glaives renfermez ne verront plus le jour, / Ou bien se verront en trophees / Par les mains de la Paix consacrez à l'Amour]" (9).

Thus far the poem reads like the pastorals that celebrated the Peace of Cateau-Cambrésis. But as Love continues to speak, something new happens.

The poem becomes both an ode to peace and a celebration of military achievement. Lamentation over the lands laid waste by war yields to jarring tributes to Louis's preeminence in battle: "I know all that his victorious arm has done, and that even several of our Gods by lesser feats have merited the Heavens! [Je sçay tout ce qu'a fait son bras victorieux, / Et que plusieurs de nos Dieux mesmes, / Par de moindres exploits ont merité les Cieux]" (7). The earlier poems, like the treaties themselves, stressed the mutuality of the settlement, the fact that both the French and Spanish kings had decided to surrender their arms and seal a treaty through the marriage of their children. In Racine, the Spanish are strikingly absent. As we saw in chapter 4, Marc-Claude de Buttet's *Epithalame* signaled the shift from war to peace by representing the heroes of the Italian wars walking peacefully in the wedding procession. Nothing similar happens in Racine. He places so much emphasis on Louis's victories over the Spanish that the treaty appears more as a Spanish surrender than a settlement between two major European powers, a direct reminder that France enjoyed a greater military advantage over Spain in 1659 than it had in 1559.

But the contrast involves more than a difference in the balance of power between the two belligerents. As in Richelieu's diplomatic theory and Louis XIV's comments on the usefulness of diplomatic marriages, Racine's poem commemorates the treaty only as a temporary reprieve from violence in a Europe where alternating periods of war and peace, particularly between France and Spain, have become the status quo. It celebrates the immediate fact of peace without suggesting its permanence. In honoring a king like Louis XIV, Racine had no reason to embrace the millenarian post-epic pastoral that characterized the poetry of Cateau-Cambrésis. Although obviously contradictory, his poetry mirrors and reinforces the contradictory diplomatic discourses that dominated the treaty's negotiation, in which the ambassadors declared a peace that might soon erupt in another war.

The contradictions of *La Nymphe de la Seine a la Reyne* may have suited Louis XIV and his ministers, but they offered a strange compliment to Maria Teresa. Much as her great-grandfather Philip II had stripped Elisabeth de Valois of her traditional role as a mediator between French and Spanish interests to render her more subject to his authority, Racine compromises Maria Teresa. Although he hails her as the source of the restored peace, he also presents her as a war trophy in passages where the celebration of diplomatic achievement relapses into glorification of war:

Spain knew well enough the valor of his [Louis's] arm; she has provided enough Laurels for his glory. He must demand something else of Spain in his turn, and for a final victory, she provides a Myrtle for his love.

Teresa is the illustrious conquest, where all his vows must meet. Never a more famous Myrtle could crown his head. . . . And never did such a beautiful Conquest merit the vows of so great a conqueror.

[L'Espagne sçait assez la valeur de son bras,
Assez elle a fourny de Lauriers à sa gloire;
Il faut qu'il en exige autre chose en ce tour,
Et que pour derniere victoire,
Elle fournisse encore un Myrthe à son amour.
Therese est l'illustre conqueste,
Où doivent tendre tous les voeux,
Jamais un Myrthe plus fameux
Ne sçauroit couronner sa teste. . . .
Et jamais Conqueste si belle
Ne merita les voeux d'un si grand Conquerant.] (7–8)

Maria Teresa's status swerves between exaltation as the numinous presence who restores a long-awaited peace and abjection as the highest trophy of Spain's humiliation. Within the longstanding ethos of European marriage diplomacy, she is destined to unite her countries of origin and descent. But her significance in a world where war has become an ongoing norm is not clear. The poem effectively takes its readers back to the blurriness of the early Middle Ages, when the boundaries between the peace-weaving bride, the hostage, and the sheer spoil of battle were not clear. Something of Rosamund's degradation threatens to resurface in the interplay of competing diplomatic visions.

In retrospect, the early modern French monarchy can look like a "disappearing mediator" separating the Middle Ages from the modern constitutionalist world we know today. On both sides of the Channel, the Tudors, the Stuarts, and the Bourbons developed state bureaucracies to govern the realm. These men replaced the provincial aristocrats on whom medieval monarchs typically depended, and with whom they shared significant authority. Bureaucratization enhanced the monarch's prestige by eliminating that dependence and simultaneously constraining aristocratic power. Versailles became an emblem of this process in France, with its famously idle marquis and counts whose ancestors had rivaled kings as the de facto rulers of their provinces.

It would be a mistake, however, to read the history of bureaucratization solely as a monarchical triumph over the aristocratic past. Ministers posed their own threat to absolutist myth, the fantasy that the king ruled with more than mortal capability. The monarch finally was not omnipotent, omniscient, and omnipresent throughout his or her realm, but the state that he or she brought into being reached deep into the country and touched the lives of ordinary subjects. As the threat of aristocratic rebellion receded into the past, the threat that the state could finally supplant the monarchy loomed.

The foreign queen's loss of her place as a peacemaker and mediator is one aspect of this transition. In seventeenth-century Europe, secretaries like Hugues de Lionne and Arnauld de Pomponne carried out the work that had once been done by royal women like Louise of Savoie and Marguerite of Austria, who had negotiated the 1529 "Paix des Dames" between France and Spain. The effect of this development on European monarchy is hard to judge. As we have seen, Louis XIII and his minister Richelieu mistrusted Anne of Austria's peacemaking efforts as a betrayal of French interests. They would have hailed Maria Teresa's exclusion from political conversation as an enhancement of the king's authority. But the old monarchy had gained considerable prestige from its association with powerful, even saintly women like Blanche of Castile, who bequeathed her own reputation for piety to her son, Saint Louis IX. However much Louis XIV stood to gain from representing his wife as a French spoil, he also stood to lose by making a less exalted woman the mother of his heir. The fact that Maria Teresa did not meddle in the king's affairs, for example, might have reduced confidence in her as a regent if Louis had predeceased her during his son's minority. Her diminished status also limited the future king's ability to claim descent from two equally exalted royal lines. The clearest benefactors from the new diplomatic culture were not the king and his heirs but the new ministers of state, whose growing authority threatened to eclipse the monarchy it presumably served.

The *Bérénice* Project: Corneille, Racine, and the Secret Treaty of Dover

Louis XIV had reasons to worry about monarchical prestige. Just a few months before his seventy-two-year reign began, the British civil wars that eventually cost Charles I of England both his throne and his life had begun. Charles was married to Henrietta Maria, Louis's aunt. Louis's brother Philippe later married Charles and Henrietta Maria's daughter Henriette of England, who had fled to the French court as an exile when she was three years old. Anglo-French interdynastic marriages were relatively rare after the High

Middle Ages. But Franco-Scottish ones were not. Charles I and his family were Stuarts, the hereditary kings of Scotland. Charles's great-grandmother was Marie of Guise, and his grandmother Mary had been queen of France before her husband's early death. The cluster of marriages linking Louis XIV with Charles marked nothing less than a renewal of the Auld Alliance that had linked the French and Scottish crowns since 1295.[36]

The close personal and historic links between the Bourbon and Stuart monarchies meant that Louis and his family registered in a direct and personal way every shock of the wars, the regicide, the Stuart exile, the Restoration, the post-Restoration constitutional struggles, and the forced abdication of James II and his life as an exile at St. Germain. French and English politics developed in the later seventeenth century in inverse relation with each other. The specter of republicanism across the Channel fueled French worries about religious dissent, while accounts of French absolutism exacerbated English fears of popery and arbitrary government. It was a dangerous symbiosis whose effects were registered differently on opposite sides of the Channel. In France, it contributed to renewed persecution of the Huguenot community. In England, it drove a vicious cycle of self-fulfilling paranoias. The men who formed the nucleus of the Whig party accused the king and his ministers of refashioning English political life on a French absolutist model. But the more they threatened the monarchy and fanned its fears of another rebellion, the more Charles II turned to his French cousin for assistance.[37]

By 1670, the declining fortunes of the Stuart monarchy, coupled with Louis's need for allies in an escalating struggle against William of Orange and the Dutch Republic, prompted one of the period's most notorious diplomatic engagements, the so-called Secret Treaty of Dover. Scholars have generally written about the treaty as a fatal miscalculation on the English side, since it convinced important sectors of the country that Charles really was in a dangerous alliance with Louis.[38] I look at the treaty instead here as a telling exception in the decline of marriage diplomacy, one with important literary and political consequences. As we have seen, Louis repeatedly insisted on the importance of excluding women from the business of state. Throughout his reign he relied exclusively on his male ministers to orchestrate what had become the fulfillment of Richelieu's vision: a perpetual cycle of war and negotiation. But that changed with the 1670 Treaty of Dover. This time, Louis turned to a woman: his sister-in-law, Henriette of England. Like many treaties, the Treaty of Dover did not deliver on all of its promises. But its marginal, supplemental character renders visible a rare moment of cultural reflection on the clash between two different attitudes toward interdynastic marriage, one older and one newer, and the role of women in state affairs.

The same year that Henriette returned to England as an emissary for the French king, Pierre Corneille and Jean Racine each wrote a play about the Judean queen Berenice, whom the Roman emperor Titus loved but abandoned because Roman law banned even the emperor from marrying a foreign queen. French theatrical companies often spied on one another and tried to scoop their rivals by premiering plays on the same subject. Two *Comédie des Comédiens* appeared in 1633, two *Place Royales* in 1634, and two *Rodogunes* in 1644. But usually one of the contenders was a relatively unknown playwright hoping to make his name by challenging a more famous one.[39] In the case of the *Bérénice* plays, Corneille and Racine were established masters, the greatest tragic writers of their age, and longtime rivals. By the early eighteenth century, critics claimed that Henriette of England herself had encouraged the competition and even proposed the subject. Since the earliest of these claims postdates the event by almost five decades, there has been room for ample debate among historians of the French stage about Henriette's role.[40] Although extant sources do not prove that Henriette set up the competition, the plays repeatedly engage questions about dynastic alliance, monarchical dignity, and the relationship between the monarch and representative assemblies that all factored into the negotiations that resulted in the Treaty of Dover.

Readers and audiences have dismissed Corneille's *Tite et Bérénice* as a failure and have much preferred Racine's *Bérénice*.[41] But once again, marginalization can be significant. Corneille's play holds more overt interest for the historian of diplomacy because his Bérénice is a savvy political player who grasps and can exploit the constitutional differences between Rome and her native Judea. Racine's Bérénice, by contrast, retreats from the political sphere into an erotic anguish that incapacitates her as a queen but has captivated audiences for generations. Her exquisite but ultimately ineffectual laments create a space for the diva on the French stage, one that expanded the next year with the first performance at the Académie d'Opéra.

The development of a taste for divas in place of daring women politicians is at stake in the competition between the older Corneille and the younger Racine. But few things are as hard to trace as the relationship between high politics and the history of tastes. Correlations can be obvious, but exact lines of causality and impact are unclear. If we talk about plays reflecting history, we place them outside of history by ignoring the social circumstances of their patronage and production and by denying them the ability to influence later historical developments. But when we start talking about a play's political work, we often base our speculations more on what happens in the play and what we think might have been its impact rather than on actual evidence of its reception. Although critics, other playwrights, and members of the French Academy said much about seventeenth-century plays, they used a neo-Aristotelian discourse that put questions of decorum and form before topical significance. In true neoclassical fashion, the universal trumped the topical in ways that can frustrate scholars trying to reconstruct histories of political culture.

I want to be especially wary about narrow topical claims, since the earliest surviving reference to Henriette's commission dates from 1704, long after the plays were written. Such commissions happened, and it is not at all improbable that Henriette asked Corneille and Racine to write the plays. At the least, the appearance of two plays dealing with the same interdynastic marriage and the place of women in foreign relations in the same year that Henriette undertook her mission to England is suggestive. Regardless of her precise role in the plays' inception, reading the Secret Treaty of Dover against them and vice versa encourages scholars of diplomacy to look beyond the synchronic interests at play in the 1670 negotiations and to consider their *longue durée* implications. The cross-reading foregrounds a problem in the relationship between women's diplomatic agency and the integrity of monarchical authority: Did the diva's eloquent abjection foreshadow the degradation of monarchy itself? This is the question that Corneille's play raises and whose evasion underwrites Racine's success.

The Treaty of Dover had an immediate purpose: enlisting the English navy in one of Louis's recurring wars against the Dutch. But on the French side, and even more on the English, deeper questions about monarchical prerogative, gender, and interdynastic marriage lay behind the treaty. Louis's troubles with the Dutch began when they impeded his efforts to annex the Spanish Netherlands. Louis claimed this land by right of his wife's inheritance as the daughter of the deceased Spanish king. The Dutch wanted to preserve it as a Spanish buffer zone between them and Louis's powerful armies. Louis insisted that the territory was his by inviolable natural right: no monarch had the power to cede away his inheritance. From the French perspective, moreover, the republican Dutch still bore the stigma of having rebelled against the king of Spain, their hereditary overlord.

On the English side, the offer of a French stipend promised a way for Charles II to break his financial dependence on Parliament. Recent English history confronted Louis with the epitome of monarchical degradation in Charles I's 1649 execution. Although Charles II restored the monarchy in 1660, Parliament enjoyed a power of the purse that constrained his foreign and domestic policy. Above all, he could not go to war without Parliament's grant of subsidies. Given the fact that a rabidly anti-Catholic Parliament was unlikely to underwrite an alliance with France against the Protestant Dutch, Louis would have to pay for England's intervention in the pending war. If the scheme worked, Louis would gain an ally, enhance the prestige and freedom of the English king, and restore foreign policy as a distinctly royal prerogative.

Despite Louis's often stated distaste for women politicians, Henriette was the ideal person to carry out the negotiations. Like her brother Charles II, she had suffered firsthand the outrages of the English Parliament against her family. Born two years into the British civil wars, she was taken to France as an infant and grew up in exile. Her English father was executed when she was only four years old. At the same time, Henriette was loyal to French interests. She bore the name of her French mother, Henrietta Maria, had spent her life at the French court, and was married to Louis's brother Philippe.

Nothing in extant historical sources suggests that Louis was thinking about much besides an English alliance against the Dutch, or that he worried about his inconsistent use of a woman as a negotiator.[42] Henriette answered a present political need. But she carried in her name, her bloodlines, and her personal and familial experience the potential for a more complex reflection on the history of Anglo-French relations, in which the degradation of queenship preceded the degradation of monarchy. Henriette derived her effectiveness as a negotiator from her place in a network of Anglo-French royal marriages that dated back generations, most obviously in the marriage between her parents. As an English princess petitioning for help from her royal brother to aid France, she stepped into a role played over a century before by Henry VIII's sister Mary Tudor, the consort of Louis XII.[43] More ominously, that *longue durée* history revealed that the degradation of such royal women and the diminution of their intercessory powers presaged dangers for kings. In their contempt for women meddling in politics, Richelieu and later Louis XIV, the great champion of royal *gloire*, came close to reproducing the antifeminism of English Parliamentarians. They too disliked women who meddled in politics and had denounced Henriette's mother as a French Catholic goading her husband to subvert the English church and constitution. Louis now found himself relying on a woman who was the product of multiple Anglo-French marriages to bolster the fortunes of both monarchies.

As far as we know, nobody at the French court pointed out the multiple ironies in this return to the diplomatic culture of prior generations or suggested that Louis shared antifeminist attitudes with English Parliamentarians. But the plays that Henriette may have encouraged Corneille and Racine to write portray conflicts between rulers and representative bodies. They also depict the denigration of foreign queens. Corneille's play in particular links queenship so closely to the dignity of kingship that the degradation of one entails the degradation of the other.

The fairly obscure story of Berenice comes from two short passages in Suetonius and Dio Cassius. They recount how Titus fell in love with Berenice, a Herodian client ruler of Judea and sister of Agrippa II, when she assisted Titus and his father, Vespasian, in crushing a rebellious Jewish faction. She later moved to Rome and lived with Titus in expectation of marrying him. But the Roman people rejected her, and Titus sent her away. Berenice had three strikes against her: she was Jewish, a foreigner, and a queen. Rome had rejected monarchy centuries before, at the beginning of the Roman Republic. Even though the Caesars wielded enormous power, they were not technically monarchs. Berenice's tragedy hinged in part on that technicality. The story may have appealed to Henriette as the exiled daughter of a hated foreign queen and an English king whose murder marked the beginning of an English republic.

Corneille and Racine treat Titus's inability to marry the foreign queen he loves as a mark of his answerability to Roman law, custom, popular opinion, and, especially in Corneille's case, the Roman Senate. An emperor might control more legions and hold more lands than a king, but he does not enjoy the freedom to form marital alliances with foreign dynasties that enhance the prestige of other, lesser rulers. Both plays revolve around this central paradox: the man who wields all cannot marry as he wishes, but only as the Roman political situation demands. Corneille's Tite sums it up in one pathetic epithet: "Maître de l'Univers, sans l'être de moi-meme" (2.1.407). Titus's inability to marry Berenice provides the perfect image for the isolation of sovereignty in what would become the dominant state system: a monarch might aspire to total control, but the inability to marry a foreign queen reminds him of the growing inaccessibility and alienation of everything that lies beyond his borders. Renouncing Berenice sacrificed cosmopolitanism for the sake of Rome.

Critics have often argued that the rival playwrights reached a kind of aesthetic rapprochement in their Bérénice plays.[44] But generic and tonal differences between Corneille's "heroic comedy" and Racine's tragedy arise from different diplomatic orientations in a world where the nature of sovereignty, of peacemaking, and of women's role in foreign alliances had changed. Corneille's extended cast of principals, doubled, intersecting plots, and tonal instabilities figure Rome's abandonment of interdynastic marriage as both a moral and a political absurdity. The paradox of an emperor who can do anything but marry the woman he loves exposes even deeper contradictions in the Roman constitution. As a foreign queen who holds to the prerogatives of her rank, Corneille's Bérénice embodies the dignity of a monarchical order, reinforced by interdynastic marriage, which the Romans have traded for something at once grander and less morally substantial. In Racine, Bérénice's histrionics detach queenly grandeur from governance and confirm Louis XIV's recurrent statements about women's political inadequacies. Yet the impassioned speeches that undermine our sense of Bérénice's ability to rule also endow her with a dramatic intensity that has made her a more memorable character than her Cornelian counterpart and earned Racine's play a greater place in the French theatrical canon.

Corneille's *Tite et Bérénice* differs most from Racine's play in its expansion of Titus and Berenice's love story into an interlocking lovers' quadrangle. Tite is in love with Bérénice, but for political reasons must not only abandon her but also marry Domitie, the daughter of a popular general once offered the imperial throne. The ruthlessly ambitious Domitie is eager to marry Tite, since she longs to be empress. But she is also in love with Domitian, Tite's brother. Domitie is a comic villain in her ambitious excess. She is willing to betray herself and the man she loves in her lust for the diadem, and to throw Rome into a civil war if Tite resumes his relationship with Bérénice. Her beloved, Domitian, is the most traditionally comic character in the play, an *eiron* who works continually to win back Domitie and to reunite Tite and Bérénice. At one point he even woos Bérénice himself to make both Tite and Domitie jealous in the hope of winning back Domitie and restoring Tite to Bérénice. The play's denouement, however, is only half-comic. Domitie and Domitian are united because Tite and Bérénice decide to remain celibate after their separation. Tite's refusal to marry anyone guarantees Domitian's succession to the imperial throne. Domitie will have her cake and eat it too, since the man she loves will eventually become emperor and she herself will reign as empress. As for Tite and Bérénice, they go their separate ways and leave intact the law banning marriage between the emperor and foreign royalty.

Tite et Bérénice figures the conflict between an older, sacramental diplomacy that honored foreign queens as mediators and a newer one more suspicious of such cosmopolitanism in the rivalry between its two leading women, Bérénice and Domitie. The opposition could not be sharper. Bérénice loves Tite for himself, Domitie for his office; Bérénice brings realms together; Domitie threatens to divide Rome. Bérénice embodies the East as everything that Rome is not: cosmopolitan rather than imperial; monarchical and dynastic rather than factionlized and sentimentally attached to a lost republican past; and, since Bérénice is a Jew, monotheistic rather than pagan. Domitie instead embodies the history of the factionalized empire. As she often reminds us, her father, Gnaeus Domitius Corbulo, served as a consul under Caligula, and a general under Claudius and Nero, and suffered a heroic disgrace for his implication in the Pisonian conspiracy to murder Nero. Her mother was a member of the Julian family and a direct descendant of Augustus. Her pedigree is exalted, but tainted by the murderous politics of the Roman past.

Tite's choice between Bérénice and Domitie is a choice not just between two women but between opposite political and moral possibilities. In leaning toward Domitie, he sides with Rome, its gods, laws, and customs, and its political culture in all its factionalism and the absurdity of an ancestral constitutionalism operating now only in the ban against interdynastic marriage. As much as Tite respects Domitie's ancestry and strength of character, he agrees to marry her because she wears the mantle of a senatorial faction whose opposition could undermine his reign. Domitie is aware of this fact, and menaces him with it whenever he shows his true feelings for Bérénice. The more such manipulations influence Tite, the more they expose absurdities in his position as an emperor but not a hereditary king. The law against intermarriage turns out not to be the only thing limiting his prerogative. He also has to worry about appeasing Domitie, various factions, and even the people he nominally governs. In this play, the emperor does not intimidate the Senate; the Senate intimidates the emperor.

As Paul Strohm, David Wallace, and others have noted, the old sacramental ideal of royal marriage emphasized monarchy as a symbiosis in which queens tempered their husbands' excesses.[45] Queens, for instance, sometimes interceded with their husbands to mitigate sentences against criminals. More broadly, kings stood to learn things from their queens and their cultures of origin. In a foundational story of the French monarchy, the Burgundian princess Clothilde brought Christianity to France by converting her Merovingian husband, King Clovis. French audiences may have recognized that story as a subtext for Bérénice's belief in the God owned by Jews and Christians alike:

> . . . she hates our temples
> And serves a jealous god, who cannot stand
> That any other might be worshipped
> Besides himself.

> [elle abhorre nos Temples,
> Et sert un Dieu jaloux, qui ne peut endure
> Qu'aucun autre que lui se fasse révérer.] (4.1.1068–70)

Bérénice's enemies note that she has already won over several Roman converts and fear that her influence will undermine the state religion. Bérénice introduces Rome to knowledge of the one true God and to a new vision of monarchy as a positive alternative to Roman factionalization. When she enters the play, she brings with her a virtue Tite clearly lacks: sovereign dignity. She will not stoop to either Domitie's taunts or Domitian's schemes: "But perhaps, sir, you believe Bérénice / Has a heart willing to lower itself to this artifice? [Peut-être, mais Seigneur, croyez-vous Bérénice / D'un cœur à s'abaisser jusqu'à cet artifice?]" (3.1.751–54). Aware of her hereditary prestige as a Herodian queen, she resists the bureaucracy, courtly decorum, and political maneuvering that compromise Tite's prerogatives as emperor. When Tite refuses to see her ambassadors before he is securely married to Domitie, for example, Bérénice simply barges into his presence. At a moment when more and more diplomatic responsibility was passing to French ministers of state, Corneille's fiction foregrounds a queen who submits only so far to ambassadorial representation: she prefers to speak for herself. Her act constitutes a protest against bureaucracies and protocols that extended the monarch's reach but also compromised his or her personal agency. Bérénice may be a client queen, but she exercises a more direct, and arguably more absolutist, authority that will not tolerate mediation.

Throughout the play, Bérénice laments the emptiness of Tite's claims to godlike power. From her perspective, the emperor's legions may make him more than a monarch, but his dependence on senatorial cooperation and popular acclaim makes him less than one: "Are you on this throne where all the world aspires / Only to subject the emperor to the empire? [N'êtes-vous dans ce trône où tant de monde aspire / Que pour assujettir l'Empereur à l'Empire?]" (3.5.991–92). Bérénice characterizes Tite's rule as a perversion of a truly absolutist monarchical order: the emperor submits in practice to the people he governs in a topsy-turvy theory of state. Instead of promulgating his own law, he submits to one common to him and to his subjects alike. Instead of his ruling an empire, the empire rules him.

Bérénice's refusal to stoop underlies her otherwise inexplicable decision not to marry Tite at the end of the play. Like the Princesse de Clèves, finally freed by her husband's death to marry the man she has always loved, she suddenly turns him down. Tite is stunned by her resolution. The motivations for her shocking decision lie both in practical considerations and in a signature concern with the decay of monarchical prestige. When Bérénice catalogues a history of senatorial inconstancy, however, she convinces him that they can never count on its support in the future: "We have already seen too many of its ebbs and flows [nous avons trop vu ses flux, et ses reflux]" (5.5.1685). Even if the Senate accepts their marriage today, it might not tomorrow. Nor can the Senate ever dispel the threat that an assassin might kill them in the name of thwarted Roman liberty, since "false virtue makes itself an honor out of crime [Et la fausse vertu se fait honneur du crime]" (5.5.1696).

Although such considerations help Tite understand her decision, Bérénice's final lines rise above practical considerations to defend the integrity of monarchy:

Rome has saved my glory in giving me her voice. . . .

Let us render her, you and I, this awareness:
To have weakened the law's force to please you,
To have sacrificed it to your sweeter wishes.

[Rome a sauvé ma gloire en me donnant sa voix, . . .

Rendons-lui, vous et moi, cette reconnaissance
D'en avoir pour vous plaire affoibli la puissance,
De l'avoir immolée à vos plus doux souhaits.] (5.5.1697, 1699–1701)

Bérénice ultimately refuses Tite's hand in marriage because she does not want to accept it as a senatorial favor. If she had accepted it, the Romans would know that she was empress only by their permission. But since she rejects it, they will suffer the humiliation of having offered to modify their laws to satisfy an emperor's desires for a foreign queen. In refusing the Roman Senate's offer, Tite and Bérénice have reestablished something of the imperial and monarchical dignity degraded by Roman custom. The denouement is heroic in the sense that Tite and Bérénice have sacrificed their love not for the sake of Rome but for their own imperial and monarchical dignity against the presumption of the Roman people.

Written the same year that Henriette negotiated a promising Anglo-French alliance, Corneille's *Tite et Bérénice* could support several topical readings focused on French and English affairs. Its original audience, for example, may have heard in Bérénice's contempt for the Roman Senate a critique of the English Parliaments that had executed Henriette's father, denigrated her brother, and constrained his prerogatives. But something even larger was at stake in this play: the fear that a pan-European political order, established and maintained through generations of interdynastic marriages, was splintering into the competing interests of individual states. In the language of modern international relations theory, *Tite et Bérénice* prioritizes an international society organized around common interests over the realist vision of states locked in perennial competition which Louis XIV anticipated in his comments on the unreliability of marriage alliances. Within the play, Bérénice's cosmopolitanism threatens the Roman state because it allows her to see Roman society from perspectives that are closed to the Romans themselves. Perhaps the greatest cost of Rome's opposition to intermarriage is her complex transnational vision. Within the historical moment of its composition, the play suggested that it might also be a cost of increasingly bureaucratized and monadic diplomatic practice.

The political dimensions of Corneille's *Tite et Bérénice* are easier to characterize than those of Racine's *Bérénice* in part because Corneille's heroine is an astute politician who comments explicitly on Roman affairs. Her language is the most direct, and often the flattest, in the play. Racine's Bérénice, by contrast, is not a politician. She is instead a diva, an extravagant performer of her own suffering.[46] For those interested in the diplomatic past, the challenge of this play lies in reading the political significance of her solipsism. Turning from politics to endless reflections on her misery, she reverses the cultural history that once exalted foreign brides as intercessors between their families of birth and origin. Her tears have no impact on relations between Rome and her native Judea, already a Roman satellite. Like those of the early Germanic peace-weavers, they merely register her powerlessness before historical destiny.

Compared with Corneille's play, Racine's *Bérénice* has a much simpler, elegantly disciplined plot. There are no lovers' quartets, no Domitie or Domitian, no attempts to bring the lovers together through a last-minute senatorial intervention, and no sudden shifts in tone or genre. *Bérénice* is a pure tragedy. Toward the end, Titus notes than in leaving Bérénice, he has surpassed the "austérité" of his Roman predecessors, a word that characterizes Racine's aesthetic and moral program alike (4.5.1166).[47] Austerity also captures the play's vision of interstate relations, in which Rome acquires a patronage relationship with other states without compromising the purity of its bloodlines. Titus's rejection of an interdynastic marriage with Bérénice discredits the older, sacramental diplomacy commemorated by Corneille as a personal self-indulgence in need of austerity and discipline.

The play's resistance to a hybridized genre blurring tragic and heroic conventions complements a resistance to racial miscegenation that, in Racine's version, underlies Rome's opposition to interdynastic marriage: Paulin, a trusted counselor, reminds Titus that "Rome, by a law that cannot be changed / Does not allow any foreign blood to mix with its blood [Rome, par une Loi qui ne se peut changer, / N'admet avec son sang aucun sang étranger]" (2.2.377–78). In obedience to it, Julius Caesar left "his Cleopatra sighing alone in the Orient [Seule dans l'Orient la laissa soupirer]" (2.2.390).

Even Antony, who "forgot both his glory and his country in her bosom, / Dared not call himself her husband [Oublia dans son sein sa gloire et sa Patrie, / Sans oser toutefois se nommer son Époux]" (2.2.392–93). According to Paulin, the only people who ever violated the law were two slaves. When Claudius freed them, they promptly married two queens "of Bérénice's blood [du sang de Bérénice]" (2.2.408). Paulin treats this marriage as an unspeakable violation of the rank and honor on which Roman society rests. His message is clear: in marrying Bérénice, Titus might mix his blood with that of slaves. The law gives Rome a racial purity that distinguishes it from the other, racially debased nations of the Mediterranean world it has conquered.

Characters link the perceived racial threat to a moral threat. Throughout the play, Bérénice opposes the personal denial and self-sacrifice on which Roman society rests. Titus's advisers and his conscience urge him to pattern himself after the great men of the past who put Rome before all. Titus carries a burden of history, one that neither he nor Paulin tires of rehearsing. Titus is answerable to the law against intermarriage because he is answerable to the Roman past—a past from which he derives his dignity.

Bérénice, by contrast, embodies a private life turned away from Roman duty. In a play that emphasizes Roman history and the course of empire, her divaesque focus is private. She first appears in her apartment inside the palace, where she has retreated from Titus's coronation. In contrast to Titus, who always appears on his way to or from grand public assemblies, Bérénice is either in her chamber or in transit between it and Titus's room. She is not afraid of the public per se. She dislikes crowds because they shift focus away from her and her feelings for Titus. This solipsism manifests itself in every line she speaks with her characteristic reiterations of first-person pronouns: "And as for me (the memory makes me tremble anew), / They wanted to take me away from everything I adore [Et moi (ce souvenir me fait frémir encore) / On voulait m'arracher de tout ce que j'adore]" (2.4.611–12). Although Titus has showered her with kingdoms, in part as a preemptive consolation for their inevitable separation, they mean nothing to her: "Weak comforts for so large a sorrow [Faibles amusements d'une douleur si grande!]" (2.2.528). The more kingdoms she wins, the less she cares about them.

Nothing must have seemed stranger to an early modern audience familiar with the conventions of interdynastic marriage than a queen dismissive of kingdoms. The play inverts the usual affective order of such marriages, in which a bride and groom who do not know each other, and certainly do not love each other, marry for political reasons. Here the bride and groom love each other desperately, but politics stands in their way. Their love for each other, and particularly Bérénice's extravagant, kingdom-sacrificing love for Titus, provides an argument not just against their marriage but potentially against all marriages of state.

In contrast to Corneille, here the law against intermarriage proves to be anything but absurd. It shields Titus, and by extension the Roman state, from an erotic desire that the play constructs as inimical to public life. In Corneille, the law finally matters less than popular opinion and the Senate's will to uphold it. In Racine, the law is everything. Every character except Bérénice speaks of it with veneration because it protects Rome from emasculating foreign influences.

Even at the height of despair, Titus never says that the law is unjust. He simply laments the situation in which he and the woman he loves find themselves: "Constrained by the austere laws of duty, / I had to renounce seeing you forever [Où pressé par les lois d'un austère devoir / Il fallait pour jamais renoncer à vous voir]" (5.6.1377–78). Plead as Bérénice might, Titus never offers to overturn or disregard those "austere laws." Even when he realizes she is contemplating suicide, the most he considers is abandoning the throne and running away with her. Yet that alternative proves impossible. He loves her too much to inflict on her a life with a disgraced emperor, "a vile spectacle to humanity of the frailties of love [Vil spectacle aux humains des faiblesses d'amour]" (5.6.1418–19). In short, he can only match her threats of suicide with his own.

At this point, a classical subtext that has haunted the play rises to the surface: book 4 of Virgil's *Aeneid*, the story of Dido and Aeneas.[48] In the preface to the play's first published edition, Racine notes that he has taken the Dido episode as his tragic model. The play shares with Virgil an equation of *romanitas*, the essence of being a Roman, with self-sacrifice. Rome calls its heroes to surrender the thing they love most in the interest of the imperium. But unlike Aeneas, who tried to skulk away without confronting Dido and certainly never considered suicide, Titus grows so eloquent in his expressions of pain that he reverses the Virgilian denouement and out-Didos Dido. His ardor also transforms Bérénice and pulls her back from the brink of self-destruction. Recognizing the depth of Titus's feelings, she escapes her solipsistic involvement with her own suffering just enough to surrender Titus to his imperial destiny: "I will live, I will follow your absolute orders / Farewell my Lord. Reign. I will never see you again [Je vivrai, je suivrai vos ordres absolus. / Adieu, Seigneur, régnez: je ne vous verrai plus]" (5.7.1505–6).

Why can Bérénice release Titus? His suicide threats have proven that he loves her so much that he will be miserable for the rest of his life if he marries her. In other words, even though the play ends with their separation, Bérénice remains incapable of understanding anything beyond the private language of the heart. Critics have argued that she achieves a kind of Cornelian dignity in her final lines that distinguishes her from Racine's other, even more passion-driven heroines. But that dignity is still tainted by so much self-involvement that one cannot imagine her going back to reign in Judea. Even in declaring her submission to Titus's absolute authority and that of the Roman law he must uphold, she remains a diva to the end: "*I will live, I will follow . . . I will never see you again.*"

The fact that Racine presents her recovery as a response to Titus's despair, moreover, confirms the worst suspicions of Paulin and others about the threat she poses to Roman manhood in its austere virtue. The question of the two plays' potential contributions to diplomatic history becomes most clear in their divergent fantasies of Roman manhood. In Corneille, on the one hand, the emperor rises to his highest authority through a vigorous, open cosmopolitanism associated with marital exogamy. Corneille's Bérénice enhances Tite's virtue, in the Latin etymological sense of *virtus*, by teaching him to stand up to the Roman Senate, a body of men prone to effeminizing manipulation. In Racine, on the other hand, cosmopolitanism jeopardizes a manhood that stems from an engagement with Roman institutions, Roman law, and the great men of the Roman past. Racine inscribes himself into that tradition through his debt to Virgil, the creator of a poem whose hero preserves his manhood and future empire by rejecting the passionate Semitic queen of Carthage and marrying instead the silent but safely Italian Lavinia. That marriage turns out to be more endogamous than exogamous, since the Trojan Aeneas traces his bloodlines from the Italian Dardanus.

Racine challenges the old sacramental diplomacy and queenly mediation in presenting a woman whose radical disengagement from politics emasculates a Roman emperor. He defines his own theater as a more appropriate space for female talent than the council room was. In Corneille, the two spaces never separate along clearly gendered lines. His leading actress speaks lines pregnant with wiser counsel than any actor in the play. In the process, she offers the women in his audience a model for women holding their own against the men at court. Racine's divaesque Bérénice, by contrast, speaks only of her passion:

You love me, you maintain you do,
And yet I am leaving, and you order me to do so!
What? Do you find so many charms in my despair?
Do you fear my eyes are pouring too few tears?

[Vous m'aimez, vous me le soutenez,

Et cependant je pars, et vous me l'ordonnez?

Quoi? Dans mon désespoir trouvez-vous tant de charmes?

Craignez-vous que mes yeux versent trop peu de larmes?] (5.6.1357–60)

On a metadramatic level, we do find charms in Bérénice's despair. It is essential to this tragedy with its passionate display of remediless human anguish. As we watch Racine's play, the political questions that Corneille—and Corneille's Bérénice—foregrounded recede into the background. Women are there not to rule, not to govern, but to suffer. Reigning supreme upon the stage, they need never sit at a table of counsel.

Henriette died shortly after she returned from England, and the French court went into extravagant mourning. The treaty that she negotiated ultimately failed. The English were later outraged to learn of a secret clause linking the French subsidy to Charles's agreement to become a Catholic. Instead of enhancing the British monarchy's prestige, the treaty brought it to one of its lowest levels. Eventually England pulled out of the French alliance and supported the Dutch against France. None of these subsequent developments, of course, suggests incompetence on Henriette's part. The conjunction of plays on similar topics by Corneille and Racine allows us to imagine two ways contemporaries may have judged Louis's surprising and atypical decision to entrust a sensitive negotiation to his sister-in-law. In the world that Corneille evokes, Henriette's mission to England had *longue durée* precedent and justification. It looked back to a pan-European society founded on shared dynastic interests and, at least in theory, grounded in a sacramentology that authorized women as natural mediators. Racine's world has no place for Henriette. If it does, it casts her as a mere functionary of the French state, or at best a spokesperson for her royal brother-in-law, who authorizes her every word. For a few weeks in 1670, the Cornelian interpretation may have been more accurate. But in the diplomatic culture that was emerging, Henriette's mission would have appeared increasingly atypical.

While Corneille looked to the diplomatic past, Racine looked to the future and to a Europe where the dream of an international society that reconciled the interests of individual powers seemed ever more elusive. Interdynastic marriages continued well into the twentieth century, but after the eighteenth-century wars of dynastic succession, such marriages no longer came with the promise, or even the rhetoric, of perpetual peace. In 1795 Immanuel Kant argued that, instead of fostering peace, the old interdynastic marriage system violated one of its cardinal preconditions, the principle that "no independently existing state, whether it be large or small, may be acquired by another state by inheritance, exchange, purchase or gift."[49] States cannot "marry one another" without violating the rights of their citizens. Kant wrote his essay in the form of a treaty, with preliminary articles, definitive articles, and appendices. He titled it "On Perpetual Peace," to distinguish it from the truces, cease-fires, and notoriously short-term alliances that had become the mainstay of European politics. But the title also glanced backwards to the language of the premodern marriage treaties he openly dismissed.

As a modern political philosopher, Kant rejected marriage as a basis of statecraft. But unlike Richelieu, Louis XIV, and the majority of his contemporaries, he refused to accept the Hobbesian inevitability of war. He argued instead for a rule of international law with such tenets as the abolition of standing armies, noninterference in the affairs of other states, and a ban on secret treaties.[50] Kant initiated a long tradition of international relations theory arguing that the transformation of despotisms into republics brings about the perpetual peace that the old dynastic system promised but never achieved. Over two hundred years later, a growing body of international law has adopted many of Kant's proposals. But perpetual, universal peace remains a hope rather than a lived experience.

Kant had his blind spots, and they may point to something valuable that was abandoned with the sacramental diplomacy of the past. The older diplomatic culture acknowledged a role for the emotions in interstate relations. Monarchs spoke of their alliances with one another in terms of friendship and familial love. Clerics called on rulers to renounce their enmities and embrace one another as Christian brothers and sisters. Interdynastic marriage gave a genealogical grounding to these emotional claims. In advocating instead a legal regime grounded in reason, Kant, and more generally the evolving Westphalian state system, banished feelings like love and hatred to the realm of the irrational and the politically irrelevant. In short, they banished them to the literary. Rulers might act on the basis of love, affection, jealousy, and hatred on the stage and in the rapidly developing historical novel. But at least in legal theory, the rulers of enlightened democracies should act on the basis of reason, law, and dedication to the common good.

In its resistance to the irrational, the legal regime that emerged in the Enlightenment reinforced a larger cultural equation between the emotional and the feminine in opposition to masculine rationality. Although later international lawyers looked back on Louis XIV as the quintessentially lawless despot, they typically shared his assumption that women had no place in public life. A new generation of diplomatic historians has helped us to see the extent to which the wives of statesmen and ambassadors remained important behind-the-scenes-players. But such influence was increasingly subject to public outcry and condemnation as unwarranted meddling.

The legal regime's refusal to engage the passions has often left it powerless before the irrational forces that continue to shape relations between states. Policy makers around the world are now struggling with the question of how to dispel or contain long-standing ethnic and religious hatreds that destabilize entire regions. In much the same way, the tacit assumption that state affairs were primarily about relations between and among men blinded generations of statesmen to gendered injustices around the world. Only in the past few decades has a new discourse of human rights brought questions about the rights of women and sexual minorities to the fore. Perhaps at this particular historical juncture, which many have hailed as the end of the Westphalian state system, we are in a position to address the intertwined roles of gender, the passions, and more generally the irrational that we have long banished to literature.

Conclusion

I wrote this book in the shadow of the United States' long wars in Iraq and Afghanistan. Nothing makes you think more about the difficulty of achieving a firm and durable peace than living in a country fighting an interminable war. Early in the project, and early in the wars, I once used a contemporary analogy to explain my work to a neighbor: "Imagine if George W. Bush and Saddam Hussein decided to make peace by marrying Jenna and Barbara Bush to Uday and Qusay Hussein. Sounds absurd? That's how many parts of the world once worked." Precisely because the analogy was so absurd, it foregrounded differences between premodern dynasticism and the modern system of states.

As the war dragged on, that admittedly flip analogy became darker and more unsettling. There was no peace. The United States and its handful of European allies conquered Iraq and set up a fragile regime that failed to contain long-standing ethnic and religious conflicts. The United States Special Forces killed Uday, Qusay, and the latter's fourteen-year-old son in the summer of 2003. Three years later, an Iraqi regime propped up by the United States and its allies hanged Saddam Hussein and broadcast pictures of his corpse around the globe. According to the official American line, victory over Saddam's regime had to be total. There could be no compromises, no truces in the global "War on Terror." The modern state system had found yet another way to validate Richelieu's belief in the perpetuity of war.

When I came up with my George W. Bush–Saddam Hussein analogy, I simply wanted to give an example of a problem in contemporary international relations that might have led to a marriage settlement in premodern Europe. But the second I proposed it, the more I realized how it exposed aspects of marriage diplomacy that appalled twenty-first-century sensibilities. The suggestion, even tongue-in-cheek, of marrying one of President Bush's daughters to Uday Hussein, an alleged serial rapist, brought the general American revulsion against arranged marriage to the fore. In the contemporary West, marriage has become an affective arrangement. At least in the popular understanding, two people get married because they love each other and want to spend the rest of their lives together. A widespread belief that affective marriage is inherently just, proper, and even "natural" underlies the disgust my students often voice when they encounter arranged marriages in Shakespeare and other premodern writers. The idea of asking—much less coercing—a young woman to marry anyone for political reasons strikes them as repulsive. I sometimes remind them that western affective marriages often end in divorce; that spousal abuse takes place every day across America; and that many Indian, Arab, and Orthodox Jewish women come to love their husbands in arranged marriages. But they remain unconvinced in their certainty that affective marriage is the better system.

In addition to their revulsion over all arranged marriages, Americans and western Europeans find the George W. Bush–Saddam Hussein analogy absurd because their countries have detached foreign policy from the family interests of individual rulers. The French, Americans, and Italians jettisoned their monarchies long ago. In Britain and the northern European countries that still retain a constitutional form of monarchy, twenty-first-century royalty now prefer their own subjects as marriage partners, even if it means marrying a commoner like Kate Middleton. In 2001, Crown Prince Haakon of Norway created a minor scandal by marrying Mette-Marit Tjessem Høiby, a Norwegian commoner and a single mother. But the scandal soon passed, and the country readily embraced Princess Mette-Marit as their future queen. Spain's Felipe VI married a news anchor whose grandfather was a taxi driver. In a period when European royal houses struggle against perceptions of privilege and obsolescence, such marriages have enhanced the standing of monarchs in the eyes of their subjects by making them seem warmer and more accessible.

To the extent that these marriages to indigenous commoners have any bearing on foreign policy, they reaffirm the nationalist sentiments of the post-Westphalian state. The last thing most Americans or Europeans would want is a foreign policy tied to the personal lives of their elected or hereditary rulers. Royal consorts and first ladies traditionally sponsor charities, patronize the arts, host banquets and garden parties, and strive to maintain goodwill between the people and the head of state. Presiding over a dinner for a foreign dignitary is one thing. Inserting themselves into policy discussions is another. One of the few foreign consorts among the younger generation of European royalty, the Argentine-born Queen Máxima of the Netherlands, has used her identity as a naturalized Dutch citizen to work for greater assimilation of immigrants into the fabric of Dutch society. But even that work, especially with its emphasis on the acquisition of the Dutch language, primarily strengthens the nation as the primary locus of individual loyalties.

The system of modern states—founded, as Max Weber famously declared, on legal rationality and bureaucracy—overcomes many of the shortcomings of the premodern dynastic order. Legislative and juridical ratifications are presumably more binding than the charisma of individual rulers, solemn promises, or even the claims of a shared posterity. Modern treaties exist between states, not individuals subject to biological, medical, or psychological caprice. Modern ratification makes the provisions of a treaty part of the law of each of the signatory states. That remains true despite changes of party, heads of state, or other personnel. The old system rested on the most intimate, but also the most vulnerable and capricious, of personal bonds. The new system rests on the impersonality of law and a balance of shared interests.

And yet, despite all the legal rationality, global peace remains as elusive now as it was when Europeans tried to settle their quarrels through interdynastic marriage. Not all countries subscribe to the Weberian regime. Many countries remain subject to dictators and theocrats whose actions defy self-proclaimed modern and rational standards of international law and human rights. Numerous theorists see this as an opposition between the modern industrialized West and the poorer, less modernized countries of Asia, Africa, and Latin America. But in the West, the state system has bred its own discontents. As humanity has repeatedly discovered in the last half century, the state's insistence on absolute sovereignty has impeded progress on everything from nuclear disarmament to immigration, human rights, the eradication of disease, the environment, and climate change. As monads suspended in anarchy, states are so mistrustful of one another's capabilities and intentions that they fail to work together as effectively as they might in a different configuration. The twentieth century witnessed repeated efforts to overcome the system's shortcomings through the creation of transnational or supranational entities like the League of Nations, the United Nations, the European Union, and the International Court of Justice. The all too familiar failures, deficiencies, and limitations of these organizations attest to a global inability to think and act beyond the interests and paranoias of the sovereign state.

Despite its many flaws, the old dynastic order had vocabularies for at least talking about two things for which the modern rational state system is still struggling to find language: gender and the emotions. As I argued in the last chapter, the rise of the diva coincided with the rise of modern bureaucratized diplomacy in telling ways. Among modern nations, diplomacy was to be conducted by men through the rational consideration of laws and common interests. Women, and the passions that supposedly animated them, belonged in the theater rather than the council room. Gone were the days when Louise of Savoy and Margaret of Austria negotiated the 1529 Treaty of Cambrai. The rational, insistently masculinist consensus has persisted into the present, even though women now regularly serve as presidents, prime ministers, foreign ministers and secretaries of state, ambassadors, and foreign officers around the globe. Women hold these jobs because they, like men, have mastered the rational discourses of the modern state system.

But in recent years, this legal discourse has found itself increasingly at an impasse with forces that defy rational analysis. About the time I began research on this project, American and western European journalists repeatedly asked a question bound up with all the passion and irrationality of the Racinian stage: "Why do they hate us?" In the neoconservative fantasy that justified President Bush's military initiatives, the only thing needed to integrate into the Westphalian state system was regime change. Instead of embracing western forms of government, with their attendant legal regimes and bureaucracies, however, Iraq and Afghanistan erupted in sectarian and ethnic hatreds that gave the lie to neoconservative theory. Often the only thing that united bitterly opposed groups of Sunnis and Shiites was a common hatred of the West and everything it represents, including secularism, gender equality, and sexual liberation. Instead of allaying the hatred, modern warfare and modern diplomacy alike have only exacerbated it.

The opposition between the West and its post–Cold War enemies challenged the assumption that states act in rational, predictable ways based on common interests. It has also brought the matter of gender once more to the center of international relations. The theocratic movements and regimes of the Middle East despise the West in part because of the freedoms enjoyed by European and American women. At the same time, westerners demonize Muslim countries because of their apparent subordination of women. Advocacy for the rights of women has become an important part of the West's more general advocacy of human rights. We are at the earliest stages of this international conversation, in part because the Westphalian state system prided itself on its gender blindness. Until very recently, statesmen and international relations scholars alike argued that human rights advocacy violated the fundamental principle of state sovereignty. From this classical Westphalian perspective, talking about women's rights harked back to the days when kings tried to tamper with the internal religious affairs of rival states. According to modern international relations doctrine, states should relate to one another as states and not ask awkward questions about one another's domestic affairs.

The West is thinking once again about gender and the place of women in international affairs, as well as about the passions, hatreds, and irrational affinities that complicate the supposedly rational actions of states. This is happening at exactly the same time the resurgence of regional and supranational jurisdictions like the EU, transnational entities like global corporations and nongovernment agencies, and transnational terrorist organizations like Al-Qaeda are all in their various ways posing a challenge to the modern state system. But as new and challenging as these developments might be, they are not without precedent. Like modern refugees, immigrants, human rights workers, missionaries, NGO officers, diplomats, and the globe-trotting corporate employees who challenge the state system now, the royal women who passed from one European court to another resisted it at its inception. They stood at the antithesis of a world order made up of passport-bearing citizens neatly housed within the borders of their respective nation-states and earnestly defending their state's interests. They experienced their transnationalism and hybridity in countless ways. Some spent their lives as de facto exiles mourning the homes their fathers had forced them to abandon. Some never really learned their husband's language. Others became so devoted to their new homelands that they all but forgot their origins in other places. A privileged few so embraced the provisionality of their identities that they treated nationality as a fiction, something that could be put on or off in the interests of helping others find a sense of home, a sense of national dignity.

We can no more overcome the impasses created by the modern state system by retreating into premodern political conditions than we can resolve gender inequities by nostalgizing high and mighty queens. But a cultural history like this one can help us resist the fictions of progress, inevitability, and transhistorical human nature that have reconciled political thinkers both within and outside the academy to a world fragmented into competing nations. The movements of royal and aristocratic women from one premodern European polity to the next depended on social, economic, and religious circumstances that we would not want to re-create if we could. The marriage system that I describe here, for example, worked best in a world where everyone shared, at least officially, a Catholic sacramental consensus. That is not the multiethnic, multi-religious world in which international settlements and alliances now unfold. Our challenge is to find our own points of ideological consensus that work effectively to balance, if not overcome, national interests that run counter to common human interests.

🍂 Notes

Introduction

1. Alan R. Schulman, "Diplomatic Marriage in the Egyptian New Kingdom," *Journal of Near Eastern Studies* 38 (1979): 177–93.

2. See Uradyn E. Bulag, *The Mongols at China's Edge: History and the Politics of National Unity* (Lanham, Md.: Rowman and Littlefield, 2002), 63–102. See also Tamara T. Chin, "Defamiliarizing the Foreigner: Sima Qian's Ethnography and Han-Xiongnu Marriage Diplomacy," *Harvard Journal of Asiatic Studies* 70 (2010): 311–54; Martin Slobodník, "The Early Policy of Emperor Tang Dezong towards Inner Asia," *Asian and African Studies* 6, no. 2 (1997): 184–96; Sechin Jagchid and Van Jay Symons, *Peace, War, and Trade along the Great Wall: Nomadic-Chinese Interaction through Two Millennia* (Bloomington: Indiana University Press, 1989), 141, 192; Kimberly Besio, "Gender, Loyalty, and the Reproduction of the Wang Zhaojun Legend: Some Social Ramifications of Drama in the Late Ming," *Journal of the Economic and Social History of the Orient* 40, no. 2 (1997): 251–82.

3. Thomas Collelo and Howard D. Nelson, *Chad: A Country Study* (Washington, D.C.: Federal Research Division, Library of Congress, 1990), 8–9.

4. Alan Kolata, *Ancient Inca* (Cambridge: Cambridge University Press, 2013), 95–96.

5. Barbara A. Somervill, *The Empire of the Aztecs* (New York: Chelsea House, 2010), 33–34.

6. Ralph S. Kuykendall, *The Hawaiian Kingdom, 1778–1854: Foundation and Transformation* (Honolulu: University of Hawaii Press, 1938), 74–75; Edward Joesting, *Kauai: The Separate Kingdom* (Honolulu: University of Hawaii Press, 1984), 98.

7. Janet L. Nelson, *Charles the Bald* (Harlow, Essex: Longman, 1992), 181–86.

8. Ibid., 203–4, 232.

9. Ibid., 181–82, 203. As Nelson notes, Charles's precise role in arranging his daughter's second marriage is not fully clear from extant sources. Nevertheless, it is highly probable that he would have at least supported the marriage to maintain the Frankish-English alliance.

10. See Patrick J. Geary, *Women at the Beginning: Origin Myths from the Virgin Mary to the Amazons* (Princeton: Princeton University Press, 2009), 51–54.

11. Eljas Oksanen, *Flanders and the Anglo-Norman World, 1066–1216* (Cambridge: Cambridge University Press, 2012), 7.

12. The marriage negotiations figure prominently in all biographies of both Henry VIII and Louis, and well as of their respective wives. In addition, see such

studies as Catherine Fletcher, *The Divorce of Henry VIII: The Untold Story from Inside the Vatican* (New York: Palgrave Macmillan, 2012); David Starkey, *Six Wives: The Queens of Henry VIII* (London: Chatto and Windus, 2003); Henry Ansgar Kelly, *The Matrimonial Trials of Henry VIII* (Stanford: Stanford University Press, 1976); Christopher James Warner, *Henry VIII's Divorce: Literature and the Politics of the Printing Press* (Woodbridge, Suffolk: Boydell and Brewer, 1998); Abby E. Zanger, *Scenes from the Marriage of Louis XIV: Nuptial Fictions and the Making of Absolutist Power* (Stanford: Stanford University Press, 1997); Claude Dulong, *Le mariage du Roi-Soleil* (Paris: Albin Michel, 1986); Madeleine Saint-René Taillandier, *Le mariage de Louis XIV* (Paris: Hachette, 1928). These lists are not exhaustive. Daniel Riches offers a more systemic discussion of marriage diplomacy between two specific early modern polities in *Protestant Cosmopolitanism and Diplomatic Culture: Brandenburg-Swedish Relations in the Seventeenth Century* (Leiden: Brill, 2013), 141–80.

13. See, for example, Glyn Redworth, *The Prince and the Infanta: The Cultural Politics of the Spanish Match* (New Haven: Yale University Press, 2003); Brennan C. Pursell, "The End of the Spanish Match," *Historical Journal* 45 (2002): 699–726; Thomas Cogswell, *The Blessed Revolution: English Politics and the Coming of War, 1621–1624* (Cambridge: Cambridge University Press, 1989): Samuel R. Gardiner, *Prince Charles and the Spanish Marriage, 1617–1623*, 2 vols. (London, 1869).

14. David L. D'Avray, *Dissolving Royal Marriages: A Documentary History, 860–1600* (Cambridge: Cambridge University Press, 2014); D'Avray, *Papacy, Monarchy, and Marriage, 860–1600* (Cambridge: Cambridge University Press, 2015).

15. For an introduction to English school and critical international society theory, see Barry Buzan, *An Introduction to the English School of International Relations: The Societal Approach* (Cambridge: Polity, 2014); Richard Little, "The English School's Contribution to the Study of International Relations," *European Journal of International Relations* 6, no. 3 (2000): 395–422; James Mayall, *Nationalism and International Society* (Cambridge: Cambridge University Press, 1990); Hedley Bull and Adam Watson, eds., *The Expansion of International Society* (Oxford: Oxford University Press, 1985); Hedley Bull, *The Anarchical Society: A Study of Order in World Politics* (New York: Columbia University Press, 1977); Martin Wight, *Systems of States*, ed. Hedley Bull (Leicester: University of Leicester Press in association with the London School of Economics, 1977).

16. See especially Andrew Hurrell, *On Global Order: Power, Values, and the Constitution of International Society* (Oxford: Oxford University Press, 2007); Andrew Linklater and Hidemi Suganami, *The English School of International Relations: A Contemporary Reassessment* (Cambridge: Cambridge University Press, 2006); Barry Buzan, *From International to World Society? English School Theory and the Social Structure of Globalisation* (Cambridge: Cambridge University Press, 2004); Edward Keene, *Beyond the Anarchical Society: Grotius, Colonialism and Order in World Politics* (Cambridge: Cambridge University Press, 2002). There is also a body of predictable realist critiques of the English school's commitment to international society and international law as fruitful foci of international relations inquiry. See Dale Copeland, "A Realist Critique of the English School," *Review of International Studies* 29, no. 3 (2003): 427–41.

17. See Bull, *Anarchical Society*, 16, 26, 27–28, 39, 269.

18. See Rebekah Clements, "Talking with the Brush: Rethinking the 'Lingua Franca' of East Asian Diplomacy through Early Modern Japanese-Korean

Encounters," in *Cultures of Diplomacy and Literary Writing in the Early Modern World: New Approaches*, ed. Tracey Sowerby and Joanna Craigwood (forthcoming).

19. On the concept of the *res publica christiana*, see Randall Lesaffer, "Peace Treaties from Lodi to Westphalia," in *Peace Treaties and International Law in European History: From the Late Middle Ages to World War One*, ed. Randall Lesaffer (Cambridge: Cambridge University Press, 2004), 29–37. Lessaffer quotes the 1515 Treaty of Paris at 29 (n. 54).

20. Emmanuel Rodocanachi, *Renée de France, Duchesse de Ferrare: Une protectrice de la réforme en Italie et en France* (Geneva: Slatkine, 1970).

21. Quoted in Karen Owens, *Franz Joseph and Elisabeth: The Last Great Monarchs of Austria-Hungary* (Jefferson, N.C.: McFarland, 2014), 142.

22. See, for example, Marie Tanner, *The Last Descendant of Aeneas: The Hapsburgs and the Mythic Image of the Emperor* (New Haven: Yale University Press, 1993).

23. See Christopher N. Warren, "Gentili, the Poets, and the Laws of War," in *The Roman Foundations of the Law of Nations: Alberico Gentili and the Justice of Empire*, ed. Benedict Kingsbury and Benjamin Straumann (Oxford: Oxford University Press, 2010), 146–62.

24. See Timothy Hampton, *Fictions of Embassy: Literature and Diplomacy in Early Modern Europe* (Ithaca: Cornell University Press, 2010). See also Joanna Craigwood's discussions of the relationship between diplomatic representation and literary representation in "Diplomatic Metonymy and Antithesis in *3 Henry VI*," *Review of English Studies* 65 (2014): 812–30, and "Sidney, Gentili, and the Poetics of Embassy," in *Diplomacy and Early Modern Culture*, ed. Robyn Adams and Rosanna Cox (Basingstoke: Palgrave Macmillan, 2011), 82–100.

25. See Stephen Wittek, "Middleton's *A Game at Chess* and the Making of a Theatrical Public," *Studies in English Literature 55*, no. 2 (2015): 423–46; Thomas Cogswell, "Thomas Middleton and the Court, 1624: *A Game at Chess* in Context," *Huntington Library Quarterly* 47 (1984): 273–88.

26. See Andrew Fichter, *Poets Historical: Dynastic Epic in the Renaissance* (New Haven: Yale University Press, 1982).

27. See Craig Kallendorf, *The Other Virgil: "Pessimistic" Readings of the* Aeneid *in Early Modern Culture* (Oxford: Oxford University Press, 2007); Adam Parry, *The Language of Achilles and Other Papers* (Oxford: Clarendon, 1989), 78–96; W. R. Johnson, *Darkness Visible: A Study of Vergil's* Aeneid (Berkeley: University of California Press, 1976); Michael C. J. Putnam, *The Poetry of the* Aeneid: *Four Studies in Imaginative Unity and Design* (Cambridge: Harvard University Press, 1965).

28. François Douaren, quoted by Alberico Gentili in *De iure belli libri tres*, trans. John C. Rolfe (Oxford: Clarendon, 1933), bk. 3, sec. 13.

29. While there has been considerable work in feminist international theory, it has yet to transform fundamental disciplinary paradigms in the way feminist theory has transformed most fields in the humanities. As Alexandra Buskie has noted, "Feminist IR [international relations] theory remains on the margins of the discipline, with mainstream IR scholars rarely engaging in productive debate about the questions raised by feminist critiques." Alexandra Buskie, "How Significant Is Feminism's Contribution to IR?" *E-International Relations Students*, March 17, 2013, http://www.e-ir.info/2013/03/17/how-significant-is-the-contribution-of-feminism-to-ir/ (accessed August 14, 2015). See also Eric M. Blanchard, "Gender, International Relations, and

the Development of Feminist Security Theory," *Signs* 28, no. 4 (2003): 1289–1312; Christine Sylvester, *Feminist Theory and International Relations in a Postmodern Era* (Cambridge: Cambridge University Press, 1994); J. Ann Tickner, *Gender in International Relations: Feminist Perspectives on Achieving Global Security* (New York: Columbia University Press, 1992); John Watkins, "Towards a New Diplomatic History of Medieval and Early Modern Europe," *Journal of Medieval and Early Modern Studies* 38, no. 1 (2008): 1–14.

1. After Rome

1. Ludovico Carbone, "Victorius Panonius et Joanna Mazon," MS Vatican City, Biblioteca Apostolica Vaticana, Ottob. Lat. 1153, 165v, quoted in Anthony F. D'Elia, "Marriage, Sexual Pleasure, and Learned Brides in the Wedding Orations of Fifteenth-Century Italy," *Renaissance Quarterly* 55, no. 2 (2002): 396.

2. "Indum sanguineo veluti violaverit ostro / si quis ebur, aut mixta rubent ubi / lilia multa / alba rosa" (*Aeneid* 12.67–69). See D'Elia, "Marriage, Sexual Pleasure, and Learned Brides." 405.

3. See Cristelle L. Baskins, *Cassone Painting, Humanism, and Gender in Early Modern Italy* (Cambridge: Cambridge University Press, 1998), 79–84.

4. See George Gömöri, "'A Memorable Wedding': The Literary Reception of the Wedding of the Princess Elizabeth and Frederick of Pfalz," *Journal of European Studies* 34 (2004): 215–24.

5. See Andrew Fichter, *Poets Historical: Dynastic Epic in the Renaissance* (New Haven: Yale University Press, 1982); John Watkins, *The Specter of Dido: Spenser and Virgilian Epic* (New Haven: Yale University Press, 1995).

6. See Anna Cox Brinton, *Maphaeus Vegius and His Thirteenth Book of the* Aeneid: *A Chapter on Virgil in the Renaissance* (Stanford: Stanford University Press, 1930); Craig Kallendorf, *In Praise of Aeneas: Virgil and Epideictic Rhetoric in the Early Italian Renaissance* (Hanover: University Press of New England, 1989), 100–128.

7. See Charles S. Ross, "Maffeo Vegio's 'schort Cristyn wark,' with a Note on the Thirteenth Book in Early Editions of Vergil," *Modern Philology* 78 (1981): 215–26.

8. Early medievalists typically use the word "barbarians" to describe the various peoples who lived on the borders of the Roman Empire. Literary scholars sometimes refer to them as "Germanic peoples." I find both terms problematic. "Germanic" resonates with nineteenth-century ethnic fantasies of a German nation before there was a Germany. To my ear, "barbarian" sounds potentially condescending, although my medievalist colleagues assure me it is standard usage and does not imply a savagery that contrasts with Roman civilization. I use it with some reservation as the lesser of two evils.

9. Craig Kallendorf, *The Other Virgil: "Pessimistic" Readings of the* Aeneid *in Early Modern Culture* (Oxford: Oxford University Press, 2007).

10. Francis Cairns, *Virgil's Augustan Epic* (Cambridge: Cambridge University Press, 1989), 114–21.

11. See Kristina Milnor, *Gender, Domesticity, and the Age of Augustus: Inventing Private Life* (Oxford: Oxford University Press, 2005), 140–85.

12. See Susan Treggiari, *Roman Marriage: Iusti Coniuges from the Time of Cicero to the Time of Ulpian* (Oxford: Oxford University Press, 1991), 43–49.

13. Seneca, *De beneficiis*, 4.35.1. See Treggiari's discussion of this example in *Roman Marriage*, 47.

14. *The Oxford Study Bible: Revised English Bible with the Apocrypha*, ed. M. Jack Suggs et al. (Oxford: Oxford University Press, 1992).

15. See Ruth Mazo Karras, "Marriage, Concubinage, and the Law," in *Law and the Illicit in Medieval Europe*, ed. Ruth Mazo Karras, Joel Kaye, and E. Ann Matter (Philadelphia: University of Pennsylvania Press, 2008), 118–19. See also Pauline Stafford, *Queens, Concubines, and Dowagers: The King's Wife in the Early Middle Ages* (London: Batsford, 1983), 62–71.

16. Stafford, *Queens, Concubines, and Dowagers*.

17. See Brian Swain's account of how recurrent Virgilian echoes and allusions characterize the Gothic immigration as a reenactment of the Trojan journey to Latium in the *Aeneid* in "Jordanes and Virgil: A Case Study of Intertextuality in the *Getica*," *Classical Quarterly* 60, no. 1 (2010): 243–49.

18. See Walter Goffart, *The Narrators of Barbarian History (A.D. 550–800): Jordanes, Gregory of Tours, Bede, and Paul the Deacon* (2005; repr., Notre Dame, Ind.: University of Notre Dame Press, 2012), 62–68.

19. Tacitus, *Opera minora*, ed. Henry Furneaux (Oxford: Clarendon, 1900), chap. 33.

20. Jordanes, *De origine actibusque Getarum*, ed. Alfred Holder (Freiburg im Breisgau, 1882), 21; hereafter cited parenthetically by page in the text.

21. See Goffart, *Narrators of Barbarian History*, 68–74. For even darker readings of the *Getica*'s conclusion, see Brian Croke, "Cassiodorus and the *Getica* of Jordanes," *Classical Philology* 82 (1987): 131–33; James J. O'Donnell, "The Aims of Jordanes," *Historia: Zeitschrift für Alte Geschichte* 31, no. 2 (1982): 230–33.

22. In reconstructing the *Historia*'s political valences and composition history, I am indebted to a large body of previous scholarship. See especially Roger Collins, *Charlemagne* (Houndmills, Basingstoke: Macmillan, 1998), 58–88; Rosamond McKitterick, *Charlemagne: The Formation of a European Identity* (Cambridge: Cambridge University Press, 2008), 75–90; Janet L. Nelson, "Making a Difference in Eighth-Century Politics: The Daughters of Desiderius," in *After Rome's Fall: Narrators and Sources of Early Medieval History*, ed. Alexander Callander Murray (Toronto: University of Toronto Press, 1998), 171–90; and Goffart, *Narrators of Barbarian History*, 333–47.

23. Nelson speculates about the name in "Making a Difference," 183. The fact that Charlemagne's brother Carloman was married to a woman named Gerberga who later fled to Desiderius's court led to the confused assumption by other historians that Charlemagne's Lombard bride was also named Gerberga.

24. Quoted in Latin in McKitterick, *Charlemagne*, 85.

25. *Annales Mosellani*, 770, in P. D. King, *Charlemagne: Translated Sources* (Kendal, Cumbria: King, 1987), 132.

26. *Codex Carolinus* (45), fol. 49v to 51r, ed. Wilhelm Gundlach, in Monumenta Germaniae Historica, epistolarum Merowingici et Karolini Aevi 1, Tomus 3 (Berolini: Weidmannos, 1892), 560; hereafter cited parenthetically by page in the text.

27. See Stafford, *Queens, Concubines, and Dowagers*, 60–61, 147.

28. Ibid., 34–37. As Stafford notes, Carolingian practice had an important impact on other western European societies, including pre-Conquest England.

29. Extant sources do not give us a clear sense of the extent to which Charlemagne self-consciously fashioned an imperial identify for himself before his 800

coronation. While some historians find evidence of imperial ambitions in his earliest conquests, others have stressed that conquest alone does not indicate a determination to revive the western empire. There are, of course, enormous questions about what "imperium" would have meant to anyone in eighth-century Europe. My own sense is that regardless of Charlemagne's conscious intentions, his marital practices even before 800 enhanced his later imperial aura. For an introduction to the debate, see Rosamond McKitterick, *The Frankish Kingdoms under the Carolingians, 751–987* (London: Longman, 1983), 70–72; Henry Mayr-Harting, "Charlemagne, the Saxons, and the Imperial Coronation of 800," *English Historical Review* 111 (1996): 1113–33, esp. 1118–23; McKitterick, *Charlemagne*, 114–27. See also Bernard S. Bachrach, "Charlemagne's Mediterranean Empire," in *Mediterranean Identities in the Premodern Era: Entrepôts, Islands, Empires*, ed. John Watkins and Kathryn L. Reyerson (Farnham, Surrey: Ashgate, 2014), 155–72.

30. Recent scholarship typically divides in characterizing the *Historia* either as a nostalgic celebration of the once great Lombard nation written primarily for the Benevantans or as a work intended for Franks and Frankish sympathizers. For an example of the former, see Goffart, *Narrators of Barbarian History*, 378–82. Those who see it as Carolingian propaganda have emphasized its alleged portrayal of several Lombard kings as *rois fainéants* whose incompetence created a power vacuum that the Carolingians filled. See, for example, Rosamond McKitterick, "Paul the Deacon and the Franks," *Early Medieval Europe* 8 (1999): 319–39. My own sense is that the work falls somewhere in the middle: the *Historia gentis langobardorum* is not an unambiguous celebration of Carolingian power, but neither is it a rallying cry for Beneventan resistance. It strikes a tentative and not always consistent position between commemorating the Lombard past and collaborating with the Carolingian present.

31. Goffart, *Narrators of Barbarian History*, 353–54. Although the present volume focuses on Jordanes, Gregory of Tours, Bede, and Paul the Deacon primarily for their contributions to a developing ideology of marriage diplomacy, I am indebted throughout to Goffart for first recognizing that their literariness was essential to their value as historical sources.

32. I am indebted to Francesco Borri's account of Paul's use of early sources in "Murder by Death: Alboin's Life, End(s), and Means," *Millennium* 8 (2011): 223–70. See also Goffart, *Narrators of Barbarian History*.

33. Paul the Deacon, *Historia Langobardorum*, ed. Ludwig Bethmann and Georg Waitz, in Monumenta Germaniae Historica, Scriptores Rerum Langobardicarum et Italicarum saec. VI–IX (Hanover, 1878). All references are to this edition and are given parenthetically in the text.

34. Goffart, *Narrators of Barbarian History*, 407–12.

2. Interdynastic Marriage, Religious Conversion, and the Expansion of Diplomatic Society

1. I am indebted throughout this chapter to a substantial bibliography on early medieval Europe that stresses continuities with the Roman past rather than cataclysmic disjunction. See especially Henri Pirenne, *Les villes du Moyen Âge: Essai d'histoire économique et sociale* (Brussels: Lamertin, 1927); Lucien Musset, *Les invasions: Les vagues Germaniques* (Paris: Presses Universitaires de France, 1965); Peter Brown, *The*

World of Late Antiquity: From Marcus Aurelius to Muhammad (London: Thames and Hudson, 1971); Walter Goffart, *Barbarians and Romans, AD 418–584: The Techniques of Accommodation* (Princeton: Princeton University Press, 1980); Bernard Bachrach, *Early Carolingian Warfare: Prelude to Empire* (Philadelphia: University of Pennsylvania Press, 2001); and Walter Goffart, *Barbarian Tides: The Migration Age and the Later Roman Empire* (Philadelphia: University of Pennsylvania Press, 2006). See also the numerous volumes in the European Science Foundation's Transformations of the Roman World series (Leiden: Brill, 1997–). Whether one argues for disjunction or continuity depends on the variables under investigation. For a reassertion of the case for disjunction, see Peter Heather, *The Fall of the Roman Empire: A New History of Rome and the Barbarians* (Oxford: Oxford University Press, 2006). As I note later, the case for continuity is especially strong for diplomatic practice.

2. Andrew Gillett, *Envoys and Political Communication in the Late Antique West, 411–533* (Cambridge: Cambridge University Press, 2003).

3. Hedley Bull and Adam Watson, *The Expansion of International Society* (Oxford: Oxford University Press, 1985), 1.

4. Hedley Bull, *The Anarchical Society: A Study of Order in World Politics* (New York: Columbia University Press, 1977), 178–93.

5. See Edward Keene, *Beyond the Anarchical Society: Grotius, Colonialism and Order in World Politics* (Cambridge: Cambridge University Press, 2002); Turan Kayaoglu, "Westphalian Eurocentrism in International Relations Theory," *International Studies Review* 12, no. 2 (2010): 193–217; Shogo Suzuki, Yongjin Zhang, and Joel Quirk, eds., *International Orders in the Early Modern World: Before the Rise of the West* (London: Routledge, 2013); Richard Little, "Reassessing *The Expansion of the International Society*," in *System, Society and the World: Exploring the English School of International Relations*, ed. Robert W. Murray (Bristol: e-International Relations, 2013), 19–24.

6. Christine Sylvester, *Feminist International Relations: An Unfinished Journey* (Cambridge: Cambridge University Press, 2002), 13–15; Jacqui True, "Feminism," in *International Society and Its Critics*, ed. Alex J. Bellamy (Oxford: Oxford University Press, 2005), 151–62. See also Eric Blanchard, "Why Is There No Gender in the English School?" *Review of International Relations* 37, no. 2 (2011): 855–79.

7. Early medievalists have often emphasized alliance formation as the primary purpose of interdynastic marriage. See Pauline Stafford, "Powerful Women in the Early Middle Ages: Queens and Abbesses," in *The Medieval World*, ed. Peter Linehan and Janet L. Nelson (London: Routledge, 2001), 398–415; Janet L. Nelson, *The Frankish World, 750–900* (London: Hambledon Press, 1996), 223–42; Ian N. Wood, *The Merovingian Kingdoms, 450–751* (London: Longman, 1994), 159–80. Ryan Patrick Crisp has challenged this orthodoxy by noting how few of these marriages resulted in stable alliances; see "Marriage and Alliance in the Merovingian Kingdoms, 481–639" (Ph.D. diss., Ohio State University, 2003), OhioLINK Electronic Theses and Dissertations Center (accessed October 23, 2014). Crisp stresses instead the domestic benefits that kings gained from marrying princesses, such as wealth and prestige. The latter was an especially important factor in the competition between and among Merovingian brothers ruling their various subkingdoms. By emphasizing the role marriage played in forging a diplomatic society, something more nebulous but also more general and encompassing than any individual alliance, I mean to avoid any simplistic division between foreign and domestic motivations.

8. For further background on Gregory's relationship with Brunhild, see Adriaan H. B. Breukelaar, *Historiography and Episcopal Authority in Sixth-Century Gaul: Histories of Gregory of Tours Interpreted in Their Historical Context* (Göttingen: Vandenhoeck and Ruprecht, 1994). See also Wood, *Merovingian Kingdoms*, 126–36.

9. Janet L. Nelson discusses the wide-ranging social origins of Merovingian wives with particular attention to Brunhild and Balthild in *Politics and Ritual in Early Medieval Europe* (London: Hambledon, 1986), 1–48.

10. See Pauline Stafford, *Queens, Concubines, and Dowagers: The King's Wife in the Early Middle Ages* (London: Batsford, 1983), 62–71.

11. Gregory of Tours, *Opera*, teil 1, *Libri historiarum X*, ed. Wilhelm Levison and Bruno Krusch, in Monumenta Germaniae Historica (Hanover: Hahn, 1884–85). All references are to this edition and are cited parenthetically by book and chapter in the text.

12. See Musset, *Les invasions*, 71–76; Danuta Shanzer, "Dating the Baptism of Clovis: The Bishop of Vienne vs. the Bishop of Tours," *Early Medieval Europe* 7, no. 1 (1998): 29–57; William M. Daly, "Clovis: How Barbaric? How Pagan?" *Speculum* 69, no. 3 (1994): 619–64; Ian N. Wood, "Gregory of Tours and Clovis," *Revue Belge de Philologie et d'Histoire* 63, no. 2 (1985): 249–72; Wood, *Merovingian Kingdoms*, 43–48.

13. See Santiago Castellanos, "Creating New Constantines at the End of the Sixth Century," *Historical Research* 85 (2012): 556–75.

14. Timothy D. Barnes, *Constantine and Eusebius* (Cambridge: Harvard University Press, 1981).

15. On the historiographic complexities of Gregory's gendering of religious conversion, see Cordula Nolte, "Gender and Conversion in the Merovingian Era," in *Varieties of Religious Conversion in the Middle Ages*, ed. James Muldoon (Gainesville: University Press of Florida, 1997), 81–99.

16. Crisp also discusses the problem of marriage to lower-ranked women in "Marriage and Alliance," where he treats Gregory's attitude as symptomatic of a general Merovingian preference for marrying queens of higher rank (147–52). Given that Gregory is our primary source for most of these marriages, I want to be more cautious. Gregory's prejudice against queens of low degree is so extreme that it seems to have a polemic edge. He opposes the practice with such vehemence because it was significantly widespread and he was determined to denounce it. As Nelson notes, marrying a woman without wealth and status allowed Merovingian kings to assert their freedom from the material and social constraints that limited the marital choices of their aristocratic subjects (*Politics and Ritual*, 5). Gregory may privilege one kind of marriage over another, in part because doing so favors his patron Brunhild over her nemesis Fredegond.

17. Charibert's father, Chlothar I, not only married two sisters but also lived with them simultaneously. To a modern reader living in a monogamous society, the story may sound downright lurid, but Gregory presents the case with a minimum of editorial commentary: "I will, moreover, tell how he took the sister of his own wife [Quae autem causa fuerit, ut uxoris suae sororem acciperet, dicam]" (4.3). The contrast with his condemnation of Charibert for marrying paupers is striking.

18. Theudechild came to a bad end. She hated the convent and sent messengers to "a certain Goth . . . , promising him that, if he would escort her to Spain and join with her in marriage, she would leave the nunnery with her treasures and follow him with a willing heart [Gothum quendam adivit, promittens, si se in Hispaniis

deductam coniugio copularet, cum thesauris suis de monasthirio egrediens, libenti eum animo sequeretur]" (4.26). The abbess caught her, however, and gave orders for her to be severely beaten and held in custody, where she was "worn away by no ordinary suffering until the end of her life [in qua usque ad exitum vitae praesentis, non mediocribus adtrita passionibus]" (4.26).

19. Bull, *The Anarchical Society*, 178–93.

20. See Walter Goffart, "The *Historia Ecclesiastica*: Bede's Agenda and Ours," *Haskins Society Journal: Studies in Medieval History* 2 (1990): 29–45.

21. Walter Goffart, *The Narrators of Barbarian History (A.D. 550–800): Jordanes, Gregory of Tours, Bede, and Paul the Deacon* (2005; repr., Notre Dame, Ind.: University of Notre Dame Press, 2012), 244–50. See also John M. Wallace-Hadrill, *Early Medieval History* (Oxford: Blackwell, 1975), 96–114.

22. See especially Clare A. Lees and Gillian R. Overing, *Double Agents: Women and Clerical Culture in Anglo-Saxon England* (Philadelphia: University of Pennsylvania Press, 2001), 4–6, 15–39.

23. Stacy S. Klein, *Ruling Women: Queenship and Gender in Anglo-Saxon Literature* (Notre Dame, Ind.: University of Notre Dame Press, 2006), 17–52.

24. For complementary discussions of Bertha's diminished role, see ibid., 21–30; Lees and Overing, *Double Agents*, 34–35.

25. Bede, *The Ecclesiastical History of the English People*, ed. Bertram Colgrave and Roger A. B. Mynors (1969; repr., Oxford: Clarendon Press, 1991). All references are to this edition and are cited parenthetically in the text.

26. See Wood, *Merovingian Kingdoms*, 178.

3. From Chronicle to Romance

1. Ryan Patrick Crisp, "Marriage and Alliance in the Merovingian Kingdoms, 481–639" (Ph.D. diss., Ohio State University, 2003), OhioLINK Electronic Theses and Dissertations Center (accessed October 23, 2014).

2. See Stanisław Kętrzyński, "The Introduction of Christianity and the Early Kings of Poland," in *The Cambridge History of Poland: From the Origins to Sobieski (to 1696)*, ed. W. F. Reddaway et al. (Cambridge: Cambridge University Press, 1950), 16–42; Henry Joseph Lang, "The Fall of the Monarchy of Mieszko II Lambert," *Speculum* 49 (1974): 623–39; Jerzy Kloczowski, *A History of Polish Christianity* (Cambridge: Cambridge University Press, 2000), 10–12.

3. Dudo of Saint-Quentin, *De moribus et actis primorum normanniae ducum libri tres*, in *Patrologiae cursus completus, series Latina*, vol. 141, ed. Jacques–Paul Migne (Paris, 1844), col. 647C, hereafter cited parenthetically in the text.

4. See Fabio Stok, "*L'Eneide* nordica di Dudone di San Quintino," *International Journal of the Classical Tradition* 6 (1999): 171–84; Pierre Bouet, "Dudon de Saint-Quentin et Virgile: *L'Enéide* au service de la cause normande," *Cahiers des Annales de Normandie* 23 (1990): 215–36; Eleanor Searle, "Fact and Pattern in Heroic History: Dudo of St. Quentin," *Viator* 15 (1984): 119–37. For more general discussion of Dudo's classical education, see Leah Shopkow, "The Carolingian World of Dudo of St. Quentin," *Journal of Medieval History* 15 (1989): 19–37.

5. For further discussion of the *Aeneid's* premodern reception, see Christopher Baswell, *Virgil in Medieval England: Figuring the* Aeneid *from the Twelfth Century to*

Chaucer (Cambridge: Cambridge University Press, 1995); Marilynn Desmond, *Reading Dido: Gender, Textuality, and the Medieval* Aeneid (Minneapolis: University of Minnesota Press, 1994); John Watkins, *The Specter of Dido: Spenser and Virgilian Epic* (New Haven: Yale University Press, 1995); Craig Kallendorf, *The Other Virgil: "Pessimistic" Readings of the* Aeneid *in Early Modern Culture* (Oxford: Oxford University Press, 2007).

6. See Geoffrey Barraclough, *The Crucible of Europe: The Ninth and Tenth Centuries in European History* (Berkeley: University of California Press, 1976); Howard R. Bloch, *Medieval French Literature and Law* (Berkeley: University of California Press, 1977), 566–70. More recent scholarship has challenged the earlier emphasis on feudal anarchy and stressed instead a general devolution of power to local castellans. See Tomaž Mastnak, *Crusading Peace: Christendom, the Muslim World, and Western Political Order* (Berkeley: University of California Press, 2002), 33–35. As Mastnak concludes, even if the much later concept of "feudalism" distorts the medieval political landscape, the warfare among the castellans and other local authorities was still violent and unregulated.

7. See Hartmut Hoffman, *Gottesfriede und Treuga Dei*, Monumenta Germaniae Historica, Schriften 20 (Stuttgart: Anton Hiersemann, 1964). See also the essays collected in Thomas Head and Richard Landes, eds., *The Peace of God: Social Violence and Religious Response in France around the Year 1000* (Ithaca: Cornell University Press, 1992); Mastnak, *Crusading Peace*, 2–9; Herbert E. J. Cowdrey, "The Peace and the Truce of God in the Eleventh Century," *Past and Present* 46, no. 1 (1970): 42–67.

8. Mastnak, *Crusading Peace*, 10–54.

9. Translated in Edward Peters, ed., *The First Crusade: The Chronicle of Fulcher of Chartres and Other Source Materials*, 2nd ed. (Philadelphia: University of Pennsylvania Press, 1998), 52 (Fulcher 2.3.2).

10. Translated ibid., 28.

11. See Georges Duby's classic statement of this position in *The Early Growth of the European Economy: Warriors and Peasants from the Seventh to the Twelfth Century*, trans. Howard B. Clarke (Ithaca: Cornell University Press, 1974). For a critique of the economic thesis, see Jonathan Riley-Smith, *The First Crusaders, 1095–1131* (Cambridge: Cambridge University Press, 1997).

12. See Björn Weiler, "The 'Negotium Terrae Sanctae' in the Political Discourse of Latin Christendom, 1215–1311," *International History Review* 25, no. 1 (2003): 1–36. Although the link between European peace and the need to liberate the Holy Land recurs in ecclesiastical discourse, Marcus Bull has questioned the extent to which concerns about preserving the Peace of God prompted knights themselves to go on crusade; see *Knightly Piety and the Lay Response to the First Crusade: The Limousin and Gascony, c. 970–c. 1130* (Oxford: Oxford University Press, 1993), 21–69.

13. Anselm of Canterbury, *Cur Deus Homo*, in *Alselmi Cantuariensis Archiepiscopi Opera Omnia*, ed. Franciscus S. Schmitt (Bonn: Hanstein, 1929); see also Richard Cross, *The Metaphysics of the Incarnation: Thomas Aquinas to Duns Scotus* (Oxford: Oxford University Press, 2002). My focus here is primarily on the devotional tradition, which rulers and policy makers were more likely to know than the more abstract philosophical tradition.

14. Bernard of Clairvaux, *Sermones in Adventu Domini*, in *Patrologiae cursus completus, series Latina*, vol. 183, ed. Jacques-Paul Migne (Paris, 1854), col. 40B, hereafter cited parenthetically in the text.

15. See Rachel Fulton, *From Judgment to Passion: Devotion to Christ and the Virgin Mary, 800–1200* (New York: Columbia University Press, 2003), 376–78, 440–41. See also Miri Rubin, *Mother of God: A History of the Virgin Mary* (New Haven: Yale University Press, 2009), 56, 115, 266–68.

16. Bernard of Clairvaux, *Sermones in Cantica Canticorum*, in *Patrologiae cursus completus, series Latina*, vol. 183, ed. Jacques–Paul Migne (Paris, 1854), col. 787C, hereafter cited parenthetically in the text.

17. Philip of Harveng, *Commentaria in Cantica Canticorum*, in *Patrologiae cursus completus, series Latina*, vol. 183, ed. Jacques-Paul Migne (Paris, 1855), col. 184C.

18. In northwestern Europe alone, for example, Æthelred II of England married Emma, the daughter of Richard I of Normandy, in a 1002 attempt to stave off attacks by Richard's Viking allies. After Cnut conquered England in late 1016, the recently widowed Emma married him to protect the interests of her son in the eventual English succession. See Pauline Stafford, *Queen Emma and Queen Edith: Queenship and Women's Power in Eleventh-Century England* (Oxford: Blackwell, 1997). William of Normandy, the future conqueror of England, was apparently the son of a love match. But when he married Baldwin V's daughter Matilda around 1053, he ended long-standing tensions between Normandy and Flanders and turned a potential enemy into an ally against the powerful counts of Anjou. See David C. Douglas, *William the Conqueror: The Norman Impact on England* (1964; repr., Berkeley: University of California Press, 1972), 53–82; William M. Aird, *Robert "Curthose," Duke of Normandy, c. 1050–1134* (Woodbridge, Suffolk: Boydell, 2008), 24–26; Lois L. Huneycutt, *Matilda of Scotland: A Study in Medieval Queenship* (Woodbridge, Suffolk: Boydell, 2003), 50–52. In 1072, France's Philip I ended a war with Baldwin's son Robert I of Flanders by marrying Robert's stepdaughter Bertha. See Jim Bradbury, *The Capetians: Kings of France, 987–1328* (London: Continuum, 2007), 118. Across the Channel, William the Conqueror's son Henry I married Edith/Matilda of Scotland, the daughter of Malcolm III. The match pacified Henry's troubled relations with Malcolm and appeased his own English subjects—still smarting from the Conquest—because Matilda's mother hailed from the old Wessex dynasty. See Huneycutt, *Matilda of Scotland*. Henry I was one of the great diplomats of medieval Europe, who settled one of the period's major feuds, between his hereditary duchy of Normandy and the county of Anjou, by marrying his daughter Matilda to Geoffrey of Anjou, the son of his family's long-standing enemy Fulk V. See C. Warren Hollister and Thomas K. Keefe, "The Making of the Angevin Empire," *Journal of British Studies* 12, no. 2 (1973): 1–25, esp. 7–9; Charles Beem, *The Lioness Roared: The Problems of Female Rule in English History* (New York: Palgrave Macmillan, 2006).

19. See Sharon Kinoshita, *Medieval Boundaries: Rethinking Difference in Old French Literature* (Philadelphia: University of Pennsylvania Press, 2006), 194–99; Thomas Asbridge, "Talking to the Enemy: The Role and Purpose of Negotiations between Saladin and Richard the Lionheart during the Third Crusade," *Journal of Medieval History* 39 (2013): 275–96.

20. See John Carmi Parsons, "Ritual and Symbol in the English Queenship to 1500," in *Women and Sovereignty*, ed. Louise O. Fradenburg (Edinburgh: University of Edinburgh Press, 1991), 60–77.

21. For further discussion of the tympanum, see M. Cecilia Gaposchkin, "The King of France and the Queen of Heaven: The Iconography of the Porte Rouge of Notre-Dame of Paris," *Gesta* 39, no. 1 (2000): 58–72.

22. See Margaret Howell, *Eleanor of Provence: Queenship in Thirteenth-Century England* (Oxford: Wiley-Blackwell, 1998), 72–73.

23. See Helen E. Maurer, *Margaret of Anjou: Queenship and Power in Late Medieval England* (Woodbridge, Suffolk: Boydell, 2003), 17–22.

24. Erin A. Sadlack, *The French Queen's Letters: Mary Tudor and the Politics of Marriage in Sixteenth-Century Europe* (Houndmills, Basingstoke: Palgrave Macmillan, 2011), 65–72.

25. Marion Facinger, "A Study of Medieval Queenship: Capetian France, 987–1237," *Studies in Medieval and Renaissance History* 5 (1968): 3–48. For critiques of Facinger, see Miriam Shadis, "Blanche of Castile and Facinger's 'Medieval Queenship': Reassessing the Argument," in *Capetian Women*, ed. Kathleen Nolan (New York: Palgrave Macmillan, 2003), 137–61; Joanna L. Laynesmith, *The Last Medieval Queens: English Queenship, 1445–1503* (Oxford: Oxford University Press, 2004), 5–9; Kristen Geaman, "Queen's Gold and Intercession: The Case of Eleanor of Aquitaine," *Medieval Feminist Forum* 46 (2010): 10–33. See also Lois Huneycutt, "Intercession and the High Medieval Queen: The Esther Topos," and John Carmi Parsons, "The Queen's Intercession in Thirteenth-Century England," both in *Power of the Weak: Studies on Medieval Women*, ed. Jennifer Carpenter and Sally-Beth MacLean (Urbana: University of Illinois Press, 1995), 126–46 and 147–77.

26. See Margaret Howell, "Royal Women in the Mid-Thirteenth Century," in *England and Europe in the Reign of Henry III (1216–1272)*, ed. Bjorn K. U. Weiler with Ifor W. Rowlands (Aldershot: Ashgate, 2002), 163–81, esp. 176–78.

27. Ruth Mazo Karras, "Marriage and the Creation of Kin in the Sagas," *Scandinavian Studies* 4 (2003): 473–90. See also Gillian R. Overing, "The Women of *Beowulf*: A Context for Interpretation," in *Beowulf: Basic Readings*, ed. Peter S. Baker (New York: Garland, 1995), 219–60; Jane Chance, *Woman as Hero in Old English Literature* (Syracuse: Syracuse University Press, 1986), 10; Carol Parrish Jamison, "Traffic of Women in Germanic Literature: The Role of the Peace Pledge in Marital Exchange," in *Women in German Yearbook* 20 (2004): 13–36.

28. See Birgit Sawyer, "Valdemar, Absalon and Saxo: Historiography and Politics in Medieval Denmark," *Revue Belge de Philologie et d'Histoire* 63, no. 4 (1985): 685–705.

29. Saxo Grammaticus, *Saxonis Grammatici Gesta Danorum*, ed. Alfred Holder (Strasbourg, 1886), 6.201–2.

30. Friedrich Klaeber, *Klaeber's* Beowulf *and the Fight at Finnsburg*, ed. Robert D. Fulk et al. (Toronto: University of Toronto Press, 2008). All references are to this edition and are cited parenthetically by line number in the text.

31. See James A. Brundage, *Law, Sex, and Christian Society in Medieval Europe* (Chicago: University of Chicago Press, 1987), 199–226, 269–70. See also Georges Duby, *The Knight, the Lady, and the Priest: The Making of Modern Marriage in the Middle Ages*, trans. Barbara Bray (New York: Pantheon, 1983); Adhémar Esmein, *Le mariage en droit canonique*, 2 vols. (Paris, 1891).

32. Bradbury, *The Capetians*, 119–20.

33. See Ruth Mazo Karras, *Unmarriages: Women, Men, and Sexual Union in the Middle Ages* (Philadelphia: University of Pennsylvania Press, 2012), 59–67; John W. Baldwin, "The Many Loves of Philip Augustus," in *The Medieval Marriage Scene: Prudence, Passion, Policy*, Medieval & Renaissance Texts & Studies 299, ed. Sherry Roush and Cristelle Louise Baskins (Tempe: Arizona Center for Medieval and Renaissance Studies,

2005), 67–80; George Conklin, "Ingeborg of Denmark, Queen of France, 1193–1223," in *Queens and Queenship in Medieval Europe*, ed. Anne Duggan (Woodbridge, Suffolk: Boydell, 1997), 39–52.

34. David Crouch, *The Normans: The History of a Dynasty* (London: Hambledon, 2002), 27.

35. William of Jumièges, *Gesta Normannorum Ducum*, 2.6 (12), in *Gesta Normannorum Ducum of William of Jumièges, Orderic Vitalis, and Robert of Torigni*, ed. Elisabeth M. C. van Houts (Oxford: Oxford University Press, 1992–1995), 58–59.

36. See Karras, *Unmarriages*, 42–43.

37. Eleanor Searle, *Predatory Kinship and the Creation of Norman Power, 840–1066* (Berkeley: University of California Press, 1988).

38. Eleanor Searle, "Fact and Pattern in Heroic History: Dudo of St. Quentin," *Viator* 15 (1984): 75–85.

39. See Justin C. Lake, "Truth, Plausibility, and the Virtues of Narrative at the Millennium," *Journal of Medieval History* 35 (2009): 221–38. On the more general problem of the balance between historical truth and fiction in medieval writing, see Suzanne Fleischman, "On the Representation of History and Fiction in the Middle Ages," *History and Theory* 23 (1983): 278–310; Ruth Morse, *Truth and Convention in the Middle Ages: Rhetoric, Representation and Reality* (Cambridge: Cambridge University Press, 1991); Monica Otter, *Inventiones: Fiction and Referentiality in Twelfth-Century Historical Writing* (Chapel Hill: University of North Carolina Press, 1996).

40. See Lucien Musset, "L'origine de Rollon," in *Nordica et Normannica: Recueil d'études sur la Scandinavie ancienne et médiévale, les expéditions des Vikings et la fondation de la Normandie*, Studia nordica 1 (Paris: Société des études nordiques, 1997), 383–87; Musset, "Ce que l'on peut savoir du traité de Saint-Clair-sur-Ept," *Annuaires des cinq départementes de la Normandie* 139 (1982): 79–182.

41. William of Apulia, *Gesta Roberti Wiscardi*, ed. R. Wilmans, in Monumenta Germaniae Historica, Scriptores 9 (Hanover, 1851), book 1. Subsequent references are to this edition and are cited parenthetically in the text.

42. William of Malmesbury, *Chronicles of the Kings of England, From the Earliest Period to the Reign of King Stephen*, trans. John Sharpe, ed. John Allen Giles (London, 1847), preface to bk. 5, 424; hereafter cited parenthetically in the text.

43. On these alternative approaches to the *Aeneid*, see Joanna Scott, "Betraying Origins: The Many Faces of Aeneas," *LATCH: A Journal for the Study of the Literary Artifact in Theory, Culture, and History* 3 (2010): 64–84; Desmond, *Reading Dido*, 45–55; C. David Benson, *The History of Troy in Middle English Literature: Guido delle Colonne's Historia destructionis Troiae in Medieval England* (Woodbridge, Suffolk: D. S. Brewer, 1980).

44. See Karras, *Unmarriages*, 45–59; Brundage, *Law, Sex, and Christian Society*; Lianna Farber, *An Anatomy of Trade in Medieval Writing: Value, Consent, and Community* (Ithaca: Cornell University Press, 2005), 93–129.

45. See James Brundage, "Force and Fear: A Marriage Case from Eleventh-Century Aragon," in *On the Social Origins of Medieval Institutions: Essays in Honor of Joseph F. O'Callaghan*, ed. Donald J. Kaygay and Theresa M. Vann (Leiden: Brill, 1998), 11–20.

46. See Charles J. Reid, *Power over the Body, Equality in the Family: Rights and Domestic Relations in Medieval Canon Law* (Grand Rapids: Eerdmans, 2004), 37–44; Brundage, "Force and Fear."

47. I am indebted to a large body of scholarship on Eleanor. See especially James A. Brundage, "The Canon Law of Divorce in the Mid-Twelfth Century: Louis VII c. Eleanor of Aquitaine," in *Eleanor of Aquitaine: Lord and Lady*, ed. Bonnie Wheeler and John Carmi Parsons (Houndmills, Basingstoke: Palgrave Macmillan, 2002), 213–21; Constance Brittain Bouchard, "Eleanor's Divorce from Louis VII: The Uses of Consanguinity," in Wheeler and Parsons, *Eleanor of Aquitaine*, 223–35; Amy Kelly, *Eleanor of Aquitaine and the Four Kings* (Cambridge: Harvard University Press, 1950), 53–63, 73–81.

48. John Gillingham, *The Angevin Empire*, 2nd ed. (New York: Oxford University Press, 2001).

49. See Farber, *Anatomy of Trade*, 129–49.

50. On the competition between chronicle and romance, see Geraldine Heng, *Empire of Romance: Medieval Romance and the Politics of Cultural Fantasy* (New York: Columbia University Press, 2003), 6–7, 35–46.

51. Kinoshita, *Medieval Boundaries*; Gregory Heyworth, *Desiring Bodies: Ovidian Romance and the Cult of Form* (Notre Dame: University of Notre Dame Press, 2009); Kevin Sean Whetter, *Understanding Genre and Medieval Romance* (Aldershot: Ashgate, 2008), 61–64.

52. Wace, *Roman de Brut, A History of the British: Text and Translation*, ed. and trans. Judith Weiss, rev. ed. (2002; repr., Exeter: University of Exeter Press, 2010). All references are to this edition and are cited parenthetically by line number in the text.

53. Benoît de Sainte-Maure, *Le Roman de Troie*, ed. Léopold Constans (Paris: Firmin-Didot, 1908), 4.26164.

54. Françoise H. M. Le Saux, *A Companion to Wace* (Cambridge: D. S. Brewer, 2005), 110.

55. See Charlotte A. T. Wulf, "A Comparative Study of Wace's Guinevere in the Twelfth Century," in *Arthurian Romance and Gender: Selected Proceedings of the XVIIth International Arthurian Congress. Internationale Forschungen zur Allgemeinen und Vergleichenden Literaturwissenschaft*, ed. Friedrich Wolfzettel (Amsterdam: Rodopi, 1995), 66–78, esp. 68–69, 73–74.

56. The *Roman de Brut* is one of the few Anglo-Norman works we can date. The date of the *Roman d'Enéas* is harder to pinpoint. Ernst Hoepffner set out the case for Wace's influence on the *Enéas* in "L'Enéas et Wace," *Archivum romanicum* 15 (1931): 248–69. See John A. Yunck's introduction to his edition of *Enéas: A Twelfth-Century Romance* (New York: Columbia University Press, 1974), 3–7.

57. *Roman d' Enéas*, ed. Jean Jacques Salverda de Grave (Halle, 1891). All references are to this edition and are cited parenthetically in the text.

58. See Tracy Adams, *Violent Passions: Managing Love in the Old French Verse Romances* (Houndmills, Basingstoke: Palgrave Macmillan, 2005), 122–24.

59. See Jessie Crosland, "Enéas and the *Aeneid*," *Modern Literary Review* 29 (1934): 282–90; Albert Pauphilet, "Enéas and Enée," *Romania* 55 (1929): 195–213; and "L'antiquité d'Enéas," in *Le Legs du moyen âge: Études de littérature médiévale* (Paris: Melun, 1950), 91–106; Yunck, introduction to *Enéas*, 10–14.

60. For complementary discussions of the poem's Ovidian debts, see Jerome Singerman, *Under Clouds of Poesy: Poetry and Truth in French and English Reworkings of the* Aeneid, *1160–1513* (New York: Garland, 1986), 77–98; Desmond, *Reading Dido*, 117.

61. From the D ms. of the poem, Appendix 1 in *Roman d' Enéas*, 381.

62. Ibid., 382.

63. Patricia Ingham, *Sovereign Fantasies: Arthurian Romance and the Making of Britain* (Philadelphia: University of Pennsylvania Press, 2001), 14–15.

64. Peggy McCracken, *The Romance of Adultery: Queenship and Sexual Transgression in Old French Literature* (Philadelphia: University of Pennsylvania Press, 1998).

65. Sharon Kinoshita, "The Poetics of *Translatio*: French-Byzantine Relations in Chrétien de Troyes's *Cligès*," in *Exemplaria* 8 (1996): 315–54. See also Kinoshita, "Chrétien de Troyes's *Cligés* in the Medieval Mediterranean," *Arthuriana* 3 (2009): 48–61.

66. Judith Herrin, *Unrivalled Influence: Women and Empire in Byzantium* (Princeton: Princeton University Press, 2013); Ruth Macrides, "Dynastic Marriages and Political Kinship," in *Byzantine Diplomacy: Papers from the Twenty-Fourth Spring Symposium of Byzantine Studies, Cambridge, March 1990*, ed. Jonathan Shepard and Simon Franklin (Aldershot: Variorum, 1992), 263–80. For the protocols of the bride show in Byzantium and later in Russia, see, respectively, Warren Treadgold, "The Problem of the Marriage of Emperor Theophilos," *Greek, Roman, and Byzantine Studies* 16, no. 3 (1975): 325–41; and Russell Martin, *A Bride for the Tsar: Bride Shows and Marriage Politics in Early Modern Russia* (DeKalb: Northern Illinois University Press, 2012).

67. See Christopher MacEvitt, *The Crusades and the Christian World of the East: Rough Tolerance* (Philadelphia: University of Pennsylvania Press, 2009), 70–71, 76–78, 88, 160–61; A. P. Kazhdan and Ann Wharton Epstein, *Change in Byzantine Culture in the Eleventh and Twelfth Centuries* (Berkeley: University of California Press, 1985), 178; Kinoshita, "The Poetics of *Translatio*," 325–26.

68. See Joseph J. Duggan's discussion of lineages in the poem in *The Romances of Chrétien de Troyes* (New Haven: Yale University Press, 2001), 64–69.

69. Chrétien de Troyes, *Cligès: Textausgabe mit Einleitung und Glossar*, ed. Wendelin Foerster (Halle, 1888). All references are to this edition and are cited parenthetically in the text by line number.

70. See McCracken, *The Romance of Adultery*, 25–51. See also Wendelin Foerster's introduction to his edition of *Cligès*; Anthime Fourrier, *Le courant realiste dans le roman courtois en France au Moyen Age* (Paris: Nizet, 1960).

4. Marriage Diplomacy, Print, and the Reformation

1. See Robert A. Kann, "Dynastic Relations and European Power Politics, 1848–1918," *Journal of Modern History* 45 (1973): 387–410.

2. See Robert K. Massie, *Nicholas and Alexandra* (New York: Atheneum, 1967), 362–66.

3. See James Laidlaw, ed., *The Auld Alliance: France and Scotland over 700 Years* (Edinburgh: University of Edinburgh Press, 1999); Norman Macdougall, *An Antidote to the English: The Auld Alliance, 1295–1560* (East Linton, East Lothian: Tuckwell Press, 2001); Elizabeth Bonner, "Scotland's 'Auld Alliance' with France, 1295–1560," *History* 84, no. 273 (1999): 5–30.

4. See Elizabeth Bonner, "French Naturalization of the Scots in the Fifteenth and Sixteenth Centuries," *Historical Journal* 40 (1997): 1085–1115; Macdougall, *An Antidote to the English*, 79–86; Louis A. Barbé, *Margaret of Scotland and the Dauphin*

Louis (London: Blackie and Son, 1917); J. H. Baxter, "The Marriage of James II," *Scottish Historical Review* 25 (1928): 69–72.

5. Macdougall, *An Antidote to the English*, 78.

6. "Francisci Valesi et Mariae Stuartae, Regum Franciae et Scotiae, Epithalamium," in George Buchanan, *George Buchanan: The Political Poetry*, ed. Paul J. McGinnis and Arthur H. Williamson (Edinburgh: Lothian Print, 1995), ll. 208, 211–14, 225–26.

7. Muriel Canallas, "The Auld Alliance (1295–1560): Commercial Exchanges, Cultural and Intellectual Influences between France and Scotland" (M.A. thesis, Université de Toulon et de Var, 2009), 31–39, HAL: Archives ouvertes, http://dumas.ccsd.cnrs.fr/file/index/docid/429946/filename/Canallas_-_The_Auld_Alliance.pdf (accessed October 7, 2014).

8. See Paula Sutter Fichtner, "Dynastic Marriage in Sixteenth-Century Habsburg Diplomacy and Statecraft: An Interdisciplinary Approach," *American Historical Review* 81 (1976): 243–65.

9. For further discussion of the dynastic background, see Jonathan Sumption, *The Hundred Years War*, vol. 1, *Trial by Battle* (Philadelphia: University of Pennsylvania Press, 1991), 100–122; Malcolm Vale, "England, France, and the Origins of the Hundred Years War," in *England and Her Neighbours, 1066–1453*, ed. Michael Jones and Malcolm Vale (London: Hambledon, 1989), 199–216.

10. Much later, in the mid-fifteenth century, the French invoked a Merovingian law code stating that neither women nor those who inherited their claims from women could inherit "Salic land," or lands that belonged to the Salian Franks, the putative ancestors of all French kings. As numerous historians have noted, women had often ruled France in various capacities. But the often forgotten law provided the French aristocracy with a convenient way of avoiding a foreign succession, since the English claims to the French throne derived from Edward's mother, Isabelle of France. See Craig Taylor, "The Salic Law and the Valois Succession to the French Crown," *French Historical Studies* 15 (2001): 358–77; Taylor, "The Salic Law, French Queenship, and the Defense of Women in the Late Middle Ages," *French Historical Studies* 29 (2006): 543–64.

11. See Theodor Meron, "The Authority to Make Treaties in the Late Middle Ages," *American Journal of International Law* 89, no. 1 (1995): 1–20, esp. 11–13; Anne Curry, "Two Kingdoms, One King: The Treaty of Troyes (1420) and the Creation of a Double Monarchy of England and France," in *"The Contending Kingdoms": France and England, 1420–1700*, ed. Glenn Richardson (Aldershot: Ashgate, 2008), 23–42.

12. See Georges Minois, *La guerre de cents ans: Naissance de deux nations* (Paris: Perrin, 2008).

13. Quoted by Tracy Adams in *The Life and Afterlife of Isabeau of Bavaria* (Baltimore: Johns Hopkins University Press, 2010), 47.

14. See J. L. Laynesmith, *The Last Medieval Queens: English Queenship, 1445–1503* (Oxford: Oxford University Press, 2004), 10–15, 42–44; Helen E. Maurer, *Margaret of Anjou: Queenship and Power in Late Medieval England* (Woodbridge, Suffolk: Boydell Press, 2003), 17–38; Maurice Keen, "The End of the Hundred Years War: Lancastrian France and Lancastrian England," in Jones and Vale, *England and Her Neighbours*, 297–311.

15. See John Watts, *Henry VI and the Politics of Kingship* (Cambridge: Cambridge University Press, 1996), 205–51.

16. John D. Fudge, *Commerce and Print in the Early Reformation* (Leiden: Brill, 2007); Ian Green, *Print and Protestantism in Early Modern England* (Oxford: Oxford University Press, 2000); Peter M. Soergel, *Wondrous in His Saints: Counter-Reformation Propaganda in Bavaria* (Berkeley: University of California Press, 1993); Clifford S. L. Davies, *Peace, Print and Protestantism, 1450–1558* (London: Hart-Davis MacGibbon, 1976); Davies, *Papist Pamphleteers: The Allen-Persons Party and the Political Thought of the Counter-Reformation in England, 1572–1615* (Chicago: Loyola University Press, 1964).

17. See Joad Raymond, *Pamphlets and Pamphleteering in Early Modern England* (Cambridge: Cambridge University Press, 2003).

18. Robert J. Knecht, *The Rise and Fall of Renaissance France, 1483–1610*, 2nd ed. (Oxford: Blackwell, 2001), 67–76.

19. I am indebted to a substantial prior bibliography on Cateau-Cambrésis. See especially Frederic J. Baumgartner, *Henry II, King of France, 1547–1559* (Durham: Duke University Press, 1988), 218–30; Clifford S. L. Davies, "England and the French War," in *The Mid-Tudor Polity, 1540–1560*, ed. Jennifer Loach and Robert Tittler (London: Macmillan, 1980), 159–85; Susan Doran, *England and Europe in the Sixteenth Century* (New York: St. Martin's, 1999); John H. Elliott, *Europe Divided, 1559–1598*, 2nd ed. (Oxford: Blackwell, 2000); David Loades, *The Reign of Mary Tudor: Politics, Government, and Religion in England, 1553–1558* (New York: St. Martin's, 1979); Knecht, *The Rise and Fall of Renaissance France*, 230–45; Wallace T. MacCaffrey, *The Shaping of the Elizabethan Regime: Elizabethan Politics, 1558–1572* (Princeton: Princeton University Press, 1968), 46–49, 58; Jocelyne G. Russell, *Peacemaking in the Renaissance* (London: Duckworth, 1986), 133–223; Richard Bruce Wernham, *The Making of Elizabethan Foreign Policy, 1558–1603* (Berkeley: University of California Press, 1980); Wernham, *Before the Armada: The Emergence of the English Nation, 1485–1588* (New York: Harcourt, Brace & World, 1966); Wernham, *After the Armada: Elizabethan England and the Struggle for Western Europe, 1588–1595* (Oxford: Clarendon Press, 1984).

20. I am indebted throughout to previous scholarship on Elisabeth de Valois. See especially Agustín G. de Amezúa y Mayo, *Isabel de Valois, reina de España (1546–1568)*, 3 vols. (Madrid: Gráficas Ultra, 1949); Santiago Nadal, *Las cuatro mujeres de Felipe II* (Barcelona: Ediciones Mercedes, 1944), 133–208; Antonio Martinez Llamas, *Isabel de Valois, reina de España: Una historia de amor y enfermedad* (Madrid: Ediciones Temas de Hoy, 1996). See also my discussion of Elisabeth's career in "Marriage à la Mode, 1559: Elizabeth I, Elisabeth de Valois, and the Changing Patterns of Dynastic Marriage," in *Queens and Power in Medieval and Early Modern England*, ed. Carole Levin and Robert Buckholz (Lincoln: University of Nebraska Press, 2009), 76–97.

21. Henry Kamen, *Philip of Spain* (New Haven: Yale University Press, 1997), 205–8. On William of Orange's accusation, see Peter Arnade, *Beggars, Iconoclasts, and Civic Patriots: The Political Culture of the Dutch Revolt* (Ithaca: Cornell University Press, 2008), 299–303.

22. See Frederic J. Baumgartner, *France in the Sixteenth Century* (New York: St. Martin's Press, 1995), 117–33; Bernard Barbiche, *Les institutions de la monarchie française à l'époque moderne: XVIe–XVIIIe siècle* (Paris: Presses universitaires de France, 1999); Joël Cornette, ed., *La monarchie entre Renaissance et Révolution, 1515–1792* (Paris: Seuil, 2000); J. Russell Major, *From Renaissance Monarchy to Absolute Monarchy: French Kings, Nobles, and Estates* (Baltimore: Johns Hopkins University Press, 1994).

23. For further discussion of Elizabeth's complex marriage politics, see Susan Doran, *Monarchy and Matrimony: The Courtships of Elizabeth I* (New York: Routledge, 1996); Carole Levin, *The Heart and Stomach of a King: Elizabeth I and the Politics of Sex and Power* (Philadelphia: University of Pennsylvania Press, 1994), 39–65.

24. *Calendar of Letters and State Papers Relating to English Affairs . . . in the Archives of Simancas*, ed. Martin A. S. Hume (London, 1892), 1:35n16.

25. For a more extensive discussion of this negotiation, see my "Marriage à la Mode, 1559."

26. See Ian Green's summary and critique of this position in *Print and Protestantism*, 553–90.

27. See Dena Goodman, *The Republic of Letters: A Cultural History of the French Enlightenment* (Ithaca: Cornell University Press, 1994).

28. Timothy Hampton, *Literature and the Nation in the Sixteenth Century: Inventing Renaissance France* (Ithaca: Cornell University Press, 2001), 1–34.

29. François Habert, *Eglogue pastorale sur l'union nuptialle de treshault, & trespuissant Seigneur, Philippes, Roy d'Hespagne, & de tresexcellente, & tresvertuose princesse, madame Elisabeth, premiere fille du Roy Henry II* (Paris, 1559), A.iii; hereafter cited parenthetically in the text.

30. Marc-Claude de Buttet, *Epithalame, ou Nosses de Tresillustre et magnanime Prince Emanuel Philibert Duc de Savoye, et de tresvertueuse Princesse Marguerite de France* (Paris, 1559), A.ii; hereafter cited parenthetically in the text.

31. For a full bibliographic survey of the poems and other writings commemorating the treaty, see D. J. Hartley, "La Célébration Poétiques du Traité du Cateau-Cambrésis (1559): Document Bibliographique," in *Bibliothèque d'Humanisme et Renaissance* 43 (1981): 303–18.

32. Hélène Fernandez, "Une paix suspecte: La célébration littéraire de la paix du Cateau-Cambrésis," *Nouvelle Revue du Seizième Siècle* 15, no. 2 (1997): 325–41.

33. I am indebted to several discussions of print and literary patronage in France during the Italian wars. See especially Adrian Armstrong, *Technique and Technology: Script, Print, and Poetics in France, 1470–1550* (Oxford: Clarendon, 2000); Cynthia J. Brown, *The Shaping of History and Poetry in Late Medieval France: Propaganda and Artistic Expression in the Works of the* Rhétoriquers (Birmingham, Ala.: Summa Publications, 1985); Brown, *Poets, Patrons, and Printers: Crisis and Authority in Late Medieval France* (Ithaca: Cornell University Press, 1995).

34. Pierre de Ronsard, *Exhortation au Camp du Roy pour Bien Combattre le Jour du Bataille* (Paris, 1558), A.ii; hereafter cited parenthetically in the text.

35. Quoted and discussed by P. A. Hansen in "*Ille ego qui quondam . . .* Once Again," *Classical Quarterly* 22, no. 1 (1972): 139–49; the quotation appears on 139.

36. Translators often render the Middle French word *musette* as "bagpipe." Although the *musette de cour* was a small member of the bagpipe family, it was closer in tone to the modern oboe than to the more familiar Highland bagpipe. To prevent indecorous confusion, I have chosen to retain the French word in my translation.

37. Vergil, *Opera*, ed. R. A. B. Mynors (Oxford: Clarendon, 1969), 1.493–97. All references to Virgil's poetry are from this edition and are hereafter cited parenthetically in the text.

38. Remy Belleau, "Chant Pastoral de la paix," in *Oeuvres poétiques*, ed. Guy Demerson et al. vol. 1, *Petites inventions—Odes d'Anacréon, Oeuvres diverses, 1554–1561* (Paris: Honoré Champion, 1995), 259–66.

39. Pierre de Ronsard, *Exhortation pour la paix* (Paris, 1558), B.r.

40. Mack P. Holt, *The Duke of Anjou and the Politique Struggle during the Wars of Religion* (Cambridge: Cambridge University Press, 1986), 113–65; Doran, *Monarchy and Matrimony*, 130–94; Natalie Mears, "Counsel, Debate, and Queenship: John Stubbs's *The discoverie of a gaping gulf*, 1579," *Historical Journal* 44 (2001): 629–50; Ilona Bell, "'Souereaigne Lord of lordly Lady of this land': Elizabeth, Stubbs, and the *Gaping Gulf*," in *Dissing Elizabeth: Negative Representations of Gloriana*, ed. Julia M. Walker (Durham: Duke University Press, 1998), 99–117.

41. John Stubbs, *The discoverie of a gaping gulf whereinto England is like to be swallowed by another French mariage, if the Lord forbid not the banes, by letting her Maiestie see the sin and punishment thereof* (London, 1579), C.4.r; hereafter cited parenthetically in the text.

42. Paul E. McLane, *Spenser's* Shepheardes Calender: *A Study in Elizabethan Allegory* (Notre Dame: University of Notre Dame Press, 1961); David Norbrook, *Poetry and Politics in the English Renaissance* (1984; repr., Oxford: Oxford University Press, 2002), 53–81.

43. Edmund Spenser, "October," in *The Yale Edition of the Shorter Poems of Edmund Spenser*, ed. William Oram et al. (New Haven: Yale University Press, 1989), 170–73, ll. 40–42, 55–59.

44. Edmund Spenser, "Aprill," ibid., 70–84, ll. 50–51, 54.

5. Shakespeare's Adumbrations of State-Based Diplomacy

1. For further discussion of the fall of Calais and its international significance, see Clifford S. L. Davies, "England and the French War," in *The Mid-Tudor Polity, c. 1540–1560*, ed. Jennifer Loach and Robert Tittler (London: Macmillan, 1980), 159–85; David Loades, *The Reign of Mary Tudor: Politics, Government, and Religion in England, 1553–1558* (New York: St. Martin's, 1979).

2. John Foxe offers the earliest account of this remark; see *The Acts and Monuments of John Foxe*, ed. Stephen Reed Cattley (London, 1839), 8:625.

3. For further discussion of this Atlanticist reorientation, see David Harris Sacks, *The Widening Gate: Bristol and the Atlantic Economy, 1450–1700* (Berkeley: University of California Press, 1991); Robert Brenner, *Merchants and Revolution: Commercial Change, Political Conflict, and London's Overseas Traders, 1550–1653* (Princeton: Princeton University Press, 1993).

4. See Richard Helgerson, *Forms of Nationhood: The Elizabethan Writing of England* (Chicago: University of Chicago Press, 1992); Andrew Hadfield, *Literature, Politics and National Identity: Reformation to Renaissance* (Cambridge: Cambridge University Press, 1994); Claire McEachern, *The Poetics of English Nationhood, 1590–1612* (Cambridge: Cambridge University Press, 1996); Philip Schwyzer, *Literature, Nationalism and Memory in Early Modern England and Wales* (Cambridge: Cambridge University Press, 2004).

5. See Andrew Gurr, *Playgoing in Shakespeare's London*, 3rd ed. (Cambridge: Cambridge University Press, 2004); John Orrell, *The Quest for Shakespeare's Globe* (Cambridge: Cambridge University Press, 1983), 127–38.

6. See Adrian Poole, *Shakespeare and the Victorians* (London: Arden, 2004), 21–26; Stuart Hampton-Reeves, "Theatrical Afterlives," in *The Cambridge Companion to Shakespeare's History Plays*, ed. Michael Hattaway (Cambridge: Cambridge University

Press, 2002), 229–44; Graham Holderness, "Agincourt 1944: Readings in the Shakespearean Myth," *Literature and History* 10, no. 1 (1984): 24–45.

7. John Stubbs, *The discoverie of a gaping gulf whereinto England is like to be swallowed by another French mariage, if the Lord forbid not the banes, by letting her Maiestie see the sin and punishment thereof* (London, 1579), C4r and v.

8. For prior discussion of Shakespeare's relationship to France, see Deanne Williams, *The French Fetish from Chaucer to Shakespeare* (Cambridge: Cambridge University Press, 2004); Linda Gregerson, "French Marriages and the Protestant Nation in Shakespeare's History Plays," in *A Companion to Shakespeare's Works*, vol. 2, *The Histories*, ed. Richard Dutton and Jean E. Howard (Oxford: Blackwell, 2003), 246–62. See also the essays collected in the special issue "France in the English and French Theater of the Renaissance," *Renaissance Studies* 9 (1995). See also the "Shakespeare and France" special issue of *Shakespeare Yearbook* 5 (1994), edited by Holger Klein and Jean-Marie Maguin.

9. There is a substantial bibliography on the development of the Elizabethan French policy. See especially Richard Bruce Wernham, *The Making of Elizabethan Foreign Policy, 1558–1603* (Berkeley: University of California Press, 1980); Wernham, *Before the Armada: The Emergence of the English Nation, 1485–1588* (New York: Harcourt, Brace & World, 1966); Wernham, *After the Armada: Elizabethan England and the Struggle for Western Europe, 1588–1595* (Oxford: Clarendon Press, 1984); Susan Doran, *England and Europe in the Sixteenth Century* (New York: St. Martin's, 1999); Wallace T. MacCaffrey, *The Shaping of the Elizabethan Regime: Elizabethan Politics, 1558–1572* (Princeton: Princeton University Press, 1968); MacCaffrey, *Queen Elizabeth and the Making of Policy, 1572–1588* (Princeton: Princeton University Press, 1981); MacCaffrey, *Elizabeth I: War and Politics, 1588–1603* (Princeton: Princeton University Press, 1992).

10. See Leah Marcus, *Puzzling Shakespeare: Local Reading and Its Discontents* (Berkeley: University of California Press, 1988), 51–105; Williams, *The French Fetish*, 189–93.

11. See Gregerson, "French Marriages and the Protestant Nation."

12. Thomas Cogswell, *The Blessed Revolution: English Politics and the Coming of War, 1621–1624* (Cambridge: Cambridge University Press, 1989).

13. In one famous formulation, seventeenth-century radicals discounted the entire period between the Conquest and the fall of Charles I as a foreign occupation, a "Norman Yoke" finally doffed by Parliamentarians committed to a contractual theory of government. See Christopher Hill, "The Norman Yoke," in *Puritanism and Revolution: Studies in Interpretation of the English Revolution of the Seventeenth Century* (1958; repr., Houndmills, Basingstoke: Palgrave, 1997), 46–111.

14. Jean E. Howard and Phyllis Rackin, *Engendering a Nation: A Feminist Account of Shakespeare's English Histories* (London: Routledge, 1997), 119. See also David Womersley's discussion of the Bastard as a response to political fracture in "The Politics of Shakespeare's *King John*," *Review of English Studies* 40 (1989): 497–515; Michael Manheim, "The Four Voices of the Bastard," in *King John: New Perspectives*, ed. Deborah T. Curren-Aquino (Newark: University of Delaware Press, 1989), 126–35.

15. All citations refer to *The Riverside Shakespeare*, ed. G. Blakemore Evans, 2nd ed. (Boston: Houghton Mifflin, 1997).

16. For a useful general survey of the political dynamics of Angevin state formation, see Robert Bartlett, *England under the Norman and Angevin Kings, 1075–1225*, New

Oxford History of England (Oxford: Oxford University Press, 2000), 1–102. See also John Gillingham, *The Angevin Empire*, 2nd ed. (New York: Oxford University Press, 2001).

17. See Amy Kelly, *Eleanor of Aquitaine and the Four Kings* (1950; repr., Cambridge: Harvard University Press, 1978), 75–81; Gillingham, *Angevin Empire*, 18–21.

18. See Gillingham's discussion of the nomenclature problem in *Angevin Empire*, 2–5.

19. Ibid., 3–4.

20. John Gillingham, *Richard I*, Yale English Monarchs (1999; repr., New Haven: Yale University Press, 2002), 24–40.

21. Gillingham, *Angevin Empire*, 86–115; Frederick M. Powicke, *The Loss of Normandy*, 2nd ed. (Manchester: University of Manchester Press), 1960; Wilfred L. Warren, *King John*, Yale English Monarchs (1961; repr., New Haven: Yale University Press, 1997), 64–99; Ralph V. Turner, *King John* (London: Longman, 1994). See also the essays in Stephen D. Church, ed., *King John: New Interpretations* (Woodbridge: Boydell Press, 1999).

22. Ralph Higden, *Polychronicon Ranulphi Higden*, ed. Churchill Babington and Joseph Rawson Lumby, 9 vols. (1865–1886), 5:336.

23. Raphael Holinshed et al., *The Chronicles of England, Scotland, and Ireland*, vol. 2 (London, 1807), 266; John Speed, *The Historie of Great Britain* (London, 1611), 531, 550. I am indebted to Gillingham's excellent discussion of Angevin historiography in *Richard I*, 1–14.

24. See Carole Levin, *Propaganda in the English Reformation: Heroic and Villainous Images of King John*, Studies in British History 11 (New York: Edwin Mellen, 1987).

25. Samuel Daniel, *The Collection of the Historie of England* (London, 1618), 107.

26. Katherine Eggert, *Showing Like a Queen: Female Authority and Literary Experiment in Spenser, Shakespeare, and Milton* (Philadelphia: University of Pennsylvania Press, 2000), 51–99. My thinking about *King John* is generally indebted to the substantial body of criticism on gender and Shakespeare's history plays. See especially Howard and Rackin's chapter on *King John* in *Engendering a Nation*, 119–33; Juliet Dusinberre, "*King John* and Embarrassing Women," *Shakespeare Survey* 42 (1990): 37–52.

27. Several scholars have commented on the disappearance of women after the third act and the sudden masculinist turn in the action. See Dusinberre, "*King John* and Embarrassing Women," 51–52; Howard and Rackin, *Engendering a Nation*, 125–26; Virginia M. Vaughan, "*King John*: A Study in Subversion and Containment," in Curren-Aquino, King John: *New Perspectives*, 72.

28. Eggert, *Showing Like a Queen*.

29. There is now a large body of scholarship on the "black legends" of various medieval and early modern queens consort. See especially Helen E. Maurer, *Margaret of Anjou: Queenship and Power in Late Medieval England* (Woodbridge, Suffolk: Boydell, 2003); Lynn Hunt, "The Many Bodies of Marie Antoinette: Political Pornography and the Problem of the Feminine in the French Revolution," in *Eroticism and the Body Politic*, ed. Lynn Hunt (Baltimore: Johns Hopkins University Press, 1991), 108–30.

30. Kelly, *Eleanor of Aquitaine*, 356–64; Warren, *King John*, 54–56.

31. See Peter Saccio's discussion of Shakespeare's adaptation of the historical sources in *Shakespeare's English Kings: History, Chronicle, and Drama* (Oxford: Oxford

University Press, 1976), 192–93. For more general discussion of Shakespeare's selective approach to his sources, see Albert R. Braunmuller, "*King John* and Historiography," *English Literary History* 55 (1988): 309–32.

32. See James L. Calderwood's discussion of the "commodity" theme in "Commodity and Honor in *King John*," *University of Toronto Quarterly* 29 (1960): 341–56.

33. See Howard and Rackin, *Engendering a Nation*, 124.

34. Warren, *King John*, 76–84.

35. See Williams's complementary reading of the Bastard as "a figure of exogamous hybridity" whose "vocabulary of conquest . . . [ties his] conception closely to England's history with France, and underscore[s] the general difficulty in articulating an English identity that is not overshadowed by conquest" (*The French Fetish*, 205, 202–3).

36. Niccolò Machiavelli, *Istorie fiorentine*, in *Tutte le opera*, ed. Mario Martelli (Florence: Sansoni, 1971), 2.5, 1.7, 6.1.

37. Alberico Gentili, *De legationibus libri tres*, trans. Gordon J. Laing (New York: Oxford University Press, 1924), 1.1.

38. See, for example, Diego Panizza, "Machiavelli e Alberico Gentili," in *Machiavellismo e antimachiavellismo nel cinquecento: Atti del Convegno di Perugia* (Florence: Olschki, 1970), 148–55; Peter Schröder, "Vitoria, Gentili, Bodin: Sovereignty and the Law of Nations," in *The Roman Foundations of the Law of Nations: Alberico Gentili and the Justice of Empire*, ed. Benedict Kingsbury and Benjamin Straumann (Oxford: Oxford University Press, 2010), 163–186; Schröder, "Taming the Fox and the Lion: Some Aspects of the Sixteenth Century's Debate on Inter-State Relations," in *War, the State and International Law in Seventeenth-Century Europe*, ed. Olaf Asbach and Peter Schröder (Farnham, Surrey: Ashgate, 2010), 83–102. For further discussion of the particular history of just war theory, see James Turner Johnson, *Ideology, Reason, and the Limitation of War: Religious and Secular Concepts, 1200–1740* (Princeton: Princeton University Press, 1975); Johnson, *Just War Tradition and the Restraint of War: A Moral and Historical Inquiry* (Princeton: Princeton University Press, 1981).

39. Alberico Gentili, *De iure belli libri tres*, trans. John C. Rolfe (Oxford: Clarendon, 1933), cited parenthetically in the text by book and section number.

40. Paola Pugliatti, *Shakespeare and the Just War Tradition* (Farnham, Surrey: Ashgate, 2010), 197–228; Rosanna Camerlingo, "*Henry V* and the Just War: Shakespeare, Gentili and Machiavelli," in *Machiavellian Encounters in Tudor and Stuart England: Literary and Political Influences from the Reformation to the Restoration*, ed. Alessandro Arienzo and Alessandra Petrina (Farnham, Surrey: Ashgate, 2013), 103–20. See also Franziska Quabeck, *Just and Unjust Wars in Shakespeare* (Berlin: de Gruyter, 2013); David L. Perry, "Using Shakespeare's *Henry V* to Teach Just-War Principles," http://home.earthlink.net/~davidlperry/henryv.htm (accessed July 31, 2015). Numerous scholars have written about the play's ambiguities of characterization, tone, and ethos. See especially Norman Rabkin, "Ducks, Rabbits, and *Henry V*," *Shakespeare Quarterly* 28 (1977): 279–96; Stephen Greenblatt, *Shakespearean Negotiations: The Circulation of Social Energy in England* (Oxford: Clarendon, 1988), 21–65.

41. For further discussion of the play's theatrical self-consciousness, see James Calderwood, *Metadrama in Shakespeare's* Henriad: Richard II *to* Henry V (Berkeley: University of California Press, 1979), 162–81.

42. Holinshed et al., *The Chronicles*, 3:85.

43. See Walter Nash, *The Language of Humour* (Abingdon: Routledge, 2013), 13–22.

44. See Holinshed et al., *The Chronicles*, 3:92: "In this meane time that the king of England was occupied about Caen, the Frenchmen had neither anie sufficient power to resist him, nor were able to assemble an host togither in their necessitie, by reason of the dissention among themselves: for their king was so simple, that he was spoiled both of treasure and kingdome, so that everie man spent and wasted he cared not what. Charles the Dolphin being of the age of sixtéene or seaventéene yeares, bewailed the ruine and decaie of his countrie, he onelie studied the reléefe of the common-wealth, and devised how to resist his enimies; but having neither men nor monie, was greatlie troubled and disquieted in mind. In conclusion, by the advise and counsell of the earle of Arminacke the constable of France, he found a meane to get all the treasure & riches which his moother queene Isabell had gotten and hoorded in diverse secret places: and for the common defense and profit of his countrie he wiselie bestowed it in waging souldiers, and preparing of things necessarie for the warre.

"The quéene forgetting the great perill . . . upon a womanish malice, set hir husband Iohn duke of Burgognie in the highest authoritie about the king, giving him the regiment and direction of the king and his realme, with all preheminence & sovereigntie. The duke of Burgognie having the sword in his hand, in revenge of old injuries, began to make warre on the Dolphin, determining, that when he had tamed this yoong unbrideled gentleman, then would he go about to withstand, and beat backe the common enimies of the realme. The like reason mooved the Dolphin, for he minded first to represse the authours of civill discord, before he would set upon forreine enimies, and therefore prepared to subdue and destroie the duke of Burgognie, as the cheefe head of that mischeefe, whereby the realme was unquieted, decaied, and in manner brought to utter ruine. Thus was France afflicted, and in everie part troubled with warre and division, and no man to provide remedie, nor once put foorth his finger for helpe or succour."

For modern accounts of the French background to the Treaty of Troyes, see Bertrand Schnerb, *Les Armagnacs et les Bourguignon:. La maudite guerre* (Paris: Perrin, 1988); Desmond Seward, *The Hundred Years War: The English in France, 1337–1453* (Harmondsworth, Middlesex: Penguin, 1999), 143–52.

45. Holinshed et al., *The Chronicles*, 6:560.

46. For history and analysis of the black legend, see Tracy Adams, *The Life and Afterlife of Isabeau of Bavaria* (Baltimore: Johns Hopkins University Press, 2010), esp. 38–72.

6. Divas and Diplomacy in Seventeenth-Century France

1. Bernard du Rosier, *Ambaxiator brevilogus*, in *De legatis et legationibus tractatus varii*, ed. Vladimir E. Hrabar (Dorpat: Mattiesen, 1905), 1–28. See also Garrett Mattingly, *Renaissance Diplomacy* (1955; repr., New York: Dover, 1988), 42–44.

2. See Stephen Wilson's introduction to his edition of *Saints and Their Cults: Studies in Religious Sociology, Folklore and History* (Cambridge: Cambridge University Press, 1983), 35–37; Jocelyne Gledhill Russell, *The Congress of Arras: A Study in Medieval Diplomacy* (Oxford: Clarendon, 1955), 205–8.

3. *Corps universel diplomatique du droit des gens, contenant un recueil des traités de paix, d'alliance, &c., faits en Europe, depuis Charlemagne jusqu'à present*, ed. Jean Dumont, 8 vols. (Amsterdam, 1726), 8:265.

4. Treaty of Cateau-Cambrésis, ibid., 6:38.

5. See Frederick H. Russell, *The Just War in the Middle Ages* (Cambridge: Cambridge University Press, 1977); Anthony Pagden, *Spanish Imperialism and the Political Imagination: Studies in European and Spanish American Social and Political Theory, 1513–1830* (New Haven: Yale University Press, 1998); Ryan Martin Greenwood, "Law and War in Late Medieval Italy: The *Jus Commune* on War and Its Application in Florence, c. 1150–1450" (Ph.D. diss., University of Chicago, 2011).

6. For examples, see Margaret Howell, *Eleanor of Provence: Queenship in Thirteenth-Century England* (Oxford: Wiley-Blackwell, 1998); Helen E. Maurer, *Margaret of Anjou: Queenship and Power in Late Medieval England* (Woodbridge, Suffolk: Boydell, 2003), 17–22; Erin A. Sadlack, *The French Queen's Letters: Mary Tudor and the Politics of Marriage in Sixteenth-Century Europe* (Houndmills: Palgrave Macmillan, 2011), 65–72.

7. Treaty of the Pyrenees, article 33, in *Corps universel diplomatique*, 6:268.

8. See Arnaud Blin's discussion of this transition in *1648, La Paix de Westphalie, ou la naissance de L'Europe politique moderne* (Paris: Éditions Complexe, 2006), 62–77. See also Lucien Bély's discussion of the sometimes complementary, sometimes contradictory dynastic and strategic "logics" that governed later seventeenth-century politics in *L'art de la paix en Europe: Naissance de la diplomatie moderne XVIe–XVIIe siècle* (Paris: Presses universitaires de France, 2007), 377–90.

9. Duc de Richelieu, *Testament Politique de Richelieu*, ed. Françoise Hildesheimer (Paris: Société de l'histoire de France, 1995), 265.

10. Bély, *L'art de la Paix*, 45–49; Mattingly, *Renaissance Diplomacy*, 87–102.

11. Richelieu, *Testament Politique*, 270.

12. Ibid.

13. Ibid., 248.

14. For further discussion of Anne's difficulties, see Ruth Kleinman, *Anne of Austria, Queen of France* (Columbus: Ohio State University Press, 1985), 95–104; Claude Dulong, *Anne d'Autriche: Mère de Louis XIV* (Paris: Hachette, 1980), 118–45; Victor L. Tapié, *La France de Louis XIII et de Richelieu* (Paris: Flammarion, 1952), 342–47.

15. This question of Corneille's relationship with Richelieu has produced an immense bibliography in both French and English. See especially Louis Batiffol, *Richelieu et Corneille: La légende de la persécution de l'auteur du Cid* (Paris: Calmann-Lévy, 1936); H. Carrington Lancaster, "The Richelieu-Corneille Rapport," *PMLA* 65, no. 2 (1950): 322–328; M. Amelia Klenke, "The Richelieu-Corneille Rapport," *PMLA* 64, no. 4 (1949): 724–45; Katherine Ibbett, "Italy versus France; or, How Pierre Corneille Became an Anti-Machiavel," *Renaissance Drama* 36–37 (2010): 379–95. Both in the last article and in her book *The Style of the State in French Theater: Neoclassicism and Government, 1630–1660* (Farnham: Ashgate, 2009), Ibbett argues for a more nuanced understanding of the relationship between Corneille and Richelieu, and more generally, of Corneille's relationship to the French state as a symbiosis rather than an ongoing conflict.

16. See especially Hélène Merlin, "*Horace*: L'équivoque et la dédicace," *Dix-septième Siècle* 182 (1994): 121–34; Christian Jouhaud, "L'écrivain et le ministre:

Corneille et Richelieu; Note sur l'épître dédicatoire d'*Horace* et tout particulièrement sur la place qu'y tient le visage du cardinal de Richelieu," *Dix-Septième Siècle* 182 (1994): 135–42; Dulong, *Anne d'Autriche*, 125–26.

17. See Georges Couton's discussion of topical allusions to Anne of Austria in his edition of Corneille's *Oeuvres complètes*, 3 vols. (Paris: Gallimard, 1980–1987), 1:1542–44.

18. Pierre Corneille, *Horace*, in *Théâtre complet*, ed. Georges Couton, vol. 1 (Paris: Bordas, 1993), cited parenthetically in the text by act, scene, and line.

19. Livy, *The History of Rome*, bks. 1–2, Loeb Classical Library (London: Heinemann; New York: Putnam, 1919–1959), cited parenthetically in the text.

20. See Robert R. Williams, *Tragedy, Recognition, and the Death of God: Studies in Hegel and Nietzsche* (Oxford: Oxford University Press, 2012), 120–36. See also Michel Prigent's reading of *Horace* as a tragic opposition between the heroism of nature and the heroism of the state in *Le héros et l'état dans la tragédie de Corneille* (Paris: Presses Universitaires de France, 1986), 45–55.

21. For discussion of the controversy, see Georges Forestier, *Essai de génétique théâtrale: Corneille à l'oeuvre* (Paris: Klincksieck, 1996), 113–23; and Couton's commentary in Corneille, *Oeuvres*, 1:1538–39.

22. John D. Lyons, *The Tragedy of Origins: Pierre Corneille and Historical Perspective* (Stanford: Stanford University Press, 1996), 38–70.

23. See Kleinman, *Anne of Austria*, 140–47; Dulong, *Anne d'Autriche*, 202–8; John B. Wolf, *Louis XIV* (New York: Norton, 1968), 13–22.

24. Wolf, *Louis XIV*, 96–130; Claude Dulong, *Le mariage du Roi-Soleil* (Paris: Albin Michel, 1986).

25. Peter Sahlins, *Boundaries: The Making of France and Spain in the Pyrenees* (Berkeley: University of California Press, 1989), 1–2.

26. See Frederik Dhondt, "Contract to Treaty: The Legal Transformation of the Spanish Succession (1659–1713)," *Journal of the History of International Law* 12 (2011): 347–75; Lucien Bély, *La société des princes XVIe–XVIIIe siècle* (Paris: Fayard, 1999); Wolf, *Louis XIV*, 116–19.

27. Wolf, *Louis XIV*, 198.

28. For a general account of the War of Devolution and the subsequent and related Dutch war, see John A. Lynn, *The Wars of Louis XIV, 1667–1714* (Edinburgh: Longman, 1999), 105–59; Wolf, *Louis XIV*, 199–212.

29. On the propaganda campaign, see Wolf, *Louis XIV*, 199–201; Dhondt, "Contract to Treaty," 355–60.

30. Louis XIV, *Mémoires de Louis XIV pour l'instruction du Dauphin*, ed. Charles Louis Dreyss, 2 vols. (Paris, 1860).

31. Ibid., 2:315.

32. Joan DeJean, *Tender Geographies: Women and the Origin of the Novel in France* (New York: Columbia University Press, 1991). See also Sharon L. Jansen, *Debating Women, Politics, and Power in Early Modern Europe* (New York: Palgrave Macmillan, 2008), 155–69. Louis's successors did not always heed his advice and sometimes allowed mistresses like Madame de Pompadour to influence diplomatic appointments and decisions. See Eva Kathrin Dade, *Madame de Pompadour: Die Mätresse und die Diplomatie* (Cologne: Böhlau, 2010). In contrast to the sacramental diplomacy of the Middle Ages and the Renaissance, this kind of female influence was never officially sanctioned.

33. Abby E. Zanger, *Scenes from the Marriage of Louis XIV: Nuptial Fictions and the Making of Absolutist Power* (Stanford: Stanford University Press, 1997).

34. Ibid., 111–30.

35. Jean Racine, *La Nymphe de la Seine à la Reyne: Ode* (Paris, 1660), 5; hereafter cited parenthetically in the text by page number.

36. See James Laidlaw, ed., *The Auld Alliance: France and Scotland over 700 Years* (Edinburgh: University of Edinburgh Press, 1999); Norman Macdougall, *An Antidote to the English: The Auld Alliance, 1295–1560* (East Linton, East Lothian: Tuckwell Press, 2001); Elizabeth Bonner, "Scotland's 'Auld Alliance' with France, 1295–1560," *History* 84 (1999): 5–30.

37. For further discussion of Anglo-French relations during the reign of Charles II, see Ronald Hutton, *Charles II* (Oxford: Oxford University Press, 1989), 157–60, 215–17, 229–31, 247–90; Sir Keith Feiling, *British Foreign Policy, 1660–1672* (London: Macmillan, 1930); David Ogg, *England in the Reign of Charles II*, 2nd ed. (1956; repr., Oxford: Oxford University Press, 1984), 322–56; John Miller, *Popery and Politics in England* (Cambridge: Cambridge University Press, 1973).

38. Ronald Hutton offers a valuable account of the treaty negotiations, as well as a summary of the historiographical debates it has generated, in "The Making of the Secret Treaty of Dover, 1668–1670," *Journal of British Studies* 29 (1986): 297–318. See also Ogg, *England in the Reign of Charles II*, 242–48; Miller, *Popery and Politics in England*, 108–14.

39. See Georges Forestier, *Racine* (Paris: Gallimard, 2006), 284–88.

40. See Couton's discussion of the competition between the two plays in his edition of Corneille, *Oeuvres complètes*, 3:1607–16; Forestier, *Racine*, 288–89. See also Philip J. Yarrow, *Racine* (Oxford: Blackwell, 1978), 50–51; Raymond Picard, *La carrière de Jean Racine* (Paris: Gallimard, 1956), 154–61.

41. See especially Gordon Pocock, *Corneille and Racine: Problems of Tragic Form* (Cambridge: Cambridge University Press, 1973), 211–15. For further discussion of the contrasting receptions, see Forestier, *Racine*, 399–402.

42. As Hutton stresses, however, the record is incomplete. Many of the letters that were exchanged between Henriette and Charles II are not extant; see "The Making of the Secret Treaty of Dover," 297–98.

43. See Erin A. Sadlack, *The French Queen's Letters: Mary Tudor and the Politics of Marriage in Sixteenth-Century Europe* (Houndmills, Basingstoke: Palgrave Macmillan, 2011).

44. See, for example, Richard Goodkin, *Birth Marks: The Tragedy of Primogeniture in Pierre Corneille, Thomas Corneille, and Jean Racine* (Philadelphia: University of Pennsylvania Press, 2000); John Campbell, "A Marriage Made in Heaven? 'Racine' and 'Love,'" *Modern Language Review* 101, no. 3 (2006): 682–90, esp. 688–89. For a particularly useful articulation of this thesis, see Gérard Defaux, "The Case of Bérénice: Racine, Corneille, and Mimetic Desire," trans. Michael Metteer, *Yale French Studies* 76 (1989): 211–39. Defaux sees the rapprochement as Racine's means to expose the darker aspects of Cornelian heroism.

45. Paul Strohm, *Hochon's Arrow: The Social Imagination of Fourteenth-Century Texts* (Princeton: Princeton University Press, 1992), 95–119; David Wallace, *Chaucerian Polity: Absolutist Lineages and Associational Forms in England and Italy* (Stanford: Stanford University Press, 1997), 363–76.

46. See Forestier's observation, "Bérénice is not a queen . . . she is solely an amorous woman [Bérénice n'est pas une reine . . . elle est exclusivement une femme amoureuse]," in *Racine*, 396.

47. Jean Racine, *Bérénice*, in *Oeuvres complètes*, ed. Georges Forestier, vol. 1 (Paris: Gallimard, 1999), 454–509, cited parenthetically in the text by act, scene, and line.

48. For prior discussion of *Bérénice*'s debts to Virgil, see Henry T. Barnwell, *The Tragic Drama of Corneille and Racine* (Oxford: Clarendon, 1982), 44–46.

49. Immanuel Kant, "Perpetual Peace," in *Kant: Political Writings*, 2nd ed., ed. Hans S. Reiss, trans. Hugh B. Nisbett (Cambridge: Cambridge University Press, 1991), 93.

50. I am indebted to a large bibliography on Kant's theory of international law. See especially Michael W. Doyle, "Kant, Liberal Legacies, and Foreign Affairs, Part I," *Philosophy and Public Affairs* 12, no. 3 (1983): 205–35; Doyle, "Kant, Liberal Legacies, and Foreign Affairs, Part II," *Philosophy and Public Affairs* 12, no. 4 (1983): 323–53; Howard Williams and Ken Booth, "Kant: Theories beyond Limits," in *Classical Theories of International Relations*, ed. Ian Clark and Iver B. Neumann (Basingstoke: Palgrave Macmillan, 1999), 71–98.

✿ BIBLIOGRAPHY

Primary Sources

Anselm of Canterbury. *Alselmi cantuariensis archiepiscopi liber cur deus homo*. Edited by Franciscus S. Schmitt. Bonn: Hanstein, 1929.

Bede. *The Ecclesiastical History of the English People*. Edited by Bertram Colgrave and Roger A. B. Mynors. 1969. Reprint, Oxford: Clarendon Press, 1991.

Belleau, Remy. *Œuvres poétiques*. Edited by Guy Demerson. 6 vols. Paris: Honoré Champion, 1995–2003.

Benoît de Sainte-Maure. *Le roman de Troie*. Edited by Léopold Constans. Paris: Firmin-Didot, 1908.

Bernard of Clairvaux. *Sermones in Adventu Domini*. In *Patrologiae cursus completus, series Latina*. Edited by Jacques-Paul Migne. Vol. 183. Paris, 1854.

———. *Sermones in Cantica Canticorum*. In *Patrologiae cursus completus, series Latina*. Edited by Jacques-Paul Migne. Vol. 183. Paris, 1854.

Buchanan, George. *George Buchanan: The Political Poetry*. Edited by Paul J. McGinnis and Arthur H. Williamson. Edinburgh: Lothian Print, 1995.

Buttet, Marc-Claude de. *Epithalame, ou Nosses de Tresillustre et magnanime Prince Emanuel Philibert Duc de Savoye, et de tresvertueuse Princesse Marguerite de France*. Paris, 1559.

Calendar of Letters and State Papers Relating to English Affairs . . . in the Archives of Simancas. Edited by Martin A. S. Hume. 4 vols. London, 1892–1899.

Chrétien de Troyes. *Cligès: Textausgabe mit Einleitung und Glossar*. Edited by Wendelin Foerster. Halle, 1888.

Codex Carolinus. Edited by Wilhelm Gundlach. In Monumenta Germaniae Historica. Epistolarum Merowingici et Karolini Aevi 1. Berlin, 1892.

Corneille, Pierre. *Œuvres complètes*. Edited by Georges Couton. 3 vols. Paris: Gallimard, 1980–1987.

———. *Théâtre complet*. Edited by Georges Couton. Vol. 1. Paris: Bordas, 1993.

Corps universel diplomatique du droit des gens, contenant un recueil des traités de paix, d'alliance, &c., faits en Europe, depuis Charlemagne jusqu'à present. Edited by Jean Dumont. 8 vols. Amsterdam, 1726.

Daniel, Samuel. *The Collection of the Historie of England*. London, 1618.

Dudo of St. Quentin. *De moribus et actis primorum normanniae ducum libri tres*. In *Patrologiae cursus completus, series Latina*. Edited by Jacques-Paul Migne. Vol. 41. Paris, 1844.

Enéas: A Twelfth-Century Romance. Translated by John A. Yunck. New York: Columbia University Press, 1974.

Foxe, John. *The Acts and Monuments of John Foxe*. Edited by Stephen Reed Cattley. London, 1839.

Gentili, Alberico. *De iure belli libri tres*. Translated by John C. Rolfe. Oxford: Clarendon, 1933.

——. *De legationibus libri tres*. Translated by Gordon J. Laing. New York: Oxford University Press, 1924.

Gregory of Tours. *Opera*. Edited by Wilhelm Levison and Bruno Krusch. Monumenta Germaniae Historica. Scriptores rerum Merovingicarum 1. Hanover, 1884–85.

Habert, François. *Eglogue Pastorale sur l'union nuptialle de treshault, & trespuissant Seigneur, Philippe, Roy d'Hespagne, & de tresexcellente, & tresvertuose princesse, madame Elisabeth, premiere fille du Roy Henry II*. Paris, 1559.

Higden, Ralph. *Polychronicon Ranulphi Higden*. Edited by Churchill Babington and Joseph Rawson Lumby. 9 vols. London, 1865–1886.

Holinshed, Raphael, et al. *The Chronicles of England, Scotland, and Ireland*. 6 vols. London, 1807–8.

Jordanes. *De origine actibusque Getarum*. Edited by Alfred Holder. Freiburg im Breisgau, 1882.

Kant, Immanuel. *Kant: Political Writings*. Edited by Hans S. Reiss and translated by Hugh B. Nisbett. 2nd ed. Cambridge: Cambridge University Press, 1991.

King, P. D. *Charlemagne: Translated Sources*. Kendal, Cumbria: King, 1987.

Livy. *The History of Rome*. London: Heinemann; New York: Putnam, 1919–1959.

Louis XIV. *Mémoires de Louis XIV pour l'instruction du Dauphin*. Edited by Charles Louis Dreyss. 2 vols. Paris, 1860.

Machiavelli, Niccolò. *Tutte le opera*. Edited by Mario Martelli. Florence: Sansoni, 1971.

Paul the Deacon. *Historia Langobardorum*. Edited by Ludwig Bethmann and Georg Waitz. In Monumenta Germaniae Historica. Scriptores rerum Langobardicarum et Italicarum saec. VI–IX. Hanover, 1878.

Philip of Harveng. *Commentaria in Cantica Canticorum*. In *Patrologiae cursus completus, series Latina*. Edited by Jacques-Paul Migne. Vol. 183. Paris, 1855.

Racine, Jean. *La Nymphe de la Seine à la Reyne: Ode*. Paris, 1660.

——. *Oeuvres complètes*. Edited by Georges Forestier. Vol. 1. Paris: Gallimard, 1999.

Richelieu, Duc de. *Testament Politique de Richelieu*. Edited by Françoise Hildesheimer. Paris: Société de l'histoire de France, 1995.

Roman d'Enéas. Edited by Jean Jacques Salverda de Grave. Halle, 1891.

Ronsard, Pierre de. *Exhortation au Camp du Roy pour Bien Combattre le Jour de la Bataille*. Paris, 1558.

——. *Exhortation pour la paix*. Paris, 1558.

Rosier, Bernard du. *Ambaxiator brevilogus*. In *De legatis et legationibus tractatus varii*. Edited by Vladimir E. Hrabar. Dorpat: Mattiesen, 1905.

Saxo Grammaticus. *Saxonis Grammatici Gesta Danorum*. Edited by Alfred Holder. Strasbourg, 1886.

Shakespeare, William. *The Riverside Shakespeare*. Ed. G. Blakemore Evans. 2nd ed. Boston: Houghton Mifflin, 1997.

Speed, John. *The Historie of Great Britain*. London, 1611.

Stubbs, John. *The discoverie of a gaping gulf whereinto England is like to be swallowed by another French mariage, if the Lord forbid not the banes, by letting her Maiestie see the sin and punishment thereof*. London, 1579.

Tacitus. *Opera minora*. Edited by Henry Furneaux. Oxford: Clarendon, 1900.

Vergil. *Opera*. Edited by Roger A. B. Mynors. Oxford: Clarendon, 1969.

Wace. *Roman de Brut, A History of the British: Text and Translation*. Edited and translated by Judith Weiss. Rev. ed. 2002. Reprint, Exeter: University of Exeter Press, 2010.

William of Apulia. *Gesta Roberti Wiscardi*. Edited by R. Wilmans. In Monumenta Germaniae Historica. Scriptores 9. Hanover, 1851.

William of Jumièges. *Gesta normannorum Ducum of William of Jumièges, Orderic Vitalis, and Robert of Torigni*. Edited by Elisabeth M. C. van Houts. Oxford: Oxford University Press, 1992–1995.

William of Malmesbury. *Chronicles of the Kings of England, From the Earliest Period to the Reign of King Stephen*. Edited by John Allen Giles and translated by John Sharpe. London, 1847.

Secondary Literature

Adams, Tracy. *The Life and Afterlife of Isabeau of Bavaria*. Baltimore: Johns Hopkins University Press, 2010.

——. *Violent Passions: Managing Love in the Old French Verse Romances*. Houndmills, Basingstoke: Palgrave Macmillan, 2005.

Aird, William M. *Robert "Curthose," Duke of Normandy, c. 1050–1134*. Woodbridge, Suffolk: Boydell, 2008.

Amezúa y Mayo, Agustín G. de. *Isabel de Valois, reina de España (1546–1568)*. 3 vols. Madrid: Gráficas Ultra, 1949.

Armstrong, Adrian. *Technique and Technology: Script, Print, and Poetics in France, 1470–1550*. Oxford: Clarendon, 2000.

Arnade, Peter. *Beggars, Iconoclasts, and Civic Patriots: The Political Culture of the Dutch Revolt*. Ithaca: Cornell University Press, 2008.

Asbridge, Thomas. "Talking to the Enemy: The Role and Purpose of Negotiations between Saladin and Richard the Lionheart during the Third Crusade." *Journal of Medieval History* 39 (2013): 275–96.

Bachrach, Bernard S. "Charlemagne's Mediterranean Empire." In *Mediterranean Identities in the Premodern Era: Entrepôts, Islands, Empires*, ed. John Watkins and Kathryn L. Reyerson, 155–72. Farnham, Surrey: Ashgate, 2014.

——. *Early Carolingian Warfare: Prelude to Empire*. Philadelphia: University of Pennsylvania Press, 2001.

Baldwin, John W. "The Many Loves of Philip Augustus." In *The Medieval Marriage Scene: Prudence, Passion, Policy*, edited by Sherry Roush and Cristelle Louise Baskins, 67–80. Tempe: Arizona Center for Medieval and Renaissance Studies, 2005.

Barbé, Louis A. *Margaret of Scotland and the Dauphin Louis*. London: Blackie and Son, 1917.

Barbiche, Bernard. *Les institutions de la monarchie française à l'époque moderne: XVIe–XVIIIe siècle*. Paris: Presses universitaires de France, 1999.

Barnes, Timothy D. *Constantine and Eusebius*. Cambridge: Harvard University Press, 1981.

Barnwell, Henry T. *The Tragic Drama of Corneille and Racine*. Oxford: Clarendon, 1982.

Barraclough, Geoffrey. *The Crucible of Europe: The Ninth and Tenth Centuries in European History*. Berkeley: University of California Press, 1976.

Bartlett, Robert. *England under the Norman and Angevin Kings, 1075–1225.* Oxford: Oxford University Press, 2000.

Baskins, Cristelle L. *Cassone Painting, Humanism, and Gender in Early Modern Italy.* Cambridge: Cambridge University Press, 1998.

Baswell, Christopher. *Virgil in Medieval England: Figuring the* Aeneid *from the Twelfth Century to Chaucer.* Cambridge: Cambridge University Press, 1995.

Batiffol, Louis. *Richelieu et Corneille: La légende de la persécution de l'auteur du* Cid. Paris: Calmann-Lévy, 1936.

Baumgartner, Frederic J. *France in the Sixteenth Century.* New York: St. Martin's Press, 1995.

——. *Henry II, King of France, 1547–1559.* Durham: Duke University Press, 1988.

Baxter, James H. "The Marriage of James II." *Scottish Historical Review* 25 (1928): 69–72.

Beem, Charles. *The Lioness Roared: The Problems of Female Rule in English History.* New York: Palgrave Macmillan, 2006.

Bell, Ilona. " 'Souereaigne Lord of lordly Lady of this land': Elizabeth, Stubbs, and the *Gaping Gulf.*" In *Dissing Elizabeth: Negative Representations of Gloriana,* edited by Julia M. Walker, 99–117. Durham: Duke University Press, 1998.

Bély, Lucien. *L'art de la paix en Europe: Naissance de la diplomatie moderne, XVIe–XVIIe siècle.* Paris: Presses universitaires de France, 2007.

——. *La société des princes, XVIe–XVIIIe siècle.* Paris: Fayard, 1999.

Benson, C. David. *The History of Troy in Middle English Literature: Guido delle Colonne's* Historia destructionis Troiae *in Medieval England.* Woodbridge, Suffolk: D. S. Brewer, 1980.

Besio, Kimberly. "Gender, Loyalty, and the Reproduction of the Wang Zhaojun Legend: Some Social Ramifications of Drama in the Late Ming." *Journal of the Economic and Social History of the Orient* 40, no. 2 (1997): 251–82.

Blanchard, Eric M. "Gender, International Relations, and the Development of Feminist Security Theory." *Signs* 28, no. 4 (2003): 1289–1312.

——. "Why Is There No Gender in the English School?" *Review of International Relations* 37 (2011): 855–79.

Blin, Arnaud. *1648, La Paix de Westphalie, ou la naissance de L'Europe politique moderne.* Paris: Éditions Complexe, 2006.

Bloch, Howard R. *Medieval French Literature and Law.* Berkeley: University of California Press, 1977.

Bonner, Elizabeth. "French Naturalization of the Scots in the Fifteenth and Sixteenth Centuries." *Historical Journal* 40 (1997): 1085–1115.

——. "Scotland's 'Auld Alliance' with France, 1295–1560." *History* 84, no. 273 (1999): 5–30.

Borri, Francesco. "Murder by Death: Alboin's Life, End(s), and Means." *Millennium* 8 (2011): 223–70.

Bouchard, Constance Brittain. "Eleanor's Divorce from Louis VII: The Uses of Consanguinity." In *Eleanor of Aquitaine: Lord and Lady,* edited by Bonnie Wheeler and John Carmi Parsons, 223–35. New York: Palgrave Macmillan, 2003.

Bouet, Pierre. "Dudon de Saint-Quentin et Virgile: L'*Enéide* au service de la cause normande." *Cahiers des Annales de Normandie* 23 (1990): 215–36.

Bradbury, Jim. *The Capetians: Kings of France, 987–1328.* London: Continuum, 2007.

Braunmuller, Albert R. "*King John* and Historiography." *English Literary History* 55 (1988): 309–32.

Brenner, Robert. *Merchants and Revolution: Commercial Change, Political Conflict, and London's Overseas Traders, 1550–1653.* Princeton: Princeton University Press, 1993.

Breukelaar, Adriaan H. B. *Historiography and Episcopal Authority in Sixth-Century Gaul: Histories of Gregory of Tours Interpreted in Their Historical Context.* Göttingen: Vandenhoeck and Ruprecht, 1994.

Brinton, Anna Cox. *Maphaeus Vegius and His Thirteenth Book of the Aeneid: A Chapter on Virgil in the Renaissance.* Stanford: Stanford University Press, 1930.

Brown, Cynthia J. *Poets, Patrons, and Printers: Crisis and Authority in Late Medieval France.* Ithaca: Cornell University Press, 1995.

——. *The Shaping of History and Poetry in Late Medieval France: Propaganda and Artistic Expression in the Works of the Rhétoriquers.* Birmingham, Ala.: Summa Publications, 1985.

Brown, Peter. *The World of Late Antiquity: From Marcus Aurelius to Muhammad.* London: Thames and Hudson, 1971.

Brundage, James A. "The Canon Law of Divorce in the Mid-Twelfth Century: Louis VII c. Eleanor of Aquitaine." In *Eleanor of Aquitaine: Lord and Lady*, edited by Bonnie Wheeler and John Carmi Parsons, 213–21. Houndmills, Basingstoke: Palgrave Macmillan, 2003.

——. "Force and Fear: A Marriage Case from Eleventh-Century Aragon." In *On the Social Origins of Medieval Institutions: Essays in Honor of Joseph F. O'Callaghan*, edited by Donald J. Kagay and Theresa M. Vann, 11–19. Leiden: Brill, 1998.

——. *Law, Sex, and Christian Society in Medieval Europe.* Chicago: University of Chicago Press, 1987.

Bulag, Uradyn E. *The Mongols at China's Edge: History and the Politics of National Unity.* Lanham, Md.: Rowman and Littlefield, 2002.

Bull, Hedley. *The Anarchical Society: A Study of Order in World Politics.* New York: Columbia University Press, 1977.

Bull, Hedley, and Adam Watson, eds. *The Expansion of International Society.* Oxford: Oxford University Press, 1985.

Bull, Marcus. *Knightly Piety and the Lay Response to the First Crusade: The Limousin and Gascony, c. 970–c. 1130.* Oxford: Oxford University Press, 1993.

Buskie, Alexandra. "How Significant Is Feminism's Contribution to IR?" *E-International Relations Students*, March 17, 2013, http://www.e-ir.info/2013/03/17/how-significant-is-the-contribution-of-feminism-to-ir/ (accessed August 14, 2015).

Buzan, Barry. *From International to World Society? English School Theory and the Social Structure of Globalisation.* Cambridge: Cambridge University Press, 2004.

——. *An Introduction to the English School of International Relations: The Societal Approach.* Cambridge: Polity, 2014.

Cairns, Francis. *Virgil's Augustan Epic.* Cambridge: Cambridge University Press, 1989.

Calderwood, James L. "Commodity and Honor in *King John.*" *University of Toronto Quarterly* 29 (1960): 341–56.

——. *Metadrama in Shakespeare's Henriad: Richard II to Henry V.* Berkeley: University of California Press, 1979.

Campbell, John. "A Marriage Made in Heaven? 'Racine' and 'Love.' " *Modern Language Review* 101, no. 3 (2006): 682–90.

Camerlingo, Rosanna. *"Henry V* and the Just War: Shakespeare, Gentili and Machia-velli."* In *Machiavellian Encounters in Tudor and Stuart England: Literary and Political Influences from the Reformation to the Restoration,* edited by Alessandro Arienzo and Alessandra Petrina, 103–20. Farnham, Surrey: Ashgate, 2013.

Canallas, Muriel. "The Auld Alliance (1295–1560): Commercial Exchanges, Cultural and Intellectual Influences between France and Scotland." M.A. thesis, Université de Toulon et de Var, 2009. HAL: Archives ouvertes, http://dumas.ccsd.cnrs.fr/file/index/docid/429946/filename/Canallas_-_The_Auld_Alliance.pdf (accessed October 7, 2014).

Castellanos, Santiago. "Creating New Constantines at the End of the Sixth Century." *Historical Research* 85 (2012): 556–75.

Chance, Jane. *Woman as Hero in Old English Literature.* Syracuse: Syracuse University Press, 1986.

Chin, Tamara T. "Defamiliarizing the Foreigner: Sima Qian's Ethnography and Han-Xiongnu Marriage Diplomacy." *Harvard Journal of Asiatic Studies* 70 (2010): 311–54.

Church, Stephen D. *King John: New Interpretations.* Woodbridge: Boydell Press, 1999.

Clements, Rebekah. "Talking with the Brush: Rethinking the 'Lingua Franca' of East Asian Diplomacy through Early Modern Japanese-Korean Encounters." In *Cultures of Diplomacy and Literary Writing in the Early Modern World: New Approaches,* edited by Tracey Sowerby and Joanna Craigwood. (forthcoming).

Cogswell, Thomas. *The Blessed Revolution: English Politics and the Coming of War, 1621–1624.* Cambridge: Cambridge University Press, 1989.

——. "Thomas Middleton and the Court, 1624: *A Game at Chess* in Context." *Huntington Library Quarterly* 47 (1984): 273–88.

Collelo, Thomas, and Howard D. Nelson, *Chad: A Country Study.* Washington, D.C.: Federal Research Division, Library of Congress, 1990.

Collins, Roger. *Charlemagne.* Houndmills, Basingstoke: Macmillan, 1998.

Conklin, George. "Ingeborg of Denmark, Queen of France, 1193–1223." In *Queens and Queenship in Medieval Europe,* edited by Anne Duggan, 39–52. Woodbridge, Suffolk: Boydell, 1997.

Copeland, Dale. "A Realist Critique of the English School." *Review of International Studies* 29, no. 3 (2003): 427–41.

Cornette, Joël, ed. *La monarchie entre Renaissance et Révolution, 1515–1792.* Paris: Seuil, 2000.

Cowdrey, Herbert E. J. "The Peace and the Truce of God in the Eleventh Century." *Past and Present* 46, no. 1 (1970): 42–67.

Craigwood, Joanna. "Diplomatic Metonymy and Antithesis in *3 Henry VI.*" *Review of English Studies* 65 (2014): 812–30.

——. "Sidney, Gentili, and the Poetics of Embassy." In *Diplomacy and Early Modern Culture,* edited by Robyn Adams and Rosanna Cox, 82–100. Basingstoke: Palgrave Macmillan, 2011.

Crisp, Ryan Patrick. "Marriage and Alliance in the Merovingian Kingdoms, 481–639." Ph.D. dissertation, Ohio State University, 2003. OhioLINK Electronic Theses and Dissertations Center (accessed October 23, 2014).

Croke, Brian. "Cassiodorus and the *Getica* of Jordanes." *Classical Philology* 82 (1987): 117–34.

Crosland, Jessie. "Enéas and the *Aeneid*." *Modern Literary Review* 29 (1934): 282–90.

Cross, Richard. *The Metaphysics of the Incarnation: Thomas Aquinas to Duns Scotus.* Oxford: Oxford University Press, 2002.

Crouch, David. *The Normans: The History of a Dynasty.* London: Hambledon, 2002.

Curren-Aquino, Deborah T., ed. King John: *New Perspectives.* Newark: University of Delaware Press, 1989.

Curry, Anne. "Two Kingdoms, One King: The Treaty of Troyes (1420) and the Creation of a Double Monarchy of England and France." In *"The Contending Kingdoms": France and England, 1420–1700*, edited by Glenn Richardson, 23–42. Aldershot: Ashgate, 2008.

Dade, Eva Kathrin. *Madame de Pompadour: Die Mätresse und die Diplomatie.* Cologne: Böhlau, 2010.

Daly, William M. "Clovis: How Barbaric? How Pagan?" *Speculum* 69, no. 3 (1994): 619–64.

Davies, Clifford S. L. "England and the French War." In *The Mid-Tudor Polity, 1540–1560*, edited by Robert Tittler and Jennifer Loach, 159–85. London: Macmillan, 1980.

——. *Papist Pamphleteers: The Allen-Persons Party and the Political Thought of the Counter-Reformation in England, 1572–1615.* Chicago: Loyola University Press, 1964.

——. *Peace, Print and Protestantism, 1450–1558.* London: Hart-Davis MacGibbon, 1976.

D'Avray, David L. *Dissolving Royal Marriages: A Documentary History, 860–1600.* Cambridge: Cambridge University Press, 2014.

——. *Papacy, Monarchy, and Marriage, 860–1600.* Cambridge: Cambridge University Press, 2015.

Defaux, Gérard. "The Case of Bérénice: Racine, Corneille, and Mimetic Desire." Translated by Michael Metteer. *Yale French Studies* 76 (1989): 211–39.

DeJean, Joan. *Tender Geographies: Women and the Origin of the Novel in France.* New York: Columbia University Press, 1991.

D'Elia, Anthony F. "Marriage, Sexual Pleasure, and Learned Brides in the Wedding Orations of Fifteenth-Century Italy." *Renaissance Quarterly* 55, no. 2 (2002): 379–433.

Desmond, Marilynn. *Reading Dido: Gender, Textuality, and the Medieval* Aeneid. Minneapolis: University of Minnesota Press, 1994.

Dhondt, Frederik. "Contract to Treaty: The Legal Transformation of the Spanish Succession (1659–1713)." *Journal of the History of International Law* 12 (2011): 347–75.

Doran, Susan. *England and Europe in the Sixteenth Century.* New York: St. Martin's, 1999.

——. *Monarchy and Matrimony: The Courtships of Elizabeth I.* New York: Routledge, 1996.

Douglas, David C. *William the Conqueror: The Norman Impact on England.* 1964. Reprint, Berkeley: University of California Press, 1972.

Doyle, Michael W. "Kant, Liberal Legacies, and Foreign Affairs, Part I." *Philosophy and Public Affairs* 12, no. 3 (1983): 205–35.

——. "Kant, Liberal Legacies, and Foreign Affairs, Part II." *Philosophy and Public Affairs* 12, no. 4 (1983): 323–53.

Duby, Georges. *The Early Growth of the European Economy: Warriors and Peasants from the Seventh to the Twelfth Century.* Translated by Howard B. Clarke. Ithaca: Cornell University Press, 1974.

——. *The Knight, the Lady, and the Priest: The Making of Modern Marriage in the Middle Ages.* Translated by Barbara Bray. New York: Pantheon, 1983.

Duggan, Joseph J. *The Romances of Chrétien de Troyes*. New Haven: Yale University Press, 2001.

Dulong, Claude. *Anne d'Autriche: Mère de Louis XIV*. Paris: Hachette, 1980.

——. *Le mariage du Roi-Soleil*. Paris: Albin Michel, 1986.

Dusinberre, Juliet. "*King John* and Embarrassing Women." *Shakespeare Survey* 42 (1990): 37–52.

Eggert, Katherine. *Showing Like a Queen: Female Authority and Literary Experiment in Spenser, Shakespeare, and Milton*. Philadelphia: University of Pennsylvania Press, 2000.

Elliott, John H. *Europe Divided, 1559–1598*. 2nd ed. Oxford: Blackwell, 2000.

Esmein, Adhémar. *Le mariage en droit canonique*. 2 vols. Paris, 1891.

Facinger, Marion. "A Study of Medieval Queenship: Capetian France, 987–1237." *Studies in Medieval and Renaissance History* 5 (1968): 3–48.

Farber, Lianna. *An Anatomy of Trade in Medieval Writing: Value, Consent, and Community*. Ithaca: Cornell University Press, 2005.

Feiling, Keith. *British Foreign Policy, 1660–1672*. London: Macmillan, 1930.

Fernandez, Hélène. "Une paix suspecte: La célébration littéraire de la paix du Cateau-Cambrésis." *Nouvelle Revue du Seizième Siècle* 15, no. 2 (1997): 325–41.

Fichter, Andrew. *Poets Historical: Dynastic Epic in the Renaissance*. New Haven: Yale University Press, 1982.

Fichtner, Paula Sutter. "Dynastic Marriage in Sixteenth-Century Habsburg Diplomacy and Statecraft: An Interdisciplinary Approach." *American Historical Review* 81 (1976): 243–65.

Fleischman, Suzanne. "On the Representation of History and Fiction in the Middle Ages." *History and Theory* 23 (1983): 278–310.

Fletcher, Catherine. *The Divorce of Henry VIII: The Untold Story from Inside the Vatican*. New York: Palgrave Macmillan, 2012.

Forestier, Georges. *Essai de génétique théâtrale: Corneille à l'oeuvre*. Paris: Klincksieck, 1996.

——. *Racine*. Paris: Gallimard, 2006.

Fourrier, Anthime. *Le courant realiste dans le roman courtois en France au Moyen Age*. Paris: Nizet, 1960.

Fudge, John D. *Commerce and Print in the Early Reformation*. Leiden: Brill, 2007.

Fulk, Robert D., et al., eds. *Klaeber's* Beowulf *and the Fight at Finnsburg*. Toronto: University of Toronto Press, 2008.

Fulton, Rachel. *From Judgment to Passion: Devotion to Christ and the Virgin Mary, 800–1200*. New York: Columbia University Press, 2003.

Gaposchkin, M. Cecilia. "The King of France and the Queen of Heaven: The Iconography of the Porte Rouge of Notre-Dame of Paris." *Gesta* 39 (2000): 58–72.

Gardiner, Samuel R. *Prince Charles and the Spanish Marriage, 1617–1623*. 2 vols. London, 1869.

Geaman, Kristen. "Queen's Gold and Intercession: The Case of Eleanor of Aquitaine." *Medieval Feminist Forum* 46 (2010): 10–33.

Geary, Patrick J. *Women at the Beginning: Origin Myths from the Virgin Mary to the Amazons*. Princeton: Princeton University Press, 2009.

Gillett, Andrew. *Envoys and Political Communication in the Late Antique West, 411–533*. Cambridge: Cambridge University Press, 2003.

Gillingham, John. *The Angevin Empire.* 2nd ed. New York: Oxford University Press, 2001.
——. *Richard I.* 1999. Reprint, New Haven: Yale University Press, 2002.
Goffart, Walter. *Barbarians and Romans, AD 418–584: The Techniques of Accommodation.* Princeton: Princeton University Press, 1980.
——. *Barbarian Tides: The Migration Age and the Later Roman Empire.* Philadelphia: University of Pennsylvania Press, 2006.
——. "The *Historia Ecclesiastica*: Bede's Agenda and Ours." *Haskins Society Journal: Studies in Medieval History* 2 (1990): 29–45.
——. *The Narrators of Barbarian History (A.D. 550–800): Jordanes, Gregory of Tours, Bede, and Paul the Deacon.* 2005. Reprint, Notre Dame, Ind.: University of Notre Dame Press, 2012.
Gömöri, George. "'A Memorable Wedding': The Literary Reception of the Wedding of the Princess Elizabeth and Frederick of Pfalz." *Journal of European Studies* 34 (2004): 215–24.
Goodkin, Richard. *Birth Marks: The Tragedy of Primogeniture in Pierre Corneille, Thomas Corneille, and Jean Racine.* Philadelphia: University of Pennsylvania Press, 2000.
Goodman, Dena. *The Republic of Letters: A Cultural History of the French Enlightenment.* Ithaca: Cornell University Press, 1994.
Green, Ian. *Print and Protestantism in Early Modern England.* Oxford: Oxford University Press, 2000.
Greenblatt, Stephen. *Shakespearean Negotiations: The Circulation of Social Energy in England.* Oxford: Clarendon, 1988.
Greenwood, Ryan Martin. "Law and War in Late Medieval Italy: The *Jus Commune* on War and Its Application in Florence, c. 1150–1450." Ph.D. dissertation, University of Chicago, 2011.
Gregerson, Linda. "French Marriages and the Protestant Nation in Shakespeare's History Plays." In *A Companion to Shakespeare's Works.* Vol. 2, *The Histories,* edited by Richard Dutton and Jean E. Howard, 246–62. Oxford: Blackwell, 2003.
Gurr, Andrew. *Playgoing in Shakespeare's London.* 3rd ed. Cambridge: Cambridge University Press, 2004.
Hadfield, Andrew. *Literature, Politics and National Identity: Reformation to Renaissance.* Cambridge: Cambridge University Press, 1994.
Hampton, Timothy. *Fictions of Embassy: Literature and Diplomacy in Early Modern Europe.* Ithaca: Cornell University Press, 2010.
——. *Literature and the Nation in the Sixteenth Century: Inventing Renaissance France.* Ithaca: Cornell University Press, 2001.
Hampton-Reeves, Stuart. "Theatrical Afterlives." In *The Cambridge Companion to Shakespeare's History Plays,* edited by Michael Hattaway, 229–44, Cambridge: Cambridge University Press, 2002.
Hansen, Peter A. "*Ille ego qui quondam* . . . Once Again." *Classical Quarterly* 22, no. 1 (1972): 139–49.
Hartley, David J. "La Célébration Poétiques du Traité du Cateau-Cambrésis (1559): Document Bibliographique." *Bibliothèque d'Humanisme et Renaissance* 43 (1981): 303–18.
Head, Thomas, and Richard Landes, eds. *The Peace of God: Social Violence and Religious Response in France around the Year 1000.* Ithaca: Cornell University Press, 1992.

Heather, Peter. *The Fall of the Roman Empire: A New History of Rome and the Barbarians.* Oxford: Oxford University Press, 2006.

Helgerson, Richard. *Forms of Nationhood: The Elizabethan Writing of England.* Chicago: University of Chicago Press, 1992.

Heng, Geraldine. *Empire of Romance: Medieval Romance and the Politics of Cultural Fantasy.* New York: Columbia University Press, 2003.

Herrin, Judith. *Unrivalled Influence: Women and Empire in Byzantium.* Princeton: Princeton University Press, 2013.

Heyworth, Gregory. *Desiring Bodies: Ovidian Romance and the Cult of Form.* Notre Dame: University of Notre Dame Press, 2009.

Hill, Christopher. *Puritanism and Revolution: Studies in Interpretation of the English Revolution of the Seventeenth Century.* 1958. Reprint, Houndmills, Basingstoke: Palgrave, 1997.

Hoepffner, Ernst. "L'*Enéas* et Wace." *Archivum romanicum* 15 (1931): 248–69.

Hoffman, Hartmut. *Gottesfriede und Treuga Dei.* In Monumenta Germaniae Historica. Schriften 20. Stuttgart: Anton Hiersemann, 1964.

Holderness, Graham. "Agincourt 1944: Readings in the Shakespearean Myth." *Literature and History* 10, no. 1 (1984): 24–45.

Hollister, C. Warren, and Thomas K. Keefe. "The Making of the Angevin Empire." *Journal of British Studies* 12, no. 2 (1973): 1–25.

Holt, Mack P. *The Duke of Anjou and the Politique Struggle during the Wars of Religion.* Cambridge: Cambridge University Press, 1986.

Howard, Jean E., and Phyllis Rackin. *Engendering a Nation: A Feminist Account of Shakespeare's English Histories.* London: Routledge, 1997.

Howell, Margaret. *Eleanor of Provence: Queenship in Thirteenth-Century England.* Oxford: Wiley-Blackwell, 1998.

——. "Royal Women in the Mid-Thirteenth Century." In *England and Europe in the Reign of Henry III (1216–1272),* edited by Bjorn K. U. Weiler with Ifor W. Rowlands, 163–81. Aldershot: Ashgate, 2002.

Huneycutt, Lois. "Intercession and the High Medieval Queen: The Esther Topos." In *Power of the Weak: Studies on Medieval Women,* edited by Jennifer Carpenter and Sally-Beth MacLean, 126–46. Urbana: University of Illinois Press, 1995.

——. *Matilda of Scotland: A Study in Medieval Queenship.* Woodbridge, Suffolk: Boydell, 2003.

Hunt, Lynn. "The Many Bodies of Marie Antoinette: Political Pornography and the Problem of the Feminine in the French Revolution." In *Eroticism and the Body Politic,* edited by Lynn Hunt, 108–30. Baltimore: Johns Hopkins University Press, 1991.

Hurrell, Andrew. *On Global Order: Power, Values, and the Constitution of International Society.* Oxford: Oxford University Press, 2007.

Hutton, Ronald. *Charles II.* Oxford: Oxford University Press, 1989.

——. "The Making of the Secret Treaty of Dover, 1668–1670." *Journal of British Studies* 29 (1986): 297–318.

Ibbett, Katherine. "Italy versus France; or, How Pierre Corneille Became an Anti-Machiavel." *Renaissance Drama* 36–37 (2010): 379–95.

——. *The Style of the State in French Theater: Neoclassicism and Government, 1630–1660.* Farnham, Surrey: Ashgate, 2009.

Ingham, Patricia. *Sovereign Fantasies: Arthurian Romance and the Making of Britain*. Philadelphia: University of Pennsylvania Press, 2001.

Jagchid, Sechin, and Van Jay Symons. *Peace, War, and Trade along the Great Wall: Nomadic-Chinese Interaction through Two Millennia*. Bloomington: Indiana University Press, 1989.

Jamison, Carol Parrish. "Traffic of Women in Germanic Literature: The Role of the Peace Pledge in Marital Exchange." *Women in German Yearbook* 20 (2004): 13–36.

Jansen, Sharon L. *Debating Women, Politics, and Power in Early Modern Europe*. New York: Palgrave Macmillan, 2008.

Joesting, Edward. *Kauai: The Separate Kingdom*. Honolulu: University of Hawaii Press, 1984.

Johnson, James Turner. *Ideology, Reason, and the Limitation of War: Religious and Secular Concepts, 1200–1740*. Princeton: Princeton University Press, 1975.

——. *Just War Tradition and the Restraint of War: A Moral and Historical Inquiry*. Princeton: Princeton University Press, 1981.

Johnson, W. R. *Darkness Visible: A Study of Vergil's Aeneid*. Berkeley: University of California Press, 1976.

Jouhaud, Christian. "L'écrivain et le ministre: Corneille et Richelieu; Note sur l'épître dédicatoire d'*Horace* et tout particulièrement sur la place qu'y tient le visage du cardinal de Richelieu." *Dix-Septième Siècle* 182 (1994): 135–42.

Kallendorf, Craig. *In Praise of Aeneas: Virgil and Epideictic Rhetoric in the Early Italian Renaissance*. Hanover: University Press of New England, 1989.

——. *The Other Virgil: "Pessimistic" Readings of the Aeneid in Early Modern Culture*. Oxford: Oxford University Press, 2007.

Kamen, Henry. *Philip of Spain*. New Haven: Yale University Press, 1997.

Kann, Robert A. "Dynastic Relations and European Power Politics, 1848–1918." *Journal of Modern History* 45 (1973): 387–410.

Karras, Ruth Mazo. "Marriage, Concubinage, and the Law." In *Law and the Illicit in Medieval Europe*, edited by Ruth Mazo Karras, Joel Kaye, and E. Ann Matter, 117–30. Philadelphia: University of Pennsylvania Press, 2008.

——. "Marriage and the Creation of Kin in the Sagas." *Scandinavian Studies* 4 (2003): 473–90.

——. *Unmarriages: Women, Men, and Sexual Union in the Middle Ages*. Philadelphia: University of Pennsylvania Press, 2012.

Kayaoglu, Turan. "Westphalian Eurocentrism in International Relations Theory." *International Studies Review* 12 (2010): 193–217.

Kazhdan, A. P., and Ann Wharton Epstein. *Change in Byzantine Culture in the Eleventh and Twelfth Centuries*. Berkeley: University of California Press, 1985.

Keen, Maurice. "The End of the Hundred Years War: Lancastrian France and Lancastrian England." In *England and Her Neighbours, 1066–1453: Essays in Honour of Pierre Chaplais*, edited by Michael Jones and Malcolm Vale, 297–311. London: Hambledon Press, 1989.

Keene, Edward. *Beyond the Anarchical Society: Grotius, Colonialism and Order in World Politics*. Cambridge: Cambridge University Press, 2002.

Kelly, Amy. *Eleanor of Aquitaine and the Four Kings*. Cambridge: Harvard University Press, 1950.

Kelly, Henry Ansgar. *The Matrimonial Trials of Henry VIII*. Stanford: Stanford University Press, 1976.

Kętrzyński, Stanisław. "The Introduction of Christianity and the Early Kings of Poland." In *The Cambridge History of Poland: From the Origins to Sobieski (to 1696)*, edited by William F. Reddaway et al., 16–42. Cambridge: Cambridge University Press, 1950.

Kinoshita, Sharon. "Chrétien de Troyes's *Cligés* in the Medieval Mediterranean." *Arthuriana* 3 (2009): 48–61.

——. *Medieval Boundaries: Rethinking Difference in Old French Literature*. Philadelphia: University of Pennsylvania Press, 2006.

——. "The Poetics of *Translatio*: French-Byzantine Relations in Chrétien de Troyes's *Cligès*." *Exemplaria* 8 (1996): 315–54.

Klein, Holger, and Jean-Marie Maguin, eds. "Shakespeare and France." *Shakespeare Yearbook* 5. Special issue. Lewiston, N.Y.: E. Mellen Press, 1994.

Klein, Stacy S.. *Ruling Women: Queenship and Gender in Anglo-Saxon Literature*. Notre Dame: University of Notre Dame Press, 2006.

Kleinman, Ruth. *Anne of Austria, Queen of France*. Columbus: Ohio State University Press, 1985.

Klenke, M. Amelia. "The Richelieu-Corneille Rapport." *PMLA* 64, no. 4 (1949): 724–45.

Kloczowski, Jerzy. *A History of Polish Christianity*. Cambridge: Cambridge University Press, 2000.

Knecht, Robert J. *The Rise and Fall of Renaissance France, 1483–1610*. 2nd ed. Oxford: Blackwell, 2001.

Kolata, Alan. *Ancient Inca*. Cambridge: Cambridge University Press, 2013.

Kuykendall, Ralph S. *The Hawaiian Kingdom, 1778–1854: Foundation and Transformation*. Honolulu: University of Hawaii Press, 1938.

Laidlaw, James, ed. *The Auld Alliance: France and Scotland over 700 Years*. Edinburgh: University of Edinburgh Press, 1999.

Lake, Justin C. "Truth, Plausibility, and the Virtues of Narrative at the Millennium." *Journal of Medieval History* 35 (2009): 221–38

Lancaster, H. Carrington. "The Richelieu-Corneille Rapport." *PMLA* 65, no. 2 (1950): 322–28.

Lang, Henry Joseph. "The Fall of the Monarchy of Mieszko II Lambert." *Speculum* 49 (1974): 623–39.

Laynesmith, J. L. *The Last Medieval Queens: English Queenship, 1445–1503*. Oxford: Oxford University Press, 2004.

Lees, Clare A., and Gillian R. Overing. *Double Agents: Women and Clerical Culture in Anglo-Saxon England*. Philadelphia: University of Pennsylvania Press, 2001.

Lesaffer, Randall. "Peace Treaties from Lodi to Westphalia." In *Peace Treaties and International Law in European History: From the Late Middle Ages to World War One*, edited by Randall Lesaffer, 29–37. Cambridge: Cambridge University Press, 2004.

Le Saux, Françoise H. M. *A Companion to Wace*. Cambridge: D. S. Brewer, 2005.

Levin, Carole. *The Heart and Stomach of a King: Elizabeth I and the Politics of Sex and Power*. Philadelphia: University of Pennsylvania Press, 1994.

——. *Propaganda in the English Reformation: Heroic and Villainous Images of King John*. New York: Edwin Mellen, 1987.

Linklater, Andrew, and Hidemi Suganami. *The English School of International Relations: A Contemporary Reassessment*. Cambridge: Cambridge University Press, 2006.

Little, Richard. "The English School's Contribution to the Study of International Relations." *European Journal of International Relations* 6, no. 3 (2000): 395–422.

——. "Reassessing *The Expansion of the International Society*." In *System, Society and the World: Exploring the English School of International Relations*, edited by Robert W. Murray, 19–24. Bristol: e-International Relations, 2013.

Llamas, Antonio Martinez. *Isabel de Valois, reina de España: Una historia de amor y enfermedad*. Madrid: Ediciones Temas de Hoy, 1996.

Loades, David. *The Reign of Mary Tudor: Politics, Government, and Religion in England, 1553–1558*. New York: St. Martin's, 1979.

Lynn, John A. *The Wars of Louis XIV, 1667–1714*. Edinburgh: Longman, 1999.

Lyons, John D. *The Tragedy of Origins: Pierre Corneille and Historical Perspective*. Stanford: Stanford University Press, 1996.

MacCaffrey, Wallace T. *Elizabeth I: War and Politics, 1588–1603*. Princeton: Princeton University Press, 1992.

——. *Queen Elizabeth and the Making of Policy, 1572–1588*. Princeton: Princeton University Press, 1981.

——. *The Shaping of the Elizabethan Regime: Elizabethan Politics, 1558–1572*. Princeton: Princeton University Press, 1968.

Macdougall, Norman. *An Antidote to the English: The Auld Alliance, 1295–1560*. East Linton, East Lothian: Tuckwell Press, 2001.

MacEvitt, Christopher. *The Crusades and the Christian World of the East: Rough Tolerance*. Philadelphia: University of Pennsylvania Press, 2009.

Macrides, Ruth. "Dynastic Marriages and Political Kinship." In *Byzantine Diplomacy: Papers from the Twenty-Fourth Spring Symposium of Byzantine Studies, Cambridge, March 1990*, edited by Jonathan Shepard and Simon Franklin, 263–80. Aldershot: Variorum, 1992.

Major, J. Russell. *From Renaissance Monarchy to Absolute Monarchy: French Kings, Nobles, and Estates*. Baltimore: Johns Hopkins University Press, 1994.

Manheim, Michael. "The Four Voices of the Bastard." In *King John: New Perspectives*, edited by Deborah T. Curren-Aquino, 126–35. Newark: University of Delaware Press, 1989.

Marcus, Leah. *Puzzling Shakespeare: Local Reading and Its Discontents*. Berkeley: University of California Press, 1988.

Martin, Russell. *A Bride for the Tsar: Bride Shows and Marriage Politics in Early Modern Russia*. DeKalb: Northern Illinois University Press, 2012.

Massie, Robert K. *Nicholas and Alexandra*. New York: Atheneum, 1967.

Mastnak, Tomaž. *Crusading Peace: Christendom, the Muslim World, and Western Political Order*. Berkeley: University of California Press, 2002.

Mattingly, Garrett. *Renaissance Diplomacy*. 1955. Reprint, New York: Dover, 1988.

Maurer, Helen E. *Margaret of Anjou: Queenship and Power in Late Medieval England*. Woodbridge, Suffolk: Boydell, 2003.

Mayall, James. *Nationalism and International Society*. Cambridge: Cambridge University Press, 1990.

Mayr-Harting, Henry. "Charlemagne, the Saxons, and the Imperial Coronation of 800." *English Historical Review* 111 (1996): 1113–33.

McCracken, Peggy. *The Romance of Adultery: Queenship and Sexual Transgression in Old French Literature*. Philadelphia: University of Pennsylvania Press, 1998.

McEachern, Claire. *The Poetics of English Nationhood, 1590–1612*. Cambridge: Cambridge University Press, 1996.

McKitterick, Rosamond. *Charlemagne: The Formation of a European Identity*. Cambridge: Cambridge University Press, 2008.

——. *The Frankish Kingdoms under the Carolingians, 751–987*. London: Longman, 1983.

——. "Paul the Deacon and the Franks." *Early Medieval Europe* 8 (1999): 319–39.

McLane, Paul E. *Spenser's* Shepheardes Calender: *A Study in Elizabethan Allegory*. Notre Dame, Ind.: University of Notre Dame Press, 1961.

Mears, Natalie. "Counsel, Debate, and Queenship: John Stubbs's *The discoverie of gaping gulf*, 1579." *Historical Journal* 44 (2001): 629–50.

Merlin, Hélène. "*Horace*: L'équivoque et la dédicace." *Dix-Septième Siècle* 182 (1994): 121–34.

Meron, Theodor. "The Authority to Make Treaties in the Late Middle Ages." *American Journal of International Law* 89, no. 1 (1995): 1–20.

Miller, John. *Popery and Politics in England*. Cambridge: Cambridge University Press, 1973.

Milnor, Kristina. *Gender, Domesticity, and the Age of Augustus: Inventing Private Life*. Oxford: Oxford University Press, 2005.

Minois, Georges. *La guerre de cents ans: Naissance de deux nations*. Paris: Perrin, 2008.

Morse, Ruth. *Truth and Convention in the Middle Ages. Rhetoric, Representation and Reality*. Cambridge: Cambridge University Press, 1991.

Mulryne, Ronnie, ed. "France in the English and French Theater of the Renaissance." *Renaissance Studies* 9 (1995). Special issue.

Musset, Lucien. "Ce que l'on peut savoir du traité de Saint-Clair-sur-Ept." *Annuaires des cinq départementes de la Normandie* 139 (1982): 79–182.

——. *Les invasions: Les vagues Germaniques*. Paris: Presses Universitaires de France, 1965.

——. *Nordica et Normannica: Recueil d'études sur la Scandinavie ancienne et médiévale, les expéditions des Vikings et la fondation de la Normandie*. Studia nordica 1. Paris: Société des études Nordiques, 1997.

Nadal, Santiago. *Las cuatro mujeres de Felipe II*. Barcelona: Ediciones Mercedes, 1944.

Nash, Walter. *The Language of Humour*. Abingdon: Routledge, 2013.

Nelson, Janet L. *Charles the Bald*. Harlow, Essex: Longman, 1992.

——. *The Frankish World, 750–900*. London: Hambledon Press, 1996.

——. "Making a Difference in Eighth-Century Politics: The Daughters of Desiderius." In *After Rome's Fall: Narrators and Sources of Early Medieval History*, edited by Alexander Callander Murray, 171–90. Toronto: University of Toronto Press, 1998.

——. *Politics and Ritual in Early Medieval Europe*. London: Hambledon, 1986.

Nolte, Cordula. "Gender and Conversion in the Merovingian Era." In *Varieties of Religious Conversion in the Middle Ages*, edited by James Muldoon, 81–99. Gainesville: University Press of Florida, 1997.

Norbrook, David. *Poetry and Politics in the English Renaissance*. 1984. Reprint, Oxford: Oxford University Press, 2002.

O'Donnell, James J. "The Aims of Jordanes." *Historia: Zeitschrift für Alte Geschichte* 31, no. 2 (1982): 223–40.

Ogg, David. *England in the Reign of Charles II*. 1956. 2nd ed. Oxford: Oxford University Press, 1984.

Oksanen, Eljas. *Flanders and the Anglo-Norman World, 1066–1216*. Cambridge: Cambridge University Press, 2012.

Orrell, John. *The Quest for Shakespeare's Globe*. Cambridge: Cambridge University Press, 1983.

Otter, Monika. *Inventiones: Fiction and Referentiality in Twelfth-Century Historical Writing*. Chapel Hill: University of North Carolina Press, 1996.

Overing, Gillian R. "The Women of *Beowulf*: A Context for Interpretation." In Beowulf: *Basic Readings*, edited by Peter S. Baker, 219–60. New York: Garland, 1995.

Owens, Karen. *Franz Joseph and Elisabeth: The Last Great Monarchs of Austria-Hungary*. Jefferson, N.C.: McFarland, 2014.

Pagden, Anthony. *Spanish Imperialism and the Political Imagination: Studies in European and Spanish American Social and Political Theory, 1513–1830*. New Haven: Yale University Press, 1998.

Panizza, Diego. "Machiavelli e Alberico Gentili." In *Machiavellismo e antimachiavellismo nel Cinquecento: Atti del Convegno di Perugia*, edited by Jan Malarczyk. Florence: Olschki, 1970.

Parry, Adam. *The Language of Achilles and Other Papers*. Oxford: Clarendon, 1989.

Parsons, John Carmi. "The Queen's Intercession in Thirteenth-Century England." In *Power of the Weak: Studies on Medieval Women*, edited by Jennifer Carpenter and Sally-Beth MacLean, 147–77. Urbana: University of Illinois Press, 1995.

———. "Ritual and Symbol in the English Queenship to 1500." In *Women and Sovereignty*, edited by Louise O. Fradenburg, 60–77. Edinburgh: University of Edinburgh Press, 1991.

Pauphilet, Albert. "*Enéas* and *Enée*." *Romania* 55 (1929): 195–213.

———. *Le legs du moyen âge: Études de littérature médiévale*. Paris: Melun, 1950.

Perry, David L. "Using Shakespeare's *Henry V* to Teach Just-War Principles." http://home.earthlink.net/~davidlperry/henryv.htm (accessed July 31, 2015).

Peters, Edward, ed. *The First Crusade: The Chronicle of Fulcher of Chartres and Other Source Materials*. 2nd ed. Philadelphia: University of Pennsylvania Press, 1998.

Picard, Raymond. *La carrière de Jean Racine*. Paris: Gallimard, 1956.

Pirenne, Henri. *Les villes du Moyen Âge: Essai d'histoire économique et sociale*. Brussels: Lamertin, 1927.

Pocock, Gordon. *Corneille and Racine: Problems of Tragic Form*. Cambridge: Cambridge University Press, 1973.

Poole, Adrian. *Shakespeare and the Victorians*. London: Arden, 2004.

Powicke, Frederick M. *The Loss of Normandy*. 2nd ed. Manchester: University of Manchester Press, 1960.

Prigent, Michel. *Le héros et l'état dans la tragédie de Corneille*. Paris: Presses Universitaires de France, 1986.

Pugliatti, Paola. *Shakespeare and the Just War Tradition*. Farnham, Surrey: Ashgate, 2010.

Pursell, Brennan C. "The End of the Spanish Match." *Historical Journal* 45 (2002): 699–726.

Putnam, Michael C. J. *The Poetry of the Aeneid: Four Studies in Imaginative Unity and Design.* Cambridge: Harvard University Press, 1965.

Quabeck, Franziska. *Just and Unjust Wars in Shakespeare.* Berlin: de Gruyter, 2013.

Rabkin, Norman. "Ducks, Rabbits, and *Henry V.*" *Shakespeare Quarterly* 28 (1977): 279–96.

Raymond, Joad. *Pamphlets and Pamphleteering in Early Modern England.* Cambridge: Cambridge University Press, 2003.

Redworth, Glyn. *The Prince and the Infanta: The Cultural Politics of the Spanish Match.* New Haven: Yale University Press, 2003.

Reid, Charles J. *Power over the Body, Equality in the Family: Rights and Domestic Relations in Medieval Canon Law.* Grand Rapids: Eerdmans, 2004.

Riches, Daniel. *Protestant Cosmopolitanism and Diplomatic Culture: Brandenburg-Swedish Relations in the Seventeenth Century.* Leiden: Brill, 2013.

Riley-Smith, Jonathan. *The First Crusaders, 1095–1131.* Cambridge: Cambridge University Press, 1997.

Rodocanachi, Emmanuel. *Renée de France, Duchesse de Ferrare: Une protectrice de la réforme en Italie et en France.* Geneva: Slatkine, 1970.

Ross, Charles S. "Maffeo Vegio's 'schort Cristyn wark,' with a Note on the Thirteenth Book in Early Editions of Vergil." *Modern Philology* 78 (1981): 215–26.

Rubin, Miri. *Mother of God: A History of the Virgin Mary.* New Haven: Yale University Press, 2009.

Russell, Frederick H. *The Just War in the Middle Ages.* Cambridge: Cambridge University Press, 1977.

Russell, Jocelyne Gledhill. *The Congress of Arras: A Study in Medieval Diplomacy.* Oxford: Clarendon, 1955.

——. *Peacemaking in the Renaissance.* London: Duckworth, 1986.

Saccio, Peter. *Shakespeare's English Kings: History, Chronicle, and Drama.* Oxford: Oxford University Press, 1976.

Sacks, David Harris. *The Widening Gate: Bristol and the Atlantic Economy, 1450–1700.* Berkeley: University of California Press, 1991.

Sadlack, Erin A. *The French Queen's Letters: Mary Tudor and the Politics of Marriage in Sixteenth-Century Europe.* Houndmills, Basingstoke: Palgrave Macmillan, 2011.

Sahlins, Peter. *Boundaries: The Making of France and Spain in the Pyrenees.* Berkeley: University of California Press, 1989.

Sawyer, Birgit. "Valdemar, Absalon and Saxo: Historiography and Politics in Medieval Denmark." *Revue Belge de Philologie et d'Histoire* 63, no. 4 (1985): 685–705.

Schnerb, Bertrand. *Les Armagnacs et les Bourguignons: La maudite guerre.* Paris: Perrin, 1988.

Schröder, Peter. "Taming the Fox and the Lion: Some Aspects of the Sixteenth Century's Debate on Inter-State Relations." In *War, the State and International Law in Seventeenth-Century Europe,* edited by Olaf Asbach and Peter Schröder, 83–102. Farnham, Surrey: Ashgate, 2010.

——. "Vitoria, Gentili, Bodin: Sovereignty and the Law of Nations." In *The Roman Foundations of the Law of Nations: Alberico Gentili and the Justice of Empire,* edited by Benedict Kingsbury and Benjamin Straumann, 163–86. Oxford: Oxford University Press, 2010.

Schulman, Alan R. "Diplomatic Marriage in the Egyptian New Kingdom." *Journal of Near Eastern Studies* 38 (1979): 177–93.

Schwyzer, Philip. *Literature, Nationalism and Memory in Early Modern England and Wales.* Cambridge: Cambridge University Press, 2004.

Scott, Joanna. "Betraying Origins: The Many Faces of Aeneas." *LATCH: A Journal for the Study of the Literary Artifact in Theory, Culture, and History* 3 (2010): 64–84.

Searle, Eleanor. "Fact and Pattern in Heroic History: Dudo of St. Quentin." *Viator* 15 (1984): 119–37.

——. *Predatory Kinship and the Creation of Norman Power, 840–1066.* Berkeley: University of California Press, 1988.

Seward, Desmond. *The Hundred Years War: The English in France, 1337–1453.* Harmondsworth, Middlesex: Penguin, 1999.

Shadis, Miriam. "Blanche of Castile and Facinger's 'Medieval Queenship': Reassessing the Argument." In *Capetian Women*, edited by Kathleen Nolan, 137–61. New York: Palgrave Macmillan, 2003.

Shanzer, Danuta. "Dating the Baptism of Clovis: The Bishop of Vienne vs. the Bishop of Tours." *Early Medieval Europe* 7, no. 1 (1998): 29–57.

Shopkow, Leah. "The Carolingian World of Dudo of St. Quentin." *Journal of Medieval History* 15 (1989): 19–37.

Singerman, Jerome. *Under Clouds of Poesy: Poetry and Truth in French and English Reworkings of the Aeneid, 1160–1513.* New York: Garland, 1986.

Slobodník, Martin. "The Early Policy of Emperor Tang Dezong towards Inner Asia." *Asian and African Studies* 6, no. 2 (1997): 184–96.

Soergel, Peter M. *Wondrous in His Saints: Counter-Reformation Propaganda in Bavaria.* Berkeley: University of California Press, 1993.

Somervill, Barbara A. *The Empire of the Aztecs.* New York: Chelsea House, 2010.

Stafford, Pauline. "Powerful Women in the Early Middle Ages: Queens and Abbesses." In *The Medieval World*, edited by Peter Linehan and Janet L. Nelson, 398–415. London: Routledge, 2001.

——. *Queens, Concubines, and Dowagers: The King's Wife in the Early Middle Ages.* London: Batsford, 1983.

——. *Queen Emma and Queen Edith: Queenship and Women's Power in Eleventh-Century England.* Oxford: Blackwell, 1997.

Starkey, David. *Six Wives: The Queens of Henry VIII.* London: Chatto and Windus, 2003.

Stok, Fabio. "L'*Eneide* nordica di Dudone di San Quintino." *International Journal of the Classical Tradition* 6 (1999): 171–84.

Strohm, Paul. *Hochon's Arrow: The Social Imagination of Fourteenth-Century Texts.* Princeton: Princeton University Press, 1992.

Sumption, Jonathan. *The Hundred Years War.* Vol. 1. *Trial by Battle.* Philadelphia: University of Pennsylvania Press, 1991.

Suzuki, Shogo, Yongjin Zhang, and Joel Quirk, eds. *International Orders in the Early Modern World: Before the Rise of the West.* London: Routledge, 2013.

Swain, Brian. "Jordanes and Virgil: A Case Study of Intertextuality in the *Getica*." *Classical Quarterly* 60, no. 1 (2010): 243–49.

Sylvester, Christine. *Feminist International Relations: An Unfinished Journey.* Cambridge: Cambridge University Press, 2002.

——. *Feminist Theory and International Relations in a Postmodern Era.* Cambridge: Cambridge University Press, 1994.

Taillandier, Madeleine Saint-René. *Le mariage de Louis XIV.* Paris: Hachette, 1928.

Tanner, Marie. *The Last Descendant of Aeneas: The Hapsburgs and the Mythic Image of the Emperor.* New Haven: Yale University Press, 1993.

Tapié, Victor L. *La France de Louis XIII et de Richelieu.* Paris: Flammarion, 1952.

Taylor, Craig. "The Salic Law, French Queenship, and the Defense of Women in the Late Middle Ages." *French Historical Studies* 29 (2006): 543–64.

——. "The Salic Law and the Valois Succession to the French Crown." *French Historical Studies* 15 (2001): 358–77.

Tickner, J. Ann. *Gender in International Relations: Feminist Perspectives on Achieving Global Security.* New York: Columbia University Press, 1992.

Treadgold, Warren. "The Problem of the Marriage of Emperor Theophilos." *Greek, Roman, and Byzantine Studies* 16, no. 3 (1975): 325–41.

Treggiari, Susan. *Roman Marriage: Iusti Coniuges from the Time of Cicero to the Time of Ulpian.* Oxford: Oxford University Press, 1991.

True, Jacqui. "Feminism." In *International Society and Its Critics*, edited by Alex J. Bellamy, 151–62. Oxford: Oxford University Press, 2005.

Turner, Ralph V. *King John.* London: Longman, 1994.

Vale, Malcolm. "England, France, and the Origins of the Hundred Years War." In *England and Her Neighbours, 1066–1453*, edited by Michael Jones and Malcolm Vale, 199–216. London: Hambledon, 1989.

Vaughan, Virginia M. *"King John: A Study in Subversion and Containment."* In *King John: New Perspectives*, edited by Deborah T. Curren-Aquino, 62–75. Newark: University of Delaware Press, 1989.

Wallace, David. *Chaucerian Polity: Absolutist Lineages and Associational Forms in England and Italy.* Stanford: Stanford University Press, 1997.

Wallace-Hadrill, John M. *Early Medieval History.* Oxford: Blackwell, 1975.

Warner, Christopher James. *Henry VIII's Divorce: Literature and the Politics of the Printing Press.* Woodbridge, Suffolk: Boydell and Brewer, 1998.

Warren, Christopher N. "Gentili, the Poets, and the Laws of War." In *The Roman Foundations of the Law of Nations: Alberico Gentili and the Justice of Empire*, edited by Benedict Kingsbury and Benjaman Straumann, 146–62. Oxford: Oxford University Press, 2010.

Warren, Wilfred L. *King John.* 1961. Reprint, New Haven: Yale University Press, 1997.

Watkins, John. "Marriage à la Mode, 1559: Elizabeth I, Elisabeth de Valois, and the Changing Patterns of Dynastic Marriage." In *Queens and Power in Medieval and Early Modern England*, edited by Carole Levin and Robert Buckholz, 76–97. Lincoln: University of Nebraska Press, 2009.

——. *The Specter of Dido: Spenser and Virgilian Epic.* New Haven: Yale University Press, 1995.

——. "Towards a New Diplomatic History of Medieval and Early Modern Europe." *Journal of Medieval and Early Modern Studies* 38, no. 1 (2008): 1–14.

Watts, John. *Henry VI and the Politics of Kingship.* Cambridge: Cambridge University Press, 1996.

Weiler, Björn "The 'Negotium Terrae Sanctae' in the Political Discourse of Latin Christendom, 1215–1311." *International History Review* 25, no. 1 (2003): 1–36.

Wernham, Richard Bruce. *After the Armada: Elizabethan England and the Struggle for Western Europe, 1588–1595*. Oxford: Clarendon Press, 1984.

———. *Before the Armada: The Emergence of the English Nation, 1485–1588*. New York: Harcourt, Brace & World, 1966.

———. *The Making of Elizabethan Foreign Policy, 1558–1603*. Berkeley: University of California Press, 1980.

Whetter, Kevin Sean. *Understanding Genre and Medieval Romance*. Aldershot: Ashgate, 2008.

Wight, Martin. *Systems of States*. Edited by Hedley Bull. Leicester: University of Leicester Press in association with the London School of Economics, 1977.

Williams, Deanne. *The French Fetish from Chaucer to Shakespeare*. Cambridge: Cambridge University Press, 2004.

Williams, Howard, and Ken Booth. "Kant: Theories beyond Limits." In *Classical Theories of International Relations*, edited by Ian Clark and Iver B. Neumann, 71–98. Basingstoke: Palgrave Macmillan, 1999.

Williams, Robert R. *Tragedy, Recognition, and the Death of God: Studies in Hegel and Nietzsche*. Oxford: Oxford University Press, 2012.

Wilson, Stephen, ed. *Saints and Their Cults: Studies in Religious Sociology, Folklore and History*. Cambridge: Cambridge University Press, 1983.

Wittek, Stephen. "Middleton's *A Game at Chess* and the Making of a Theatrical Public." *Studies in English Literature* 55, no. 2 (2015): 423–46.

Wolf, John B. *Louis XIV*. New York: Norton, 1968.

Womersley, David. "The Politics of Shakespeare's *King John*." *Review of English Studies* 40 (1989): 497–515.

Wood, Ian N. "Gregory of Tours and Clovis." *Revue Belge de Philologie et d'Histoire* 63, no. 2 (1985): 249–72.

———. *The Merovingian Kingdoms, 450–751*. London: Longman, 1994.

Wulf, Charlotte A. T. "A Comparative Study of Wace's Guinevere in the Twelfth Century." In *Arthurian Romance and Gender: Selected Proceedings of the XVIIth International Arthurian Congress. Internationale Forschungen zur Allgemeinen und Vergleichenden Literaturwissenschaft*, edited by Friedrich Wolfzettel, 66–78. Amsterdam: Rodopi, 1995.

Yarrow, Philip J. *Racine*. Oxford: Blackwell, 1978.

Zanger, Abby E. *Scenes from the Marriage of Louis XIV: Nuptial Fictions and the Making of Absolutist Power*. Stanford: Stanford University Press, 1997.

❧ INDEX

CPSIA information can be obtained
at www.ICGtesting.com
Printed in the USA
LVHW09*1938150918
590267LV00004B/133/P